Churchill and the Anglo-American Special Relationship

This book examines Winston Churchill's role in the creation and development of the Anglo-American special relationship.

Drawing together world leading and emergent scholars, this volume offers a critical celebration of Churchill's contribution to establishing the Anglo-American special relationship. Marking the seventieth anniversary of Churchill's pronouncement in 1946 of that special relationship in his famous Iron Curtain speech, the book provides new insights into old debates by drawing upon approaches and disciplines that have hitherto been marginalised or neglected. The book foregrounds agency, culture, values, ideas and the construction and representation of special Anglo-American relations, past and present. The volume covers two main themes. First, it identifies key influences upon Churchill as he developed his political career, especially processes and patterns of Anglo-American convergence prior to and during World War Two. Second, it provides insights into how Churchill sought to promote a post-war Anglo-American special relationship, how he discursively constructed it and how he has remained central to that narrative to the present day. From this analysis emerges new understanding of the raw material from which Churchill conjured special UK–US relations and of how his conceptualisation of that special relationship has been shaped and re-shaped in the decades after 1946.

This book will be of much interest to students of Anglo-American relations, Cold War Studies, foreign policy, international history and IR in general.

Alan P. Dobson is an Honorary Professor at Swansea University, UK, and author of *Franklin D. Roosevelt and Civil Aviation 1933–1945* (2011).

Steve Marsh is Reader in International Relations at Cardiff University, UK, and editor of *Anglo-American Relations: Contemporary Perspectives* (2013, with Alan P. Dobson).

Series: Cold War History
Series Editors: Odd Arne Westad
and
Michael Cox

In the new history of the Cold War that has been forming since 1989, many of the established truths about the international conflict that shaped the latter half of the twentieth century have come up for revision. The present series is an attempt to make available interpretations and materials that will help further the development of this new history, and it will concentrate in particular on publishing expositions of key historical issues and critical surveys of newly available sources.

Mao, Stalin and the Korean War
Trilateral communist relations in the 1950s
Shen Zhihua; translated by Neil Silver

The Iran–Iraq War
New international perspectives
Edited by Nigel Ashton and Bryan R. Gibson

International Summitry and Global Governance
The rise of the G7 and the European Council, 1974–1991
Edited by Emmanuel Mourlon-Druol and Federico Romero

Human Rights in Europe during the Cold War
Edited by Kjersti Brathagen, Rasmus Mariager and Karl Molin

NATO and Western Perceptions of the Soviet Bloc
Alliance analysis and reporting, 1951–69
Evanthis Hatzivassiliou

The Cuban Missile Crisis
A critical reappraisal
Edited by Len Scott and R. Gerald Hughes

Neutrality and Neutralism in the Global Cold War
Between or within the blocs?
Edited by Sandra Bott, Jussi M. Hanhimäki, Janick Marina Schaufelbuehl and Marco Wyss

The Trilateral Commission and Global Governance
Informal elite diplomacy, 1972–82
Dino Knudsen

German Reunification
A multinational history
Edited by Frédéric Bozo, Andreas Rödder and Mary Elise Sarotte

Churchill and the Anglo-American Special Relationship
Edited by Alan P. Dobson and Steve Marsh

Churchill and the Anglo-American Special Relationship

Edited by
Alan P. Dobson and
Steve Marsh

LONDON AND NEW YORK

First published 2017
by Routledge

2 Park Square, Milton Park, Abingdon, Oxfordshire OX14 4RN
711 Third Avenue, New York, NY 10017

Routledge is an imprint of the Taylor & Francis Group, an informa business

First issued in paperback 2018

Copyright © 2017 selection and editorial matter, Alan P. Dobson and Steve
Marsh; individual chapters, the contributors

The right of the editor to be identified as the author of the editorial matter,
and of the authors for their individual chapters, has been asserted in
accordance with sections 77 and 78 of the Copyright, Designs and Patents
Act 1988.

All rights reserved. No part of this book may be reprinted or reproduced or
utilised in any form or by any electronic, mechanical, or other means, now
known or hereafter invented, including photocopying and recording, or in
any information storage or retrieval system, without permission in writing
from the publishers.

Notice:
Product or corporate names may be trademarks or registered trademarks,
and are used only for identification and explanation without intent to infringe.

British Library Cataloguing in Publication Data
A catalogue record for this book is available from the British Library

Library of Congress Cataloging in Publication Data
Names: Dobson, Alan P. | Marsh, Steve.
Title: Churchill and the Anglo-American special relationship / edited by
Alan P. Dobson and Steve Marsh.
Description: New York, NY : Routledge, 2016. | Series: Cold War history |
Includes bibliographical references and index.
Identifiers: LCCN 2016030723| ISBN 9781138188143 (hardback) |
ISBN 9781315642673 (ebook)
Subjects: LCSH: Great Britain–Foreign relations–United States. |
United States–Foreign relations–Great Britain. | Churchill, Winston,
1874-1965–Influence. | Great Britain–Foreign relations–1936-1945.
| Britain–Foreign relations–1945-1964. | United States–Foreign
relations–1933-1945. | United States–Foreign relations–1945-1989. |
Cold War.
Classification: LCC DA566.9.C5 C47628 2016 | DDC 327.41073–dc23
LC record available at https://lccn.loc.gov/2016030723

ISBN: 978-1-138-18814-3 (hbk)
ISBN: 978-1-138-32786-3 (pbk)

Typeset in Times New Roman
by Wearset Ltd, Boldon, Tyne and Wear

Contents

Notes on contributors		vii
Introduction		1
ALAN P. DOBSON AND STEVE MARSH		
Prologue – the ghost in the attic: Churchill, the Soviet Union, and the Anglo-American Special Relationship		10
WARREN F. KIMBALL		
1	**'Strategic culture' on the road to (and from) Fulton: institutionalism, emotionalism, and the Anglo-American special relationship**	19
	DAVID G. HAGLUND	
2	**Churchill's Fulton speech and the context of shared values in a world of dangers**	43
	ALAN P. DOBSON	
3	**Manipulating the Anglo-American civilizational identity in the era of Churchill**	64
	ROBERT M. HENDERSHOT	
4	**The Fulton address as racial discourse**	96
	SRDJAN VUCETIC	
5	**Personal diplomacy at the summit**	116
	STEVE MARSH	
6	**Churchill's ambassadors – from Fulton to Suez**	142
	TONY McCULLOCH	

vi *Contents*

7 Churchill's inter-subjective special relationship: a corpus-assisted discourse approach 171

ANNA MARCHI, NURIA LORENZO-DUS AND STEVE MARSH

8 The architecture of a myth: constructing and commemorating Churchill's special relationship, *c.*1919–69 202

SAM EDWARDS

9 Curtains, culture and 'collective' memory 223

DAVID RYAN

Conclusion 247

ALAN P. DOBSON AND STEVE MARSH

Primary sources 253
Index 275

Contributors

Alan P. Dobson is an honorary Professor, Swansea University. He has written extensively on Anglo-American relations, civil aviation, and the Cold War. His most recent monograph is *Franklin D. Roosevelt and Civil Aviation 1933–1945* (Palgrave 2011). He was awarded the John A. Adams Cold War essay prize, Virginia Military Institute, in 2014 and has held fellowships at St Bonaventure and Baylor University (Fulbright Scholar), and the Nobel Institute Oslo. He is editor of the *Journal of Transatlantic Studies* and the *International History Review*.

Sam Edwards is Senior Lecturer in American History at Manchester Metropolitan University. His research explores transatlantic relations, commemoration and memory, and the cultural history of war. He is co-editor of *D-Day in History and Memory* (2014), and author of *Allies in Memory: World War II and the Politics of Transatlantic Commemoration, c.1941–2001* (2015), which has been shortlisted for the Royal Historical Society's Gladstone Prize. Sam is a Fellow of the Royal Historical Society and a former Fulbright Scholar.

David G. Haglund is a Professor of Political Studies at Queen's University (Kingston, Ontario). His research focuses on transatlantic security, and on Canadian and American international security policy. His most recent book, entitled *Ethnic Diasporas and the Canada–US Security Community: From the Civil War to Today*, was published in 2015.

Robert M. Hendershot is a Professor of history at the Grand Rapids Community College. He earned his PhD in the transnational history programme jointly administered by Central Michigan University and the University of Strathclyde, Glasgow, and is the author of *Family Spats: Perception, Illusion and Sentimentality in the Anglo-American Special Relationship*. His current research is focused on the roles of culture and public opinion in twentieth-century international relations.

Warren F. Kimball is Robert Treat Professor (emeritus) at Rutgers University and formerly Pitt Professor at Cambridge, 1987–8. He edited the Churchill–Roosevelt correspondence (with commentaries) and is author of *Forged in* viii *Contributors*

War (1997), *The Juggler* (1991), and of books on the Morgenthau Plan and the origins of Lend–Lease. He has published over fifty essays on Churchill, Roosevelt and the era of the Second World War. His institutional history of the US Tennis Association is in press for 2017.

Nuria Lorenzo-Dus holds a Personal Chair in Linguistics at Swansea University. She is the founding Director of the Language Research Centre, a global hub for research into language data and processes. Her area of expertise is discourse analysis, with a focus on media discourse. She is the author of several books and over fifty articles and book chapters in this area.

Tony McCulloch is Senior Fellow in North American Studies at the UCL Institute of the Americas where he teaches US foreign policy and leads the Canadian Studies programme. He has published widely on US and Canadian political history, and his book on Franklin D. Roosevelt and the Anglo-American 'special relationship' before Churchill is due to be published by Edinburgh University Press in 2017.

Anna Marchi is an adjunct lecturer of English at Bologna University. She has extensive experience in corpus linguistics and has collaborated with the Universities of Siena, Cardiff, Swansea and Lancaster. Her main area of interest is the corpus-assisted discourse study of news and she has a practical and theoretical background in journalism.

Steve Marsh is Reader in International Relations at Cardiff University. His books include *Anglo-American Relations: Contemporary Perspectives* edited with Alan Dobson (2013), *The European Union in European Security* co-authored with Wyn Rees (2012), *US Foreign Policy since 1945* co-authored with Alan Dobson (second edition 2006), *International Relations of the European Union* co-authored with Hans Mackenstein (2006) and *Anglo-American Relations and Cold War Oil* (2003).

David Ryan is Professor and Chair of Modern History at University College Cork. His books include *Obama, US Foreign Policy and the Dilemmas of Intervention* co-authored with David Fitzgerald (2014), *US Foreign Policy and the Other* edited with Michael Cullinane (2015), *Frustrated Empire: US Foreign Policy from 9/11 to Iraq* (2007), *Vietnam in Iraq: Tactics, Lessons, Legacies and Ghosts* edited with John Dumbrell (2007), *The United States and Europe in the Twentieth Century* (2003), *US Foreign Policy in World History* (2000) and *US–Sandinista Diplomatic Relations: Voice of Intolerance* (1995).

Srdjan Vucetic is Associate Professor at the Graduate School of Public and International Affairs, University of Ottawa, Canada. He received his PhD in Political Science from the Ohio State University in 2008. He is author of *The Anglosphere: A Genealogy of a Racialized Identity in International Relations* (2011) and has further research interests in Canadian foreign policy and international security.

Introduction

Alan P. Dobson and Steve Marsh

Aboard the USS *Williamsburg* as guest of President Harry Truman in January 1952, British Prime Minister Winston Churchill speculated – as was his frequent wont – how deep in alcohol he and his colleagues would be standing were the dining saloon of the presidential yacht to be filled with the equivalent of his life-time consumption. Secretary of State Acheson recalled Churchill's disappointment upon learning that rather than drowning all present in champagne and brandy, the anticipated flood would rise only to knee height.[1] Nevertheless, he would likely have drawn several measures of consolation had he known that the *Williamsburg* would probably have sunk if loaded with the subsequent cumulative works of scholars, commentators and political pundits on him and his life. He might also have detected a wry irony in the different contemporary fates of the vessel and himself. At the time of writing the steel-hulled former gunboat and presidential yacht is a rusty unseaworthy wreck moored at La Spezia, Italy; she faces imminent scrapping after her historic value proved insufficient for two former White House Staffers to crowd-source a last-minute $40 million rescue fund. Meantime, Church-ill lives on. His speeches, writings, art and politics are passed down through history. His image remains more instantly recognizable than many contemporary politicians. Even his death marked a rebirth, the ceremony at St Paul's Cathedral in London being the largest state funeral to date, a global broadcast event and a point of subsequent (inter)national commemoration.

This book is in some ways part of the commemorative renewal of Churchill, being occasioned as it is by the seventieth anniversary of his famous Iron Curtain speech at Fulton in March 1946. One might ask, of course, why it is necessary given a literal weight of extant literature likely capable of sinking a 244-foot long presidential yacht. For us there are two principal reasons. First, there is still much to be understood about the man and about the need to navigate cautiously through the interpretative waves of scholarship that too often neglect his flaws, forget his humanity and appropriate him to various ends. Second, Churchill is a connector of status, space and time. He was a soldier, a journalist, a politician, a builder of walls, a war leader, a painter, a prime minister and a splendid Eliza-bethan. He enjoyed Britain at its height, manifested its pride, and presided 'with the roar of a wounded lion' over its relative decline and the indignities that it suffered.[2] And long after his death, his image, experiences, arguments and global impact are looked to for insights into contemporary problems and harnessed to particular causes.

Our particular concern is the Anglo-American special relationship, specifically Churchill's role in practising it during World War Two and promoting it in the aftermath of conflict when it seemed that Britain and America might once more become less intimately entwined. His Fulton speech is one of Churchill's earliest and most important public pronouncements of, and elaborations upon, the special relationship and the historic role of the English-speaking peoples. For us, though, it marks both a beginning and a mid-point. It marked a beginning in terms of a concerted effort to construct a self-conscious Anglo-American special relationship that was at once function and nature in form. It was a mid-point for Churchill in this creation. He had to look backwards to his past and to Anglo-American history to discern what could – and should not – be used in demonstrating the unique connections between Britain and America and in arguing the naturalness of close partnership. At the same time he had to look forward, recognizing the shift in power between the UK and US and their different needs, and that it was largely the exogenous influence of a common enemy that had drawn them into the unique wartime cooperation symbolized by the Destroyers for Bases deal in September 1940. And then, of course, he needed opportunity to convince his fellow Britons and Americans that he was right. Few would have guessed on this count that it would be a little-known college in mid-West America that would give Churchill the stage he desired.

'All aboard'?

Frank Lewis McCluer was the President of Westminster College, Fulton, Missouri, from 1933 to 1947. One of the advantages of being President was the opportunity to invite distinguished people to speak and lecture at the College in the John Findley Green lecture series that had begun in 1936. In late 1945 he began to cast around for a candidate for the lectures and rather boldly decided that he would approach Winston Churchill. The great man was now out of office leading His Majesty's Loyal Opposition, but as he himself was only too quick to confirm, he was the world's greatest living celebrity. In the mid-1950s when his grandson Nicholas Soames, then about six years old, had the temerity to enter his grandfather's study at Chartwell uninvited and then compounded his impudence by asking if his granddad really were the greatest man in the world, without any hesitation whatsoever Churchill replied: 'Yes, and now bugger off.'[3] Churchill's response to McClure's enquiry about giving lectures was more polite.

McClure went about the invitation by engaging the good offices of his friend Major General Harry Vaughan, who just happened to be on President Harry Truman's White House staff. The ploy worked and Truman himself pressed Churchill to accept the offer, writing a short note in his own hand at the end of the formal invitation issued by McClure: 'This is a wonderful school in my home state. Hope you can do it. I'll introduce you.' Churchill was persuaded, though only on condition that it would be one rather than a short series of addresses.

Introduction 3

The scene was set for what came to be universally known as Churchill's Iron Curtain speech.[4]

Early 1946 was a decisive moment in world affairs. Decisions were taken, stances adopted, words uttered, symbols invoked and images projected that helped shape the world for decades to come, not least in terms of the relationship that developed between the USA and Britain. Mounting tensions over Poland, Germany, Iran and Turkey as well as reparations and ideological and personal antagonisms bitterly soured relations between the Soviets on the one hand and the USA and Britain on the other. Churchill was deeply worried that there might be a replay of the 1930s, but on this occasion with the Soviets cast in the role of totalitarian aggressors, and who this time would need to be resisted rather than appeased. He travelled to the US with such thoughts on his mind, but also with deep concern about Britain's economic weakness and above all about the future of Anglo-American relations. Even in 1946 Britain's trajectory as a world power was clear for those who wished to see. Kipling's foresight was now manifest:

> Far-called, our navies melt away,
> On dune and headland sinks the fire,
> Lo, all our pomp of yesterday
> Is one with Nineveh and Tyre!
> Judge of the Nations, spare us yet,
> Lest we forget, lest we forget!
> > Rudyard Kipling,
> > 'Recessional' (1897)

Unlike Kipling, Churchill was little disposed to look to religion for help. More practically, he looked to the USA. He believed that a prerequisite not only for peace, security and prosperity in Britain, but for the entire world too, depended on a close Anglo-American relationship of broad and deep mutual cooperation – a special relationship. Consequently he thought long and hard about what he would do in the USA: he was going to be there for some considerable time, arriving on 14 January and leaving on 20 March. While much of his time was spent in rest and recreation, including much painting, he also meticulously choreographed his public appearances.

In his early seventies in 1946, Churchill had done and achieved much in his life and, significantly, he had been a journalist in his youth and had developed technical skills and flair in composing his paintings: both would stand him in good stead in choosing the right words, phrases and suitable images to present to the world. These as well as his more obvious rhetorical and verbal communication skills would be drawn on while he was in the US, not just for the Fulton speech but in all his other public engagements as well. Churchill was near on the complete performer when it came to delivering public messages. He knew that it was not just the message that counted. It was not even the way the message was crafted linguistically – though he was a master at that. It also involved conjuring up symbolism appropriate to the occasion and the

4   *A.P. Dobson and S. Marsh*

projection of carefully contrived images – visual as well as verbal – that would resonate with his audience.

Churchill and Truman steamed into Fulton, and history, aboard the train *Ferdinand Magellan*. Nominally an American president escorted an elderly private British citizen to an educational event; in reality Truman lent the presidential seal to the words of the man most Americans still regarded as representing Britain. At Fulton, and elsewhere during his stay in the US, Churchill duly conjured his rhetorical magic, courted the press and exuded an authority derived not from office but from his immense personal popularity in the US. Of course, this did not mean that his warnings or prescriptions were universally well received. Far from it, especially among those who thought that a less confrontational approach to the Soviets was possible, or were suspicious of British imperialism, or felt excluded by the 'othering' language of Churchill's English-speaking peoples. Yet this is no critique of Churchill's performance. He and Truman recognized, and even desired, beforehand that his words should create a stir such that popular support might be mustered to enable democratic leaders to develop what they saw as crucially important new security policies. Moreover, that the Fulton speech has impact and significance seventy years later is testimony not only to the power of its appreciation of events in 1946 but also to how Churchill wove the Anglo-American way of life as a non-temporally specific thread throughout his presentation. It is this timelessness that enabled Prime Minister Blair to speak of 9/11 as an attack on a shared way of life in the same way as Churchill did of the looming Cold War threat: 'The target of the terrorists was not only New York and Washington but the very values of freedom, tolerance and decency which underpin our way of life.'[5]

Structure and contributors

'From Stettin in the Baltic to Trieste in the Adriatic, an iron curtain has descended across the continent.'[6] Churchill's speech and particularly that phrase have resonated down the years in various guises and mutated forms and always with important impact. This series of essays, provided by an eminent array of historians, political scientists and language specialists, is geared to providing original and stimulating thoughts on the Iron Curtain speech, Churchill, the Anglo-American special relationship and the place of the speech in the unfolding Cold War and beyond. It deliberately eschews the traditional and well-trodden scholarly focus on functional Anglo-American cooperation, such as nuclear, military and intelligence ties. After the lucid and sure touch of the Prologue by Warren Kimball, and consistent with its conceptualization of the Fulton speech being for Churchill both a starting and a mid-point for the special relationship, the book develops insights in two broad parts. The first section focuses mainly on the pre-World War Two period, teasing out some of the raw material that Churchill had to work with, as well as controversies to avoid, in developing a discourse of natural special relations between Britain and America. The second section looks broadly at agency and legacy in Churchill's post-World War Two development of the special relationship. This spans what Churchill did, be it through personal

Introduction 5

diplomacy, discourse or ambassadorial appointments, through to the impact of his legacy developed in terms of collective memory and memorialization.

Kimball's Prologue takes the position that the Fulton speech 'cannot be understood without a firm grounding in the alliance politics of the Second World War'. It was in war that the Anglo-American relationship became truly special. But complicating that special relationship was the need to engage in a working alliance with the Soviet Union, which was the ally that would effectively defeat the *Wehrmacht*. Working with the Soviets led Churchill in particular into some pretty complicated diplomatic contortions given his virulent opposition to the Soviets in the past and his continuing suspicions and distaste of them. Kimball develops how all this played out during the war in the triangular relationship between Churchill, Franklin Roosevelt and Joseph Stalin and through to the eve of the Fulton speech.

With the scene set, the first section of the book examines the foundations of the Anglo-American special relationship and comprises contributions from David Haglund, Alan Dobson, Robert Hendershot and Srdjan Vucetic.

Haglund explores the concept of strategic culture and what it might contribute to understanding the origins and development of the special relationship, which Churchill spoke of several times during the war, but most famously in the Fulton speech. The question of when the special Anglo-American relationship emerged is important for his thesis. That is not to say that one has to pinpoint the actual year, but more to identify variables in historical context, which result in what is known as path dependency emerging within a shared security community. For Haglund, claims about the Great Rapprochement between Britain and the USA at the end of the nineteenth century resulting in a special relationship are not persuasive. And they are not because path dependency creates a form of 'lock-in' created by positive feedback from the emergence of path dependency, and he sees insufficient evidence of that in the nineteenth century and indeed in the interwar period. He suggests 1940 with the Destroyers for Bases deal, or the Fulton speech in 1946, or even 1949 and the creation of NATO as possible candidates for the emergence of path dependency, but his actual vote goes to 1940. He does not over-exaggerate the efficacy of his thesis concerning the importance of strategic culture and path dependency. He simply presents it as worthy of consideration for adding to our understanding of the Anglo-American special relationship: at the very least it has some utility. In the editors' views, such claims are unduly modest.

Dobson takes the line that Churchill's paramount aim at Fulton was to help consolidate and develop a special relationship between the US and Britain. All his other objectives hinged on consummating such a special relationship. Churchill largely succeeded, and Dobson demonstrates that a significant part of the reason for that success was Churchill's ability to invoke commonly held political values. While acknowledging some different substantive concerns such as slavery and imperialism in the nineteenth century and explaining how different institutional frameworks in the US and Britain seemed to engender differences in preponderant political concerns and values, he goes on to argue that

6 *A.P. Dobson and S. Marsh*

underlying value trajectories were the same, though often moving at different and variable speeds. In doing this he introduces a broad range of American and British political theorists who together produced traditions of thought and practice which, while not identical, did speak to each other widely. The result of all this was British and American ability to work together in World War Two to iterate and implement the values that infused the Atlantic Charter, the UN, the IMF, the GATT and other post-war regulatory forms of governance. Not surprisingly, then – or so Dobson argues – confronted by a common alien form of totalitarianism, Churchill was able to invoke common political traditions and values that had resonance in the US and facilitated the consolidation of the special relationship.

Hendershot engages with complex issues concerning cultural affinity and what he calls civilizational identity. His starting point is that Churchill operated in a context where a strong sense of civilizational identity between Britain and the US already existed. In this he builds on his own previous ground-breaking work and is very much in tune with work done by Haglund on the conscious re-establishment of ties with Britain that occurred among Americans of British descent in the latter part of the nineteenth century.[7] Providing compelling evidence such as the Britain's Day celebrations in the US in December 1918, which evinced an outpouring of admiration and affection for Britain and the role it had played in the Great War, Hendershot goes on to demonstrate how Churchill built on such foundations. Churchill consciously manipulated things to promote an ever-stronger sense of a common civilizational identity, of which, Hendershot claims, he became the ultimate living embodiment. The contribution by Edwards (see below) lends much support to that view. For Hendershot the Anglo-American special relationship is thus not simply about economic, military and diplomatic ties. Rather, these functional dynamics are undergirded by an Anglo-American civilizational identity that encourages commonality of view and a powerful undercurrent that cushions inevitable ups and downs in the relationship occasioned by specific events, personalities and large-scale changes in the configuration of world economic and military power. This, among other things, is what Churchill intended and succeeded in projecting on many occasions, but none more successfully than when he spoke at Westminster College in Fulton, Missouri.

Vucetic analyses the Fulton speech and its language as an integral part of an ongoing racial discourse. Not surprisingly, Joseph Stalin's reaction to the speech was outrage at the way Churchill used language to establish an 'us' composed of the English-speaking peoples and 'othered' the Russians as not only outsiders, but also as bearers of a dire potential threat to what Churchill described as good in the world. Stalin even went so far as to claim Churchill was articulating a Hitlerite racial theory. However, the Russians were not the only ones to take profound offence at the way Churchill portrayed the world. The leading African-American celebrity, Paul Robeson, along with probably the majority of his fellow elite African Americans, saw the framing of the English-speaking peoples as the embodiment of liberty, democracy and human rights in the world

Introduction 7

as a brazen attempt to sustain white Anglo-Saxon racial supremacy. Similar arguments could be applied to the sensibilities of those Africans and Asians, and indeed anyone else who did not fit Churchill's category of Anglo-Saxon and English-speaking. Much of the chapter interrogates the use of racial language by Churchill both before and in the Fulton speech. Vucetic is aware of the sensitivity of this line of interpretation of Churchill, but he declares his view that Churchill's racialism should be acknowledged as a central part of his political life. Failure to do so would not only be dishonest to history but also neglect how Churchill's views on race informed his world view and how he evolved them – at least publicly – over time. His Fulton address epitomized this, Churchill choosing not to mention the British Empire and presenting the English-speaking peoples with far less of the overt Anglo-Saxonism that accompanied the Great Rapprochement.

The second section considers how the special relationship underwent further construction on some of the foundations spelt out in Fulton and is comprised of contributions from Steve Marsh, Tony McCulloch, Anna Marchi and Nuria Lorenzo-Dus, Sam Edwards and David Ryan.

Marsh takes as his starting point Churchill's penchant for personal diplomacy and confidence not only in his own powers of persuasion, but also in the capacity for intimate and friendly talks between leading statesmen to steer international relations in positive directions. He develops this in the context of Churchill's conviction of the need for close personal relations between Anglo-American leaders and that they should enjoy regular informal and intimate dialogue across the spectrum of global affairs. Marsh demonstrates how for Churchill the pinnacle of this endeavour was Anglo-American summitry. Furthermore, by examining his peacetime bilateral meetings with Presidents Truman and Eisenhower, Marsh reveals how Churchill fashioned a style and expectation of regularized Anglo-American summits that has persisted through to the present day. This, Marsh contends, provided a pseudo-institutionalization of the special relationship. He also contends that to achieve this Churchill consciously exploited his 'brand' in the US to develop simultaneously a public diplomacy of special relations and a private diplomacy of message-sending that British support should not be assumed and that the White House needed to treat Britain as a global partner rather than as a European supplicant.

McCulloch provides a wide-ranging perspective on the impact of Churchill's Fulton speech and on the contribution to the special relationship generally through public diplomacy. He looks at Churchill's concept of the special relationship, and evaluates the debate in the US sparked by Churchill's speech and the public diplomacy of British ambassadors in its aftermath. He also examines the 'descent to Suez' and the possible flaws in Churchill's concept of the special relationship, which might have contributed to the problems experienced in 1956. All of this is tied in with detailed analyses of five successive British ambassadors to Washington: Lord Lothian, Lord Halifax, Lord Inverchapel, Sir Oliver Franks and Sir Roger Makins. He suggests that while the 1954 Potomac Charter might be seen as embodying what Churchill aspired to in his vision of the special relationship, only two years later relations were mired in the Suez debacle. He draws an interesting contrast between the way public diplomacy made major contributions to the strength of the special relationship and the way covert diplomacy in 1956 brought on its post-war nadir.

Marchi, Lorenzo-Dus and Marsh develop an ambitious interdisciplinary approach to the special relationship, conceptualizing it as a discursive construction and interrogating that discourse quantitatively and qualitatively. This analytic corpus of *c.*500,000 words consists of US and UK government and newspaper records of Churchill's summit meetings with Truman in January 1952 and with Eisenhower in December 1953 and June 1954. Combining Diplomatic History with Corpus Assisted Discourse Analysis enables the language and images in these records to be examined to reveal how notions of special Anglo-American relations were subsequently evolved discursively. Focusing in particular on Churchill's role in the articulation and mediation of a special relationship, the authors demonstrate that in the early 1950s the nomenclature 'special relationship' had yet to gain currency. At the same time, political and media elites were beginning to develop a lexicon of a unique Anglo-American relationship, one that often rehearsed words and phrases developed in the Fulton speech. They also suggest both that the media ascribe roles to Churchill and that there are interesting early differences in British and American discourses of special relations, with the latter being more functionally and action orientated.

Edwards also provides a highly original take on Anglo-American relations in his work on what he aptly terms the landscape of Anglo-American memory. His chapter opens with a portrayal of Churchill's state funeral in 1965. It was at St Paul's Cathedral, which housed the American Memorial Chapel dedicated in 1958. The music included 'The Star-Spangled Banner', ex-president and close wartime comrade Dwight Eisenhower attended, and obviously the funeral centred on Churchill himself – half-American and since 1963 an honorary American citizen. It is difficult to imagine a more potent image of Anglo-Americanism. Edwards then takes the reader on a tour from the establishment of the Lincoln statue in London's Parliament Square in 1920 through an ever more memorial- and commemoration-populated landscape. He sees such acts of commemoration and memorial as an integral part of mythologizing the Anglo-American special relationship, but not in the sense of it producing an untruth. Churchill throughout much of his career contributed to the expansion of this myth by his rhetoric and performance and did this nowhere better than in Fulton, Missouri.

Ryan makes the final contribution to this collection of essays, and it is most appropriate that he does so as he engages with the concept of collective memory and how it can resonate from its origins down the decades, morphing along the way into new forms for application and use in new settings. The kind of collective memory which Churchill's Fulton speech did so much to engender has had a limiting effect by constraining possibilities. The Iron Curtain content of the speech helped to create a Manichean view of international relations that became so potent that it straightjacketed diplomats and politicians alike. It

Introduction 9

established an identity of good pitched against an alterity of evil that continued to resonate decades after Fulton in the rhetoric of Presidents John F. Kennedy and Ronald Reagan. Even after work by the historical revisionists of the 1970s and 1980s, the polarization of the Cold War conflict remained deeply embedded in many official minds and as a manner of thinking continued even after the Cold War faded out. This is not to say that during these years leaders were unable to escape these othering narratives. Clearly, as Ryan points out, President George Herbert Walker Bush, while hesitant and wary at times, overcame his inhibitions and traditional Iron Curtain imagery and developed a degree of empathy for Gorbachev and the Soviets sufficient to enable the gradual dismantling of Cold War institutions and armament systems. It is not that leaders cannot escape the imperatives of collective memory: it is just that one needs to recognize how difficult it can be to do so. Statesmen need to be careful in what they ask for. Their language can mobilize images, ideas and concepts, especially of 'us and them', which take on robust and enduring lives of their own that outlast their original purpose and serve later to constrain and limit possibilities for good. Whether this applies to Churchill's special relationship has proven an eternal font of analysis and media/popular speculation.

Notes

1 Dean Acheson, *Present at the Creation. My Years in the State Department*, London: Hamilton, 1970, p. 597.
2 This description was made in the context of Conservative Party handling of the Iranian oil crisis upon its coming to power in autumn 1951. *Foreign Relations of the United States* Iran 1952–54, vol. 10, Secretary of State to State Dept, 10 November 1951, pp. 278–9.
3 Roy Jenkins, *Churchill*, London: Macmillan, 2001, p. 849, footnote.
4 Philip White, *Our Supreme Task: How Winston Churchill's Iron Curtain Speech Defined the Cold War Alliance*, New York: Public Affairs, 2012, p. 60, citing source National Churchill Museum Archives, Fulton Missouri, Churchill, Truman, McCluer Day Collection, folder 7, image 267.
5 'Attacks remembered: in quotes', BBC News, 11 September 2002, http://news.bbc. co.uk/1/hi/world/americas/2251406.stm.
6 White, p. 192.
7 See essays by Haglund and Hendershot in Alan P. Dobson and Steve Marsh (eds), *Anglo-American Relations: Contemporary Perspectives*, London and New York: Routledge, 2013.

Prologue – the ghost in the attic
Churchill, the Soviet Union, and the Anglo-American Special Relationship

Warren F. Kimball

> All wisdom is not new wisdom.
>
> Winston Churchill, 1938[1]

In the past decade or so, we have been inundated with newly written scholarly and popular histories of Winston Churchill, Franklin Roosevelt – and, since the bulk of those studies have focused on the Second World War – many histories of Churchill and Roosevelt together. The documentation for their relationship, joint actions, and international diplomacy has been available, with a few exceptions, since the early 1970s, despite breathless dust-jacket claims of 'new, secret' documents. Once the late John Costello failed to find the fabled cache of Hitler's secrets at the bottom of some Swiss lake, it was clear we pretty much had it all. Even Russian historians now working on Stalin's correspondence with FDR and Churchill admit there are no revelations in the Soviet era archives, though there are invaluable new insights into Stalin's reasoning and reactions.

Perhaps Second World War historians are now firmly in the age of 'nuance', of rethinking its history – when interpretation (usually that of the author) is all that's truly new. The cliché is that each generation writes its own history. Churchill evidently contributed mightily to penning his. And this is certainly not to denigrate the exercise. But it is to sound a note of caution in the transition from insight via new documentation to originality through (re-)interpretation. As Churchill noted well, not all wisdom is new.

The famous 'Iron Curtain' – 'Sinews of Peace' – speech made by Winton Churchill on 5 March 1946, in Fulton, Missouri, cannot be understood without a firm grounding in the alliance politics of the Second World War, and Winston Churchill's differing assessments (somersaults, as one historian put it) regarding the Soviet Union since 1917. The *longue durée* of the Anglo-American Special Relationship (AASR) that Churchill christened and addressed in that speech is essential to any understanding of that continuing, very special, unique relationship. But it was the Second World War, and the immediate post-war political situation in Europe, that set the stage for his performance.

To steal a phrase from myself, 'the eternal triangle is as much a threat to statesmen as it is to lovers'.[2] Throughout the Second World War, the ghost in the

Prologue: the ghost in the attic 11

attic for the British and the Americans, and particularly for the AASR, were the Soviet Union and Josef Stalin. Can't live with him; can't live (win) without him. Franklin Roosevelt and Winston Churchill, the wartime leaders of the United States and Great Britain, quickly recognized that the German attack on the Soviet Union on 22 June 1941 offered a far better chance to defeat rather than just contain Hitler's Germany. Churchill famously quipped that 'If Hitler invaded hell I would at least make a favourable reference to the devil in the House of Commons.' FDR quickly dispatched his key adviser, Harry Hopkins, to Moscow to assess Stalin's mettle. Hopkins came back and reported that, yes, Stalin was a dictator, but he and the Russians would go the distance against Hitler.[3]

There is a long background to Churchill's speech, but let us not make that more complex than it was. It was written in an atmosphere of what Churchill described as 'poverty and privation', a desperate situation well known to any American who read a newspaper. He spoke of the 'the awful ruin of Europe'; of 'the prevailing anxiety' about economic issues; and to 'the 46 millions in our island being harassed about their food supply' with 'difficulty in restarting our industries and export trade'. He followed those descriptions in the closing paragraph with an appeal for Anglo-American cooperation. These were strong statements, but they were dwarfed by the length and power of his remarks on war and tyranny. They fell short of an appeal for help – however much that appeal was being made by the Attlee Government.

Churchill's condemnation of Soviet behaviour in Eastern Europe garnered greater attention from his American audience than he expected. So much so that the speech will forever be known as the 'Iron Curtain' speech, not the 'We Need Help' address, though Churchill himself titled it 'The Sinews of Peace'.

The receptivity of the American public and its leaders to confronting the Soviet Union was not created by Churchill's oration; it was there waiting for a champion.[4] It is worth noting that, in 'Sinews of Peace', Churchill specifically rejected the legitimacy of the Soviet Union acting as one of the world's constables or sheriffs (the four policemen), that he, Soviet leader Josef Stalin, and President Roosevelt had agreed to at the Teheran and Yalta conferences.[5] Churchill placed great emphasis on the AASR as a tool, a means by which Britain and Europe could survive their economic crisis, while standing up to what he feared was a Soviet threat to expand Bolshevism and, at the same time, Russian influence (and security). Ideology and geopolitics, all mixed up together.

Yet this was the same Winston Churchill who had just finished five years in a political alliance with the USSR that defeated Hitler's Germany and Imperial Japan; the same Winston Churchill who, in the mid- and late-1930s, had advocated allying with the 'Russians', as he referred to the Bolsheviks when he looked to get along with them.

Whether that was 'appeasement', practical power politics, prudence, or some other loaded label, it was a remarkable somersault for the man who had famously despised the Bolshevik revolution in Russia from the start.[6] Churchill's initial anger at that time stemmed from their refusal to rejoin the fight against Imperial Germany in the First World War, but it quickly gave way to a more ideological condemnation, as he called for military intervention. Describing, in 1920, the Bolsheviks as a 'vile group of cosmopolitan fanatics', he promised that 'the policy I will *always advocate is the overthrow and destruction* of that criminal regime'. The criminal acts were, presumably, the execution of Russian royal family – the Romanovs (regicide was anathema to Churchill). Churchill's angry riffs on the Bolsheviks ran the gamut of animals and disease: they were 'a pestilence', 'swarms of typhus-bearing vermin', 'a foul combination of criminality and animalism', ferocious baboons', and vampires. Yet he was eager to have them as allies in 1917–18, looked to make them allies against Hitler in the 1930s, and allied with them during the Second World War.[7]

By 1946, Churchill had concluded that the Stalin he had 'trusted' at the Yalta conference, had betrayed that trust.[8] The reference to an iron curtain was, like so many of his catch-phrases, a well-rehearsed label. Whatever Stalin's well-documented and quite logical, perhaps accurate, conviction that the capitalist nations were dedicated to the containment and/or destruction of the Soviet state and system (Churchill clearly advocated a restoration of the *cordon sanitaire*), the Soviet leader had ignored the spirit and sense of the Yalta agreements.[9] His brutal installation of Soviet puppet states, under the guise of liberation, particularly in Poland, had ignored the facade that both Churchill and Roosevelt had constructed. Granted, both Churchill and Stalin acknowledged that 'the right to guide the course of history is the noblest prize of victory' (Churchill's phrase) and that, according to Stalin, 'everyone imposes his own system as far as his army can reach'. Just before the Yalta talks, Churchill wrote, 'it is understood that the Russians were to work their will in this sphere [the Balkans]. Anyhow we cannot prevent them'.[10]

The unwritten rule that Stalin ignored was that in return for acceptance of Soviet dominance in Eastern Europe, the Anglo-Americans expected cosmetics that would make Soviet control politically tolerable in the UK and the USA. Stalin, hardly sensitive to the domestic pressures of a democratic society, ignored unstated nuances and ploughed ahead to establish subservient states that would not challenge Russian/Soviet dominance. In March 1945, a few weeks after the Yalta meeting, Churchill, predisposed to distrust socialism of any kind and Communism in particular, swung away from a cooperative approach towards the USSR, and campaigned to get the United States to take the lead in confronting the Soviet Union. FDR, desperately ill, stuck to his guns, hoping to preserve what he called the 'family circle' approach to post-war great power relationships – his 'Four Policemen'.[11]

Both Churchill and Roosevelt were probably wrong. Stalin's fatalism was set out bluntly after the Hiroshima and Nagasaki bombings, when he instructed his bureaucracy to ignore American coercive hints about their superweapon (i.e. 'atomic diplomacy') and to develop an atomic bomb. His logic was flawless given his premise that the West was unwavering in its commitment to destroy the Soviet (Bolshevik/Communist) revolution. Ignore the hints and threats and

Prologue: the ghost in the attic 13

build our own bomb, he instructed. If we do not develop a bomb, they will destroy the Revolution. If we do develop a bomb and they attack us, we are all destroyed. Only having a bomb gives us a chance to preserve the Revolution, a remark that presaged MAD – mutual assured destruction.[12] In the same spirit, both Churchill and Roosevelt consistently and firmly rejected proposals to 'internationalize' the bomb. Sharing such information was not one of the 'sinews of peace' and Churchill flatly said so in that so-titled Fulton speech. 'God has willed' that the Anglo-Americans hold the atomic secret, and 'it would be criminal madness' (and blasphemy?) to allow 'some Communist or neo-Fascist State' to frighten other nations 'with consequences appalling to human imagination'.[13]

This is not the place to berate or praise the Anglo-Americans, or to argue about moral equivalency, though quite obviously they had been conducting their own form of atomic diplomacy, a tactic that had failed to mitigate Soviet brutality in Eastern Europe. What matters here is that Churchill had somersaulted back to his earliest nightmares about the Bolsheviks – 'criminal madness' and unimaginable consequences constitute an unequivocal position statement.

Nor is this the place for a comprehensive summary of Churchill and the Soviet Union. Fortunately, the historian David Carlton published in 2000 a study that remains the best survey of the title subject, *Churchill and the Soviet Union*. Carlton neatly traces Churchill's 'somersaults' (flip-flops in today's media jargon) with his chapter titles: initially 'Irreconcilable adversary'. Then 'Guarded rapprochement' in the 1930s, until the Nazi–Soviet Pact ended any hope of working with the Bolsheviks, followed by 'Allied with hell' – the Second World War, when Churchill worked with the Russians. 'Preaching confrontation, 1945–49' gave way to 'Summitry' and 'Domestic politics' during Churchill's second ministry in the early 1950s.[14]

Obviously then, we should not treat the Fulton speech or Churchill's fulminations in the early 1920s as his final position. The same Churchill who is depicted as a 'fanatical enemy of Marxism–Leninism' once again counselled for talks with Soviet leaders following Stalin's death in 1953. Deeply worried about the possibility of thermonuclear war, he counselled that 'meeting jaw to jaw is better than war' (the accurate version of that famous quip).[15] Then President Dwight Eisenhower, who spoke of the evil of the Soviet Union long before Ronald Reagan, dismissed Churchill's plea as that of an old man. The inference was palpable. Alzheimer's would have been today's label.[16]

Boxing in Winston Churchill is a difficult fit. Emerson posited that 'foolish consistency is the hobgoblin of small minds', On the Soviet Union, Churchill hardly seemed consistent, foolishly or otherwise. Or was he? If the destruction of the Soviet system, which he vigorously advocated in his younger years, was a consistency, then what about his later flirtations with rapprochement and even alliance with the Bolsheviks in Moscow, and his plea for discussions with Stalin's successors where he counselled geopolitical peace rather than ideological war?

The answer is that his consistency was not foolish, but primarily (perhaps decisively) reserved to the interests of the United Kingdom or, perhaps more narrowly, England, and its traditions. Claims that he was a great defender of liberty and human rights make no sense except within that tight restraint. He was, in every sense of the word, a nationalist steeped in British tradition. No wonder the Fulton speech combined hint of a plea for economic aid with a condemnation of Soviet excesses.

We must be careful to distinguish between Churchill's rhetoric and writings and his actions, particularly when in high office and when he was responsible for Britain and its Empire. As 'Ziggy' once asked in the comic strip: 'Ever notice how politicians only make promises before they're elected?'

The Soviet Union – adversary, rapprochement, ally, confrontation, politics – the contradictory images are obvious. Churchill never let ideology get in the way of practical and prudent politics. He was Cicero, not Cato.

But where does that leave the Anglo-American Special Relationship?

Churchill's long-standing affection for the United States and his repeated calls for an alliance with America make it seem as if he disagreed with Lord Palmerston's epigram: 'Nations have no permanent friends or allies, they only have permanent interests.' Critics have accused him of a sentimental commitment to a relationship that ensured that Britain would 'lose' the Second World War even as the Allies won it. Just as Joseph 'Kennedy wanted to "appease" Hitler ... Churchill wanted to appease Roosevelt,' wrote one.[17] That distorts Churchill's thinking. He sought to preserve and expand what he later christened the 'Special Relationship' because it already existed and because Britain's interests benefited from that policy. Put another way, it is always better to have as a partner someone who shares your values and ideals in addition to having the wherewithal to help you.

To start with, the AASR was not a creation of the Second World War or of the 'Sinews of Peace' speech. It was and has been very real from the beginning. Common sense dictates that there is a permanent 'special' relationship between a colonizer and its colonials, between the 'mother' country and its offspring. Simultaneously, there are significant differences between this and that empire, this and that colony. The long-term relationship may be positive, may be combative, may be benign, may be competitive. But that it is different and special needs no footnote.[18] *'Special' does not mean good, positive, negative, or exploitative. It just means unique, in the proper sense of the word.*

Once the War of 1812 (the North American version of the Napoleonic War) ended, disagreements between the United States and Great Britain were relegated to details, not territory and legitimacy – whatever the sometimes overheated rhetoric. Even the disputes during the American Civil War never rose to crisis level. Without offering a litany of examples (see any good history), suffice to say that, for two centuries, the reality has been that the Special Relationship has been 'the *tendency* to work together and rise above discord'. Routinely, Britain and America have come to the same broad conclusions, though it 'was always a negotiation, not a dictation'.[19] Economic/commercial competition was a given, but never a war. The apogee of that relationship may have come during the Second World War, but its origins and present persistence suggest that there is much more to it than just a necessary alliance against a clear and present danger.

Prologue: the ghost in the attic 15

Certainly Josef Stalin treated the AASR as a very real thing. When Roosevelt tried to distance himself from Churchill in attempts to convince the Soviet leader that the British and Americans were not ganging up on him, Stalin routinely cautioned associates that the Anglo-Americans were working together. Initiatives proposed by just FDR prompted Stalin to ask about Churchill's thoughts.

But was the AASR as tight as Stalin thought it was? Roosevelt and Churchill were not in lock-step on how to deal with their indispensable ally. But both recognized that victory over Hitler's Germany required the Red Army. End of discussion. Compromise and consideration for each other's arguments were in order, always facilitated by the growing personal relationship between Churchill and Roosevelt.

Immediately after the German attack on Soviet forces in 1941, both agreed, Roosevelt a bit more quickly than Churchill, that the survival of the Soviet Union was essential if Germany was to be contained and defeated. Despite the gloomy predictions of their military advisors, both made commitments to ensure that aid went to the Russians. Presciently, Roosevelt had successfully prevented attempts to exclude the Soviet Union from obtaining Lend–Lease aid (March 1941), but US war production was only beginning to gear up and there was not much aid to send. Churchill, understandably reluctant to share the military aid going to Britain, agreed to limited diversions of those supplies.

Once the Battle of Moscow (December 1941) stopped the German advance, Stalin revived his efforts for a formal wartime alliance and for agreement on restoration of the Soviet boundaries as of the German attack, particularly the return of the Baltic states (which had been ruled by the Russian czars for some two centuries). Churchill initially agreed while Roosevelt demurred, saying such boundary adjustments should await the end of the war and a peace conference. By war's end, the two had switched their positions, Roosevelt agreeing to Soviet rule of the Baltics, Churchill moving towards challenging expanding Soviet control. Those differences have been discussed and debated extensively, but often without alluding to the key point: the AASR was not broken or even challenged by their differences.[20]

That pattern continued throughout the war; during the period of rough Anglo-American equality, then after the US contribution of manpower and machines became overwhelming, and at the great wartime conferences between Churchill and Roosevelt as well as their tripartite meetings with Stalin at Teheran and Yalta. Even Churchill's two private get-togethers with Stalin (meetings to which FDR had no objections) caused not a ripple in the AASR. Roosevelt once tried secretly to arrange a private meeting with Stalin, fearing Churchill's pre-war open hostility toward the 'Bolsheviks' would work against agreement. Churchill's feelings were hurt when he found out, but the AASR hardly wobbled.

The much publicized great arguments within the AASR over grand and even theatre/operational strategy were fully and well argued, and settled amiably (though sometimes amiability took a few months). The military staffs of both leaders were told at the Atlantic conference (August 1941) and thereafter that they had to work together and not bring disagreements directly to the President

16 *W.F. Kimball*

or the Prime Minister to settle, an injunction that Roosevelt and Churchill themselves followed by working together.

The over-argued matter of an all-out versus a series of peripheral invasions of Western Europe always related to the Russians. By the end of 1942, Roosevelt and Churchill had reached broad agreement on using the wartime alliance (coalition) as a way to build confidence among Soviet leaders that they could work with the Anglo-Americans during the war and in the peace that would follow. Not only did Roosevelt and Churchill consistently fear that Stalin might negotiate with the Germans, but FDR believed that, in the long term, such confidence was the only way to build a lasting (fifty years or so was his prediction) peace. Churchill was cautious, sometimes edgy, but he loyally stuck with that agreement until after the Yalta conference (February 1945). Following FDR's death (April 1945), Churchill and the successor Labour Government moved towards challenging Soviet expansion and policies in East–Central Europe, as did the Truman administration. The personal relationship of British and US leaders became more formal, but the AASR rolled on.

What is clear is that almost all of the great debates within the AASR during the war depended or at least touched on wartime and/or post-war relations with the Soviet Union. Even the sometimes angry debate over European colonialism prompted Stalin to jump in, saying that

> after this war all States would be very nationalistic.... The feeling to live independently would be the strongest. Later, economic feelings would prevail, but in the first period they would be purely nationalistic and therefore groupings would be unwelcome. The fact that Hitler's regime had developed nationalism could be seen in the example of Yugoslavia where Croats, Montenegrins, Slovenes, &c. all wanted something of their own. It was a symptom.[21]

Stalin was right. A half-century after the Second World War, nationalism would confront and confound the Soviet Union and then the Russian republic. But nationalism had another face. In August 1941 the challenge seemed to come from the Atlantic Charter. That informal but widely publicized agreement between Churchill and Roosevelt stated 'they respect the right of all peoples to choose the form of government under which they will live'. Churchill knew that old-style empire was a thing of the past, but he could not figure out what should come next. He was angered by what he viewed as FDR's interference in imperial affairs, just as FDR was annoyed that Churchill seemed not to understand the international tensions created by European empires. But they agreed to disagree. FDR stopped his public pushing – for a while, Churchill moved on and the AASR continued – strong as ever.

Churchill's prescriptions set out in the 'Sinews of Peace' speech pivoted on the AASR. American economic leadership and help was a *sine qua non*. Standing up to (containing) the Soviet Union took US military strength and statesmanship. The AASR ensured that Great Britain would be part of the process, not merely party to it.[22]

Prologue: the ghost in the attic   17

Notes

1 Richard M. Langworth (ed.), *Churchill By Himself*, St Ives: Ebury Press, 2008, p. 29. My thanks to Richard Langworth, Lloyd Gardner, James Muller, Fred Pollock, and the editors of this volume for their indispensable help.

2 As I have warned elsewhere, it is hard not to repeat myself on these issues, even though historians are masters at saying the same thing under various guises. Portions of this essay have been borrowed and/or paraphrased from a number of my earlier pieces, particularly, 'Principles and Compromises: Churchill, Roosevelt and Eastern Europe', in Richard Langworth (ed.), *Churchill Proceedings, 1994–95*, Washington, DC: The Churchill Center, 1998, pp. 98–106, and my review of David Carlton, *Churchill and the Soviet Union*, Manchester and New York: Manchester University Press, 2000, in *Finest Hour: Journal of the Churchill Center and Societies*, 107, Summer 2000, 24–5. My thanks to Carlton for the somersault image. See also 'The "Special" Anglo-American Special Relationship: "A Fatter, Larger Underwater Cable"', *Journal of Transatlantic Studies*, 3:1, 2005, 1–5; '"Fighting with Allies": The Hand-care and Feeding of the Anglo-American Special Relationship', in David Schmitz and T. Christopher Jesperson (eds), *Architects of the American Century*, Chicago: Imprint Publications, 2000; and 'Dangerously Contagious? The Anglo-American Special Relationship', a debate with Alex Danchev, *The British Journal of Politics and International Relations*, 7:3, 2005, 437–41. For the 'eternal triangle' quote, see my introduction to *Churchill and Roosevelt: The Complete Correspondence*, Princeton: Princeton University Press, 1984, 3 volumes, I, p. 9. Even the title of this piece is genially lifted from my 'The Ghost in the Attic: The Soviet Union as a Factor in Anglo-American Wartime Planning for Postwar Germany, 1943–1945', in Arthur L. Funk (ed.), *Politics and Strategy in the Second World War, International Committee for the History of the Second World War and Military Affairs/ Aerospace Historian*, 1976, pp. 88–112.

3 For Churchill's quip see Langworth (ed.), *Churchill By Himself*, p. 276. See W. Kimball, *The Juggler*, Princeton: Princeton University Press, 1991, pp. 31–6. Hopkins wrote of being 'confident' and that 'There is unbounded determination to win'; as quoted in David Roll, *The Hopkins Touch*, New York: Oxford University Press, 2013, p. 131. See also Christopher O'Sullivan, *Harry Hopkins: FDR's Envoy to Churchill and Roosevelt*, Lanham, MD: Rowman & Littlefield, 2015, ch. 4.

4 For the origins of the 'iron curtain' phrase see John Ramsden, 'Mr Churchill Goes to Fulton', in James W. Muller (ed.), *Churchill's 'Iron Curtain' Speech Fifty Years Later*, Columbia, MO: University of Missouri Press, 1999, p. 15, n. 1. Other essays in this collection address the reasons for the receptivity of American leaders and the public to Churchill's speech.

5 Robert Rhodes James (ed.), *Winston Churchill: His Complete Speeches, 1897–1963*, vol. VII, New York and London: Chelsea House, 1974, p. 7287 (hereafter 'Sinews of Peace'). For the 'Four Policemen' see Warren F. Kimball, 'The Sheriffs: FDR's Postwar World', in David Woolner, Warren F. Kimball and David Reynolds (eds), *FDR's World: War Peace, and Legacies*, New York: Palgrave Macmillan, 2008, pp. 91–121.

6 For a vigorous defence of Churchill's principled prudence see Larry P. Arnn, *Churchill's Trial: Winston Churchill and the Survival of Free Government*, Nashville, TN: Thomas Nelson, 2016.

7 Carlton, *Churchill and the Soviet Union*, p. 26 (emphasis added). The riff of insults is on page 20.

8 Langworth (ed.), *Churchill By Himself*, p. 374.

9 For documentary evidence of Stalin's firm belief in Western intentions, see Oleg Rzheshevsky (ed.), *War and Diplomacy: The Making of the Grand Alliance: Documents from Stalin's Archives*, Amsterdam: Harwood Academic Publishers/Overseas Publishers Association, 1996.

18   *W.F. Kimball*

10 'Everyone imposes his own system as far as his army can reach' is one version of Stalin's observation; 'whoever occupies a territory imposes on it his own social system' is another. The minor differences are likely due to different translations of the original source, Milovan Djilas, *Conversations with Stalin* (1961). For Churchill on the Balkans see Carlton, *Churchill and the Soviet Union*, p. 121 (quoting from Martin Gilbert, *Road to Victory*, see note 21).

11 Kimball, *The Juggler*, pp. 159–83, and 'Sheriffs and Constables: Churchill's and Roosevelt's Postwar World', *Finest Hour: The Journal of Winston Churchill*, 141, 2008–9, pp. 36–42. I argue the 'cosmetics' thesis in *The Juggler*, ch. 8.

12 I have constructed statements by Stalin for which there is problematic evidence. Suffice to say that what I have written comports with David Holloway's extensive research in Soviet and Western sources; for example see Holloway, 'The Atomic Bomb and the End of the Wartime Alliance', in Ann Lane and Howard Temperley (eds), *The Rise and Fall of the Grand Alliance, 1941–45*, London: Macmillan, 1995, pp. 207–25.

13 'Sinews of Peace', pp. 7287–8.

14 David Carlton and I have some interpretive disagreements, but his summary of Churchill's statements and actions is spot on.

15 Quotations from Carlton, *Churchill and the Soviet Union*, p. 142, and Langworth (ed.), *Churchill By Himself*, p. 19.

16 Warren F. Kimball, 'Churchill and Eisenhower: Sentiment and Politics', in Richard Langworth (ed.), *Churchill Proceedings*, 1998–2000, Washington, DC: The Churchill Center, 2004, pp. 64–74. See also Klaus Larres, *Churchill's Cold War*, New Haven: Yale University Press, 2002.

17 The phrase is that of John Charmley as quoted in W. Kimball, 'Sentimental Relations?' a review of Charmley, *Churchill's Grand Alliance* (1995), *Times Literary Supplement*, 21 July 1995.

18 Of course I am happy to provide a citation: see Kimball, 'Dangerously Contagious? The Anglo-American Special Relationship'.

19 Warren F. Kimball, 'The Anglo-American Relationship: Still Special after All these Years', in Antoine Capet (ed.), *The 'Special Relationship' – La 'relation spéciale' entre le Royaume-Uni et les États-Unis*, Rouen: Université de Rouen, 2003, pp. 207–24.

20 The latest entry into the lists is Kaarel Piirmäe, *Roosevelt, Churchill, and the Baltic Question: Allied Relations during the Second World War*, New York: Palgrave Macmillan, 2014.

21 Minutes of the TOLSTOY Conference, Moscow, 17 October 1944, as quoted in Martin Gilbert, *Road to Victory*, Boston: Houghton Mifflin, 1986, p. 1026.

22 The AASR has, in the last two decades or so, generated a corps of British sceptics. John Charmley and Alex Danchev, representing two very different starting points, come to mind, though there are more recent, more vocal voices. In some cases that stems from searching for an explanation of why Britain went from Great to not-so-Great despite winning World War Two. Their answer? The Americans. For others, those who view the European Union as Britain's future, escaping the AASR is essential to redirecting Britain's focus towards Europe.

1 'Strategic culture' on the road to (and from) Fulton

Institutionalism, emotionalism, and the Anglo-American special relationship

David G. Haglund

Introduction

The purpose of this chapter is a simple one. It is to ask what, if anything, the somewhat voguish if ambiguous conceptual touchstone known as 'strategic culture' can add to the debate over the central focus of this book, the 'Anglo-American special relationship' (hereafter, AASR). Many have taken it to be self-evident that the bilateral security and defence linkage that has been constructed between the US and UK constitutes a development of sufficient singularity to stand out as one of the most important (a few would even say *the* most important) among the myriad geostrategic 'institutions' to have arisen over the course of the past century. Questions have abounded regarding this geostrategic institution, some related to the AASR's chronology, others to its 'causal' mechanisms, and still others to its normative implications. As well, there is even a smattering of analysts who make so bold as to deny that there ever *has* been an AASR, or if there has been, they say, it has effectively drawn to an end. But for the most part, the AASR is accepted as an ongoing fixture of the international political scene. How it came to be such, and what its policy and normative implications might be, remain topics of debate.

This debate, regarding the AASR's existence and evolution, I discuss in the second part of this chapter, which sets the stage for the ensuing discussion of the strategic cultural dimension(s) of the AASR. In the third part I turn to a conceptual analysis of strategic culture, where I endeavour to suggest how we might broach the nexus between our master concept and the AASR, *inter alia* by illustrating how strategic culture should *not* be applied. The core of the chapter's argument is to be found in part four, in which I claim that strategic culture, properly understood, can assist our scholarly inquiry into the AASR in two main ways. The first of these involves an analysis of 'institutional' dynamics associated with a theoretical approach known as 'path dependence', one that at first blush may seem to have nothing at all to do with culture (strategic or otherwise), but which I am going to argue deserves being considered as a subset of 'relational culture', this latter being itself an attribute of strategic culture. Following directly upon this I introduce the relative importance of 'affect' for the functioning of the AASR, a putatively recent line of inquiry among certain International

20 *D.G. Haglund*

Relations (IR) scholars. Its novelty aside, there is a lengthy academic pedigree for a related category, 'national character', a concept that rounds out my discussion in this part of the chapter, where I reflect upon some recent research into what 'collective identity' might mean for the AASR. The concluding part draws together the various threads of the argument, and recapitulates the two themes highlighted in the chapter's subtitle – institutionalism and emotionalism.

Both of these latter themes were adumbrated in Churchill's March 1946 speech in Missouri, and for symbolic reasons alone a case might be made for considering the Fulton address as a logical point of departure for any strategic–cultural assessment of the AASR. At the very least, if culture can be thought of as a system of symbols and meanings – in one writer's apt words, as 'the semiotic dimension of human social practice in general'[1] – then surely the particularized variant of culture under discussion in these pages, *strategic* culture, has never been more well serviced than it was on that day back in March 1946 when the wartime prime minister waxed so eloquently about two powerful tropes, summoning forth emotionalism so as to serve the purposes of institutionalism.

Most memorable of the two, of course, was the metaphor 'iron curtain', invoked to draw attention to the need for Western countries to adopt a robust response to what was looking very much like an attempt of the quondam Soviet ally to reserve for itself as much of Central and Eastern Europe as it was capable of bringing into its political and military orbit. Although we invariably remember Churchill as the originator of this figure of speech, we would do better to regard him as being simply its most successful merchandiser. As early as 1920 the metaphor had been employed by Ethel Snowden, a member of a Labour Party delegation travelling to the Soviet Union, thrilled as she announced herself to be 'behind the "iron curtain" at last!' A generation later, it was recycled by none other than Joseph Goebbels, warning German readers in the pages of *Das Reich* on 24 February 1945 that should their country surrender, the recently concluded Yalta agreement between the American, British, and Soviet leaders would 'allow the Soviets to occupy all east and southeast Europe, together with the major part of the Reich. An iron curtain would at once descend on this territory.' Lest it be thought that he was taking symbolic cues from Hitler's chief propagandist, it should be noted that Churchill, too, had been wont to deploy the metaphor himself, in speeches made during the year leading up to Fulton.[2]

Symbolically powerful as the iron curtain was, it was another Churchillian figure of speech at Fulton that concerns us more in this book, revealing as it did the lineaments of the emerging geostrategic institution we know of as the AASR – in Churchill's words, a 'fraternal association of the English-speaking peoples. This means a special relationship between the British Commonwealth and Empire and the United States.'[3] This time, no one appears to have beaten Churchill to the semiotic punch, for 'it is clear that the term itself was a Churchillian invention'.[4] However, Fulton did not mark, as so many like to think, his first uttering of it in public; according to the *Oxford English Dictionary*, he had used it in a speech in the House of Commons a quarter of a year earlier, when Prime Minister Clement Attlee was preparing to pay a visit to the United States.

Churchill had in mind both the US and Canada, and wanted to remind his Downing Street successor about the existence of one of the strongest security bonds between Britain and North America, the one forged in trilateral wartime collaboration to build nuclear weapons: 'We should fortify in every way our special and friendly connections with the United States,' he remarked on 7 November 1945. '[W]e should not abandon our special relationship with the United States and Canada about the atomic bomb.'[5]

But if the phrase, 'special relationship' was Churchill's own, the idea intended to be advanced by its invocation had a considerably longer pedigree than simply the recent global war. Indeed, as we shall see in the section below, visions of special security relations between the two large English-speaking countries had been dancing in the heads of quite a few intellectuals and policy elites on either side of the Atlantic, beginning in the late nineteenth century. These visions were nothing if not grandiose ones.[6]

What would Epictetus say? Debating the AASR

Among those analysts, and they are numerous, who accept the existence of the geostrategic institution we call the AASR, there remains widespread disagreement over some key aspects of its biography, beginning with, but hardly limited to, the question of its birthday. Some believe it made its appearance in the transatlantic and global security environment as long ago as the end of the nineteenth century. Others hold it to have originated later than that – by some accounts, a half-century later (which, if so, would be yet another reason commending the Fulton address for particular attention in a chapter such as mine). No one could or would be able to sustain the claim that the AASR's origins ought to be situated much earlier than the second quinquennium of the nineteenth century's final decade, notwithstanding prior instances of transitory Anglo-American harmony (of a sort), as for instance around the start of that same century.[7] Yet there might be some utility here in our peering way back in time, into the very mists of antiquity, in quest of heuristic guidance. Specifically, we might benefit from pondering, in respect of the ongoing debate over our geostrategic institution, a bit of advice proffered some two millennia ago by the Stoic philosopher Epictetus, whose *Discourses* contain wisdom from which contemporary students of international security can derive benefit. For what Epictetus had to say about appearances and realities *in general* can inspire creative thinking about particular features of recent and contemporary political reality, and no more so than when we confront the existential debate over the AASR.[8]

Apropos that debate, consider a couple of strong claims made by some observers of the international security scene, who tend to doubt that the AASR ever has existed – or, if it has existed, has done so only in a fashion radically different from the manner in which it is usually described, and sometimes 'evangelized' (to use Alex Danchev's dismissive term).[9] In a word, the AASR has been a lie. We might refer to this class of scholar as the 'AASR-denier'. Conspicuous members of the class would include Erwan Lagadec and Edward Ingram. In the

22 D.G. Haglund

case of the former, there is only one thing that can be said to be 'special' about the relationship between the US and the UK, and it resides not in the cluster of behavioural qualities suggestive of cooperation and friendship, but rather the reverse. Somewhat joyfully, Lagadec tells us that the

> litany of insults, misunderstandings, and clashes between the UK and the US suggests that their relationship' is only 'special' insofar as it has been *more* contentious than any other in the recent past. As a result, the political 'special relationship' is but a futile exercise in deluded nostalgia. It leans on the altar of a past that never was, though it yields but the flimsiest results in the present, and is a useless tool to shape the future.[10]

Strong words, one might think. But Lagadec's acerbic scepticism regarding the AASR can look positively celebratory when contrasted with that of Edward Ingram, who in an epistemological broadside directed against political scientists and a policy one aimed at enthusiasts of the special relationship has gone so far as to dismiss as nonsense what some IR theorists like to regard as one of their discipline's rare 'iron laws'.[11] I refer here to the notion that liberal democracies do not resort to force or even to the threat of same when they are involved in disputes with fellow liberal democracies (an ostensible law captured in the acronym DPT – for democratic peace theory). For Ingram, this claim is not only theoretically preposterous, but it flies in the face of empirical reality, for as he tells it, '[b]etween 1916 and 1945 ... the two most powerful so-called democratic states, the United States and Britain, had gone to war with one another, to fight until one of them was destroyed'. Nor is that all, for he adds, in a passage that will have many students of the AASR adjusting their reading classes, that '[a]lthough the United States did not formally declare war against Britain during World War II, it did destroy Britain and may have done so deliberately'.[12] Seen in this light, the AASR was nothing but a snare and a delusion for Britain and its leaders, and the road to Fulton, epitomized by the wartime relationship between Churchill and Franklin D. Roosevelt, turned out to be a pot-holed dead end, with the AASR representing nothing other than 'so extreme a version of an alliance as a tool of management that it became a strangling alliance in which one party uses the alliance to destroy the other'.[13]

So, what *would* Epictetus say about such claims? He would say that '[t]hings either are what they appear to be; or they neither are, nor appear to be; or they are and do not appear to be; or they are not, and yet appear to be'.[14] Applied to the AASR, this quadripartite dictum alerts us to the following menu of choice: (1) that the AASR is self-evidently a feature of the modern international security system, and is widely recognized to be so; or (2) that it is hogwash taken seriously by no one, save perhaps a few superannuated cheerleaders of Anglo-American condominium (Danchev's 'evangelists'); or (3) that it actually does possess ongoing theoretical and policy significance, though to date its existence has transcended our ability to comprehend it intellectually, much less to explain it; or (4) that it is devoid of content, but is mistakenly thought to be otherwise.

'Strategic culture' on the road to Fulton 23

If *ur*-sceptics such as Lagadec and Ingram belong in the menu's second category (and possibly its fourth), we are still left with a couple of parts of the Epictetian list from which to select when we set out to analyse the debate over the AASR in a systematic fashion – all the more so when we insist, as this chapter does, upon mustering strategic culture into the labour of systematic analysis. As I will argue below, a good case can be made for slotting the AASR into Epictetus's third category, namely of things that exist but whose workings and logic have not been sufficiently comprehended. The AASR-deniers apart, there really is a large body of scholarly and policy writing testifying to the frequency with which this geopolitical institution, even if only cloaked in mythical raiment,[15] has been brought into discussions of transatlantic and even global security arrangements, on the part of analysts bent on understanding how the AASR might figure into the calculus of the US or UK national interest(s), or more broadly what might be its consequences for regional and global security, writ large.

Indeed, if taken purely in a consequential sense – that is, when it has been envisioned as a necessary and sufficient component of whatever stability is to be found in the international system[16] – you could even say that the AASR attained the height of its policy allure well prior to its having earned its name, much less any rightful claim to importance in the councils of transatlantic or global security (both of which, the name and the claim, date from the 1940s). Taken only in this consequentially aspirational sense, the AASR was being extolled by some as *the* central and indispensable cog in the apparatus of global peace and security decades before the Fulton address and its specific invocation of the special relationship. There never *was* a moment when the luminous promise of Anglo-American security collaboration shone more brightly – again, from the purely aspirational point of view – than the decade and a half preceding the onset of the First World War, the era of the 'Great Rapprochement' between the erstwhile English-speaking geopolitical antagonists.[17] Many were the voices raised in a chorus of praise for the advent of a new international age, one in which nothing short of the 'universal peace' was finally going to be ushered into existence, thanks to the combined energies of the two most powerful states on earth, the UK and the US.

As expressed by one of the acolytes of this uplifting vision, H. Perry Robinson, the British, much like Barkis in Dickens' *David Copperfield*, were 'willin'' – willing, that is, to take the plunge and enter into an alliance with the Peggotty of their own choosing, the Americans. Should such an alliance be constructed, no power on earth could take it on, with the happy result being the dawning of peace for all time. It really was all a matter of America's opting to do the right and necessary thing, argued Robinson.

> I believe that it has it in its power to do no less a thing than to abolish war for ever – to give to the peoples of the earth the blessing of Perpetual Peace.... The ultimate domination of the world by the Anglo-Saxon (let us call him so) seems to be reasonably assured; and no less assured is it that at

24   *D.G. Haglund*

some time wars will cease. The question for both Englishmen and Americans to ask themselves is whether, recognising the responsibility that already rests upon it, the Anglo-Saxon race dare or can for conscience' sake … hang back and postpone the advent of the Universal Peace which it is in its power to bring about to-day.[18]

Compared with this vision of an AASR not yet born, the special relationship that emerged from the Second World War, and was anointed at Fulton, cannot help but pale; for rather than the deus ex machina of the early twentieth century, which would engender 'systems change' and abolish the international balance of power itself via an Anglo-American imperium, what Churchill was advocating a half-century later was a much more modest version of change. What Churchill was promoting in Missouri was change of a 'systemic' variant whereby the two partners would combine forces in a bid not to eradicate the anarchical system (and with it, war) but rather to ensure that the familiar logic of the balance of power could be fashioned in such a way as to yield them a favourable margin of safety against the Soviet Union, if necessary by threatening war.[19]

Thus if one sought to substantiate, *pace* the AASR-deniers, the 'objective' existence of the special relationship, it would require starting with the alliance between the two countries and then going on to specify how this particular bilateral security bonding might coexist, but in a behaviourally (and observably) distinct fashion, with the other bilateral alliances that the two countries have compacted and maintained.[20] One need not invoke strategic culture to undertake such a demonstration, and indeed many scholars have happily eschewed the rubric altogether, when they advance claims about the specialness of the Anglo-American alliance, often dependent upon particular modes of sharing, in both military technology – namely nuclear weaponry – and intelligence.[21] But if one wanted to go a bit further, and probe not just *why* the AASR is said to be so singular, but also *when* it could be remarked to have come into existence, then strategic culture might have a legitimate claim for inclusion in the theoretical and empirical debate over our geostrategic institution, not least because it provides us with some conceptual tools with which to address what is the most important theoretical question posed in respect of the 'ties that bind' the two countries in pursuit of common aims. That question, an old if not easily answerable one, turns on whether analysts incline more towards those things we call 'interests' when we posit bonding elements, as opposed to putting the emphasis upon something (presumably) different, 'sentiment'.[22] I return to this point in this chapter's fourth section.

No better platform can be found for embarking on this line of inquiry than the body of IR scholarship broadly lumped under the category of 'stable peace theorizing'. Not exactly an offshoot of DPT, this variant of theory is similar to it in that it, too, is concerned with the necessary and (to its adherents) sufficient causes of peaceful change in the international system, predicated on assumptions related to 'collective identity'. According to one of its prominent thinkers, Charles A. Kupchan, there are three stages through which a bilateral relationship progresses on its way to a condition of stable peace between its members: rapprochement, security community, and union[23] – which latter, in the case of the AASR, can be comprehended as meaning alliance rather than a reconstitution of the first British Empire, something that a literal reading of union would seemingly compel. Illustratively, the AASR might be considered 'modal' for all three stages of the stable peace, with perhaps the first more than the other two stages being where the uniqueness of Anglo-American relations stands out, given that, in Kupchan's words, '[r]approchement between the United States and Great Britain demonstrates that hegemonic transitions can occur peacefully – but it represents the only case of peaceful transition on record'.[24] Seen thus, a relationship does not get more 'special' than this, when we consider empirically observable reality, and indeed, it is precisely for this reason – to wit, its happy ending – that some analysts these days turn hopefully to the contemplation of the record of the 'rapprochement' when they speculate about the future of great power relations, especially those involving the US and China.[25]

But there is more to the theory than this, and as it relates the rise and staged evolution of this variant of irenic relations, Kupchan's depiction of the stable peace is apt for our purposes in this volume, and certainly for mine in this chapter. For what it does is to draw our attention to two matters that I am going to argue invite (even if they do not oblige) a strategic–cultural perspective on the workings of the AASR. The first of these concerns the matter of timing and directs us to this question: how would we know when the AASR came into existence, and what would our so knowing tell us about the significance of the Fulton address, particularly in terms of its bearing upon 'institutionalization'? The second (and as hinted above, more important) question relates to what it is that is thought to hold the AASR together, and what if anything this bonding element might have to do with 'emotion'.

These, respectively, are the topics covered in the fourth part of this chapter, but before we get to them, one more matter requires our attention: the manner in which we comprehend strategic culture.

What good is strategic culture?[26]

Strategic culture is one of a long list of ambiguous and sometimes confusing concepts to which students of IR turn when they seek to explain or otherwise understand the complex realities of the international system. It has had little to do, so far, with the scholarship on the AASR, and there is no reason to imagine that either the scholars or the relationship have suffered as a result. Still, there may be something to commend this rubric's applicability to the topic of this book.[27] Of course, this will require, first, a bit of discussion as to how we might usefully employ the rubric, and why. This is the challenge I face in this portion of the chapter, to make the case for strategic culture's being invited into the discussion of the rise, evolution, and future of the AASR.

To begin this conceptual–analytical foray into strategic culture, it is useful to engage in something of a definitional skirmish *a contrario*. By this I mean that we

26 *D.G. Haglund*

are better advised if we demand of our concept that it stand for what some social scientists like to call an 'independent variable', i.e. a postulated cause of an effect (or, to use more formalistic – or at least non-English – wording, the *explanans* said to account for the *explanandum*). This is not always how our concept has been employed, for all too frequently it is encountered as something roughly synonymous with 'grand strategy' or even just with a particular country's (or, sometimes, international organization's) way of doing something. This is not necessarily spurious, but treating strategic culture more as an 'output' of policy – or, worse, as just another name for the policy – rather than as a *shaper* of policy raises the obvious question: what is the point of invoking this concept instead of some more serviceable (because familiar) one? Instances of epiphenomenal articulations of policy or strategy in terms of 'culture' are not hard to find. Indeed, they have had an uncanny way of turning up in discussions as to whether the Atlantic was 'widening' because of what was, especially around the time of the Iraq War and for several years afterwards, widely regarded as a divergence within the Western alliance on the utility of force in a country's statecraft.

No one expressed that divergence more memorably than Robert Kagan, in his pithy and widely cited monograph *Of Paradise and Power*, which triggered a polemic not only because of the planetary imagery he offered to support his thesis of a growing gulf between America's strategic culture and that of its various European allies (Britain possibly excepted), with America famously being from 'Mars' and the Europeans from 'Venus', but also because of the manner in which he interpreted the cause of this gulf – primarily to be found in relative capability (otherwise known as power among those analysts who do not choose to equate power with something else, namely 'influence').[28] Nor was Kagan alone in imagining that strategic culture was, and would *have* to be, interesting primarily because of its dependence upon relative capability; legions of European analysts have similarly, though more admiringly than did Kagan, bought into the notion that European strategic culture really did differ, empirically as well as normatively, from America's, because it was predicated upon 'soft power' and a commitment to multilateralism lacking, or so they maintained, in American diplomacy.[29]

For sure, there is nothing wrong and likely a lot right with analysis that places a premium upon 'third-image' (or structural) variables, both in IR theory generally and in the study of that upon which we concentrate in this book, the AASR. Who, just to take some very recent cases, would dare to deny that, say, a Scottish departure from the UK would have serious repercussions upon the AASR, not only because of the problems it would pose for the British nuclear deterrent, berthed at HMNB *Clyde* in Faslane, but also because of the logical supposition that a diminished Britain would, all things being equal, be a less interesting security partner for the US? *Mutatis mutandis*, something similar has been argued to be in the offing should Britain itself exit the European Union – not an outcome very much desired by the US, for a variety of reasons.[30] The upshot of contemporary worries about a downsizing of Britain, even if 'merely' in the budgetary sense, is clear enough; as expressed by John Bew, the UK's stock in Washington, DC, is diminishing. Foot-dragging and defense-cutting Britain is not the ally to America it once was.... The United Kingdom is now hand-wringing about its role in the world in a way not witnessed for many decades.[31]

So, obviously, relative capability counts for a great deal. But the point is, given this, why should anyone feel the need to dress up as 'strategic culture' whatever policy choices are said to be fashioned in strict accord with the presumed dictates of relative capability? We have enough words in the English language to do justice to the thoughts expressed by structural theorists. Thus in this chapter I am going to put the emphasis upon strategic culture as itself the thing that accounts for the strategic choice, and not the other way around. In short, I am going to elevate the concept and treat is as an *explanans*.

How to do this? The first task is some elementary semantic brush-clearing, to facilitate careful grooming of the terrain upon which strategic culture's two component elements display themselves. Of the adjectival component, little need be said save to note that 'strategy' should never be thought to be a word whose meaning resides primarily in the domain of things military. It obviously can and does work its way often into discussion of very 'high' politics indeed – of the sort that conjure up aircraft overhead and troops on the ground, and most of all planners back in headquarters, poring over their maps – but it need not be so wedded to the most martial of arts. For to 'strategize' simply means that one is seeking to identify and promote the most 'rational' linkage possible between whatever ends one seeks to attain and the means available for their attainment. John Lewis Gaddis has said it best: 'by "strategy", I mean quite simply the process by which ends are related to means, intentions to capabilities, objectives to resources'.[32]

If only matters could be so simple when it comes to the noun, 'culture'! Alas, the simplicity inherent in the adjective is nowhere to be encountered, once the focus shifts from one class of word to another. 'Culture' is nothing if not a notoriously ill-disciplined concept. Now, as much the same might be said of so many of our concepts in IR, let us move from lamentation to refinement, and at least attempt to suggest some ways that culture might credibly be employed as an *explanans*. Three such ways come to mind, and we have glimpsed one of them already in the introduction to this chapter, where reference was made to two powerful images employed by Winston Churchill.

In discussing the *cognitive* dimension of strategic culture, we could do much worse than to reflect upon the semantic career of a very similar social-science concept that came into use a generation earlier than strategic culture – the concept of 'political culture'. If strategic culture did not acquire its name until the latter part of the 1970s,[33] political culture got off this particular mark two decades earlier; yet even though it might have been baptized by Gabriel Almond in 1956, it still remained far from obvious what it meant. Was it the 'generalized personality' of a people? Their collective history? Something else altogether? No one could say, and so rampant grew the confusion surrounding

28   D.G. Haglund

the exotic new rubric of political culture that within a decade of its naming it had become nearly extinct as a currency of serious exchange. Though the concept might have gone into eclipse shortly after its baptism, its primary question never did decline in importance – the question of how one goes about tapping the stubbornly subjective orientations of societies' members so as to account for political differences cross-nationally. What *had* changed in the period between political culture's decline and its re-emergence was that a new element was being highlighted whenever political scientists gathered to ponder how they were to assess this thing they called culture. That new element was symbolism.[34]

Symbolism helped resuscitate political culture in two ways. First, it solved the 'level-of-analysis' problem hobbling political culture, for much of the early work by Almond and his associates relied upon survey data that, while it might indicate much of value about the perceptions and psychological state of *individuals*, seemed incapable of generating usable knowledge about the cognitive patterns of collectivities. Individuals, after all, had personalities, but only collectivities could be said to possess cultures, and the trick was to find a way to go from the individual to the collective level of analysis if culture was to mean anything. Symbolism provided the answer, enabling theorists to explore the *social* ideas of individuals.[35]

Symbolism could do this because of its second major contribution, which was to alert us to the cognitive devices that social groupings rely upon, as Lowell Dittmer so astutely phrased it, to 'transmit meanings from person to person despite vast distances of space and time'. Dittmer invited us to think of those devices, which include but are not limited to imagery and metaphor, as being identical to what the poet T.S. Eliot called 'objective correlatives', i.e. mechanisms for the efficient expression of feelings. In this regard, symbols become a 'depository of widespread interest and feeling'. And for Dittmer, the task of those who would employ political culture must be nothing other than the systematic, scientific analysis of society's key symbols.[36] Or as Michael Walzer so eloquently put the same thought, symbols and images tell us 'more than we can easily repeat'.[37]

What occurred with respect to political culture did not take long to recur in connection with strategic culture. Indeed, to the extent (unlikely) that there is or even can be a consensual definition of the latter term, no one has ever filled the bill better than Alastair Iain Johnston, who has presented us with the most ambitious and sophisticated attempt at defining strategic culture. This latter he holds to be

> an integrated system of symbols (i.e., argumentation structures, languages, analogies, metaphors, etc.) that acts to establish pervasive and long-lasting grand strategic preferences by formulating concepts of the role and efficacy of military force in interstate political affairs, and by clothing these conceptions with such an aura of factuality that the strategic preferences seem uniquely realistic and efficacious.[38]

'Strategic culture' on the road to Fulton 29

Now, if all there was to the concept of strategic culture was its cognitive applicability, that would be grounds enough, as noted earlier, for invoking the rubric in a book such as ours, given the widely recognized significance of the Fulton address from the point of view of the imagery to which it made appeal, with the additional contention of some analysts being that it was Churchill's employment of metaphor – his 'discursive' technique as some might be tempted to label it – that served to reinvigorate if not launch *ab ovo* the AASR project.

But there is more to strategic culture than its cognitive dimension, as significant as that assuredly is. More importantly for my purposes here are what can be taken to be the *contextual* uses of strategic culture. Surprisingly for such a seemingly banal word as 'context', there has been a fairly robust epistemological duel from within the very ranks of 'strategic culturalists' – a duel pitting as its chief sword-flashers the 'positivist' Alistair Iain Johnston against the 'interpretivist' Colin Gray. Gray insists that strategic culture must imply the 'context' within which security decision-making occurs, if it is to imply anything at all. For his part, Johnston has been known to object strenuously to what he takes to be the tautological nature of culture-as-context arguments, and not only those made by Gray. Nor is he without supporters,[39] but then so too does Gray have his backers – for one, Stuart Poore, who has entered this fray with a clear, but not unqualified, endorsement of Gray. As he puts it, the 'Gray–Johnston debate illustrates the futility of thinking about strategic culture in terms of causal explanations and falsifiable theory, whilst confirming the potential of a contextual or constitutive framework'.[40]

Poore's comment suggests that the 'contextual' side of the strategic–cultural dwelling must contain the living quarters of the 'anti-positivists', with their estranged family members, the cognitivists, occupying rooms in the wing reserved for 'positivists', these latter folk said to be characterized by their pursuit of 'reliable causality' (otherwise known as 'explanation'), with their contextualizing kin undertaking the more modest task of 'interpreting' social reality.[41] This probably overstates things: not all cognitivists are positivists, and by the same token, as we will soon see, not all contextualists are anti-positivists. Moreover, there is one matter upon which cognitivists like Johnston and contextualists like Gray can be said to be in agreement: 'history' must always constitute a foundational element of strategic culture. Beyond, this, however, there is little common understanding of the meaning of history. This observation is hardly a withering critique of strategic culturalists, for it is obvious that historians themselves cannot come to an agreement on the meaning or nature of their scholarly enterprise. I make the observation here merely to advance the claim that taking history seriously does not necessarily mean that one is 'anti-positivist', any more than the converse. In the next section of this chapter, I am going to show how history can be employed to buttress a particular 'contextualist' argument about the AASR that relies upon the concepts of 'path-dependence' and 'relational culture' – each of which, in its own way, makes powerful claims regarding the origins, evolution, and likely future of the AASR.

30   D.G. Haglund

But before we get to that discussion, one more item of a classificatory nature needs to be introduced, to complete our contextualist inventory of the strategic-culture cupboard with greatest applicability to the AASR. That item is ethnicity, which we will also encounter in the fourth part of this chapter. The dividing line of most significance for my argument in this next, and penultimate, portion of the chapter is the one separating those contextualists whose inquiry into strategic culture inclines them to seek explication of foreign policies in terms of how particular states have acted in the past (i.e. their previous behaviour is argued to have great bearing on their current and future options) from those contextualists who prefer to inquire into how states are thought by their own and other peoples as being likely to act based on the 'way they are' (i.e. their identity, or character, is said to predispose them towards certain policies).

Obviously, this last category, ethnicity, has hardly been *terra incognita* for students of the AASR, notwithstanding their otherwise indifference to strategic culture, and irrespective of whether they put the emphasis upon 'race' or language as the 'ethnic' marker of greatest significance.[42] The point is that ethnicity, whatever we take it to mean, has mattered for a long time among those who contemplate the meaning of the AASR, with Bismarck's hardly representing a solitary voice descrying an Anglo-American alliance as representing nothing other than the 'logic of history' – and this simply because the transatlantic countries shared a common language.[43]

To sum up this section, strategic culture, properly interpreted, can be of use to those of us professing an interest in the AASR. Nor does strategic culture have to be considered the preserve of IR specialists; indeed, probably the most thorough-going strategic culturalist of them all, though he would likely have been the first to spurn the label, is the late Christopher Hitchens, whose masterly study of the AASR managed, with precision and wit, to touch all the cognitive and the contextual bases of relevance to the relationship. In respect of the former domain (the cognitive), he memorably referred to the way in which imagery, much as Johnston would have it, shaped the thinking of decision-makers.

> They [the images] formed part of the common stock of allusion and reference – one might call it the unacknowledged legislation – which underlay the ways in which people thought and responded, and the ways in which they made up their minds regarding the AASR.[44]

In respect of the contextual dimension, Hitchens' analysis had a place for both path dependence and ethnicity, the first in his insistence upon the legacy of role-mediated behaviour that had become the 'endowment from a prolonged engagement with empire, war, and nationalism' and the second because the two peoples' 'main inheritance in the coming polycentric century will be the English language – even if as a final irony this is transmitted through American cultural media and artifacts'.[45]

Path dependence, relational culture, and 'emotion' in the AASR

One of the more innovative of recent applications of strategic culture has been the corpus of contextualizing thinking that has gone under the label of 'path dependence'. In this respect, a seminal figure (though one who, like Hitchens, would be unlikely to don willingly the mantle of strategic culturalist) is the American political scientist Paul Pierson, neither a specialist in the AASR nor a theorist of IR. Yet what this expert in comparative (and American) politics has to tell us about the importance of context is more than germane to those whose scholarly interests incline them towards the AASR. On no particular matter is Pierson's theoretical guidance more poignant than on the very origins of the AASR, in terms both of its chronology and its very *raison d'être*. So let us briefly turn to what he has to say.

In short, what Pierson has to say, both about how history might be taken to matter and especially about the importance of context, should comfort even the most hard-bitten anti-positivist, notwithstanding that Pierson himself dances to a different epistemological rhythm and very much aspires to establish reliable causality (i.e. is much more attuned to the virtues of positivism than one comes to expect from the ranks of contextualizers). Context, acknowledges Pierson, has become a 'bad word' among many social scientists, and this he laments, because to him context is central, not peripheral (or even in opposition) to the scientific enterprise. Context carries in its train a theoretically powerful signification: it concerns those things that surround and therefore define matters of great interest to social scientists, and seen in this light, it is nothing short of a 'scientific disaster' to effect, as the 'decontextualizers' wish to do, the 'removal of defining locational information'.[46]

For Pierson and many others, to place 'politics in time' requires thinking in terms of path dependence. This latter, it is true, hardly constitutes a straightforward or uncontested logic.[47] Nevertheless, path dependence can be consistent with strategic culture, and its logic is so often embedded, however implicitly and even intuitively, in analyses of the AASR that is high time its position be given explicit recognition, as I do in this section. Path dependence is a wonderful intellectual vehicle for the transportation of two very apposite debates about the AASR: to say again, these are the ones concerning its origins and its binding element(s).

Apropos the first of these, the AASR's origins, the two most important aspects of path dependence are 'temporal sequencing' and 'contingency'. For path dependence to mean anything, it cannot simply connote sensitive dependence upon 'initial conditions' set down in some distant past; rather, it must suggest a break point after which the ability of those initial conditions to shape the future can be shown to have altered substantially.[48] Now, whether that inflection point is called 'contingency' or a 'critical juncture' is not terribly important. What does matter is the idea that the inflection point constitutes a moment in time when choices get made that prove to have lasting impact, because they bend

32   *D.G. Haglund*

the 'arc of the future' in a way that no one could have predicted from a sedulous reading of the initial conditions. This is accomplished through the generation of 'self-reinforcing path-dependent processes',[49] referred to varyingly as 'positive feedback' or 'lock-in' or 'increasing returns' (this third formulation often being favoured by economists). Although there is no necessary reason for the logic of positive feedback to yield positive outcomes for interstate cooperation, usually the tendency of those who are enamoured of path-dependent approaches is to dwell upon 'efficient cooperation' as that which is being locked in, and hence to forget that sometimes path dependency can consist in 'reactive sequences' capable of generating negative outcomes for cooperation.[50]

Although there is no shortage of bilateral relationships in the international system to which the ascription of reactive sequences would hardly be out of place (for only one such, consider the US–Iranian tandem), when thoughts turn to the topic of this book, the AASR, it is almost invariably lock-in leading to positive outcomes that captures analytical attention. Scholars can and do disagree as to why there should be this positive sign attached to outcomes (sentiment as opposed to interest, as mentioned above, being the leading binary choice), but few apart from the AASR-deniers doubt that somewhere along the line, the two historic adversaries, the US and the UK, fundamentally reshaped the course of the future, transforming what had been, between 1776 and the ending of the nineteenth century, a bilateral relationship characterized by no little snarling and ill will (and occasionally warfare) into something else, a rapprochement, in the process becoming the very 'poster' candidate for stable peace theory.[51]

When, exactly, the future became changed – that is to say, what the contingent moment turned out to be – is an important question, and path-dependence theorizing can help us think more clearly as to how we should approach this business of putting a date on the AASR's inception, a point of no trifling importance given that, for so many, Churchill's Fulton speech *must* have been an important step on the road to the AASR. Here, on this matter of the timing of the AASR's onset, we find the scholars literally all over the map, or at least the clock's face. Some (Kupchan, ironically, for one) see its origins developing in the last half-decade of the nineteenth century, even if they disagree as to which particular one – 1895, 1896, or 1898 – truly merits the accolade of 'hinge year' for the AASR.[52] Usually, it is the earliest year that is selected for the contingent moment among scholars who date the AASR's onset from this particular *fin de siècle*, because of the bilateral crisis that erupted over the Venezuela–British Guiana boundary, and for a brief period at the end of 1895 looked, improbably as it must otherwise have seemed in light of the absence of any *direct* US territorial stake in the dispute, as if it might lead to a third Anglo-American war. Thus choosing 1895 as the contingent moment represents more than a simple chronological decision; it carries with it a theoretical presumption that among certain kinds of states (here one can take one's pick, among liberal democracies or among Anglo-Saxon countries) war is or should be impossible, for reasons associated with collective identity.[53] This is an important presumption, one to which I return later in this section of the chapter.

'Strategic culture' on the road to Fulton   33

For the moment, though, let us see why it might make more sense to vest contingency in a period closer to our own, possibly early 1946, possibly even later than that. The reason I reported, in the paragraph above, a certain irony associated with Kupchan's assertion regarding the Great Rapprochement's having constituted our contingent moment,[54] is that there really did not seem to be any lock-in detectable in the three post-Rapprochement decades that preceded the Second World War. True, the long-running Anglo-American neuralgia had become mightily soothed by the onset of more pleasant diplomatic interchanges, but if the stable peace is to require, as the theory tells us it does, two subsequent stages in its construction – the first being security community and second, union (or alliance) – then it is obvious that even as late as the interwar period this second stage could not have been taken for granted. Significantly, none other than Winston Churchill himself provides evidence of a non-existent security community, witness his oft-cited remark made to cabinet colleagues on 20 July 1927, '[n]o doubt it is quite right in the interests of peace to go on talking about war with the United States being "unthinkable". Everyone knows that this is not true.'[55]

And this is precisely the point about security community (stage two of stable-peace theorizing): war between the members has to be 'unthinkable'. To the extent it *is* conceivable, then there exists *no* security community, by definition. The list of contentious items on the Anglo-American agenda during the interwar years, coupled not only with Churchill's statement but with the continuation until 1937 of war planning in Washington that presupposed Britain might be a future enemy, means that one should definitely not ascribe too early a birthdate to the AASR.[56] So where might we find the contingent moment, and how would this relate to the Fulton address? If we agree that contingency needs, logically, to be situated neither at the first nor the second stage of stable peace theory – important though rapprochement and security community must be – and insist it must be to the third stage that we turn our attention, we have a reduced range of choice before us, one moreover that is much closer in time to the Fulton speech than it is to the Great Rapprochement.

Candidate 'hinge' years could include 1940, because of the Destroyers for Bases exchange which effectively put paid to American isolationism and led to the de facto alliance (union, in terms of stable-peace theory) between the two that would take them through the Second World War and beyond.[57] Or it could be 1946, because of the Churchillian call for a post-war alliance. Or it could be 1949, because of the formation that year of NATO, a development that one of the alliance's founders, Ernest Bevin, considered to be constitutive for the AASR.[58] It might even be later, perhaps the time of Suez and possibly not until the closing years of the 1950s, this final choice reflecting the assumption that what was *truly* 'special' about the AASR was and remains the nuclear-sharing arrangements that lie at the very heart of the two states' 'union' and that were developed subsequent to the US decision to extend to Britain what it extended to no other ally, access to sensitive nuclear weapons technology.[59]

How to select from this list? Not easily, it would appear, for one's manner of dating the onset of the AASR can also reveal something significant about how

34   *D.G. Haglund*

one understands the causal mechanisms supposedly responsible for making the relationship so special. But if we follow the logic of path dependence with the view, this time, of trying to unravel causal rather than chronological mysteries, we could employ it in such a manner as to provide us leverage upon the somewhat novel idea that among those many items that can be 'cultured' in the international political sphere, *relationships* occupy a prominent place. Thus, through pursuing a path-dependent logic that stimulates expectations of lock-in yielding positive outcomes, we come to the study of what a few writers have recently been terming 'relational culture'. Prominent among these writers is Lucile Eznack, who adopts an approach bearing clear hallmarks of such logic, in making an intriguing case for why and how we might subsume relational dynamics into a strategic–cultural framework.

In a study of how 'affect' (or emotion) can come to figure in state interaction, particularly during moments of crisis within alliances, Eznack stresses the need for there to be some 'defining moment' that sets in motion a different sort of future, one in which states will incorporate into their own culture 'emotional beliefs'[60] that effectively constitute lock-in mechanisms for the restoration of cooperative interaction. In sum, decision-makers will shape policy as it relates to the AASR (or other important bilateral relationships) in response to how they emotionally assess the value of the relationship(s) in question. More than this, she says: '[A]ffective attachment to specific interstate relationships is *part of a given state's culture and practice of foreign policy*, and it is internalized and reproduced by the individuals in charge.'[61] Although she is less clear about what it actually *is* that sets in motion this affect-charged relationship in any specific sense, she makes it obvious that she relies upon the path-dependence concept of contingency, albeit under a different name: '[F]irst, and most important, is what I call a "defining moment", that is, an event that had a particularly significant impact on a given relationship, either by founding it or by determining the development of its special quality.'[62]

Affect theory such as Eznack's may not tell us when the AASR *came* into existence, but it speaks to why it *stays* in existence. Significantly, much recent work on emotion and IR can be associated with scholars whose paradigm of choice is a constructivist one, and while it would be rash to conclude that there is any consensual policy (or normative) message emanating from these theoreticians, it is clear that they tend to be dismissive of arguments, ventured by many realists, to the effect that geostrategic institutions such as NATO and the AASR must face an uncertain future whenever the 'threat' that brought them into being vanishes. Indeed, what was being said by many realists about NATO in the aftermath of the Cold War's ending a generation ago was echoed, nearly verbatim, in respect of the AASR.[63] Neither institution was expected to have much of a future ahead of it, which is why the latter's track record over the past quarter-century has led some analysts to liken it to that of Lazarus, showing an uncanny knack for returning to life after being pronounced dead.[64]

The emotion-in-IR camp, as I have argued above, can well and truly be linked with the scholarship on path dependence, especially as that latter leads to a focus

'Strategic culture' on the road to Fulton 35

upon relational culture, basically one way of asserting that institutional lock-in can and does exert a powerful impact upon how individual decision-makers value the geostrategic institution in question – in our case, the AASR. And *pace* certain realists who think that increased appeals to sentiment (or, 'shared values') presage nothing so much as the impending end of the AASR,[65] constructivists prefer often to understand sentiment as a guarantor of the long-term stability of the relationship, and this because of the power (some even say the 'power politics') of collective identity. To phrase it slightly differently, institutional lock-in gets a mighty boost if the cooperating partners happen to share in a collective identity.

This is the reason why, for instance, Janice Bially Mattern could interpret one of those alliance crises that Eznack and others examine, Suez in 1956, as being rather 'therapeutic' for the AASR, instead of something that shook it to its foundations. Her answer to the puzzling question of why this falling out left in its wake not rancour and disunity but rather a reinforced desire to solidify the AASR bears some resemblance to how the 'near miss' in 1895 itself proved therapeutic, save for the important distinction that in the Venezuela dispute there was no extant alliance to serve as an institutional check upon disarray and discord. But in 1956 there *was* such a union, and its preservation constituted a prima facie objective of both American and British decision-makers, who because of the 'power politics of identity' found themselves essentially trapped in an ideological cage of their own design, one in which how they thought and talked about the AASR exerted a 'representation force' upon them, forcing them 'into complying with the status quo narrative of their friendship'. This, she tells us, fortified the collective 'Anglo-American identity', holding in check future fissiparous pressures that might have imperilled both the security community and the alliance.[66]

I noted earlier in this chapter, when introducing the debate over 'context' that has fuelled the passions of certain adherents to the strategic–cultural approach, the proposition that context can and does appeal both to positivists and anti- (or 'post-') positivists. While it may be open to contestation whether any constructivists worthy of the name would boast of being positivists, what is less disputable is that the master variable of constructivism, which we can take to be 'identity', is no newcomer to the study of Anglo-American relations. Quite the contrary: to the extent that there has been a common theme built into assumptions (aspirational or otherwise) regarding Anglo-American geostrategic unity, it has been the notion of a 'kindred folk', which as we saw earlier used regularly, a century and more ago, to get brought under the 'Anglo-Saxon' heading. For sure, that descriptive became more than a little shopworn as time went on, not least because even in its heyday it was far from clear who qualified, and who did not, for membership in this collective identity – memorably lampooned in Mr Dooley's classificatory scheme as 'a German that's forgot who was his parents'.[67] And even among those who self-styled as 'Anglo-Saxonists' on either side of the Atlantic, it still could matter whether one happened to be an American, as opposed to an English, exponent of the creed; in other words, as

36 *D.G. Haglund*

Paul Kramer has brilliantly demonstrated, even this 'collective' identity was not immune to the pull of divergent national identities, especially as these latter rested on narratives of national 'exceptionalism'.[68]

If we can accept that an analytical orientation and approach might actually pre-exist its own naming (something that turns out to be more common than one would think), then it is clear that when what later would become known as strategic culture attained its initial burst of popularity, it did so around the time of the Second World War and under the label of 'national character'.[69] Hardly a noncontroversial rubric, national character has, like so many related categories, experienced its ups and downs, sometimes finding itself stigmatized for being a veiled form of racism (or at least, racialism),[70] other times for being too confusing to 'operationalize' and still other times for simply being *dépassé*. But it has had its defenders, as well,[71] and one could argue that the constructivist challenge to IR theory of the post-Cold War years, because of the emphasis laid upon collective identity, including national identity,[72] has served to reinvigorate scholarly interest in, among other matters, ethnicity.

If this is so, then the recent group of theorists who have been expanding the bounds of inquiry along frontiers that were once thought conceptually inhospitable for IR students – frontiers that in particular have been skirting difficult terrain associated with 'emotionalism'[73] – have injected a new and fascinating element into the scholarship on the AASR. What this research does is to call into question the distinction that once used so regularly to be drawn between 'rationality' and emotion, and in so dissolving the barriers hitherto so prominent a feature in IR analysis, not excluding that appertaining to the AASR, the research has opened up new vistas upon topics that used to be thought, to put it mildly, rather strange. One such topic, of course, is the notion of 'friendship' between states, something usually relegated to the category of exotic species by scholars smitten with the dictum associated with Palmerston, about states having no permanent friends or enemies, only permanent interests.[74] For reasons linked with assumptions of 'we-feeling' among 'kin countries' – no matter what may be said to be the emotional bonding element of greatest significance (and here one could do much worse than to reflect about the Bismarckian observation cited earlier in this chapter) – the roots of this collective identity can be found imbedded in the fertile soil of ethnicity, if only as this latter gets conveyed through shared language.

Conclusions

To say again, no one needs to invoke strategic culture as an *essential* approach to understanding the AASR; there are any number of paths one might follow in a bid to take the measure – or even to deny the existence – of the AASR. No one should imagine that pride of analytical place could or should be given to those professing to approach the relationship from a strategic–culture coign of vantage. Instead, the argument of this chapter has simply been the more moderate assertion that there might be some utility in our rubric, when all is said and done. It is obvious that there is nothing new in the dichotomy – false or genuine – so often postulated (at least by those who accept the reality of the AASR) between 'interest' and 'sentiment' as the effective bonding agent between the two states. The debate over which it is that 'truly' binds the two countries can at times become an impassioned one, as witnessed by the manner in which one leading scholar of the AASR, Harry Cranbrook Allen, took another leading scholar, Donald Cameron Watt, to task three decades ago for what the former regarded as an excessively grudging and mean-spirited assessment of the AASR being presented in the latter's magnum opus, *Succeeding John Bull* – an assessment he felt paid far too much attention to narrow self-interest and not enough to transatlantic collective identity.[75]

In this chapter, I have concentrated on demonstrating that strategic culture can play a part in advancing our comprehension of the AASR. It can do this in three ways, though most of my attention has been dedicated only to the pair of approaches I associated with a 'contextualist' appreciation of strategic culture. Nevertheless, it warrants repeating, especially in a volume such as this, marking the seventieth anniversary of the Fulton address, that the 'cognitive' camp among strategic culturalists would have absolutely no difficulty in embracing the claim that both Churchill and Fulton were seminal from the strategic–cultural perspective, if for no other reason than the semiotic one. Symbolism, as I tried to argue, rarely comes in stronger doses than those administered by Winston Churchill in March 1946.

Mostly, though, the chapter has concentrated upon context, in two senses. First, I have advanced the argument, counterintuitive as it might otherwise seem to some, that path-dependent logic so often associated with historical-institutionalism (as well as historical sociology) must itself be regarded as congruent with, indeed a part of, the strategic–culture perspective. This, I said, was so not only for what path dependence might tell us about the origins of the AASR, but also for what it says about the mechanisms that are held to sustain the relationship. Second, I have linked relational-culture assessments of the AASR to a more broadly based corpus of scholarship paying tribute to the importance of identity in IR. That corpus is neither old nor new; or to put it better, it is *both* old and new. Embedded within it, though, is the contention that collective identity and the 'we-feeling' it spawns can be and is central, not epiphenomenal, to the existence of the AASR.

Notes

1 William H. Sewell, Jr, 'The Concept(s) of Culture', in Victoria E. Bonnell and Lynn Hunt (eds), *Beyond the Cultural Turn: New Directions in the Study of Society and Culture*, Berkeley: University of California Press, 1999, pp. 35–61, quote at p. 48.
2 Henry Butterfield Ryan, 'A New Look at Churchill's "Iron Curtain" Speech', *Historical Journal*, 22, December 1979, pp. 895–920, citing from pp. 897–8.
3 Quoted in David Reynolds, 'Re-thinking Anglo-American Relations', *International Affairs*, 65, Winter 1988–9, pp. 89–111, quote at p. 94.
4 Eric Edelman, 'A Special Relationship in Jeopardy', *American Interest*, 5, July/ August 2010, pp. 25–34, quote at p. 29.

38 D.G. Haglund

5 Cited in Jorgen Rasmussen and James M. McCormick, 'British Mass Perceptions of the Anglo-American Special Relationship', *Political Science Quarterly*, 108, Autumn 1993, pp. 515–41, quote at p. 516.

6 See Stuart Anderson, *Race and Rapprochement: Anglo-Saxonism and Anglo-American Relations, 1895–1904*, Rutherford, NJ: Fairleigh Dickinson University Press, 1981, as well as Chapter 4 in this volume by Srdjan Vucetic, 'The Fulton Address as Racial Discourse'.

7 Bradford Perkins, *The First Rapprochement: England and the United States, 1795–1805*, Berkeley: University of California Press, 1967.

8 I borrow this idea from an earlier article of mine, David Haglund, 'Relating to the Anglosphere: Canada, "Culture", and the Question of Military Intervention', *Journal of Transatlantic Studies*, 3, Autumn 2005, pp. 179–98.

9 Alex Danchev, 'On Specialness', *International Affairs*, 72, October 1996, pp. 737–50.

10 Erwan Lagadec, *Transatlantic Relations in the 21st Century: Europe, America and the Rise of the Rest*, London: Routledge, 2012, p. 80.

11 Some, but not all; for a decidedly different assessment of this 'iron law', see Errol A. Henderson, *Democracy and War: The End of an Illusion?* Boulder: Lynne Rienner, 2002.

12 Edward Ingram, 'The Wonderland of the Political Scientist', *International Security*, 22, Summer 1997, pp. 53–63, quote at pp. 56–7.

13 Edward Ingram, 'Hegemony, Global Reach, and World Power: Great Britain's Long Cycle', in Colin Elman and M.F. Elman (eds), *Bridges and Boundaries: Historians, Political Scientists, and the Study of International Relations*, Cambridge, MA: MIT Press, 2001, pp. 223–51.

14 Quoted in John C. Farrell and Asa P. Smith, 'Foreword', in J.C. Farrell and A.P. Smith (eds), *Image and Reality in World Politics*, New York: Columbia University Press, 1967, p. v.

15 With myths here meaning not 'lies' but rather symbolic assertions, necessarily ambiguous, such that they can be labelled neither true nor false; see John Baylis, 'The "Special Relationship": A Diverting British Myth?' in C. Buffet and B. Heuser (eds), *Haunted by History: Myths in International Relations*, Oxford: Berghahn, 1998, pp. 117–34.

16 For examples, see James E. Cronin, *Global Rules: America, Britain and a Disordered World*, New Haven: Yale University Press, 2014; and Walter Russell Mead, *God and Gold: Britain, America, and the Making of the Modern World*, New York: Alfred A. Knopf, 2008.

17 The standard work on that reconciliatory era remains Bradford Perkins, *The Great Rapprochement: England and the United States, 1895–1914*, New York: Atheneum, 1968.

18 H. Perry Robinson, *The Twentieth Century American: Being a Comparative Study of the Peoples of the Two Great Anglo-Saxon Nations*, Chautauqua, NY: Chautauqua Press, 1911, p. 19. For a similar full-throated call for Anglo-American alliance during the pre-First World War era, see John Randolph Dos Passos, *The Anglo-Saxon Century and the Unification of the English-Speaking Peoples*, second edition, New York: G.P. Putnam's Sons, 1903.

19 For the difference between 'systems change', which seeks to alter the very organizational principle of international order, and 'systemic change', which applies to shifting power relations within an international order that is otherwise unaltered, see Robert G. Gilpin, *War and Change in World Politics*, Cambridge: Cambridge University Press, 1981, pp. 39–43.

20 For instances of this line of argumentation, see John Dumbrell and Axel R. Schäfer, *America's 'Special Relationships': Foreign and Domestic Aspects of the Politics of Alliance*, London: Routledge, 2009.

'Strategic culture' on the road to Fulton   39

21 See, for example, Richard J. Aldrich, 'British Intelligence and the Anglo-American "Special Relationship" during the Cold War', *Review of International Studies*, 24, July 1998, pp. 331–51; John Baylis, 'The Anglo-American Relationship and Alliance Theory', *International Relations*, 8, January 1985, pp. 368–79; and Raymond Dawson and Richard Rosecrance, 'Theory and Reality in the Anglo-American Alliance', *World Politics*, 19, October 1966, pp. 21–51.

22 Of course, some scholars, including the co-editors of this volume, will tell us, correctly, that it is not so easy to distinguish interests from values. See, for instance, their reminder that '[w]hat comes to be seen as an interest is often moulded by common sentiment and the existence of friendly sentiments often leads on to common interests'; Alan P. Dobson and Steve Marsh, 'Anglo-American Relations: End of a Special Relationship?' *International History Review*, 36, August 2014, pp. 673–97, quote at p. 683.

23 Charles A. Kupchan, *How Enemies Become Friends: The Sources of Stable Peace*, Princeton: Princeton University Press, 2010, pp. 30–4.

24 Ibid., p. 5.

25 See especially Feng Yongping, 'The Peaceful Transition of Power from the UK to the US', *Chinese Journal of International Politics*, 1, 2006, pp. 83–108. More generally, see Stephen R. Rock, *Why Peace Breaks Out: Great Power Rapprochement in Historical Perspective*, Chapel Hill: University of North Carolina Press, 1989.

26 Portions of this section are based on my article, 'What Good Is Strategic Culture? A Modest Defence of an Immodest Concept', *International Journal*, 59, Summer 2004, pp. 479–502.

27 I have made an effort in this direction previously, in a chapter titled 'Is There a "Strategic Culture" of the Special Relationship? Contingency, Identity, and the Transformation of Anglo-American Relations', in A. Dobson and S. Marsh (eds), *Contemporary Anglo-American Relations: A 'Special Relationship'?* London: Routledge, 2013, pp. 26–51.

28 Robert Kagan, *Of Paradise and Power: America and the New World Order*, New York: Alfred A. Knopf, 2003, especially pp. 27–8, where Kagan cites one British analyst's bon mot to make his point about strategic choice being driven by relative capability: 'When you have a hammer, all problems start to look like nails.'

29 See, for instance, Per M. Norheim-Martinsen, 'EU Strategic Culture: When the Means Becomes the End', *Contemporary Security Policy*, 32, December 2011, pp. 517–34. Also see Adrian Hyde Price, 'European Security, Strategic Culture and the Use of Force', *European Security*, 13, January 2004, pp. 323–43; and Janne Haaland Matlary, 'When Soft Power Turns Hard: Is an EU Strategic Culture Possible?' *Security Dialogue*, 37, March 2006, pp. 105–21.

30 See Anand Menon, 'Littler England: The United Kingdom's Retreat from Global Leadership', *Foreign Affairs*, 94, November/December 2015, pp. 93–100; and 'Little Britain', *Economist*, 4 April 2015, pp. 53–5.

31 John Bew, 'Pax Anglo-Saxonica', *American Interest*, 10, May/June 2015, pp. 40–9, quote at p. 41. This notion of a shrinking Britain, even if not necessarily in any territorial sense, recurs periodically, and was a fixture during the latter part of the 1960s and well into the 1970s; see Thomas Robb, 'The "Limit of What Is Tolerable": British Defence Cuts and the "Special Relationship"', *Diplomacy and Statecraft*, 22, June 2011, pp. 321–37.

32 John Lewis Gaddis, *Strategies of Containment: A Critical Appraisal of Postwar American National Security Policy*, Oxford: Oxford University Press, 1982, p. viii.

33 Jack Snyder is often credited with being the first writer explicitly to employ the rubric, in his *The Soviet Strategic Culture: Implications for Nuclear Options*, Santa Monica: RAND Corporation, 1977.

34 Ronald Inglehart, 'The Renaissance of Political Culture', *American Political Science Review*, 82, December 1988, pp. 1203–30.

40 *D.G. Haglund*

35 On the level-of-analysis problem, see David J. Elkins and Richard E.B. Simeon, 'A Cause in Search of Its Effect, or What Does Political Culture Explain?' *Comparative Politics*, 11, July 1979, pp. 127–45; and Ruth Lane, 'Political Culture: Residual Category or General Theory?' *Comparative Political Studies*, 25, October 1992, pp. 362–87.

36 Lowell Dittmer, 'Political Culture and Political Symbolism', *World Politics*, 29, July 1977, pp. 552–83.

37 Michael Walzer, 'On the Role of Symbolism in Political Thought', *Political Science Quarterly*, 82, June 1967, pp. 191–204, quote at p. 196.

38 Alastair Iain Johnston, *Cultural Realism: Strategic Culture and Grand Strategy in Chinese History*, Princeton: Princeton University Press, 1995, pp. 36–7. Also see his 'Thinking about Strategic Culture', *International Security*, 19, Spring 1995, pp. 32–64.

39 For instance, Christopher P. Twomey, 'Lacunae in the Study of Culture in International Security', *Contemporary Security Policy*, 29, August 2008, pp. 338–57.

40 Stuart Poore, 'What Is the Context? A Reply to the Gray–Johnston Debate on Strategic Culture', *Review of International Studies*, 29, April 2003, pp. 279–84, quote at p. 284.

41 For my own precinct of social science (IR), this dichotomy has been best captured in Martin Hollis and Steve Smith, *Explaining and Understanding International Relations*, Oxford: Clarendon Press, 1990.

42 See, respectively, Srdjan Vucetic, *The Anglosphere: A Genealogy of a Racialized Identity in International Relations*, Stanford: Stanford University Press, 2011; and James C. Bennett, 'Networking Nation-States: The Coming Info-National Order', *National Interest*, 74, Winter 2003/4, pp. 17–30.

43 Quoted in William Clark, *Less than Kin: A Study of Anglo-American Relations*, Boston: Houghton Mifflin, 1958, p. 2.

44 Christopher Hitchens, *Blood, Class, and Empire: The Enduring Anglo-American Relationship*, New York: Nation Books, 2004, pp. 44–5.

45 Ibid., pp. 150–1, 371.

46 Paul Pierson, *Politics in Time: History, Institutions, and Social Analysis*, Princeton: Princeton University Press, 2004, pp. 167–9.

47 See, for instance, the thoughtful critique by Andrew R. Rutten, 'Review Essay: Politics in Time', *Independent Review*, 11, Fall 2006, pp. 299–305.

48 See Jack A. Goldstone, 'Initial Conditions, General Laws, Path Dependence, and Explanation in Historical Sociology', *American Journal of Sociology*, 104, November 1998, pp. 829–45.

49 Giovanni Capoccia and R. Daniel Kelemen, 'The Study of Critical Junctures: Theory, Narrative, and Counterfactuals in Historical Institutionalism', *World Politics*, 59, April 2007, pp. 341–69, quotes at p. 341.

50 James Mahoney, 'Path Dependence in Historical Sociology', *Theory and Society*, 29, August 2000, pp. 507–48.

51 The classic work on the history of the bilateral relationship remains Harry Cranbrook Allen, *Great Britain and the United States: A History of Anglo-American Relations, 1783–1952*, London: Oldhams, 1954. Also see Kathleen Burk, *Old World, New World: Great Britain and America from the Beginning*, New York: Grove Press, 2009; Kenneth Bourne, *Britain and the Balance of Power in North America, 1815–1908*, Berkeley: University of California Press, 1967; and Charles S. Campbell, Jr, *From Revolution to Rapprochement: The United States and Great Britain, 1783–1900*, New York: John Wiley & Sons, 1974.

52 Hitchens, *Blood, Class, and Empire*, p. 166.

53 See, for instance, Marshall Bertram, *The Birth of Anglo-American Friendship: The Prime Facet of the Venezuelan Boundary Dispute – A Study of the Interrelation of Diplomacy and Public Opinion*, Lanham, MD: University Press of America, 1992.

'Strategic culture' on the road to Fulton   41

54 Of the rapprochement, he writes that it was generative of a 'strategic partnership that has lasted to this day'; Kupchan, *How Enemies Become Friends*, p. 2.
55 Quoted in Reynolds, 'Re-thinking Anglo-American Relations', p. 92.
56 On interwar Anglo-American dissension, see Christopher M. Bell, 'Thinking the Unthinkable: British and American Naval Strategies for an Anglo-American War, 1918–1931', *International History Review*, 19, November 1997, pp. 789–808; Brian J.C. McKercher, '"Our Most Dangerous Enemy": Great Britain Pre-eminent in the 1930s', *International History Review*, 13, November 1991, pp. 751–83; David Reynolds, 'Competitive Co-operation', *Historical Journal*, 23, March 1980, pp. 233–45; Alfred George Gardiner, 'England and America: Their Misunderstandings and Their Opportunity', *Harper's*, 149, July 1924, pp. 145–52; 'The Source of Anti-Britishism', *New Republic*, 52, 16 November 1927, pp. 325–6; and George H. Knoles, *The Jazz Age Revisited: British Criticism of American Civilization during the 1920s*, Stanford: Stanford University Press, 1955. On the 1937 revision of American war planning, see Louis Morton, 'Germany First: The Basic Concept of Allied Strategy in World War II', in Kent Roberts Greenfield (ed.), *Command Decisions*, Washington: Office of the Chief of Military History, Department of the Army, 1960, pp. 12–22.
57 I have opted for this myself, in 'Is There a "Strategic Culture" of the Special Relationship?'
58 Bevin made this claim in 1950; see Geoffrey Warner, 'The Anglo-American Special Relationship', *Diplomatic History*, 13, October 1989, pp. 479–99, citing from p. 479.
59 William Wallace and Christopher Phillips, 'Reassessing the Special Relationship', *International Affairs*, 85, March 2009, pp. 263–84, quoting from p. 270: 'There are enormous advantages to the UK in this relationship. The UK has gained access to US technology, warhead and submarine design, as well as to US missiles at a price well below that of a fully independent system.'
60 The term is not hers, but rather Jonathan Mercer's, who defines it thus: 'An emotional belief is one where emotion constitutes and strengthens a belief and which makes possible a generalization about an actor that involves certainty beyond evidence.' See Jonathan Mercer, 'Emotional Beliefs', *International Organization*, 64, Winter 2010, pp. 1–31, quote at p. 2.
61 Lucile Eznack, 'Crises as Signals of Strength: The Significance of Affect in Close Allies' Relationships', *Security Studies*, 20, April 2011, pp. 238–65, quote at p. 242 (emphasis added).
62 Ibid.
63 The best case in point being Christopher Coker, 'The Special Relationship in the 1990s', *International Affairs*, 68, July 1992, pp. 407–21.
64 Steve Marsh and John Baylis, 'The Anglo-American "Special Relationship": The Lazarus of International Relations', *Diplomacy and Statecraft*, 17, April 2006, pp. 173–211.
65 Alex Danchev, 'Shared Values in the Transatlantic Relationship', *British Journal of Politics and International Relations*, 7, August 2005, pp. 429–36.
66 Janice Bially Mattern, 'The Power Politics of Identity', *European Journal of International Relations*, 7, September 2001, pp. 349–97, quote at p. 351. Also see her 'The Difference that Language-Power Makes: Solving the Puzzle of the Suez Crisis', in François Debrix (ed.), *Language, Agency, and Politics in a Constructed World*, Armonk, NY: M.E. Sharpe, 2003, pp. 143–70.
67 Finley Peter Dunne, *Mr Dooley in Peace and War*, Boston: Small, Maynard, 1898, p. 54.
68 Paul A. Kramer, 'Empires, Exceptions, and Anglo-Saxons: Race and Rule Between the British and US Empires, 1880–1910', *Journal of American History*, 88, March 2002, pp. 1315–53.
69 See Michael C. Desch, 'Culture Clash: Assessing the Importance of Ideas in Security Studies', *International Security*, 23, Summer 1998, pp. 141–70.

42 D.G. Haglund

70 Most famously by Hamilton Fyfe, *The Illusion of National Character*, London: Watts, 1940.
71 Dean Peabody, *National Characteristics*, Cambridge: Cambridge University Press, 1985; Morris Ginsberg, 'National Character', *British Journal of Psychology*, 32, January 1942, pp. 183–205; and Kenneth W. Terhune, 'From National Character to National Behavior: A Reformulation', *Journal of Conflict Resolution*, 14, June 1970, pp. 203–63.
72 Peter Mandler, 'What Is "National Identity"? Definitions and Applications in Modern British Historiography', *Modern Intellectual History*, 3, August 2006, pp. 271–97; and Philip Gleason, 'Identifying Identity: A Semantic History', *Journal of American History*, 69, March 1983, pp. 910–31.
73 See, in particular, Neta C. Crawford, 'The Passion of World Politics: Propositions on Emotion and Emotional Relationships', *International Security*, 24, Spring 2000, pp. 116–56; Rose McDermott, 'The Feeling of Rationality: The Meaning of Neuroscientific Advances for Political Science', *Perspectives on Politics*, 2, December 2004, pp. 691–706; and Andrew A.G. Ross, 'Coming in from the Cold: Constructivism and Emotions', *European Journal of International Relations*, 12, June 2006, pp. 197–222. Also useful are Roland Bleiker and Emma Hutchison, 'Fear No More: Emotions and World Politics', *Review of International Studies*, 34, January 2008, pp. 115–35; and Jean-Marc Coicaud, 'Emotions and Passions in the Discipline of International Relations', *Japanese Journal of Political Science*, 15, September 2014, pp. 485–513.
74 See especially Felix Berenskoetter, 'Friends, There are No Friends? An Intimate Reframing of the International', *Millennium: Journal of International Studies*, 35, September 2007, pp. 647–76; as well as Brent E. Sasley, 'Theorizing States' Emotions', *International Studies Review*, 13, September 2011, pp. 452–76.
75 Harry Cranbrook Allen, 'A Special Relationship', *Journal of American Studies*, 19, December 1985, pp. 403–13. This was a review essay of Donald Cameron Watt, *Succeeding John Bull: America in Britain's Place, 1900–1975*, Cambridge: Cambridge University Press, 1984.

2 Churchill's Fulton speech and the context of shared values in a world of dangers[1]

Alan P. Dobson

Churchill's trip to the US in early 1946 was an unusually long one, much of it being for rest and recuperation, but he also had an agenda. Exactly what that agenda was is not immediately clear. One might simply say that it was primarily the delivery of his Iron Curtain speech of 5 March 1946 at Westminster College, Fulton, Missouri. However, that simply begs more questions and he did more than just speak at Fulton. A more exhaustive reply would be that his overall aims during the time he was in the US were threefold. First, he wanted to give a clarion call for robust defence measures as he had in the 1930s, but this time targeting the Soviet Union and the bourgeoning threat arising therefrom. Second, he wanted to try to ease the terms and facilitate the ratification of the Anglo-American Loan Agreement that would provide Britain with essential financial support to the tune of $3.75 billion. Third, and something that undergirded the first two, he wanted to consolidate what he saw as the indispensable foundation for security, prosperity and peace – a special relationship between the US and the UK – by invoking the cultural and political values that made their people akin. These values were the common font from which would issue coordinated action in a world of growing troubles and help persuade the Americans to render economic and other support to Britain. In many ways the first objective and the one retrospectively with the highest profile – the warning about the Soviets that he uttered in Fulton – was actually more to do with achieving the second two objectives than with the need to energise and warn the Americans of the Soviet menace. In fact both the warning and securing financial help from the US were primarily means to an end.

Churchill arrived in the US on 14 January and travelled on to Florida where he spent his time mainly socialising and painting. However, on the 15th he addressed the press and immediately began to conjure up a commonality of Anglo-American interests and lay out Britain's need for financial help. In response to a question about whether he held a negative view about the 1940 Destroyers for Bases deal between Britain and the US, he replied: 'No, we didn't trade the islands for fifty old destroyers. We did it for strategic use by the United States and for your safety and ours.' He later went on to speak of Britain's need to recover its strength: 'If we are not given opportunity to get back on our feet again we may never be able to take our place among other nations.'[2] At his first

44   *A.P. Dobson*

formal engagement, which was at the University of Miami on 26 February, the idea of the entanglement of British and American security was yet again invoked. In the meantime he had requested both Secretary of State James Byrnes and his longstanding friend and eminent financier and government adviser Bernard Baruch to come and visit, and they did. He tried to convince them to ease the conditions of the Loan Agreement and, regarding Baruch, more importantly tried to persuade him to stop opposing the Loan. On both counts Churchill only had limited success, but a factor that was becoming ever clearer to him was the growing fear of the Soviets in America and specifically among the Truman administration. Such fears could be grist for the mill of closer Anglo-American relations and achieving that could help consummate all he sought.[3]

On 3 March Churchill arrived in Washington, DC, and the following day he set off with the President for Fulton, and so the central business part of his trip began and continued more or less unabated until his last day in the States on 20 March.

The crux of his Fulton speech was security through Anglo-American cooperation, involving:

> not only the growing friendship and mutual understanding between our vast but kindred systems of society, but the continuance of the intimate relationship between our military advisers, leading to common study of potential dangers, to the similarity of weapons and manuals of instructions, and to the interchange of officers and cadets at technical colleges. It should carry with it continuance of the present facilities for mutual security by the joint use of all Naval and Air Force bases in the possession of either country all over the world.[4]

This was incendiary among US Isolationists and Anglophobic anti-imperialists. However, conjoined with Churchill's finger pointing at the Soviets as the immediate security threat, it also lit a veritable and wider conflagration. Delivered on the same podium on which sat the President of the US, Harry S. Truman, it issued a powerful warning to British and American domestic audiences and to the Soviet Union. Even though Churchill was no longer prime minister of Britain, he led the Conservative Party and was probably the most celebrated living human being. His words always carried weight: standing beside the President of the United States his impact was guaranteed to be enormous. And so it was.

In Moscow Stalin was outraged and dubbed the speech warmongering. In London Labour MP William Warberg collected ninety-three signatures for what was eventually an unsuccessful vote of censure in the Commons. In Washington Senators Kilgore, Taylor and Pepper warned of a new Anglo-American imperialism, while others such as Joseph H. Ball and Walter George were equally critical. Influential journalist Walter Lippmann labelled it as 'an almost catastrophic blunder'. The journal *The Nation* was severely critical, as were mid-Western papers such as the *Chicago Tribune* and the *Chicago Sun*. Even *The Wall Street*

Journal decried the idea of any kind of alliance with Britain.[5] In this furore of criticisms in the US, Truman tried to distance himself by falsely claiming to the press that he had not read the text of the speech ahead of its delivery and Byrnes tried to indicate that there was clear water between State Department policy and what Churchill had said, although then current and subsequent US actions belied that. Notwithstanding the Labour MPs who sought a vote of censure, most of the press in Britain was favourably disposed to Churchill's sentiments, as were US east coast publications such as the *New York Times* and *Pittsburg Post-Gazette.* In private Truman and his close entourage in fact wholeheartedly agreed with Churchill and contrary to some public denials were well aware of the content of Churchill's speech before it was delivered. For example, Truman's Chief of Staff, Admiral Leahy, wrote in his diary on 3 March: 'I could find no fault in his proposed address.'[6] Byrnes had briefed the President about the speech and the President had sight of the text on the way to Fulton, when he accompanied Churchill aboard the train the *Ferdinand Magellan.* He declared it 'admirable', though it would 'make a stir'.[7]

So, aware of the likely difficulties for the Truman administration and the international controversy he was about to ignite, why did Churchill deliver such a controversial and potentially problem-laden speech? The most provocative aspect of it was the invoking of the security threat posed by the USSR to Britain, the US and the wider world in general, but the Americans hardly needed to be told. Scholars such as Fraser Harbutt and Randall Bennett Woods, among others, have argued that Britain, largely in the shape of Foreign Secretary Ernest Bevin, carried the lead flag in opposing the Soviets and helped draw the US into a more confrontational stance and there is undoubtedly much truth in that, but the trajectory of US policy came primarily from indigenous concerns about the Soviets and that trajectory was already gaining momentum before Churchill's Fulton speech.[8] US Secretary of the Navy James Forrestal circulated the Long Telegram of 22 February 1946 from George Kennan, the Soviet specialist and Counsellor at the US Embassy in Moscow, to all members of the Cabinet, and that made the case for a strong line against the Soviets in much more detail than Churchill was to do. Even before the Kennan analysis was circulated, evidence indicates that Truman had already radically shifted his views on the Soviets. After believing he could do business with Stalin at Potsdam in 1945, by January 1946 he felt: 'There isn't a doubt in my mind that Russia intends an invasion of Turkey and a seizure of the Black Sea Straits to the Mediterranean.' 'Only one language do they understand: How many divisions have you?' 'I'm tired babying the Soviets.'[9]

In the light of the above evidence it seems unlikely that warning the world of the Soviet threat, something already widely acknowledged in London, Paris and Washington, was Churchill's main concern at Fulton, though one might argue that the public dissemination of the fear of Soviet intentions could have been important to him. Even if that were so, there seem to have been two much more significant factors on his mind. The first was that there was a clear polar-like difference between the values Churchill believed that the English-speaking peoples

46   *A.P. Dobson*

shared and those held by the Soviets: a view also clearly held and disseminated by George Kennan. The second was his determination to connect the Soviet threat to what he saw as its only possible solution: Anglo-American solidarity in an ever-closer special relationship. That is why he took such pains to conjure up the image of a shared political, moral and cultural inheritance facilitated and enhanced by a shared language. His speech resonated with common political and moral values, especially when he invoked Jefferson's Declaration of Independence as a supreme example of the values of the English-speaking peoples.

Ironically, in the scholarship of Anglo-American relations, and it is very extensive, there is little about the political traditions that the two might share. And when the term 'political tradition' is used here it goes beyond the institutional settings, clearly very different in Washington and London, to encompass underpinning values, which lie at the very heart of their respective versions of democracy. In mid-September 2012 at Baylor University, Texas, the Constitution Day Address was given by one of the US's leading constitutional scholars, Akhil Reed Amar of Yale University. In the course of his delivery he argued that after the Declaration of Independence and the establishment of the Constitution of the United States, nowhere else really contributed anything of significance to the development of democracy except for the USA. At the heart of its democratic trajectory was the founding principle of the USA, 'We the people', reformulated by Abraham Lincoln decades later as 'government of the people, by the people, for the people'. If Amar is right then the idea that there was and still is a growing and mutually cross-fertilising Anglo-American democratic political tradition looks rather vacuous, but let us see.

There is little doubt that the different institutional frameworks of government in Britain and the USA caused significant differences in political concerns during the nineteenth and early twentieth centuries. There were also some important differences in substantial issues, or at least about their timing. In Britain William Wilberforce led the campaign that abolished British participation in the slave trade in 1807 and then slavery itself in 1833. By contrast, in the US, the Missouri Compromise of 1819 sought to accommodate the continuance of slavery in the states. Even so, friction between free and slave state continued. In 1828 with 'The Tariff of Abominations' such friction became intense because the tariff protected Northern industry and discriminated against the South's agricultural economy, which happened to be based on plantation slavery. For the next thirty years American politics was dominated by the political arguments about slavery and freedom with no counterpart in Britain to such writers as William Lloyd Garrison, J.C. Calhoun and George Fitzhugh.[10] Similarly different in Britain for much of the nineteenth century was an obsession with empire that was not reflected in the US unless one sees westward expansion as comparable. Certainly there was no one in the US like Cecil Rhodes or Benjamin Disraeli. Towards the end of the century things began to change with the strategic ideas of sea power promulgated by Alfred Mahan and the eruption of the Spanish–American War, but major differences remained.[11] The substance and the nuances of those differences do not need to be assessed here: simply the point is made that in some

The Fulton speech and shared values   47

respects political thought and morality had different foci and content in the US and Britain in the nineteenth century. In addition the governmental structure in the US also seemed to have created a central, ongoing and different political struggle from the one that was germane to British experience, although this perspective needs careful inspection.

The American War of Independence was in part a reassertion of the traditional rights of Englishmen, which the British King George III was trying to subvert, and it was justified by the work of John Locke and his legitimating of revolution. So far, so good, one might argue, in terms of a common Anglo-American political tradition. But then the greatest theoretical novelty of the American War of Independence, the idea of divided sovereignty, posed problems and a possible point of departure. Clearly divided sovereignty was something very different to the British unitary state in which parliamentary supremacy became ever more embedded as the nineteenth century progressed. Federalism divided sovereignty and pitched states' rights against the power of the Washington government. Nothing like this really existed in Britain until the framework of devolution was created in the twenty-first century, with a Scottish Parliament with revenue-raising powers and a Welsh Assembly with somewhat more limited but nevertheless substantial power. Federalism set a context, which nurtured a different kind of political struggle from that possible in Britain. In hindsight one can identify three great struggles that arose in the US as a consequence: the Civil War to deny states a right to secede from the Union; the New Deal to superimpose national regulation and taxation on the states to create a more national economy; and the struggle in the Supreme Court in the 1950s and 1960s to nationalise the Bill of Rights, which among other things extended federal standards to the criminally accused, established civil rights enforceable by federal law for all including ethnic minorities, and created a limited right of abortion for women. Prima facie such developments seem distant from British experience, so how plausible was it when Churchill emphasised at Fulton a common inheritance of political and moral ideals, which underpinned the fraternity of the English-speaking peoples?

> [W]e must never cease to proclaim in fearless tones the great principles of freedom and the rights of man which are the joint inheritance of the English-speaking world and which through Magna Carta, the Bill of Rights, the Habeas Corpus, trial by jury, and the English common law find their most famous expression in the American Declaration of Independence.
> ... if all British moral and material forces and convictions are joined with your own in fraternal association, the high roads of the future will be clear, not only for us but for all, not only for our time, but for a century to come.[12]

Frank Lewis McCluer, the President of Westminster College and Churchill's formal host, anticipated some of this content when he introduced Churchill on the podium, saying that Churchill's visit would: 'emphasize the importance to all mankind of the ideals of political liberty cradled in England and nourished here

48　*A.P. Dobson*

as there'.[13] Even without McCluer's short eulogy, the very fact that Churchill spoke at a college called Westminster in America's mid-West evoked at least the possibility of connections between the US and Britain.

But what specifically should one make of the remarks by Churchill and McCluer? Did they both get it wrong? Were they simply indulging in political rhetoric, conjuring up hollow fictions that sounded stirring and pleasant on the day but in fact were just that: hollow, ineffective fictions?

Churchill's emphasis on the importance of values and common Anglo-American inheritances was something that he so consistently held to that it would be difficult to see it as a confection, though he often applied a thick coating of icing. In his *History of the English-Speaking Peoples* the central theme was premised on the development of democracies arising from the English Common Law, habeas corpus, due process and the Bill of Rights. Furthermore, by the twentieth century Churchill conceived of the British–American axis as the main carrier of that tradition. He wrote in the preface to the *History of the English-Speaking Peoples*:

> For the second time in the present century the British Empire and the United States have stood together facing perils of war on the largest scale known among men, and since the cannons ceased to fire and the bombs to burst we have become more conscious of our common duty to the human race. Language, law, and the processes by which we have come into being already afforded a unique foundation for drawing together and portraying a concerted task. I thought when I began that such unity might notably influence the destiny of the world. Certainly I do not feel that the need for this has diminished in any way in the twenty years that have passed.[14]

Of course, this was not just Churchill describing the growth of the Anglo-American relationship: his writing was also part of its creative process.

There is no doubt, however, that there were both significant political and cultural differences between Americans and Britons. Indeed, for many years after the birth of the Republic through war, there was an understandable Anglophobia, but as American self-confidence grew, so 'othering' the mother country became less important to its sense of self. More significantly, many Americans began to conceive of themselves and their country as part of a transnational collective identity that included, rather than shunned, Britain. For some this identification came through racial Anglo-Saxonism; for a greater number it came through a community of language, ideas and principles that found expression in terms such as 'the English-speaking peoples' and cohesion before the challenge of a de-Anglicising effect upon the US of immigration from Southern and Eastern Europe with alternative identities and ideologies. Much of this was reflected in literary interactions and developments.

There was a growing and reciprocal fascination with each other's country. Possibly most famously and at times not very complimentary were the views of Charles Dickens, who while seeing much to commend in American industry,

The Fulton speech and shared values 49

energy and freedoms was dismayed by their materialism, lack of sensitivity to beauty and most of all by their popular press.[15] Perhaps most important was the huge audience in Britain that reports by Dickens and others from America reached. It was part and parcel of a new age of learning and interaction for both countries. In the US literary changes were also afoot and often with tensions surrounding the notion of identity. For some, best epitomised in works by Ralph Waldo Emerson and Walt Whitman, was a search for a distinct and unique North American identity for the people of the US. James Fenimore Cooper, among others, also did much to contribute to that project, particularly with his books *Leatherstocking Tales* and *Last of the Mohicans*, but he also emphasised the hugely important common Anglo-American literary inheritance.

> The authors, previous to the revolution, are common property, and it is quite idle to say that the American has not just as good a right to claim Milton and Shakespeare, and all the old masters of language, for his countrymen, as an Englishman.[16]

For Cooper the division between Britain and the US was a political one, but more on that as a generic issue in a little while. Others led by Henry James went much further and looked back, and indeed went back, to Europe to quarry for the cultural foundations of US Americans and how their contemporaries interacted with Europeans. They were hugely influential on the east coast elite and beyond in the USA and also in Britain and included such icons as T.S. Eliot, Raymond Chandler and Ezra Pound. The political scientist David Haglund, drawing at least partially on the literary movement represented by James, goes further to suggest that in the late nineteenth and early twentieth centuries the anti-British lobbying of American Irish and German ethnic diasporas actually drew American elite identity further into the transatlantic community rather than driving a wedge between the US and Britain.[17] Given that both Eliot and James took British nationality and that Chandler spent forty-nine of his seventy years of life as a British citizen, at least the idea of a literary if not a broader transatlantic community certainly has resonance.[18]

So at least Churchill's invoking of the importance of a common language and culture seems to have some substance in experience, but what of supposedly shared political values? Seemingly nothing similar happened in Britain compared with the triumvirate of struggles between states' rights and the expansion of the remit of the federal government, and yet if one were to recast those struggles in terms of simply containing or expanding the central state, then matters take on a rather different hue.

In Britain the focus was not centred on a struggle between central and local or regional government, but between and *within* the major political ideologies of Liberalism, Conservatism and Socialism concerning the appropriate scope of government. In conceiving of the respective parties associated with such ideologies one can place them along a continuum between libertarianism and collectivism such as Liberal – Conservative – Labour or, in the twenty-first century,

50 *A.P. Dobson*

Conservative – Liberal (Democrat) – Labour. However, equally important – and indicated by the switch in position of the parties on the spectrum just indicated – within each ideology there also developed a contest between libertarianism and collectivism. All this resulted in a gradual expansion of government regulation and provision of health, education and welfare as the collectivist ethos gradually progressed.[19] The struggle was, on the one hand, between a libertarianism that believed humanity had to be left alone in order to flourish and be free and, on the other, welfare liberalism that held humanity could only be free if provided with minimum standards of health education and welfare so people could be liberated from circumstance to make the best of themselves. This was clearly articulated in Britain especially in the conflict between the social Darwinist and laissez-faire views of Herbert Spencer on the one hand and the welfare liberalism of Thomas Hill Green and L.T. Hobhouse on the other. It was never so clearly argued on the American side in the nineteenth century, though Spencer's American acolyte W.G. Sumner articulated an equally harsh version of social Darwinism, claiming that the drunk in the gutter was where he naturally should be. Couching such sentiments in more general terms he wrote:

> In general, however, it may be said that those whom humanitarians and philanthropists call the weak are the ones through whom the productive and conservative forces of society are wasted. They constantly neutralize and destroy the finest efforts of the wise and industrious, and are a dead-weight on the society in all its struggles to realize any better things.[20]

Sumner wrote in the Gilded Age, a time of rampant individualistic, domestic laissez-faire capitalism. As Richard Hofstadter put it in his classic work on the American political tradition: 'There is no other period in the nation's history when politics seems so completely dwarfed by economic changes ... in politics the reformers were both isolated and sterile.'[21] Any idea that government should regulate anything in order to achieve a form of distributive justice or set standards of public welfare seemed alien, at least until the 1880s. So, again, experiences in the US and Britain seemed radically different but were actually simply on a different time scale.

Interestingly, if we track forward well after the period of our current concern with the Fulton speech, ironically it was in the US that the most complete version of the controversy between libertarianism and collectivism developed with John Rawls' *A Theory of Justice* and Robert Nozick's *Anarchy State and Utopia*. Rawls tried to square the circle to encompass economic competition, individual liberty and distributive justice that would provide health, education and welfare by arguing that this is the kind of society that any rational person would choose in a state of ignorance of his or her own situation and talents, i.e. behind a veil of ignorance. Nozick forthrightly rejected this:

> Individuals have rights, and there are things no person or group may do to them (without violating their rights). So strong and far-reaching are these

The Fulton speech and shared values 51

rights that they raise the question of what, if anything, the state and its officials may do.

He argued that modern taxation was a form of slavery, whereby individuals were coerced to work for the state (paying high taxes) against their free will. And Ronald Dworkin, another American scholar, who interestingly split his time mainly between Oxford and London on the one hand and New York on the other, disagreed with both but on ground that was much nearer to Rawls than Nozick.[22] But most importantly he added to the debate, one that had originated in an acute form in Britain but reached its apogee in late twentieth-century America. In short, the traditions were and always have been speaking to each other.

Returning to the late nineteenth and early twentieth century in Britain, the libertarians believed in laissez-faire economics and the need for limiting government drastically to maintaining defence, law and order with only very restricted economic, health education and welfare roles. The welfare liberals saw government in a more positive light and as necessary for regulation and the provision of basic needs to empower people to fulfilment. In this they not only anticipated the Rawls–Nozick debate but also reflected the same kind of concerns about the virtues and vices of large and small government that was at the heart of the tension between states' rights and the federal government. Looked at this way one can see that there were indeed similarities in the way the American and British political traditions developed. They were both engaged in a similar debate about the role of government, its relationship to the individual, how the individual could best prosper, and what constituted liberty. If this is so then it seems that Britain as well as the US contributed to the development of modern democracy and, given the importance of people such as Jeremy Bentham, John Stuart Mill, Herbert Spencer, T.H. Green, L.T. Hobhouse, R.H. Tawney and the Fabians, one could say that the British contribution to democratic theory and practice – *contra* Amar – was as great if not greater than the US's contribution, at least in the nineteenth century.

But where did all this lead to by the 1930s and 1940s?

In the US American idealists such as Henry Thoreau and Walt Whitman, Edward Bellamy and his scathing critique of capitalism in *Looking Backward,* Populists such as William Jennings Bryan, Henry Demarest Lloyd and Progressives such as Eugene Debs, Herbert Croly, Woodrow Wilson and Theodore Roosevelt all contributed to a sea-change of attitudes towards laissez-faire capitalism and the Gilded Age. This was comparable to the impact of the welfare liberals and the rise of the Labour Party and its ideologues in Britain. In many ways the intellectual summation of concerns and ideas in America culminated in what many see as the only distinctive American school of philosophy – Pragmatism, nowhere better expressed than in the work of John Dewey.

Dewey recognised the way in which Liberalism as articulated in Britain had developed along two not entirely compatible paths: humanitarian and philanthropic, leading naturally into welfare liberalism; and laissez-faire economics

52   A.P. Dobson

and political libertarianism leading to advocacy of the limited 'night-watchman' state.[23] In attacking the defenders of the US economic status quo in 1935 Dewey clearly declared the superiority of the former over the latter and intellectually committed himself to a form of liberal welfare-ism.

> If one wants to know what condition of liberty is at a given time, one has to examine what persons can do and what they cannot do ... liberty is always a social question, not an individual one.... No one can do anything except in relation to what others can do and cannot do ... liberty is something that affects every phase of life – liberty of thought, of expression, of cultural opportunity – and that is not to be had, even in the economic sphere, without a degree of security that is denied to millions by the present economic system.[24]

Two years earlier in a ground-breaking study Adolf A. Berle and Gardiner C. Means exposed the changes in corporate capitalism in such a way that it demonstrated just how radically capitalism had changed in the previous half-century such that it now required new forms of regulation. These ideas had impact on both sides of the Atlantic: Berle worked for the Roosevelt administration, and in Britain the message of Berle and Means was mediated through a variety of sources with impact on both the Conservative Party and the Labour Party, notably in the latter with influence on Labour revisionist intellectual C.A.R. Crosland.

One of the central issues of the new conception of capitalism was the perceived need for more 'scientific management' of the state and the economy. One can see this very much in Dewey's pragmatism and its emphasis on the importance of applying scientific methodology to social and political issues. In Britain many were even more enthused than Dewey by the promise of science to analyse, understand and shape society; most notable here was the elitism of the Fabians, but even the Conservatives seemed to abandon their scepticism of theory and man's ability to craft widespread social change as they re-thought their position after their 1945 General Election defeat. The consequent shift to a more welfare-oriented position with increased state action was caught nicely, if by some rather unkindly, in the term 'Butskellism', a conflation of Butler, a senior Tory and Chancellor of the Exchequer in the 1950s, and Hugh Gaitskell, Attlee's successor as leader of the Labour Party. It is difficult to convey the prevailing political positions in the US and the UK in the mid-twentieth century, but two points may suffice at least to establish a line of interpretation that would need extensive rebuttal.

First, the US and Britain respectively planned for a very different society after the end of World War Two and they did so along parallel though by no means identical lines. And it is suggested here that they were able to do so precisely because of the shared political tradition of values illustrated above. Both countries worked closely with each other to plan a new post-war economic and political order and invested huge amounts of time and talent to achieve those ends.

The Fulton speech and shared values   53

As early as 1941 Churchill and Roosevelt promulgated general principles in the Atlantic Charter which were later incorporated into the charter of the United Nations and which underpinned the planning for the new economic world order established through the IMF and the GATT (WTO after 1995). In the domestic sphere both committed to a welfare state to varying degrees. It was accomplished in a more advanced form in Britain and liberals have subsequently criticised President Truman for not only betraying Roosevelt's New Deal, but also reneging on his own election pledges for social and economic reform. But both sides were reading from the same book, though not necessarily from the same page: and John Maynard Keynes had written that book, at least as far as its economic content was concerned. Keynes' influence was ubiquitous, and in a very strong sense all in the prevailing consensus on both sides of the Atlantic were Keynesians now.

Keynes contributed hugely to the understanding of and possible management of modern economies and that came from basic moral convictions as well as his wonderful grasp of economics. In a lecture in 1926 Keynes said much that speaks to the understanding of political and economic values that permeated the consensus in the US and Britain in 1946:

> Let us clear from the ground the metaphysical or general principles upon which from time to time, *laissez-faire* has been founded. It is *not* true that individuals possess a prescriptive 'natural liberty' in their economic activities. There is *no* 'compact' conferring perpetual rights on those who Have or those who Acquire. The world is *not* so governed from above that private and social interest always coincide. It is *not* so managed here below that in practice they coincide. It is *not* a correct deduction from the Principles of Economics that enlightened self-interest always operates in the public interest. Nor is it true that self-interest generally *is* enlightened; more often individuals acting separately to promote their own ends are too ignorant or too weak to attain even these. Experience does *not* show that individuals, when they make up a social unit, are always less clear-sighted than when they act separately.[25]

This was denying the truths upon which so much of the radical libertarian position lay. In the nineteenth century Green had said something of similar import but more politically:

> When we measure the progress of society by its growth in freedom, we measure it by the increasing development and exercise on the whole of those powers of contributing to social good with which we believe the members of society to be endowed; in short, by the greater power on the part of the citizens as a body to make the most and the best of themselves.[26]

Churchill and Roosevelt had set out general principles in August 1941 in the Atlantic Charter, which reflected the substance of Roosevelt's 'Four Freedoms'

54   *A.P. Dobson*

of speech and worship, and freedom from want and fear. He had set these out earlier in the year in his 1941 inaugural. The Atlantic Charter actually used the phrase 'freedom from fear and want' and asked for the securing of world-wide improved labour standards, economic advancement and social security. All this had been a general clarion call to set out what would become an alternative vision to totalitarianism for democracies in the world and those that aspired to be democratic. Roosevelt, Churchill and Truman (not to mention Clement Attlee's Labour Government) were all social democrats of varying kinds. In 1933, his first year in office, Roosevelt had spoken of the need 'of adapting existing economic organization to the service of the people'.[27] Over a quarter of a century earlier Churchill had declared:

> I do not want to impair the vigour of competition, but we can do much to mitigate the consequences of failure. We can draw a line below which we will not allow persons to live and labour yet above which they may compete with all the strength of their manhood. We do not want to pull down the structure of science and civilization – but to spread a net over the abyss.[28]

Roosevelt could just as easily have uttered that at any time during his four terms of office as president. And while his legacy seems to many to have been compromised by Truman, the latter did have notable progressive welfare achievements to his credit including the expansion of social security, a doubling of its payments, and an increase in the minimum wage. Such reforms went nowhere near as far as the National Health Service, welfare provisions and the nationalisation of swathes of industry in Britain, but the intention and arguments were cast in the same values mould. Churchill was not invoking hollow images of shared moral and political values when he spoke at Fulton: his language had traction on both sides of the Atlantic among the respective prevailing consensus of views. To see just how resilient this community of prevailing political values was, the problems over the US Loan Agreement provide some interesting indicators.

In considering possibilities for the post-war economy there emerged two radically opposed alternatives in British thinking. The first was premised on maintaining bilateral trading arrangements and currency controls that would favour the Empire and Commonwealth and members of the sterling area. For the Left in the Labour Party this had appeal as it would insulate Britain from the prescriptions of US-style capitalism and allow them independently to build a socialist Britain. Hard-line Labour MPs, albeit small in number, wanted to maintain close relations with the USSR, while others including Richard Crossman and Michael Foot sought a middle position anchored in Europe between the two superpowers.[29] For the imperial Right in the Tory Party, many of whom were not enamoured by liberal trade and currency practices, it was an attractive Empire/Commonwealth-based alternative to undue subservience to the US. However, the majority in London feared that this route, which involved monetary and trade discrimination, would lead to the kind of conflict and economic disorder that had contributed much to the outbreak of the Second World War. The Americans, led by Secretary of State Cordell Hull, had identified discrimination, particularly in the guise of British imperial preference tariffs, as an evil that led to political conflict and ultimately war, and the Americans were determined to exorcise it from the international economic system. Unsurprisingly, then, the British realised early on that this first route option would make co-operation with the US 'impossible of achievement'.[30]

Second was the option of cooperating with the US for a liberal multilateral economic system with equal access to trade, the removal of all kinds of economic discrimination, managed exchange rates and a progressive lowering of barriers to trade. This was the basic project that American and British planners had worked on since 1941. But there were problems for Britain here as well. In particular, in the condition that Britain was likely to find itself after the war, there was a danger of deflationary policies and rising unemployment. Planning in 1941 began prior to the Beveridge Report, upon which Britain's welfare state was later structured, but there was already a growing consensus on the need for improved social conditions, better health care and full employment.

> An unqualified commitment on our part to remove bilateral trading arrangements and exchange controls regardless of the position of our balance of payments might involve the danger of internal deflation and unemployment or of an excessive depreciation of sterling, and might thus lead to serious internal economic and social difficulties.[31]

A way of mitigating those dangers was to agree on liberal multilateral goals with the Americans, but also to insist on a lengthy transition period in which discriminatory and protectionist measures would be gradually abandoned. This would provide a breathing space to allow Britain to repair its economy and regain its strength for a more competitive environment. Unfortunately, Britain was in a difficult position and one that deteriorated as the war progressed. At the war's end it was critically vulnerable because of debt, exhausted capital equipment and lost export markets. The only way out so far as the majority in London was concerned was to gain financial help from the US in the form of a huge dollar loan to recuperate Britain's economic fortunes. But that need put the Americans in a strong position to demand whatever conditions they thought appropriate. In the end they brutally insisted on a short transition period as one of the conditions of a loan: a transition period that was actually shorter than the one for sterling convertibility embodied in the Bretton Woods IMF agreement. The American objective was to achieve the new multilateral world economic order as quickly as possible. On 4 December 1945, 'The US delegation made it perfectly clear that they would break off the negotiations rather than concede the point about the transitional period.'[32] Britain had to give way and on 6 December the Loan Agreement was signed. Britain was extended a $3.75 billion line of credit and a further $650 million to cover post-hostilities Lend–Lease deliveries. In return Britain accepted a short transition period, committed itself anew to cooperate

56   *A.P. Dobson*

with the Americans on building the new economic world order and after a two-year period of grace began to pay interest of 2 per cent on the Loan. Final repayment was made in December 2006.

Chancellor of the Exchequer Hugh Dalton had been under no illusion: if US dollars were not forthcoming, the British could expect: 'an Irish peasant's standard of living.... Worst of all from the point of view of morale, practically no smokes.'[33] Prime Minister Clement Attlee later laconically recollected: 'We were in no position to bargain.'[34] Even so the words of *The Economist* captured many misgivings among Tory imperialists and Labour's left wing: 'How much economic hazard is a reasonable price for continued American generosity and friendship?'[35] British imperialists laid the blame for their country's decline partly at least at America's door and deeply resented what they saw as the harsh terms of the Loan Agreement, the unreasonable insistence on Britain's early return to sterling convertibility, American support of colonial independence movements, and their damaging assault on imperial preference. Dislike of American actions was also shared by the left wing of the Labour Government. They thought that the US was determined to undermine Labour's plans for a welfare state, the NHS and nationalisation of swathes of British industry and infrastructure. These two ideologically motivated groups were not strong enough to dictate policy and reject the American Loan and its conditions, but their power was by no means inconsiderable.

Reservations by some Tories were so strong that Churchill simply asked that his party abstain from voting altogether on the Loan. Even so, seventy of them and twenty-eight others, mainly left-wing members of the Labour Party, voted against. The final vote was 345 in favour, ninety-eight against. The overriding consideration for the majority was a combination of the need for US cooperation to guarantee Britain's security and ambition for a liberal world economic order, which would be lost if Britain took the road of economic protection. In the Lords there was a renewed tussle over the path Britain should take when the IMF Agreement and the Loan Agreement came up in debate. Keynes spoke at length in the House on 18 December 1945 to press the case for joining the IMF, and more generally for following the path laid out for Anglo-American cooperation and rejecting a move back to a form of economic autarky based on preferences for Empire and Commonwealth trade and a tightly regulated sterling bloc. The argument for an Empire-based alternative to the American Loan was forcefully made by Lord Woolton, wartime Minister of Food and Conservative Party Chairman 1946–55:

> We fought at Dunkirk, but today we are surrendering what I conceive to be our just rights. We are surrendering them to the power of the dollar, because those responsible for the affairs of this country do not dare to retreat to the economic fastness of the Empire.[36]

Other Conservative luminaries such as Lord Boothby were also virulently opposed to the Loan. But, Keynes was convinced that the 'economic fastness of the Empire' option was a chimera. What Woolton proposed was simply not viable. Keynes articulated the fears of consensus opinion in London and Washington when he argued: 'The separate economic blocs and all friction and loss of friendship they must bring with them are expedients to which one may be driven in a hostile world.... But it is surely crazy to prefer that.'[37] The Lords approved of Britain's entry into the IMF and the American Loan and by implication gave its imprimatur to close Anglo-American economic cooperation.

The Loan Agreement was thus passed in Britain, but it still had to be ratified in the US, and just as ideological differences had arisen in London to oppose the agreement so did they similarly arise in Washington. There they came from an array of sources. There were the usual suspects – Anglophobe sections of the US and anti-imperialists – but fiscal conservatives worried about inflation and jobs in the US and sceptics about the virtues and benefits for the US of multilateralism also strongly opposed. Reinforcing this opposition across the array of critics of the Loan was distaste at the idea of helping to finance the Labour Government's policies on health, education, welfare and nationalisation of industries. As Bernard Baruch put it, the Labour Government 'diverted much of her resources for the task of recovery to a programme of economic experimentation'.[38] So far as Churchill and those in the cross-party Labour–Conservative consensus were concerned, ratification of the Loan was imperative. The reasons why it was imperative were multiple. As Keynes indicated in the Lords, if Britain had to fall back on currency controls, imperial preference and other forms of financial and trade discrimination then it would come into serious economic and then political conflict with the USA and other countries. It would be forced to renege on the IMF and wartime commitments and principles expressed in the Atlantic Charter, the Master Lend–Lease Agreement and the charter of the UN. Second, Britain's economic straits would worsen and its decline, relative to others, increase. Third, close relations with the US would haemorrhage, endangering not just their economic relations, but security and political relations as well. Even if that did not follow, Britain's parlous economic state would drastically reduce its capabilities and make it of less value to the US. In short, consummating the Loan Agreement was vital to the life of the special relationship and thus, in Churchill's view, to the security of the world.

As noted previously, from the outset of his visit Churchill spoke of Britain's economic needs in Florida and canvassed both Secretary of State Byrnes and Bernard Baruch there for support for the ratification of the Loan in Congress. He was working fully in conjunction with the Attlee Government on these matters and kept in close contact with Attlee and Bevin.[39] The Labour Government was prepared to go to great lengths to guarantee passage of the Loan in Congress. For example, the government had, albeit with huge reluctance, given way to the Americans in talks in Bermuda in February 1946 on a vital civil aviation agreement, reversing their position at the Chicago Civil Aviation Conference in 1944. Civil Aviation Minister Lord Winster put his finger on Britain's vulnerability when towards the end of the proceedings he wrote:

58 *A.P. Dobson*

> [I]f the Cabinet felt that the signing of the agreement was of vital import-
> ance from the point of view of our general relations with the United States
> and the consideration of the loan agreement by Congress, he was willing
> that our delegation should be authorised to sign.[40]

Winster effectively reiterated Churchill's concerns in that brief paragraph: the
need for good (read 'special') relations with the US – with all that that involved
for British security – and help for the British economy. Winster signed.

The widespread support for the Loan in the US was more fluid than in Britain.
The reasons for supporting the Loan differed from one supporting constituency
to another and changed in most constituencies over time. The Truman administration wanted the Loan to be approved, but were aware that arguing the case on
the merits of promoting the multilateral new world economic order might not be
persuasive enough. As tensions rose with the Soviets, the administration began
to give more and more emphasis to arguments about security and the important
help Britain could render the US. On the morning of 4 March, prior to the departure for Fulton, President Truman publicly endorsed the proposed Loan at the
White House and urged the Congress to ratify it because it 'represented a cornerstone in the world's structure of peace'.[41] This put Truman on a page identical to
Churchill's. The Loan was not just important because of economic reasons
alone, it had implications that went far beyond that, resonating loudly with the
need for a close Anglo-American partnership to ensure the free world's security.
Churchill memorably drove that message home in Fulton, but he did not stop
there. After his departure from Florida his progress was a parade through Washington, Fulton, Virginia, Washington again and finally New York among the
great and good of the American establishment.

After Fulton he addressed the General Assembly of Virginia on 8 March with
General Eisenhower, US Army Chief of Staff, at his side. Again he hammered
home the need for fraternal friendship between the US and Britain: 'Above all,
among the English-speaking peoples, there must be the union of hearts based
upon conviction and common ideals. That is what I offer. That is what I seek.'[42]

After this, in which Churchill uttered not a whit of repentance for what he had
stirred up in Fulton, Eisenhower paid tribute to him, saying: 'It is my earnest
conviction that only history can measure the true value ... of the service he has
rendered to all of us.'[43] Standing beside the American war hero and his personal
and clearly admiring friend, this was just what Churchill wanted and had
designed: to transmit living images of close Anglo-American fraternity. Returning to Washington, Churchill also pressed again specifically for the Loan Agreement, and then attempted again on the final leg of his journey to persuade Baruch
to support the Loan. Baruch never did, but he moderated his opposition, did not
testify to the Congress (though he was scheduled to do so) and instead submitted
a written statement that was critical of the Loan, but did not specifically call for
it to be rejected by the Congress.[44]

Churchill's final major engagement was at the Waldorf Astoria Hotel as guest
of the Mayor of New York. When he spoke he insisted: 'I do not wish to

withdraw or modify a single word' of what he had said in Fulton. The Soviet threat was real and could only be successfully countered by a close Anglo-American special relationship acting as bedrock for world peace and prosperity. When challenged that he had repeatedly called for an Anglo-American military alliance, he had yet again an opportunity to spell out the need and importance of a special relationship and invoke the necessary conditions that made it possible.

> I have never asked for an Anglo-American military alliance or a treaty. I asked for something different and in a sense I asked for something more. I asked for fraternal association, free, voluntary, fraternal association. I have no doubt it will come to pass, as surely as the sun will rise to-morrow ... in their harmonious companionship, lies the main hope of a world instrument for maintaining peace on earth and goodwill to all men.[45]

As Paul Addison perceptively remarked in his work on Churchill: 'Though convinced of the Soviet threat, Churchill was deploying it [the Fulton speech] in support of his long cherished project of Anglo-American unity.'[46] His speeches in Virginia and New York were tailored to exactly the same goal. And Churchill was wise to reject the idea of a formal alliance. As Walter Lippmann and others pointed out, no government in Washington could enter a treaty that would willy-nilly have committed the US to protecting the British Empire. Polls only weeks after Churchill's Fulton speech indicated that 52 per cent of the American people were against a formal treaty, with 33 per cent in favour. But the idea of a broad plank that included many commonalities was something that Churchill could and did effectively invoke. He repeatedly referred to values shared through the parallel development of the British and American political traditions, a common language, common perception of the threat posed by Moscow and a shared commitment to a new economic and political world order which the two countries had taken the lead in crafting. Taken together this amounted to the components of what he called the fraternal association of the British and American people – the special relationship.

On 13 July 1946 the tortuous passage of the Loan through Congress was finally completed when 219 members of the House of Representatives voted for it and 155 against, with one abstention and fifty-seven not voting. Its passage had been difficult with the most recalcitrant opposition coming not surprisingly from the mid-West. The main reason for its passage and the way that the administration argued their case for it was now largely to do with matters of security.[47] One of Churchill's goals in going to the US had been achieved, but there was more to this than just the consummation of the Loan Agreement.

Churchill did not go to the US primarily to warn the American people of the threat from the Soviets or to ease the passage of the Loan Agreement. His purpose was much more broadly construed. He was convinced that above all else the objective for British foreign policy had to be the nurturing of a close association with the US. For him this was required for both sentimental and *realpolitik* reasons. He believed in the importance of the English-speaking peoples and

60   A.P. Dobson

despite the apparent differences with the US in political institutions, he perceived that there were strong underlying commonalities. They worked under two different institutional frameworks and those had spawned differences in the form that political debates had taken place, but the underlying narrative had been the same: the appropriate scope of government, its relationship to the individual, how the individual could best prosper, and what constituted liberty. That common narrative bound the two countries together and had enabled them jointly to craft a new political and economic world order during the war. Undoubtedly that was with Britain playing the junior role, but given the cross-fertilisation of ideas and values between the two peoples the idea of a junior role might be somewhat misleading. For example it is difficult to assess just how much influence the ideas of John Maynard Keynes had among American politicians and economists. Churchill was not evoking empty vessels when he spoke of a commonality of language and literature, political and social values. In the political tradition for Herbert Spencer there was W.G. Sumner; for T.H. Green and L.T. Hobhouse there was John Dewey and Pragmatism, and mirroring British social democracy and its health education and welfare ambitions there was the New Deal and Truman's Fair Deal. Even more to the point in the Atlantic Charter, the IMF and in the UN, Anglo-American collaboration had either exclusively iterated values as in the Atlantic Charter or had done more than any other country to define values and content. From this perspective Churchill's rousing rhetoric about fraternal association had great resonance. Given America's sense of its own exceptionalism and the strength of Isolationism as late as 1941, the figure of 33 per cent of Americans in favour of an alliance with Britain in 1946 is in many ways more notable than the 52 per cent opposing.

But Churchill was no romantic delusionary, he knew that invoking fraternal relations on the basis of shared political, economic and social values and a common language would never be enough to sway a sufficient number of Americans: so *realpolitik* was part of his agenda as well. He was well aware before speaking in Fulton that Truman and Byrnes had recently shifted to a position that was more trenchantly opposed to the Soviets and their demands. Truman did not need convincing of the Soviet danger. What Churchill did at Fulton was to try to deepen the entanglement of Britain and the US and demonstrate that because of shared language and historical inheritance they needed each other to keep world peace and uphold their shared values. A prerequisite for that was financial help from the US to enable Britain to regain its feet, play a significant role in the world and help achieve security for them both. The political game was to demonstrate to the American people his closeness to the President and to war heroes such as Eisenhower, and to try to convince them of the desirability of a strong Britain working in harmony with the US to counter the imminent threat from the Soviets; this would create the foundations of a form of cooperation that would continue to provide security irrespective of where threat might arise.

Fulton was not so much about the Soviet threat, but about the potential dangers of the US and Britain failing to establish a close working relationship

The Fulton speech and shared values 61

and of British enfeeblement if the American Loan were not approved. It would be gross overstatement to claim that the special relationship that Britain and the US continued to experience over the following decades and the passage of the US Loan Agreement in Congress were all due to Churchill and what he accomplished in Fulton and elsewhere during his trip to the US in early 1946. On the other hand it is to misunderstand what he was doing in the US if Fulton is simply seen as the Iron Curtain speech, calling the free world to arms. Churchill's agenda was more subtle and expansive than that, and one could say that on balance he had considerable success in promoting it.

Notes

1 Acknowledgement: I thank Kristin Cook, Warren F. Kimball and Robert Hendershot for their constructive comments from which this paper significantly benefited.
2 *Miami News*, 16 January 1946.
3 Martin Gilbert, *Churchill and America*, London: Free Press, 2006, pp. 364–7.
4 Text quoted from Philip White, *Our Supreme Task: How Winston Churchill's Iron Curtain Speech Defined the Cold War Alliance*, New York: Public Affairs, 2012, p. 185.
5 White, *Our Supreme Task*, pp. 206–12.
6 Ibid., p. 143, citing *Leahy Diaries*, Iowa State University, entry 3 March 1946.
7 Gilbert, *Churchill and America*, p. 368.
8 F.J. Harbutt, *The Iron Curtain: Churchill, America and the Origins of the Cold War*, Oxford: Oxford University Press, 1986; and R.W. Woods, *A Changing of the Guard: Anglo-American Relations 1941–1946*, Chapel Hill: University of North Carolina Press, 1990. For recent discussion of these matters see Kathleen Britt Rasmussen, 'Great Britain and American Hegemony', in Daniel S. Margolies (ed.), *A Companion to Harry Truman*, Chichester: Wiley-Blackwell, 2012, pp. 305–27.
9 Harry S. Truman Library, Independence, Missouri, Truman to Byrnes, 5 January 1946, Truman Papers PSF, longhand memos. Further evidence of the shift of views in the administration can be found in Frank Costigliola, *Roosevelt's Lost Alliances: How Personal Politics Helped Start the Cold War*, Princeton: Princeton University Press, 2013.
10 *Selections from the Writings and Speeches of William L. Garrison*, Boston: R.F. Walcutt, 1852; J.C. Calhoun, *The South Carolina Exposition and Protest* and *A Disquisition on Government*, both in Richard K. Cralle (editor), *The Works of John C. Calhoun*, New York: D. Appleton, 1851–6 in multiple volumes; George Fitzhugh, *Sociology for the South: Or The Failure of a Free Society*, Richmond: A. Morris, 1854, and *Cannibals All: Or Slaves Without Masters*, Boston: Harvard University Press, 1966.
11 A.T. Mahan, *The Influence of Sea Power Upon History 1660–1783*, New York: Dover Publications, 1987.
12 White, *Our Supreme Task*, pp. 185, 200.
13 Ibid., p. 175
14 Winston S. Churchill, *A History of the English-Speaking Peoples, Volume 1: The Birth of Britain*, London: Cassell, 1974 (first published 1956), p. ix.
15 Charles Dickens, *American Notes*, Altenmünster: Jazzybee Verlag, 2014, May 1868. concluding remarks; similarly critical but widely read comments on America were also made by Oscar Wilde and many others.
16 James Fenimore Cooper, *Notions of the Americans: Picked up by a Travelling Bachelor*, 2 volumes, London: Henry Colburn, 1828, p. 132.

62 *A.P. Dobson*

17 David Haglund, 'Is There a "Strategic Culture" of the Special Relationship?' in Alan P. Dobson and Steve Marsh (eds), *Anglo-American Relations: Contemporary Perspectives*, London: Routledge, 2013, p. 45.

18 Resonance, of course, does not mean that the cultures were identical. There are some very obvious differences in culture more broadly, not least firearm-related deaths: UK 0.25 per 100,000 (2010); US 10.3 per 100,000 (2011). The only part of the UK that comes remotely close in violent crime is Scotland with a 48 per cent higher murder rate than in the rest of the UK with knife-related deaths composing a large part of those crimes, but this is still a long way off the overall murder rate in the US. There is also a strong sense of restless movement in the US, caught in the works of writers such as Hemingway and Cormac McCarthy. Such sentiments are rarely found in British culture.

19 The most detailed exposition of this thesis is by W.H. Greenleaf, *The British Political Tradition, Volume Two: The Ideological Heritage*, London: Methuen, 1983.

20 William Graham Sumner, *What Social Classes Owe to Each Other*, Caldwell Idaho: Caxton Printers, 1978, p. 19.

21 Richard Hofstadter, *The American Political Tradition: And the Men Who Made It*, London: Jonathan Cape, 1967, pp. 163 and 174.

22 John Rawls *A Theory of Justice*, Oxford: Oxford University Press, 1980; Robert Nozick, *Anarchy State and Utopia*, New York: Basic Books, 1974, p. ix; Ronald Dworkin, *Taking Rights Seriously*, London: Duckworth, 1996, chapter 6; and Justine Burley (ed.), *Dworkin and His Critics: With Replies by Dworkin*, Oxford: Blackwell, 2004.

23 'Future of Liberalism' from John Dewey, *Problems of Men*, New York: The Philosophical Library, 1946.

24 John Dewey, 'Liberty and Social Control' and 'Future of Liberalism', both from *Problems of Men*.

25 Quoted from Greenleaf, *Political Tradition*, pp. 173–4, source J.M. Keynes, *The End of Laissez-Faire*, London: Hogarth Press, 1926, pp. 39–40.

26 T.H. Green, *Liberal Legislation and Freedom of Contract*, Oxford: Slatery & Rose, 1861.

27 Franklin Roosevelt, 'Looking Forward', 1933, cited from Andrew M. Scott, *Political Thought in America*, New York: Rinehart, 1959, p. 577.

28 'The Cause of the Left-Out Millions', 11 October 1906, Saint Andrews Hall Glasgow, in Winston S. Churchill (ed.), *Never Give In: Winston Churchill's Speeches*, London: Bloomsbury Academic, 2013, p. 20.

29 Kenneth Morgan, *Labour in Power*, Oxford: Oxford University Press, 1985, p. 63.

30 British National Archives (BNA), FO 371 28907, 'Proposals for Anglo-American Post-War Economic Co-operation', 18 August 1941.

31 Ibid.

32 BNA, FO371/45711, Bridges to Eady, 4 December 1945.

33 H. Dalton, *High Tide and After: Memoirs 1945–1960*, London: Frederick Muller, 1962, pp. 84–5.

34 F. Williams, *A Prime Minister Remembers*, London: Heinemann, 1961, p. 134.

35 *The Economist*, 21 July 1945.

36 Benn Steil, *The Battle of Bretton Woods: John Maynard Keynes, Harry Dexter White and the Making of the New World Order*, Princeton: Princeton University Press, 2013, p. 285.

37 Quoted from Robert Skidelski, *John Maynard Keynes 1883–1946: Economist, Philosopher and Statesman*, London: Pan Books, 2004, p. 819, source *The Collected Writings of John Maynard Keynes*, Cambridge: Cambridge University Press, 2012, vol. XXIV, pp. 605–24.

38 Bernard Baruch, *The Public Years*, London: Odhams Press, 1961, p. 321.

39 Gilbert, *Churchill and America*, ch. 35.

The Fulton speech and shared values   63

40 BNA, CAB 128/5, 11(46)8, 4 February 1946 considering CP37(46) by Winster.
41 White, *Our Supreme Task*, p. 144.
42 R.S. Churchill (ed.), *The Sinews of Peace: Post-War Speeches by Winston S. Churchill*, London: Cassell, 1948, pp. 106–10
43 Robert H. Pilpel, *Churchill in America 1895–1961: An Affectionate Portrait*, London: New English Library, 1977, p. 224.
44 Woods, *A Changing of the Guard*, p. 373.
45 Gilbert, *Churchill and America*, p. 376.
46 Paul Addison, *Churchill: The Unexpected Hero*, Oxford: Oxford University Press, 2005, p. 222.
47 Woods, *A Changing of the Guard*, pp. 393 and *passim*.

3 Manipulating the Anglo-American civilizational identity in the era of Churchill

Robert M. Hendershot

This chapter explores the roles of identity and memory in the historical evolution of the Anglo-American special relationship. Through an integrated examination of diplomatic discourse, opinion polls and popular culture, it seeks to compliment the other contributions in this volume by analysing the ways in which sentiment and strategic interests have thoroughly merged in the history of American and British relations and, in turn, how this dynamic has wrought a stabilizing effect upon the unique bilateral diplomatic partnership between the two nations.

Understanding the factors of causation behind the special relationship must include careful assessment of what will be referred to here as the Anglo-American civilizational identity – a distinct imagined community based upon perceptions of shared history, culture, values, and language among the British and American peoples. While this civilizational identity emerged before Winston Churchill's career, this chapter establishes that it was nevertheless his astute perception of its existence (particularly in the United States), his early recognition that the ability to influence such an identity could be used to advance strategic goals, and his resulting effective manipulation that helped contribute to an enduring post-1945 special relationship. Indeed, Churchill and other Anglo-American leaders of the era conceptualized and laboured to produce a new cultural context in which future Anglo-American diplomacy would have to operate. In the process, Churchill successfully transformed himself into the ultimate manifestation of the identity he sought to manipulate, and the influence of his memory has ever after been detectible within the cultural ether of Anglo-American diplomacy. In terms of identity, memory, tone and attitude, the contemporary Anglo-American special relationship still functions largely within the cultural context engineered and popularized during the era of Churchill.

Britain's Day, 7 December 1918

In order to fully appreciate how mid-century leaders such as Churchill were able to manipulate the Anglo-American civilizational identity, it is essential to first understand its key components, all of which were demonstrated publicly and heartily as the Americans celebrated their victory in the First World War. In this way, analysing the events of Britain's Day establishes how pervasive this

Manipulating the Anglo-American identity   65

civilizational identity had become by 1918, and clarifies how and why it had the potential to influence the future of Anglo-American relations.

Twenty-three years to the day before the Japanese attack on Pearl Harbor, approximately 2,000 communities throughout the United States joined together in the celebration of Britain's Day on 7 December 1918. With the largest public demonstrations taking place in New York, Philadelphia, and Chicago, and thousands of smaller events at schools, churches, clubs, and fraternal organizations across the nation, the American celebrations were, as the *New York Times* declared, 'the inevitable result of the country's admiration for the splendid fighting spirit Britain has shown in the world war', as well as expressions of the goodwill and friendship that existed between Great Britain and the United States.[1] At the myriad banquets, open-air concerts, and parades, American flags flew alongside the Union Jack as speakers described the British as steadfast, gallant, and tenacious people, deserving of American loyalty, respect, and gratitude. In this moment of national triumph, the British people were praised as determined kinsmen whose essential nature was complimentary to American identity, naturally resulting in inseparable Anglo-American unity, friendship, and peace. Indeed, any historian of Anglo-American relations would be hard pressed to find another moment in which American affinity for Britain would be enacted so widely, enthusiastically, or publicly.

Britain's Day headquarters in New York City loosely coordinated these events, and corresponded with governors, mayors, school boards, and individuals from every state in the union, which prompted *The Times* to declare confidently, 'One of the surest proofs of growing good feeling and closer relations between the United States and Britain is the hearty response of the entire nation to Britain Day.'[2] At many of the celebrations, crowds cheered a message from King George V stating that he was 'deeply touched' and welcomed America's celebration of Britain's Day

> as proof of the true and lasting friendship of the United States. It will be a particular satisfaction to my Navy and Army to feel that they have won the esteem of a nation which sent so many gallant men to suffer with them in the trials of the great war, and to share the glorious victory – In the name of the Empire, I thank the people of the United States. I pray that the coming era of peace may find the two nations always united, as to-day.[3]

Britain had already paid tribute to its American and French allies earlier that year, on 4 July and Bastille Day respectively. To celebrate the Americans, the British had observed the 142nd anniversary of the Declaration of Independence in multiple ways, including flying the American flag level with the British flag from the Parliament buildings in London as well as inside Westminster Cathedral, where the flags were paired with the inscription: 'Independence 1776, Interdependence 1918, Asunder – Never!' The American media was struck by these compliments, and the *New York Times* made sure to point out that no other nation's banner had been accorded such an honour and that this was profoundly expressive of the fellowship existing between the two countries'.[4]

Similar themes of unity and friendship would be emphasized in the United States on Britain's Day. President Woodrow Wilson, then in Europe, cabled home to express his own thanks for the efforts of British soldiers and sailors,[5] as did General John Pershing, commander of American forces in Europe, who was even more effusive on the day's themes:

The achievements of the British Empire for humanity are too many fold to enumerate in a short message. Entering the war to defend the rights of nations, she has unhesitatingly given her sons and her wealth. Gathered from her loyal dominions, the men of the British Empire have carried their victorious eagles over many a bloody field. Steadfast in adversity, wounded with a thousand blows, Britain's hammer blows have never weakened or faltered. But for the tenacity of her people the war would have been lost.

To those of us who have been associated with them and who have fought beside their gallant troops, words of praise seem inadequate to express our admiration. These things our kinsmen have done, and these things have brought an inseparable union between them and ourselves. To the British people, we extend our thanks for the powerful aid her navy has given, and offer our great respect for the resolute Anglo-Saxon determination with which she has held on, and we offer our right hand of friendship that our two nations may be more firmly linked together to insure the future peace of the world.[6]

Posters designed and distributed to advertise the event also captured the spirit of the day. Some posters centred on the figure of Britannia, icon of the British Empire, and frequently depict her surrounded by Poseidon, Greek god of the seas, various symbols of her Empire, knights in armour, destroyers and planes.[7] However, the most famous and widely printed artwork associated with Britain's Day was created by artist James Montgomery Flagg and distributed by the American Lithographic Company of New York.[8] Flagg, who had created America's most iconic version of Uncle Sam in his famous recruiting poster during the war (which was itself modelled on a British poster with Lord Kitchener urging Britons to join the war effort) now portrayed his creation arm-in-arm with Britannia. Significantly, *Side by Side* places the two national icons on equal footing, with Britannia's knee slightly in advance of Uncle Sam's, but with his foot placed scarcely beyond hers.[9] They are shown in action, cresting a hilltop accompanied by their familiars, the American eagle and the British lion, which are also on equal footing. The overall theme of the artwork is that of equal and conjoined progressive movement, not of one nation following the other, nor in the other's debt. Their relationship is portrayed as platonic rather than romantic; Uncle Sam beams at Britannia as she gazes back at her ally with distinct fondness and pride. Her classic Greco-Roman helmet makes her the slightly taller figure, but this early visual representation of the special relationship (a term not yet coined) between America and Britain tells a clear story of unity, equality, and victory – foreshadowing a version of the alliance that would become ubiquitous decades later, but remarkable in 1918.

Manipulating the Anglo-American identity 67

Figure 3.1 Side by Side – Britannia! Britain's Day, 7 December 1918, James Montgomery Flagg.

Source: Library of Congress, www.loc.gov/pictures/item/2002712329/ (accessed 10 November 2015).

Though the United States had, like Britain, honoured France earlier in the year by observing Bastille Day, and French tricolours were displayed on public buildings across the nation as President Wilson and Newton Baker, Secretary of War, sent messages to France praising their nations' alliance in defence of democracy,[10] this former commemoration lacked the gusto and scale of Britain's Day, and accordingly received much less media attention. Flagg had produced a poster advertisement for Bastille Day as well, for which he chose to depict a martial version of Marianne, based largely upon the central figure in Eugène Delacroix's *Liberty Leading the People*, wearing a skirt made from the French flag and surrounded by allies singing the Marseillaise.[11] The visual imagery here succeeded in praising French allies in the war effort, but certainly did not conjure the more intense partnership and unity displayed in pieces such as *Side by Side*. In general, America's enactment of Britain's Day went beyond merely thanking Britain for its role in the war and featured a chorus of voices from throughout the United States calling for an enduring alliance with the British and expressing sentimental gratitude for the 'unyielding, unconquerable, constant, tenacious British spirit, cheerful in disaster, unboastful in victory, [that] has never been bent or weakened'.[12] Offering yet another glimpse of how history and culture would be lauded as the bedrock of the special relationship in the future, Chauncey Depew, the Pilgrims Society president in New York, described the improvement in Anglo-American relations as the 'fruitage in the centuries of the Magna Charta, the Bill of Rights, and the American Declaration of Independence, in common principles and ideals'.[13] When examined collectively in this way, the sentiments and statements of Britain's Day 1918 demonstrate that the classic discourse of the Anglo-American alliance – emphasizing shared values, democracy, history, kinship, and culture – so often axiomatically accepted as having originated with Winston Churchill's career as the British prime minister, are actually much older.

For academics interested in the history of Anglo-American relations, Britain's Day is important in two key ways. First, it reveals the positive perceptions of Britain that existed within the United States during this period. That Americans felt compelled to publicly demonstrate these feelings and stress their appreciation for British partnership is indeed significant, since it illustrates how intensely American identities had begun to shift. Until the First World War, the United States had still largely been a regional rather than a global power. But this changed dramatically in a relatively short period of time, and by 1918 Americans were struggling to come to terms with the vastly expanded military, economic, and diplomatic powers of their nation.[14] Complicating this process was the experience of joining an international coalition of allies for the first time, and then witnessing their government, and particularly President Wilson, attempt to sculpt the international order of the post-war world. The simultaneous collapse of massive empires and the spectre of Marxist-inspired revolutions only added to the sense of social disorientation Americans felt during these years.

The American people's similarities with the British were made all the more manifest in comparison with foreign powers and peoples that they perceived as so different from themselves, given the wartime propaganda about the 'Huns' in Germany and post-war news of fulfilled and stewing revolutions coming at the end of the war in Russia and other countries. As David Haglund has explained, it was in this period of the early twentieth century that 'Americans began to conceptualize their own "national" self as being embedded in a larger cognitive community, one that was impregnated with English-bestowed social and political practices'.[15] During the early years of the war, Americans with British ancestry had begun to take increased pride in this connection, particularly as a way of distancing themselves from those who favoured Germany. As the war

Manipulating the Anglo-American identity 69

continued, and particularly after the United States entered the war in the spring of 1917 while championing self-determination, this dynamic moved beyond personal family heritage and began to embrace a common identity with the British in the broader terms of shared political values, language, history, and culture as well.[16] Indeed, the Britain's Day celebrations in 1918 lauded each of these elements in turn, and cumulatively form a powerful expression of the dominant American perceptions of Britain at the war's conclusion.

Of course, this is not to argue that all Americans maintained purely positive notions of Britain during the era of the First World War. One is reminded of the story about an American artillery battery in France being inspected by the Prince of Wales and General Pershing near the end of the war. Many of Captain Harry S. Truman's soldiers had Irish heritage and apparently resented having to dress up and polish their equipment before standing at attention for two hours in the rain waiting for the Prince to appear. As Truman escorted the Prince through the inspection, a anonymous soldier shouted from the back, 'Hey, Cap'n Harry, ask that little sonuva-so-and-so when he's gonna free Ireland!'[17] Obviously, the shared experience of alliance and combat did not always guarantee complete Anglo-American cultural affinity. Nevertheless, these were not the sentiments that dominated public space and popular art, or indeed the American government, on Britain's Day in 1918, and nor would they be in the future.

Second, Britain's Day is important because it stands out in the historical record as a fascinating anomaly in the interwar period. America's sentimental praise for its wartime allies in general and Britain in particular seemed to have crested after December 1918, and in the coming months and years the national debate over the Versailles Treaty and the League of Nations would sour many on the prospects of future alliances with foreign powers. Though vague, Warren Harding's promise of a 'return to normalcy' in the 1920 presidential election was an important part of his popularity, as was his contention that the United States needed 'not submergence in internationality, but sustainment in triumphant nationality'.[18] The excitement and the jubilant Atlanticist tone of 1918 seemed to fade quickly, and the subsequent interwar distractions of economic turmoil and the New Deal led many Americans to shift their perspectives away from global relationships and towards domestic problems. It was simply easier to consider European affairs as remote and ultimately unrelated to life in America. To many observers it seemed as though, in the words of *Time* magazine, 'most Americans still thought of international diplomacy with all the repugnance of a Victorian lady contemplating sex'.[19]

Nevertheless, the perceptions, identities, and affinities on display during the Britain's Day celebrations did not completely disappear. Rather, they survived, muted but intact, and would resurface in remarkably similar forms beginning in 1939. It was at this time that perspicacious political leaders in Britain and America began to understand the capacity of identity and culture to impact international relations, and they would in turn seek to harness these powers for the first time. This would not be a simple matter to accomplish, but to anyone who had been paying attention in December of 1918, there could be little doubt that the post-WWI American world view was fertile soil for those interested in cultivating a powerful and durable transatlantic alliance. Winston Churchill was one of the earliest such leaders to reach this conclusion, and as will be explained below, this ought to be considered as one of his greatest contributions to the history of American and British diplomacy.

Manipulating an Anglo-American identity in the era of Churchill

Winston Churchill's first public reference to the 'unity of the English-speaking races' came in 1911, the year he turned thirty-seven and became the First Lord of the Admiralty.[20] The Great Rapprochement between the Unites States and the British Empire that began in the 1890s already seemed to suggest these nations' diplomatic relationship would continue to improve, and the early twentieth century offered little to persuade British leaders that these two industrial powers could not coexist harmoniously. For Churchill, however, throughout the rest of his long career in British politics, the idea that America and Britain were natural allies bound together by language, history, and culture would grow to become one of his dominant themes. Of course, given that he was half American by birth, it is entirely possible that this notion appealed to key elements of his own identity – as a way of reconciling his zealous commitment to the British Empire and his own American heritage. In this way, his early commitment to Anglo-American unity was likely a projection of his own identity and biases, but the notion itself was neither his invention nor even a novel concept when he began to speak about it openly.

Unfortunately, there is no nineteenth-century public opinion polling data to show exactly how widespread such notions may have been during his youth, but there is certainly no shortage of examples to prove that the ideas of Anglo-American connection and fellowship were quite common. For example, the famous American poet and anti-slavery advocate John Greenleaf Whittier expressed these sentiments proudly:

> O Englishmen! – in hope and creed,
> In blood and tongue our brothers!
> We, too, are heirs of Runnymede;
> And Shakespeare's fame and Cromwell's deed
> Are not alone our mother's.
> 'Thicker than water', in one rill
> Through centuries of story,
> Our Saxon blood has flowed, and still
> We share with you the good and ill,
> The shadow and the glory.[21]

Other popular Anglo-American authors went beyond sentimental references to shared history, culture, and blood to write frankly of Atlantic convergence. As Henry James said,

Manipulating the Anglo-American identity 71

I can't look at the English–American world, or feel about them, any more, save as a big Anglo-Saxon total, destined to such an amount of melting together that an insistence on their differences becomes more and more idle and pedantic.[22]

Such ideas were sufficiently ingrained to keep Churchill and others convinced of the premise of Anglo-American unity even when personal experience failed to justify it. For example, when on a lecture tour in the United States in 1900, Churchill was struck by both the low turnout at his lectures (he had not yet successfully built his brand in America) as well as the significant pro-Boer feeling he sometimes encountered, particularly among Irish and Dutch Americans. Yet such discouraging aspects of his trip were not sufficiently powerful to convince him to alter his expectations of Anglo-American connection. Indeed, he encountered more satiating opinions as well. Among the various dignitaries he met on this trip was the famous author and humourist Mark Twain, who kindly welcomed Churchill as 'a blend of America and England that makes a perfect match'. And while Twain shared many people's distress about the war in South Africa, he simultaneously saw this as no reason why his country and Britain would not remain allies. Remarking that recent British actions in the war were strikingly similar to the simultaneous American conflict in the Philippines, Twain condescended, 'England and America were kin in almost everything; now they are kin in sin.'[23] Despite their concerns, Americans like Twain were nevertheless conscious of their similarities with the British on multiple levels, and such interactions may help us to understand how Churchill's generally lukewarm reception in the United States at the turn of the century nevertheless failed to shake his perceptions of the fundamental unity of the English-speaking peoples.

The early twentieth century saw these ideas appear more frequently in public discourse, and ultimately the experience of the Great War seemed to offer more concrete evidence that the two nations would be allies in the future. Indeed, Churchill would have been highly pleased with the Britain's Day event in the United States, since the sentiments displayed were so closely aligned with his own. As the United States had entered the war in 1917, Churchill argued that having the Americans and the British fighting together in a common cause would tie 'these two branches of the Anglo-Saxon world' together on a long-lasting basis, and he described this as the logical climax of all previous English history. Moreover, the resulting 'comradeship and reconciliation' of the United States with Britain could potentially form 'the mainstay of the future of the world when the war is over'.[24] Such statements represent both an expression of his own longstanding views as well as an attempt to resolve his British audience to the strategic necessity of being on excellent terms with the United States, a nation rapidly advancing in global influence. Anglo-American camaraderie was already being acknowledged as more than a widespread cultural perception – it was also expected to be of tactical advantage to the United Kingdom in the future.

Once again, Churchill was not alone in these views, and various British leaders voiced similar ideas throughout the interwar period.[25] While such references were largely abstract and theoretical, and no specific policies were implemented to stoke transnational Anglo-American identities in the 1920s or 1930s, this would not remain the case much longer. It was in the crisis of the Second World War that Churchill, as prime minister, became fully convinced that the Anglo-American civilizational identity could be moulded into an essential tool that would ensure Britain's survival.

A series of dramatic German victories came swiftly after hostilities began in 1939, and by mid-1940 France had been defeated and the remnants of the British Army had retreated from the European mainland. The British Empire then stood alone against the Axis Powers, and the fighting in North Africa and the ongoing Battle of the Atlantic continued to go poorly for the British. German aerial bombing campaigns against Britain increased in August 1940, and the Blitz underscored the dire nature of the United Kingdom's situation. The British desperately needed American support, yet the United States remained neutral. Though President Franklin Roosevelt had already believed that the Nazi regime posed a threat to the United States before the war had begun, and in September of 1939 had told his nation bluntly that the war 'does affect the American future', he still had not succeeded in convincing enough of the American population that the United States had practical and moral reasons to help defeat the Axis Powers.[26]

Roosevelt would have to stand for re-election in November of 1940, and he was unwilling to jeopardize his campaign by involving the United States in the war without a popular mandate. An opinion poll conducted in October of 1940 revealed that 83 per cent of Americans did not believe 'the United States should enter the war against Germany and Italy at once'.[27] Accordingly, the Destroyers for Bases deal of September 1940, by which the US transferred fifty obsolete destroyers to the British Royal Navy in exchange the right to use British bases around the world, represented the extent of what the President could do at the time. While the British government was encouraged by the deal, it was certainly not enough to reverse their fortunes in the war, and Churchill was frustrated with 'those bloody Yankees' and unwilling to wait patiently for American public opinion to shift in his nation's favour.[28] During the Blitz, a German invasion seemed imminent, and time was the key factor. Accordingly, he began a campaign to manipulate American perceptions as a way of altering the course of the war.

Churchill was remarkably confident that if the Americans could be made more mindful of Britain's experiences in the war, as well as of their shared history and culture with the British, then they would identify with the British people in their desperate struggle. Logic held that this would cause American neutrality to weaken and perhaps even break down completely, in which case the United States would enter the war directly as Britain's ally once again. Indeed, he believed the Blitz itself was natural propaganda that could be relied upon to provoke the Americans to not only sympathy for the British, but action as well. As early as June 1940, his secretary's notes for a speech in a secret session of the House of Commons underscored this strategy:

Attitude of the United States.
Nothing will stir them like fighting in England.
No good suggesting to them we are down and out.
The heroic struggle of Britain
Best chance of bringing them in.[29]

That Churchill assumed British heroism in defence of the homeland would stir American attitudes like nothing else and move the American people to abandon their neutrality demonstrates his recognition that cultural affinity could be used to advance the strategic ends of the United Kingdom. This prediction would prove accurate in the months ahead as Churchill and others worked to spread awareness of the Blitz in America, and public opinion began to shift.

The scores of American pilots who chose to defy American neutrality laws by joining the Royal Air Force were an early sign of hope for the British in general and the Prime Minster in particular. The first of three 'Eagle Squadrons' was formed as the Blitz accelerated in late September 1940, and though their training was incomplete that fall, a media frenzy commenced and numerous positive articles about the American pilots appeared in newspapers and on radio programmes. In addition to the glowing BBC coverage, the American journalist Ed Murrow interviewed several of the pilots for the American network CBS.[30] While such media coverage was encouraging, more would be needed to secure the desired effect.

In the following months, three major interrelated themes of the Anglo-American civilizational identity were employed to manipulate opinions: shared political history and values, shared religious world views, and unique cultural intimacy. The United States and Britain were presented as the only remaining viable democracies in a world increasingly dominated by totalitarian regimes, and the shared Anglo-American concepts of common law, due process, religious freedom, representative government, and civil rights would be emphasized. Conversely, British imperialism was de-emphasized or, whenever necessary, presented in the best possible light for the American public, i.e. as a force for spreading these significant ideals around the world. Biblical terminology and imagery were employed to underscore cultural similarities as well as to conjure a religiously (and familiar) poetic sense of destiny and purpose for their alliance, as a thing essentially preordained by a higher power. On one hand, placing such emphasis on their shared religious world views effectively contrasted the Anglo-American identity with the heavily secular ideologies of both fascism and communism. On the other, lauding a shared language and religious tradition was a key way of emphasizing Anglo-American intimacy. The English language, as the most overt cultural similarity between the American and British peoples, and particularly the poetic cultured Jacobean English of the King James Bible, was a powerful reminder of their shared history and a symbol of their similarities in the present. The frankness, equality, shared identity, and intimate partnership Churchill and the British required would be facilitated by fluid communication between the partners.

74   *R.M. Hendershot*

It is also significant that invoking the concept of Anglo-Saxonism was becoming less common by 1940. Times were changing, and fighting for freedom and equality against racist and ethnist, genocidal totalitarian regimes made prideful references to ethnic Anglo-Saxonism, so common in previous generations, appear passé. As a result, nebulous racial allusions to Anglo-Saxon peoples or their characteristics were increasingly replaced with phrases such as 'Anglo-American' or 'English-speaking peoples' – terms that evoked the desired transnational or cultural connections between diverse populations. Occasional references to Anglo-Saxonism still appeared, and Churchill himself would continue to make such references longer than other leaders, but these instances became fewer and further between during the war. In diplomatic exchanges, government statements, and the media, the dominant discourse increasingly described Great Britain and the United States as historically and culturally linked parts of a global community with a common interest in defending freedom.

To be fully effective, these themes would need to be embedded in the hearts and minds of American decision-makers as well as in the consciousness of a majority of the American public. Accordingly, these efforts required a media campaign as well as an interpersonal campaign. Of course, Churchill kept up his extensive correspondence with Roosevelt throughout the fall of 1940, always stressing British gratitude for current American support, the need for expanded support, and the determination and resilience of the British people. With the American elections looming, however, Roosevelt remained an elusive and disappointing partner. As historian Jon Meacham has written, 'Churchill was still very much the suitor in the courtship of Franklin Roosevelt.'[31] Nevertheless, American affinity for Britain was known to exist in enough quarters for it to be used strategically, and the British worked to advance this area of diplomacy through specific channels. For example, Churchill's close friend and confidant Brendan Bracken had extensive contacts with influential Americans, and he utilized these contacts successfully during the Blitz. After Eugene Meyer, the publisher of the *Washington Post* and an American known for his pro-intervention position, had sent Bracken an article explaining how British war orphans were finding refuge in American homes, Bracken replied with the promise that 'England will never forget what America is doing for her'. Using the same types of sentiment that Churchill was using with Roosevelt, Bracken went on to stress that

> this war will not have been in vain if it ends by welding the foreign naval and military policies of England and America into an instrument which can stifle the rebirth of tyranny, race prejudice, and all other beastly systems bred by Nazis and Fascists.

He then explained that conditions were hard for the British people, but that they remained positive and determined, and would never surrender. Meyer responded with enthusiasm, explaining, 'America is profoundly impressed by the splendid defense put up by your people' and praising both Churchill and the high morale of the British. Meyer's newspaper would continue to reflect these sentiments, and, of course, President Roosevelt, like many Americans, read the *Post* daily.[32]

The British government simultaneously cultivated the sympathies of many other key figures in the American media. CBS broadcaster Edward Murrow was the greatest of these, and his famous 'This is London' reports reached millions of American homes each week, made him a celebrity, and earned him the title of 'the No. 1 man on the air' among his colleagues. Churchill had courted Murrow and other journalists since he first became Prime Minster, and now they were given unprecedented access, prompting one jealous British reporter to complain that such Americans were 'treated as tin gods because they were so useful'. Indeed, when Murrow's initial request to broadcast live during the Blitz was denied by the British government, Churchill intervened personally because Murrow's work was invaluable to the British strategy, particularly because his reports emphasized all of the themes Churchill most desired. Murrow humanized the Blitz for his American audience, describing the common people's struggle to live their lives amid the bombs; he depicted the British as suffering but hardworking, democratic and inspirational. Of course, he also routinely implied that despite their strength, the British could not go on alone for ever, and that the United States would have to do more. Hundreds of Americans wrote to Murrow to explain that it was his broadcasts, which were also printed as newspaper columns, that had moved them away from neutrality and towards support for the British people.[33]

The effective use of modern mass media was crucial to swaying American opinions, and the British government worked with reporters like Murrow, all increasingly impatient with American neutrality, to harness the power of the American media during the Blitz. The British Ministry of Information colluded with sympathetic American journalists and Warner Brothers Studios to produce a ten-minute short film, *London Can Take It!*, which continued the themes of Murrow's reports and rapidly became a great success in the United States, where it was shown at more than 12,000 theatres throughout the country beginning in November. The film's narration claimed it was an unbiased report, and the British government's involvement went unmentioned in the credits. Murrow himself simultaneously created a full-length documentary film, *This is England*, which not only became a hit but was also screened at the White House. As Lynne Olsen has argued, Murrow and other American journalists blurred the line between journalism and propaganda,[34] and the result was a marked increase in American affinity for the British.

The American debate over intervention was not only beginning to shift in favour of the British, but it was also echoing the specific themes Churchill and the Ministry of Information had worked to imbed in their media campaign. On the radio in October of 1940, Dean Acheson, noted lawyer and former Undersecretary of the Treasury, had defended the argument for aiding the British by describing them as an 'incredibly heroic and determined people ... standing between us and the greatest danger which we have ever faced'. He went on to stress that this precious time to prepare for war was 'given to us by the British'.[35]

76   R.M. Hendershot

Following his re-election in November, Roosevelt likewise embraced such descriptions of Britain and the British people. Giving one of his famous Fireside Chats in December, the President told his nation, 'in a military sense Great Britain and the British Empire are today the spearhead of resistance to world conquest. And they are putting up a fight which will live forever in the story of human gallantry.' He concluded the radio address by stating that it was time for the United States to become 'the great arsenal of democracy'.[36] Just as the British had popularized such descriptions to sway American opinion, Roosevelt now embraced the same strategy. To secure public support and Congressional approval for his next steps towards war, he too tied his strategic war aims to America's growing solidarity with the British.

Roosevelt sent his long-time friend and trusted confidant Harry Hopkins to the United Kingdom in January 1941 to assess the British situation more carefully, gauge Churchill as a leader, and determine the potential for an expanded alliance. Hopkins was fiercely loyal to Roosevelt and wielded enormous influence within his administration – he had a reputation for being a man 'who could cut short a career with the scribble of his pen'.[37] In poor health, painfully thin, a chain-smoker with a generally acidic personality, it would be Hopkins' assessment that determined the future of the Anglo-American alliance. His trip to Britain would be a great test of the power of the Blitz to cultivate the desired feelings of Anglo-American solidarity sought by the British. Churchill made it his personal business to win Hopkins over during their time together, and he was successful. He and Churchill travelled the country by rail, and Hopkins was able to study the war and the British intimately. By early 1941, even the stoical Hopkins was sympathetic to the British, and wrote to Roosevelt from London in an uncharacteristically sentimental but sincere tone, describing the British people as amazing and courageous, telling the President bluntly, 'this island needs our help now Mr President with everything we can give them'.[38] The British were acutely aware of how influential Hopkins was in his home country, and it came as a great relief when, at dinner with Churchill and his inner circle one night towards the end of his fact-finding mission, he stood and said,

> I suppose you wish to know what I am going to say to President Roosevelt on my return. Well, I'm going to quote you one verse from that Book of Books.... 'Wither thou goest, I will go; and where thou lodgest, I will lodge: thy people shall be my people, and thy God my God.'

He finished quietly: 'Even to the end.' The Prime Minister was openly weeping by the conclusion of this short speech. As Churchill's doctor, Lord Moran, wrote, 'he knew what it meant ... the words seemed like a rope thrown to a drowning man'.[39]

Indeed, Hopkins' words could not have been better chosen. Not only did they serve to confirm that he was in favour of American support for Britain, they also reflected precisely the kind of American attitudes Churchill wanted for the future. Hopkins was true to his word, and the Roosevelt administration moved

Manipulating the Anglo-American identity   77

quickly after his return to Washington. This was made all the easier because, after six months of the Blitz and efforts to stoke American sympathy, public opinion had thoroughly shifted. In early February 1941 a Gallup poll revealed that 54 per cent of Americans were in favour of Roosevelt's Lend–Lease policy 'without qualifications'. Comparatively, only 15 per cent were in favour with qualifications such as 'If it doesn't get us into war' or 'If the British can give us some security for what we give them'. A mere 22 per cent were explicitly against the President's plan.[40]

The Lend–Lease Act was signed into law in March 1941, and an unprecedented amount of American money and supplies began flowing to Britain. Simultaneously, the pro-British John Winant was made the American Ambassador to the Court of Saint James, and Averell Harriman was sent to London to coordinate Lend–Lease. Now more convinced than ever about the power of the Anglo-American civilization identity, Churchill and the British government increased their efforts to woo these new American decision-makers to their way of thinking. The same themes of shared history, values, faith, and language dominated these exchanges, and Winant and Harriman always responded in kind. Both men would begin pressing Roosevelt to do more in the months ahead. It is worth noting at this point that Winant and Harriman, like Ed Murrow, also had affairs with women of the Churchill family during this period.[41] At both popular and elite levels, Churchill had achieved a sufficient degree of Anglo-American intimacy and fellow feeling to directly impact American policy.

With Lend–Lease tying their national fortunes together and themes of Anglo-American connection dominating the diplomatic discourse, Churchill and Roosevelt would meet at sea, off the coast of Newfoundland, in August of 1941. This Atlantic Conference yielded the famous Atlantic Charter, a joint declaration to work together to promote self-determination, restore peace, and reduce trade restrictions. Neither leader got all the tactical objectives they wanted – Roosevelt stopped short of promising to declare war and Churchill was disinclined to discuss specific changes to the British sterling bloc – but the precedent, tone, and symbolism of their meeting ensured its historical significance. The Charter was an overt declaration of Anglo-American unity, objectives, and values. Britain and America would seek no territorial gains in the war, only to make the world free from oppression, fear, and want 'after the final destruction of Nazi tyranny'.[42]

Churchill in particular paid great attention to their meeting's historic nature, and he oversaw all details relating to symbolism as well as making sure that there were plentiful photographs for use later. By far the most memorable moment during the conference was the church service Roosevelt and Churchill attended together aboard HMS *Prince of Wales*. Roosevelt called it the 'keynote' of the meeting. Churchill had selected the hymns and Bible readings himself, designing the service to, as Meacham has written, work 'a kind of magic, which is one of the points of liturgy and theater: to use the dramatic to convince people of a reality they cannot see'. The Americans and the British sang 'Onward, Christian Soldiers' and listened to a reading from the book of Joshua:

78   *R.M. Hendershot*

> as I was with Moses, so will I be with thee: I will not fail thee, nor forsake thee.... Be strong and of a good courage; be not afraid: for the Lord thy God is with thee whithersoever thou goest.

British journalist H.V. Morton was there to report on the conference and was deeply struck by this service; he wrote,

> In the long frightful panorama of this war ... there had been no scene like this, a scene, it seemed, from another world, conceived on lines different from anything known to the pageant-masters of the Axis, a scene rooted in the first principles of European civilization which go back to the figure of Charlemagne kneeling before the Pope on Christmas morning.[43]

After the service, Roosevelt told his son Elliot that, 'If nothing else had happened while we were here, that alone would have cemented us. "Onward, Christian Soldiers". We *are*, and we *will* go on, with God's help.' Churchill was extremely pleased with himself after the service and was convinced that it had wrought the effect he desired:

> When I looked upon that densely packed congregation of fighting men of the same language, of the same faith, of the same fundamental laws and ideals, and now to a large extent the same interests, and certainly in different degrees facing the same dangers, it swept across me that here was the only hope, but also the sure hope, of saving the world from measureless degradation.[44]

Such feelings of aligned Anglo-American identity would be similarly emphasized time and again not only throughout the rest of the war, but routinely throughout the post-war period as well.

When the Americans finally declared war on the Axis Powers after Japan's attack on Pearl Harbor in December, Churchill seized the opportunity to replicate his success aboard the *Prince of Wales* with the American population at large. Roosevelt's quick invitation to Churchill to spend Christmas at the White House may likewise be read both as the result of the need to continue joint war planning with his key ally as well as to bolster the morale of the American people after the disaster in Hawaii. The British Prime Minister, as a symbol of British strength and resistance to the Axis Powers, was already a popular figure in America and having him in Washington during the dark days of December would cement his position as an icon of the Anglo-American alliance.

Time magazine reported that Churchill 'swept in like a breath of fresh air, giving Washington new vigour, for he came as a new hero'. Throughout his visit, the British leader maximized the power of his celebrity status, and in so doing demonstrated the value of British partnership to the American government. Churchill charmed the White House reporters with his confidence in victory while simultaneously emphasizing the familiar themes of historical, cultural, and linguistic connections between Britain and America. As he and Roosevelt lit the White House Christmas tree together, Churchill stressed the unity of the English-speaking peoples, whose strongest weapon was the 'dignity and brotherhood of man'. The President and the Prime Minister continued to attend church services together and generally engaged in various kinds of Anglo-American pageantry for the press, such as laying a wreath on George Washington's grave at Mount Vernon. The large assembly of guests at the White House Christmas dinner listened intently as Roosevelt adopted Churchill's language to praise 'the coming together of the English-speaking races' and declared that they 'would go on together after the war'.[45]

The culmination of this visit was Churchill's speech to Congress the day after Christmas, which was by all accounts a tremendous success. He began by taking pride in his American heritage and praising his American forebears, and went on to draw parallels between the 'Olympian fortitude' he sensed in Washington and the British people's resolution during the Blitz. He stressed the themes of the Anglo-American civilizational identity, denounced the Axis powers, and concluded that victory, though difficult, was assured and the future bright so long as 'in the days to come the British and American peoples will for their own safety and for the good of all walk together in majesty, in justice, and in peace'.[46] *Time* captured the mood of the moment:

> There were tears in Winnie Churchill's eyes at the ovation which greeted him, from isolationist and interventionist Congressmen alike.... Between bursts of applause in which Supreme Court Justices and diplomats joined as lustily as doormen, the galleries wondered whether ever before had such a moving and eloquent speech been made on the Senate floor. Actually it was not so much the speech as the personality that put it over.[47]

Leaving the podium, Churchill displayed his 'V for Victory' sign and, as the *Washington Post* reported, 'The effect was instantaneous, electric.... The cheers swelled into a roar' and many of those in attendance returned the salute. As presidential advisor George Elsey recalled, Churchill 'was ten times larger than life to Americans at that point'.[48]

Since the United States did not enter the war until after Japan attacked Pearl Harbor, it may be tempting for some to see Churchill's strategic use of cultural identity as a failure, but this would be distortive. His efforts successfully entrenched a particular and positive view of Britain in the American world view, made it possible for the Roosevelt administration to pass Lend–Lease, anchored himself in the centre of American perceptions of Britain, and laid the popular foundations of a continuing Anglo-American alliance after the war was over. He built his brand in America well, the power of the Anglo-American civilizational identity could not be ignored, and, accordingly, his new allies would embrace his strategies and themes wholeheartedly in the years ahead.

American commitment to the Anglo-American civilizational identity

Throughout the remainder of the war, the American government worked steadily to entrench Churchill's themes of historical Anglo-American values, shared religious perspectives, and unique cultural intimacy in the American people's collective world view. There were three primary reasons for this strategy. First, the main elements of the Anglo-American civilizational identity were already largely in place by mid-1941; the American public sympathized with the British in general and valued Churchill in particular. Accordingly, maintaining the emerging cultural themes of the special relationship, or indeed failing to do so, suggested political dividends (or consequences) for the Roosevelt administration. Second, as his words and actions suggested during Churchill's first Christmas visit in 1941, Roosevelt was convinced that British partnership had the power to bolster American morale during the war. And third, Britain remained America's closest ally, and thus an intimate and smooth working relationship between their peoples was a strategic necessity. The tactics employed by the Americans were similar to Churchill's own – they would cultivate personal relationships with high-profile British leaders as well as manipulate mass media to make the themes of the Anglo-American civilizational identity ambient in American culture.

Roosevelt had begun publicly touting Churchill as 'a brilliant and a great leader' immediately after his re-election in the fall of 1940, and he remained committed to such public descriptions throughout the remainder of his life. The two leaders met routinely during the war, and in private they often disagreed on important issues, such as the timing of Operation Overlord or the best ways to deal with Joseph Stalin and the Soviet Union. Nevertheless, each occasion featured a series of press events tailored to emphasize Anglo-American unity on both diplomatic and cultural levels, and their propaganda campaign revealed none of their disagreements. For example, despite the hectic schedule of the Casablanca Conference in 1943, ample time was built into the schedule for the leaders to be photographed together as allies on equal footing, prompting *Newsweek* to comment that the image of the Anglo-American leaders smiling together 'seemed the most natural thing in the world'. After the Quebec Conference later that year, Roosevelt had arranged for Churchill to receive an honorary degree from Harvard, his alma mater. The President personally made sure that the occasion would be one of great pomp and media attention, and Churchill predictably used the venue to stress the shared culture of the English-speaking peoples and its assurance of ultimate victory.[49]

After the Tehran Conference in late 1943, Roosevelt delivered a Fireside Chat on Christmas Eve to personally report the key events of the meeting and the status of the war. He discussed meeting Stalin and Chiang Kai-shek for the first time, praising them both and predicting positive relations with them in the future. However, he also hit the necessary notes for Anglo-American relations, stressing that 'Of course, as you all know, Mr Churchill and I have happily met many

Manipulating the Anglo-American identity   81

times before, and we know and understand each other very well. Indeed, Mr Churchill has become known and beloved by many millions of Americans.' He emphasized the integrated command of Anglo-American forces as he announced that American General Dwight Eisenhower would command allied forces from 'other points of the compass' in the near future while a British commander (not yet named) would lead American and British soldiers in the Mediterranean: 'We now pledge that new Commander that our powerful ground, sea and air forces in the vital Mediterranean area will stand by his side until every objective in that bitter theatre is attained.' Towards the end of the radio address, Roosevelt's tone ran emotional as he recalled recently flying over Bethlehem, and prayed on behalf of the American people and 'all your comrades in arms' that God would 'keep us strong in our faith that we fight for a better day for human kind – here and everywhere'.[50] In analysing Roosevelt's words, rather like Churchill's tears, it is difficult to determine which emotions were genuine and which were engineered to intensify the fellowship they believed their nations so greatly needed. In the study of the Anglo-American special relationship, and indeed of cultural history in general, sentiment and interest ought not to be treated as separate factors of historical causation – they are better seen as two sides of one coin.

Once in London, Eisenhower became a 'fanatic' for creating total Anglo-American partnership, and he ordered his British and American staff members to act as if they 'belonged to a single nation'. His work in this regard complemented the continuing efforts of Winant, Murrow, Harriman and multiple government offices to educate the American and British publics about one another.[51] For example, common soldiers from all over the United States were routinely dosed with the most desirable depiction of the United Kingdom and the British people. In 1942 the US War Department produced and distributed a seven-page pamphlet to all American servicemen sent to the United Kingdom. The government intended the pamphlet to prepare soldiers for service in Britain and, as one might expect, to fulfil the strategic goal of not offending their British hosts and allies. The language is awash with ideas of Anglo-American connection, likeness, friendship, and respect – all key components of the cultural message that permeated the Anglo-American alliance:

> The most evident truth of all is that in their major ways of life the British and American people are much alike. They speak the same language. They both believe in representative government, in freedom of worship, in freedom of speech.
> [...]
> The British are tough, strong people, and good allies.
> [...]
> The best way to get on in Britain is very much the same as the best way to get on in America. The same sort of courtesy and decency and friendliness that go over big in America will go over big in Britain. The British have seen a good many Americans and they like Americans. They will like your frankness as long as it is friendly. They will expect you to be generous.

82 *R.M. Hendershot*

They are not given to back-slapping and they are shy about showing their affections. But once they get to like you they make the best friends in the world.[52]

Such measures were clearly designed to secure high levels of Anglo-American fellowship and simultaneously indicative of the cultural bias that existed within the US War Department. As at elite levels, sentiment and strategic interest were conjoined. Maintaining the dominance of the Anglo-American civilizational identity at other levels was challenging work sometimes, since Britons usually interacted with American personnel when they were off duty, rowdy, and/or intoxicated. Yet the propaganda efforts and personal connections that formed over time ultimately combined to counteract such tensions. The dominant narrative of Anglo-American fellowship and cultural connection intensified rather than abated, and immunity to its influence proved difficult. Many British communities welcomed American soldiers warmly, and innumerable friendships grew during the build-up to the Normandy invasion.[53] One quarter of all the letters mailed by American servicemen after D-Day were sent to British homes.[54]

Hollywood, perhaps more than any other form of mass media, was responsible for much of the Anglo-American civilizational identity's cultural permeation during the war. Complementing personal connections and governmental attempts to secure fellow feeling among the allies, the American film industry, by the nature of its profession, had the ability to ply massive domestic and international audiences with dramatic themes, heart-warming stories, likeable characters, and, of course, sentiment. Just as journalists had erased the line between the news and propaganda during the Blitz, the entertainment industry would merge their desire to sell tickets with the popular theme of American solidarity with the British – a dynamic that began early.

Accurately sensing the rising levels of American interest in the British during the Blitz, Metro-Goldwyn-Mayer had begun pre-production of *Mrs Miniver* in the fall of 1940. This film, produced and directed by Americans, told the story of the war's impact on everyday people's lives. The title character, Carol Miniver, endures hardship and sacrifice, sees her country devastated during the Blitz, and is ultimately killed by shots from a German plane. At the end of the film, the surviving characters gather in their bomb-damaged church to hear their vicar deliver a passionate sermon, which in essence paraphrases Churchill's oratory about the resolution, unity, strength, and love of freedom that will see the British people through their darkest hour. At the conclusion of the sermon, the congregation sings 'Onward, Christian Soldiers', and the camera pans upward allowing the audience to see through the gaping roof as a V-formation of RAF fighter planes roar overhead.[55] After Pearl Harbor, Roosevelt recognized the propaganda value of the film, particularly for this closing scene, and requested that it be rushed into cinemas.[56] *Mrs Miniver* was a great success across the United States in 1942, became the highest-grossing MGM film at that time, and won six Academy Awards, including Best Picture.[57]

Manipulating the Anglo-American identity 83

Numerous American war movies contained references to Anglo-American partnership and camaraderie in the years ahead, and *Lifeboat*, written by John Steinbeck and directed by Alfred Hitchcock, was even less subtle than most. Released in early 1944, this film chronicled the fictional story of the survivors of a German U-boat's attack on a passenger liner, and as such, portrayed its American and British characters literally in the same boat. Their alliance in the struggle for survival is treated as self-evident throughout the film. The characters mercifully rescue a German officer from the attacking U-boat, which was also sunk, but he plots against them, causing the Americans and British to work together even harder to survive. The end of the film goes so far as to hint at enduring love between two of the leads, one British and the other American.[58]

Cumulatively, the efforts of the American and British governments, the press, and the film industry successfully entrenched the notion of a natural Anglo-American partnership. Public opinion polling provides us with clear evidence of this trend. For example, during the war a majority of American citizens became committed to a permanent military alliance with Great Britain and believed that the two allies should 'come to each other's defense immediately' if the other were attacked in the future. Gallup polling demonstrated that this majority grew from 59.68 per cent to 67.21 per cent in 1943 alone. Furthermore, American citizens favoured an enduring alliance with Great Britain considerably more than with their other major wartime allies. For example, Gallup polling in August 1943 demonstrated that only 38.68 per cent of Americans favoured such an alliance with the Soviet Union, and in April of 1944, that only 41.88 per cent favoured such an alliance with China.[59] As indicated by this data, the American public was uniquely fond of their alliance with the British, and embedded within this fondness were the alliance's distinctive notions of Anglo-American unity, equality, partnership, and inevitable success through their nations' cooperation.

The Second World War was a highly formative experience, and the resulting American world view has proven remarkably durable since 1945. As historian Andrew Bacevich has written, this conflict was the

> point of origin for the ideology of national security, the war is also the force that sustains it down to the present day. For those determined to prevent any backsliding in the never-ending quest for assured national security, the war – more specifically the Anglo-American war against Nazi Germany – is the gift that keeps on giving, the source of endlessly repeated 'lessons'.

This dynamic can be detected in a variety of areas, such as in successive generations of American leaders' refusals to 'appease' their nation's enemies, or their tendency to liken any enemy of the United States to Adolph Hitler.[60]

But perhaps nowhere are the lessons of the Second World War more evident than in the continuing American preference for Winston Churchill and partnership with the British. By the war's end, the view of Britain and America as culturally similar allies united in the quest for global freedom continued to exist and, likewise, be treated as an aspect of identity that had the power to further

84 R.M. Hendershot

strategic goals. Indeed, this was one lesson of the war that Anglo-American leaders had learned particularly well, and thus would influence the operational dynamic of the special relationship for many years to come.

American affinity for Churchill and the durability of the Anglo-American civilizational identity

Churchill's success in cementing his popularity within the United States, as well as that of the Anglo-American identity to which he was thoroughly tied, is once again clearly discernible in the public opinion survey data produced by Gallup in the post-war period. As early as 1946 and well into the 1950s, a routine survey of American opinion inquired, 'What man, living today in any part of the world, that you have heard or read about, do you most admire?' Throughout this period, the American public consistently ranked Churchill among the top five most admired men – along with various other American wartime giants such as Eisenhower, Truman, Douglas MacArthur, and George Marshall. Churchill was ranked fifth in 1946, third in 1947, fourth in 1948, and remained in third place in 1949.[61] This trend continued throughout the period Gallup asked this question in the next decade as well, and by December of 1953, polling exposed the British Prime Minister as the second most admired man among Americans, after President Eisenhower. Significantly, of the top five most frequent responses, only Churchill was not an American citizen – no other foreign leaders, nor any other Britons came close to his status.[62] His popularity also remained consistent when Gallup broke respondents into various subgroups – American men, women, and veterans all ranked the British leader similarly high.[63]

Churchill's consistent status as America's favourite foreign person speaks directly to his success in attaching his individual celebrity to the idea of a natural and permanent Anglo-American partnership within the American world view. Roughly the same percentage of Americans that esteemed Churchill personally also favoured continuing friendship with the British people. For example, a Gallup poll in January 1952 showed that, once again, nearly two-thirds of the American people (65.64 per cent) admired Winston Churchill. In February 1953, Gallup polling demonstrated that nearly two-thirds of Americans (62.73 per cent) maintained 'friendly' feelings for the people of Great Britain. In this way, fourteen years after the Blitz, Americans' affinity for Winston Churchill remained statistically correlated with American preference for Britain in general, revealing the extent to which Churchill had become a personification of the special relationship and an enduring icon of Anglo-American partnership and fraternity.[64]

Just as they had during the war, these American affinities would continue to impact British and American diplomatic relations during the peace, a fact that became clear to leaders quite early. It was apparent by 1946 that Britain required continuing American financial support for a post-war recovery, and thus securing a large loan from the United States became a British priority. The Truman administration and the State Department, for their part, sought to use the financial need of Britain as leverage, and would make the loan contingent on Britain's support of what they had termed 'multilateralism' – the British would have to open their formerly closed sterling bloc to the goods of non-sterling nations. Many in the British government were not happy with this arrangement, but they had little choice. Further complicating matters, even with these generous terms on the table, the US Congress hotly debated whether or not to provide the loan, and the American public was likewise hesitant.[65] At this point, Churchill, though without official office, intervened to alter the terms of this debate.

Having been invited, along with President Truman, by Westminster College to receive another honorary degree and make a speech in Fulton, Missouri, that March, Churchill would, without mentioning the loan directly, tie the issue of the world's future security to Anglo-American partnership. After being warmly introduced by Truman, Churchill famously announced that an 'iron curtain; of Soviet domination had descended on Eastern Europe, and argued that only 'the fraternal association of English-speaking peoples' could achieve the strength required to negate its threat. Those gathered in Fulton to hear the former British prime minister offered their applause as he asserted that this special relationship, featuring cooperation 'in the air, on the sea and in science and industry, and in moral laws' would be an 'overwhelming assurance of security' in the future.[66] As during the Blitz, Churchill believed the Anglo-American civilizational identity could be counted upon to help sway American opinion. His portrayal of the special relationship in the post-war world created a crucial new context for the Cold War; it effectively cast the British loan as an American investment in containing communism, and simultaneously, as in the war, kept the American mind focused on Britain as a stalwart friend in a dangerous world.

Many Americans were initially very concerned with Churchill's Fulton speech, and the White House was deluged with what may be accurately described as hate mail denouncing his warmongering and his recklessness,[67] but the Truman administration saw the utility of what Churchill was trying to accomplish, and since it would advance their own anti-Soviet agenda, embraced the strategy. Secretary of State Dean Acheson and Treasury Secretary Fred Vinson went on the radio to tell the public that the proposed loan to Britain was in the American people's best interests as well as in the interests of global stability. As he made the case for the loan, Acheson tapped wartime memories of the strong, resolute and worthy British people as he reminded listeners, 'all of us have great admiration for the British and we think they did a great job in the war. We have great sympathy for what they suffered', and immediately transitioned to say that the loan was about the future rather than the past, and that a healthy Britain and freer world trade were the main objectives of the loan. Vinson concluded that 'Britain is our natural ally' and stressed that the two nations were still tied together: 'a feeble impoverished Britain ... would weaken our own position'.[68]

As the Truman administration continued to make their case, Churchill kept up his usual dual programme of mass media and personal diplomacy. A few days after the widely reported speech in Fulton, he had dinner with nine influential senators and congressmen and lobbied them to support the British loan. All but

86   R.M. Hendershot

one ultimately did so, and Congressman Frank Fellows later told Churchill, 'It was the realization that the best of all that is Britain is represented in you which prompted my tearing up and discarding a speech prepared in opposition to the loan, and my vote in favor of it.'[69] Indeed, many Americans continued to conflate Churchill with the British in general, and as a result the wartime memories and the sentimental notions of natural partnership he personified would regularly characterize future discussions of Anglo-American relations.

For example, when concerned citizens wrote to Truman's White House objecting to continuing American aid to Britain, key elements of the Anglo-American civilizational identity and wartime memories of the gallant British were routinely employed to explain and justify the support. For example, when Miss C. McEwen of Cicero, Illinois, wrote to protest about aid to Britain because she thought her taxes too high already, Joseph Short, Secretary to the President, merged current American interests with *Mrs Miniver*-esque sentiment in his reply:

> We have been aiding Great Britain because it is in our interest to do so. As you remember, the British fought alone against the Nazis, after Europe had been conquered and before the United States entered the war. British losses in men, women, and children were very great. (Our civilian losses were negligible by comparison.) In addition, the British expended large quantities of money, material, and resources throughout the war and all over the world.... Their gallant fight against great odds undoubtedly contributed a major share to final victory. As you know, after the US entered the war, Britain became a vast base for the Allied liberation armies.
>
> I mention these things briefly because I think we should not forget how important an ally Britain has been, nor the tremendous sacrifices she has made, and is making, in the cause of world freedom. Britain again is raising large armies and maintaining a strong navy and air force, financed in large part out of British taxes. Certainly it is in our own national interest that we have strong friends ...
>
> If we had no allies, with fighting men ready to resist aggression along with our own men, you may be sure that American taxes would be far higher, and American defenses far less secure that they are today.[70]

Truman himself used similar tactics with the American public at large. In a nationwide broadcast from the White House in 1952, the President spoke on the topic of mutual security and sought to silence recent critical commentary about the limited defence spending of European nations compared to that of the United States. Truman praised America's allies in the Cold War and highlighted the British efforts in Malaya and French efforts in Vietnam, but he went into greater detail about the sacrifices of the British people, and significantly chose to make his argument more emotional than data-driven:

> Take the British. They're down to sixteen cents' worth of meat a week. That makes a mighty small package when the butcher wraps it up. They would have

Manipulating the Anglo-American identity 87

more if it weren't for their defense effort. Do you think we ought to ask them to cut that sixteen cents' worth of meat down to a dime's worth, or a nickel's worth? Do they have to do that to do their share? Would you want to tell them that they ought to spend less than sixteen cents a week on meat?[71]

It is easy to detect echoes of Murrow's wartime reports from London in Truman's sympathetic example drawn from the daily lives of regular British people. European defence commitments were economically and strategically important to the United States, but the best way to get the public to accept their comparatively small capabilities was to tap the empathy with the British that had been embedded in the public consciousness since the early 1940s.

Truman and Prime Minister Clement Attlee also continued to publicly enact the special relationship in the same ways Roosevelt and Churchill had done during the war. After meeting in Washington in 1950 to discuss atomic weapons and the war in Korea, the two leaders issued a joint statement that emphasized rhetoric they knew would play well with their respective publics: the American and British peoples would 'act together with resolution and unity to meet the challenge to world peace', they were in 'complete agreement' and declared that 'there can be no thought of appeasement'.[72] The State Department was pleased with reactions to the joint statement, and particularly noted the high approval expressed in the media for the communiqué's 'evidence of British–American unity' and its stern denouncement of appeasement.[73] This aping of FDR and Churchill was to become a key fixture of the special relationship throughout the post-war period – there would be little change in either tone or message as this public ritual was enacted again and again, each time revealing the enduring Anglo-American biases of contemporary people and simultaneously entrenching them in the minds of younger generations.

Churchill remained the most popular and lauded symbol of the special relationship, and the American people continued to honour him regularly throughout the remainder of his lifetime. For example, in January 1956, the city of Philadelphia awarded Sir Winston Churchill the Benjamin Franklin medal for 'the greatest contribution during the past ten years to international understanding'. Churchill appeared touched by the Americans' recognition of his efforts and took the opportunity to express his belief that the world, 'although full of difficulties, is not without hope so long as Britain and America stand together'.[74] He went on to stress his classic themes of shared history, faith, and language, but more important than Churchill's well-known views was that the people of Philadelphia chose to reward him because of those views. In this way, American behaviour towards Winston Churchill effectively demonstrated continued affinity for both Britain and the special relationship. On 9 April 1963, President Kennedy, with specific authorization from both houses of Congress, officially branded the British icon as an 'Honorary American Citizen' and explained that this was merely 'a formal recognition of the place he has long since won in the history of freedom and in the affections of my – and now his – fellow countrymen'. Significantly, Churchill was the first person ever to be honoured by the Americans in this way.[75]

88   R.M. Hendershot

Popular culture, like politics and diplomacy, also continued to demonstrate the continuity of the Anglo-American civilizational identity. For example, the same year Churchill became the first honorary American citizen, the Mirisch Company and United Artists produced and distributed *The Great Escape*, which made over $12 million in box office sales and was one of the top-earning films of the year.[76] The film was loosely based on the true story of an allied escape from a German prisoner-of-war camp in 1943, but the movie altered numerous facts in order to create a more satisfying Anglo-American narrative for audiences. No American POWs were part of this famous escape, but the screenwriters included American characters playing central roles throughout the film and strayed into allegorical territory as well.[77] For example, Steve McQueen's character, American pilot Virgil Hilts, is lean, cool, and initially reluctant to collaborate with the X Organization, which worked for a year to plan a massive escape from inside the prison under the leadership of Big X, Squadron Leader Bartlett of the Royal Air Force – portrayed as a clear Churchillian representation by the round-faced British actor Richard Attenborough.[78] After witnessing the brutal shooting of a British comrade by the Germans, Hilts changes his mind and commits to working with Bartlett's organization for the freedom of all the allies in the prison camp. The roles of other American personnel were similarly embellished in the movie, and while distortive of the historical record, the film certainly reflects the narrative of Anglo-American relations that had become dominant by the 1960s.[79]

Churchill's death in January 1965 led to many public observances of his historical role as well as frank admissions of his central place within American perceptions of Britain. Eisenhower mourned him as 'the embodiment of all that was best in the British Empire'. Joseph Harsh was the American journalist who provided commentary for ITV's coverage of the state funeral, and he took the opportunity to explain how Churchill had successfully used his celebrity in America to alter the cultural context of Anglo-American diplomacy: 'Before the days of Winston Churchill, many an American saw Britain as a selfish imperial taskmaster.... During the Churchill era that image has been transformed.' Thanks to him more than anyone else, 'we Americans who once thought of Britain as rapacious, insolent and domineering now think of Britain as sturdy, brave, and above all honorable'.[80] Churchill, as the American public perceived him, was a legend of the war, not unlike the special relationship itself. Even Fulton was little more than epilogue in the story he had successfully etched into the American national consciousness. His interpretation of the Anglo-American alliance as the natural product of shared history and culture had become ubiquitous in transatlantic discourse and popular culture alike. And significantly, he no longer needed to be living to perpetuate this view. His memory alone would be sufficient.

In the decades ahead, Anglo-American leaders routinely conjured his memory and its associations as well as his ideas and phrases at summits and in joint communiqués. His death merely elevated his celebrity to the status of a secular diplomatic saint, to be venerated with reverence in the course of political pageantry

Manipulating the Anglo-American identity 89

and diplomatic ritual. When President Richard Nixon and Prime Minister Edward Heath met in Washington, DC, during the Christmas season of 1970, their exchanges were marked by strong declarations of affinity, commitment, and cultural bonds. Predictably, this next generation of Anglo-American leaders invoked multiple references to their nation's partnership in the Second World War. In offering a toast to the President, Heath recounted yet another Anglo-American Christmas visit. In December of 1941, after the Christmas tree had been lit by President Roosevelt, Churchill had confessed that he could not 'feel other than at home' in the United States. Heath stated that these words were as pertinent in 1970 as they had been during the war, effectively implying that the levels of Anglo-American intimacy and partnership had remained consistent since the war.[81] The numerous and serious disagreements that had plagued the diplomatic partnership since 1945, like the Anglo-American divergence during the Suez crisis in 1956 or the glaring absence of joint military action in the Vietnam War, clearly did not fit into the popular and sentimental narrative of natural and perpetual Anglo-American relations and accordingly went unmentioned.

Later that decade, Britain made a point of playing a large and visible role in the celebrations of the American bicentennial, but it was the era of Churchill, far more than the American War of Independence, which was being commemorated in events such as Queen Elizabeth II's state visit in July 1976. The day after the televised state dinner at the White House, President Gerald Ford and the Queen attended church services together, dedicating the south porch in Washington Cathedral in memory of Winston Churchill. During the ceremony, workmen lowered a 1,000-year-old stone from London's Westminster Abbey as Reverend Francis B. Sayre waxed poetic about the special relationship:

> We put that English stone in yon western entrance which is our tribute and memorial to Sir Winston Churchill, who in the blood of his parentage was rooted on either side of the sea and whose dauntless defense of liberty was our glory and our salvation on both sides of the Atlantic.[82]

Bagpipers of the Scottish Black Watch and a crowd of 10,000 were on hand to join in singing Churchill's favourite American song, 'The Battle Hymn of the Republic', at the culmination of the dedication. Afterwards, thousands of onlookers cheered as President Ford led Queen Elizabeth down the front steps of the cathedral.[83]

Churchill's legacy continued to be enacted throughout the remainder of the century as well, with the high-profile friendships and close working relationships of presidents and prime ministers always triggering comparisons to FDR and Churchill in the darkest period of the twentieth century. The famous duos of Ronald Reagan and Margaret Thatcher, Bill Clinton and Tony Blair, as well as George Bush and Blair, each in their turn were conscious of how memory of Churchill had the power to impact the alliance, and thus cultivated it carefully.[84] At the end of the Clinton administration, the US State Department's Office of

Research found that 83 per cent of the British public held favourable opinions of the United States, which was predictably the highest percentage of favourable responses among the Western European allies.[85] Likewise, a Gallup survey in early 2002 found that 90 per cent of Americans held favourable opinions of Great Britain, again outstripping American affinities for any other ally.[86]

The symbolism of Churchill has remained consistently potent into the contemporary period as well. For example, President Barack Obama's administration was so plagued by rumours purporting that the President had snubbed the British people and the special relationship by choosing to send the famous White House bust of Churchill back to the British Embassy that a special section of the White House website was dedicated to dispelling the rumour in 2012. Nevertheless, the urban legend continues to circulate and inspire concerned people to contact the White House demanding its return. To settle the matter and appease all parties concerned, the White House posted a picture on their website showing President Obama and Prime Minister David Cameron closely admiring the bust together in the residence.[87] Nevertheless, hypersensitivity to Churchill's memory remains strong in the United States, even inspiring Republican presidential nominee Mitt Romney to seek votes in 2012 by promising to honour Churchill and the British alliance properly by moving the bust from the residence to the Oval Office.[88]

Conclusions

Since the 1960s, Fulton, Missouri, has been the home of America's National Churchill Museum and Memorial. Visited by between 15,000 and 20,000 people each year, the museum presents an overwhelmingly positive narrative of the British statesman, emphasizing his roles in the Second World War and his firm stance against communism at the start of the Cold War. On site are several statues of Churchill as well as a church designed by Sir Christopher Wren in 1677, the Church of St Mary Aldermanbury, which was bombed in London during the Blitz and moved brick by brick to Fulton beginning in 1964.[89] The Wren church is conspicuous in the United States, and while it had no direct connection to Churchill, its odd presence in Fulton, with its steeple towering over the other local buildings, tells a clear story of British culture embedded in the heartland of America. Former President Truman turned the first shovelful of dirt, with a golden spade, at the Fulton groundbreaking, and Presidents Eisenhower, Kennedy, and Johnson supported the memorial and served on its board as well.[90] In 2009, the United States Congress issued a resolution granting the museum its national status, and commended 'its efforts to recognize the importance of the historic legacy of Sir Winston Churchill and to educate the people of the United States about his legacy of character, leadership, and citizenship'. The memorial remains a routine stop for politicians on the campaign trail, strongly indicating the continuing political potency of the special relationship and the memory of Churchill in the United States.[91]

This museum and memorial may be viewed in essence as a microcosm of America's historical relationship with Churchill, remembering him exactly as he would have wished to be remembered by Americans – a triumphant symbol of Anglo-American cultural connection and victory. Even the gift shop reveals Churchill's position as a symbol of American affinity for Britain in general; in addition to history books, wartime posters, and British flags, visitors shop for Harry Potter toys, Dr Who Christmas ornaments, teas inspired by the BBC programme *Downton Abbey*, and various other knickknacks of British popular culture with no direct connections to Churchill. Yet their presence in the gift shop is reasonable, a marketing recognition of how Americans continue to associate Churchill with all of Britain.

As long as Americans memorialize Churchill in this way, without complexity, securely within his wartime context, and certainly not as the aristocratic politician who once called for the sterilization of the lower orders of society, as the key advocate of the atrocious Dardanelles misadventure in the Great War, or as the pro-Empire stalwart who stood against Irish and Indian freedoms, the special relationship is made more secure than it otherwise would be.

In the era of Churchill, leaders on both sides of the Atlantic came to recognize the power of culture in the Anglo-American relationship. They not only recognized and lauded the key themes of Anglo-American connection, but also found ways of harnessing it, effectively merging sentiment and strategic interest together again and again, until ultimately it became very difficult to separate cultural perceptions from diplomatic agendas. Churchill himself was an early and successful practitioner of this policy, and his work in this area wove him into the American world view as a dominant symbol of the special relationship. In politics, diplomacy, public opinion and popular culture, his ideas and themes have remained ambient since the Second World War, his memory a touchstone used in each subsequent generation of Anglo-American relations.

In the American world view, Churchill and the Anglo-American partnership had become a unified thought by 1945, and subsequently enacting the special relationship was to enact Churchill, and to honour Churchill was to honour the special relationship. In this way, his consistent popularity in the United States produced a stabilizing dynamic within Anglo-American relations. To abandon the special relationship would mean more than a break with tradition, it would mean betraying a cultural hero and failing to uphold the vision and values for which so much was sacrificed in the Second World War. With Churchill fully embedded within the popular sentimental mythology of a natural and victorious special relationship, Anglo-American relations have been sustained by not only economic, military, and diplomatic ties, they have been, and continue to be, cemented by the Anglo-American civilizational identity as well.

Notes

1 As quoted in *St Nicholas: An Illustrated Magazine for Boys and Girls*, 46:1, New York: The Century Company, 1919, p. 219.
2 Ibid.
3 ' "Britain's Day" in America', *The Queenslander*, 14 December 1918, p. 40.

92 R.M. Hendershot

4 David Monger, *Patriotism and Propaganda in First World War Britain: The National War Aims Committee and Civilian Morale*, Liverpool: Liverpool University Press, 2012, p. 147; *St Nicholas*, pp. 220–1. The primary sources describe the flags as being presented in 'Westminster Cathedral', but the context suggests that they are describing Westminster Abbey.
5 ' "Britain's Day" in America', p. 40.
6 James Elgin Wetherell (ed.), *The Great War in Verse and Prose*, Toronto: A.T. Wilgress, 1919, p. 149.
7 Elizabeth Prelinger with Barton Hacker, ' "The Spirit of Woman-Power": Representation of Women in World War I Posters', in Barton Hacker and Margaret Vining (eds), *A Companion to Women's Military History*, Leiden: Brill, 2012, p. 462.
8 'Side by side – Britannia! Britain's Day Dec. 7th 1918', Library of Congress www.loc.gov/pictures/item/2002712329/ (accessed 10 November 2015).
9 Prelinger, 'Posters', p. 462.
10 *The Press* (New Zealand), 54:16268, 19 July 1918, p. 7.
11 Prelinger, 'Posters', p. 461.
12 Ibid., p. 462.
13 *New York Times*, 8 December 1918. Numerous speeches delivered across the nation stressed similar themes; also see 'The World's Debt to Great Britain: Address of Samuel Harden Church, on Britain's Day at the Pittsburgh Exposition', 7 December 1918, Hathi Trust Digital Library, http://catalog.hathitrust.org/Record/009593532 (accessed 15 November 2015); Lynn Harold Hough, 'Address on British Day delivered before the Chicago Association of Commerce', *Bulletin, Northwestern University*, 19:22, 1919, pp. 2–14; *North Otago Times*, 106:14291, 10 December 1918, p. 3.
14 Erez Manela, *The Wilsonian Moment*, Oxford: Oxford University Press, 2009.
15 David Haglund, 'Is There a "Strategic Culture" of the Special Relationship? Contingency, Identity, and the Transformation of Anglo-American Relations', in Alan P. Dobson and Steve Marsh (eds), *Anglo-American Relations: Contemporary Perspectives*, London: Routledge, 2012, p. 37.
16 Alan P. Dobson and Steve Marsh, 'Anglo-American Relations: End of a Special Relationship?' *The International History Review*, 36:4, August 2014, p. 683.
17 During a 1945 visit to the White House, then President Truman and the Duke of Windsor (formally the Prince of Wales) reminisced about this first meeting. 'Kup's Column', *Chicago Times*, 27 August 1945; David McCullough, *Truman*, New York: Simon and Schuster, 1992, p. 136.
18 Warren G. Harding, *The White House*, www.whitehouse.gov/1600/presidents/warrenharding (accessed 15 November 2015).
19 As quoted in Lynne Olsen, *Citizens of London*, New York: Random House, 2010, p. 19.
20 Richard Toye, *Churchill's Empire: The World that Made Him and the World He Made*, New York: Henry Holt, 2010, p. 189.
21 John Greenleaf Whittier, *The Poetical Works*, London: Ward, Lock, Warwick House, 1880, p. 191.
22 Percy Lubbock (ed.), *The Letters of Henry James, Volume I*, London: Macmillan, 1920, p. 143.
23 Toye, *Churchill's Empire*, pp. 80–1.
24 Ibid., p. 136.
25 Jason Tomes, *Balfour and Foreign Policy: The International Thought of a Conservative Statesman*, Cambridge: Cambridge University Press, 1997, p. 190; Philip Williamson, 'The Doctrinal Politics of Stanley Baldwin', in Michael Bentley (ed.), *Public and Private Doctrine: Essays in British History Presented to Maurice Cowling*, Cambridge: Cambridge University Press, 1993, p. 199; Toye, *Churchill's Empire*, p. 189.

Manipulating the Anglo-American identity 93

26 David Stafford, *Roosevelt and Churchill*, New York: Overlook, 2011, p. 43; Jon Meacham, *Franklin and Winston: An Intimate Portrait of an Epic Friendship*, New York: Random House, 2003, p. 43.
27 Meacham, *Franklin and Winston*, p. 76.
28 Graham Farmelo, *Churchill's Bomb*, New York: Basic Books, 2013, p. 152.
29 Meacham, *Franklin and Winston*, p. 68.
30 Ultimately, 244 American pilots flew in the three Eagle Squadrons during the next two years; Olsen, *Citizens of London*, pp. 130–5.
31 Meacham, *Franklin and Winston*, p. 77.
32 Ibid., p. 75.
33 Stafford, *Roosevelt and Churchill*, p. 49; Olsen, *Citizens of London*, pp. 30–4.
34 Ibid., pp. 49–51.
35 'The American Forum of the Air: Shall We Give Further Aid to Great Britain?' 6 October 1940, Dean G. Acheson Papers, Publications File, 1936–71, Box 134, Truman Presidential Library, Independence, Missouri (hereafter as TPL).
36 Meacham, *Franklin and Winston*, pp. 78–9.
37 Randall Woods, *A Changing of the Guard: Anglo-American Relations, 1941–1946*, Chapel Hill: University of North Carolina Press, 1990, p. 11.
38 Stafford, *Roosevelt and Churchill*, p. 51; Meacham, *Franklin and Winston*, pp. 91–3.
39 Olsen, *Citizens of London*, p. 64; Meacham, *Franklin and Winston*, pp. 94.
40 'Bill to Aid Britain Strongly Backed', *New York Times*, 9 February 1941.
41 Olsen, *Citizens of London*, pp. 25–6, 91, 174–5, 242–4.
42 Roosevelt and Churchill, 'The Atlantic Charter', *The Avalon Project*, http://avalon. law.yale.edu/wwii/atlantic.asp (accessed 10 November 2015).
43 Meacham, *Franklin and Winston*, pp. 114–16.
44 Ibid., p. 116.
45 Farmelo, *Churchill's Bomb*, p. 205; Meacham, *Franklin and Winston*, pp. 140–56.
46 'The Address to Congress by the Rt Hon. Winston Churchill', 26 December 1941, Papers of Harry Truman, Post-Presidential Papers, Box 58, TPL.
47 'Netanyahu Will Be Speaking in Winston Churchill's Shadow', *Time*, 3 March 2015, http://time.com/3727163/netanyahu-churchill-history/ (accessed 20 November 2015).
48 Meacham, *Franklin and Winston*, p. 218.
49 *Newsweek*, 1 February 1943; Meacham, *Franklin and Winston*, pp. 97, 209, 231, 237, 300.
50 Franklin D. Roosevelt, 'Address of the President Delivered by Radio from Hyde Park, NY', 24 December 1943, Mid-Hudson Regional Information Center, www.mhric.org/fdr/chat27.html (accessed 10 November 2015).
51 Olsen, *Citizens of London*, pp. xvi–xvii, 158–84.
52 US War Department, '*Over There: Instructions for American Servicemen in Britain, 1942*, Oxford: Bodleian Library, 1994, pp. 1, 3, 7.
53 James T. Quirk Correspondence, World War II, Papers of James T. Quirk Subject File, Box 1, TPL.
54 Olsen, *Citizens of London*, pp. 278, 280–5, 290–2.
55 *Mrs Miniver*, directed by William Wyler, Metro-Goldwyn-Mayer, 1942.
56 Emily Yellin, *Our Mothers' War*, New York: Free Press, 2005, pp. 99–100.
57 'Mrs Miniver', Internet Movie Database, www.imdb.com/title/tt0035093/ (accessed 10 October 2015).
58 *Lifeboat*, directed by Alfred Hitchcock, Twentieth Century Fox, 1944.
59 *Gallup Poll #300*, 17 August 1943, Gallup Organization, http://brain.gallup.com/documents/questionnaire.aspx?STUDY=AIPO0300, (accessed 1 July 2005); *Gallup Poll #303*, 28 September 1943, The Gallup Organization, http://brain.gallup.com/documents/questionnaire.aspx?STUDY=AIPO0303, (accessed 1 July 2005); *Gallup Poll #317*, 25 April 1944, Gallup Organization, http://brain.gallup.com/documents/questionnaire.aspx?STUDY=AIPO0317, (accessed 8 July 2005).

94 *R.M. Hendershot*

60 Andrew Bacevich, 'H-Diplo Article Review 552', https://networks.h-net.org/node/28443/discussions/84104/h-diplo-article-review-552-monsters-everywhere-genealogy-national (accessed 22 November 2015).

61 'The Ten People Most Admired by the US Public', *Public Opinion News Service*, 10 March 1947, Records of the American Institute of Public Opinion (RAIPO), 1945 to 1951, Box 1, TPL; 'Voters in Poll Pick Ten Men Most Admired', *Public Opinion News Service*, 20 December 1948, RAIPO, 1945 to 1951, Box 1, TPL; 'Truman, Eisenhower Lead List of 10 Most Admired Men', *Public Opinion News Service*, 21 December 1949, RAIPO, 1945 to 1951, Box 1, TPL; 'Eisenhower Leads List of 10 Most Admired Men in World', *Public Opinion News Service*, 31 January 1951, RAIPO, 1945 to 1951, Box 1, TPL,

62 *Gallup Poll #512*, 20 February 1953, The Gallup Organization, http://brain.gallup.com/documents/questionnaire.aspx?STUDY=AIPO0512 (accessed 1 July 2005); *Gallup Poll #524*, 9 December 1953, The Gallup Organization, http://brain.gallup.com/documents/questionnaire.aspx?STUDY=AIPO0524 (accessed 1 July 2005).

63 'The Ten People Most Admired by the US Public', *Public Opinion News Service*, 10 March 1947, RAIPO, 1945 to 1951, Box 1, TPL.

64 In the December 1953 Gallup poll, Americans were also asked to identify the woman they admired most in the world. Queen Elizabeth tied with First Lady Mamie Eisenhower for fourth place, each with 4.12 per cent of the vote. *Gallup Poll #484*, 4 January 1952, The Gallup Organization, http://brain.gallup.com/documents/questionnaire.aspx?STUDY=AIPO0484 (accessed 1 July 2005); *Gallup Poll #512*, 20 February 1953, The Gallup Organization, http://brain.gallup.com/documents/questionnaire.aspx?STUDY=AIPO0512 (accessed 1 July 2005); *Gallup Poll #524*, 9 December 1953, The Gallup Organization, http://brain.gallup.com/documents/questionnaire.aspx?STUDY=AIPO0524 (accessed 1 July 2005).

65 Woods, *A Changing of the Guard*, pp. 2–10.

66 Churchill, 'The Sinews of Peace', Papers of Harry S. Truman (HST), President's Secretary's Files, Box 99, TPL.

67 Papers of HST, Official File 48, Box 293, TPL.

68 'The British Loan – What It Means to Us', Department of State Publication, 1946, Dean Acheson Papers, British Loan, 1946, Box 27, TPL.

69 Toye, *Churchill's Empire*, pp. 268–9.

70 Short to McEwen, 19 November 1951, Papers of HST, Official File 48, Box 293, TPL.

71 Truman, 'Mutual Security Speech', 6 March 1952, Papers of HST, President's Secretary's Files, Box 27, TPL.

72 Joint Communiqué by Truman and Attlee, 7 December 1950, Papers of HST, President's Secretary's Files, Box 142, TPL.

73 'Daily Opinion Summary', Department of State, 11 December 1950, Papers of HST, President's Secretary's Files, Box 142, TPL; 'Daily Opinion Summary,' Department of State, 12 December 1950, Papers of HST, President's Secretary's Files, Box 142, TPL.

74 'Award to Sir W. Churchill: Franklin Medal', *Glasgow Herald*, 12 January 1956, p. 3; Churchill was honoured similarly throughout the United States during this period. For example, the International Rescue Committee of New York awarded him the Admiral Richard E. Byrd Memorial Award in 1958 for his leadership; IRC to President Truman, 8 August 1958, Papers of HST, Post-Presidential Papers, Box 57, TPL.

75 Kay (Katherine Murphy) Halle (#94): An Inventory of Her Personal Papers (1895–1989), John Kennedy Library, National Archives and Records Administration (NARA), www.jfklibrary.org/fa_halle.html 21 August 2005; Kennedy, 'Remarks on Honorary Churchill Citizenship', 9 April 1963, Papers of HST, Post-Presidential Papers, Box 58, TPL.

Manipulating the Anglo-American identity 95

76 'The Great Escape: 50th anniversary', *The Telegraph*, www.telegraph.co.uk/culture/film/9853745/The-Great-Escape-50th-anniversary.html (accessed 10 December 2015).

77 Eric Snider, 'What's the Big Deal? The Great Escape', *Film.com*, www.film.com/movies/whats-the-big-deal-the-great-escape-1963 (accessed 10 December 2015).

78 *The Great Escape*, directed by John Sturges, The Mirisch Company, 1963.

79 Another enduring example of these dynamics in Cold War pop culture is found in the on-screen friendship between James Bond and CIA agent Felix Leiter. See James Chapman, *Licence to Thrill: A Cultural History of the James Bond Films*. New York: I.B. Tauris, 2013.

80 Toye, *Churchill's Empire*, p. 309.

81 Heath went on to explain the 'natural' reasons for Anglo-American intimacy: 'We are of the same stock, origin, and language and background, and I think the simplest thing is to say one cannot help but feel at home, and how thankful one is for it.' White House Press Release, 'Exchange of Toasts Between the President and Prime Minister Edward Heath of England, State Dining Room', 17 December 1970, VIP Visits, National Security Council Files, Nixon Presidential Materials Project, NARA; White House Press Release, 'Exchange of Remarks Between the President and Prime Minister Edward Heath of England, South Lawn', 17 December 1970, VIP Visits, National Security Council Files, Nixon Presidential Materials Project, NARA; Henry Kissinger, Memorandum for the President, 31 January 1973, VIP Visits, National Security Council Files, Nixon Presidential Materials Project, NARA.

82 Richard Growald, 'Washington Cathedral', *United Press International*, 8 July 1976, State Visits File, Sheila Weidenfeld Files, 1974–7, First Lady's Staff, GFL.

83 Ibid.

84 Philip Abbot, 'Leadership by Exemplar: Reagan's FDR and Thatcher's Churchill', *Presidential Studies Quarterly*, 27:2, Spring 1997, pp. 186–206; Kristine Miller, *Transatlantic Literature and Culture After 9/11: The Wrong Side of Paradise*, New York: Macmillan, 2014.

85 Public Broadcasting Service, 'What Does the World Think of Us?' 6 April 2007, www.pbs.org/now/shows/314/opinions-of-us.html (accessed 5 May 2011).

86 Pew Research Center, *Views of a Changing World*, Washington, DC: The Pew Research Center for the People and the Press, 2003, pp. 19, 20.

87 The bust of Churchill has been on display in the White House consistently since the 1960s. For a thorough recap of the Churchill bust controversy, see Charles Krauthammer, 'Charles Krauthammer: Busted: Mr Pfeiffer and the White House blog', *Washington Post*, 29 July 2015, www.washingtonpost.com/opinions/charles-krauthammer-busted-mr-pfeiffer-and-the-white-house-blog/2012/07/29/gJQA8M46IX_story.html (accessed 8 November 2015); Dan Pfeiffer, 'Fact Check: The Bust of Winston Churchill', The White House, 27 July 2012; www.whitehouse.gov/blog/2012/07/27/fact-check-bust-winston-churchill (accessed 2 December 2015).

88 Amy Davidson, 'The Case of the Two Churchills', *The New Yorker*, 1 August 2012; www.newyorker.com/news/daily-comment/the-case-of-the-two-churchills (accessed 5 November 2015).

89 National Churchill Museum; www.nationalchurchillmuseum.org/history-church-of-st-mary.html (accessed 10 November 2015).

90 'Churchill, Winston S. – Memorial, Fulton Missouri', Papers of HST, Post-Presidential Papers, Box 58, TPL.

91 James Williams, Executive Director of the National Churchill Museum, telephone interview with Robert M. Hendershot, Grand Rapids Community College, 26 October 2015; House Resolution 390, Congress.gov, www.congress.gov/bill/111th-congress/house-resolution/390 (accessed 3 November 2015).

4 The Fulton address as racial discourse[1]

Srdjan Vucetic

> Why be apologetic about Anglo-Saxon superiority? We are superior.
>
> Winston Churchill, 1943

Historians have long pointed out that Churchill's Fulton address was initially met with a mixture of cheers and boos around the world. The reactions tended to be politically and ideologically determined. Conservative politicians and the media praised the speech for its realism about the nature of the post-war settlement: at last someone had the courage to publicly say that the victor nations could not forever be friends. In contrast, most liberals, socialists and communists condemned the speech as inflammatory. With so many hopes pinned to the newly created United Nations Organization (UNO), the last thing the world needed was geopolitical tension between the Western powers and the Soviet Union, they argued. That was not all. Some leftists went further still. Churchill's notion the Anglo-American 'special relationship' and 'fraternal association' constituted the ultimate sinew of world peace smacked of racial supremacism, they said.

What do we know about this last group? In his interview in *Pravda*, which was translated and published by the *New York Times* on 14 March, Stalin chastised Churchill for articulating a Hitlerite 'racial theory' that could incite another war. For many historians, this event stands for the sort of over the top propaganda that lays bare Soviet cynicism, malfeasance and hostility. This interpretation is not wrong, but it sidesteps the fact that many non-communists wholeheartedly agreed with Stalin on this point. For the African-American elite at the time, the Fulton address sounded like another ballad in the chorus of Anglo-Saxon supremacy. The sociologist Horace Cayton likened the speech to the 'master race game'.[2] Paul Robeson, then the most renowned African-American figure in the world, agreed. What Churchill was selling, Robeson argued, was an elaborate schema for maintaining the racist status quo globally – 'a more highly developed kind of benevolent Anglo-American imperialism'.[3]

It would be a mistake to dismiss these denouncements as Kremlin agitprop even if one accepts that Robeson, for example, had certain sympathies for the Soviet point of view.[4] Indeed, what Robeson publicly said and wrote in response

The Fulton address as racial discourse   97

to Churchill's speech in his capacity as the chairman of the 'radical' Council on African Affairs (CAA) is strikingly similar to the opinions expressed by the executive secretary of the 'moderate' National Association for the Advancement of Colored People (NCAAP)[5] or the editors and commentators in the 'mainstream' *Pittsburgh Courier*, one of the highest-circulating 'American Negro newspapers' in 1946.[6] In other words, it is probably safe to say that the majority of those who spoke on behalf of this particular fourteen million-strong English-speaking people strongly viewed the Fulton address as a 'paean to white racial superiority'.[7] Furthermore, it is reasonable to speculate that similar interpretations would have emerged throughout the colonized world at the time.[8]

The purpose of this chapter is to examine some ways in which race and racism were implicated in the Fulton address. This is a difficult topic because how Churchill is remembered matters to many, and for perfectly good reasons: he is the saviour of Britain and Western civilization in 1940, a 1953 Nobel laureate in literature, one of history's supreme orators, the greatest Briton of all time, the twentieth century's most valuable figure, and so on.[9] The stardust surrounding the man's name often makes critical reflection difficult. Some like to consign any number of Churchill's 'controversial' statements and decisions to one-liners or footnotes in which the focus is always presentism rather than racism. Others temporize the problem by juxtaposing the brash young Churchill, whose views on human difference were appalling even by the standards of his time, to Churchill the Nazi slayer from 1940 to 1945 – an image that further eulogizes the man by showcasing his capacity for political and moral growth. Still others argue that Churchill was a force for good 'overall'.

My view is that Churchill-watchers stand to benefit from a more systematic engagement with the vast literature on the history and constitution of a racialized world order. This means that Churchill's Anglo-Saxon supremacism should not be obscured, relativized or otherwise finessed, but rather acknowledged as a manifestation of one of the defining political forces of the modern age. This acknowledgement, I hasten to add, does not spell 'forget Churchill' nor does it imply that the worst of Churchill should take precedence over the best of Churchill.

I begin by reviewing the mainline rhetorical strategies in academic and popular representations of Churchill's racism. Next I consider the Fulton address itself, focusing on Churchill's references to the English-speaking peoplehood, fraternity and unity. In the third section, I contextualize this dimension of the address in relation to Churchill's experience of 'Greater Britain'. My main contention here is that Churchill's appeal for the Anglo-American special relationship was a racialized political utopia – a cross between re-imagining a Greater British past and a programmatic statement on, to borrow one of Robeson's phrases, 'Anglo-Saxon world domination' for an era marked by communism, decolonization and the UNO.

A quick caveat is in order from the outset: the reader has noticed the lack of scare quotes around the word race. In contemporary academic communication this and similar warning practices are a method of signalling awareness about the social and political construction of knowledge and reality and, in turn, about

98   S. Vucetic

the problems of essentialism and reification.[10] Scare-quoting is unnecessary so long as race is defined from the outset as a socially and politically constructed, historically evolving, and cross-culturally variable identity that orders human beings on the basis of a mixture of bodily appearance and ancestral links.[11]

Let's talk about Churchill

Labelling and un-labelling Churchill is an inherently political act. Today, some see Churchill as an icon of modern conservatism (and, *sotto voce*, of sound aristocratic paternalism). For others, he symbolizes the twentieth-century liberal democratic triumph. For others still, he is an embodiment of civilizational discontents like militarism and colonial imperialism.[12] Some of these labels are more established than others. In the years after the man's death in 1965, most commentators ignored the themes of race and racism altogether. Whether this was wilful or not can be debated, but it is more relevant to remember that at that time the majority of intellectuals either themselves subscribed to racial bigotry or at least found dependable ways of hiding from the reality of racial discrimination. This approach is no longer an option. In today's Western societies, you can call Churchill the great twentieth-century beacon of liberty, but sooner or later you will be asked to reflect on the 'irony' of defending and promoting human freedom in the context of his 'Victorian' views of humanity.[13] The range and nuance of such reflections are considerable, but they tend to be expressed on the basis of one or more of the three ideal-typical rhetorical strategies: 'contextualization', 'temporization' and 'balancing'.

Contextualization works to curb evaluations of the past by the political and moral norms and experiences of the present – a fallacy known as anachronism or presentism. In this case, the purpose of contextualization is to suggest that it is absurd to blame Churchill for what were prototypical views in his time.[14] The argument is rhetorical, but it can be evaluated historically. One approach is to juxtapose public alongside private statements made by the person under study. Comb through the mountain of speeches the great man left behind – all 2,360 of them – and overt racism never jumps out the way it does in the equivalent documents penned by some of his contemporaries, to say nothing of his predecessors. The same cannot be said about Churchill's confidential memoranda, letters and, especially, conversations recorded by others – the outstanding case in point being the quotation in the epigraph of this chapter, which was recorded by the vice president of the United States Henry Wallace on 22 May 1943.[15]

While prime facie interesting, observable discrepancies between private and public statements can also be seen as trivial. Political leaders have always known how to talk out of both sides of their mouths, and Churchill is no outlier. A potentially more satisfying inquiry requires further context: how do Churchill's private statements compare to those left behind by his contemporaries? Yes, this approach, too, is problematic since it hinges on an agreed-upon point of moral stability – the most appropriate standard – from which to interpret a given historical figure. If the benchmark is someone like Woodrow Wilson, then Churchill certainly emerges as 'racially prejudiced' rather than as a 'malignant racist'.[16] But what of Mohandas Gandhi? Here, Churchill is not the one who comes off as 'merely' racially prejudiced.[17]

Contextualization also guides attempts to unpack the historical meanings of race and racism as a way of defending the British leader. Consider what Robin W. Winks said in his 1995 Crosby Kemper Lecture at Westminster College with regards to 'Churchill's real feelings about race':

> Churchill was a behaviorist: there were people he liked and disliked, indeed entire peoples he liked and disliked, and he was unrepentant in his belief that the English possessed a culture superior to any other. Further, in the darkest hours of Britain, he frequently referred to the 'British race' in a way that would make many participants in the political scene today blanch. Yet, when looked at in context, all his statements related to behavior, not to inherency.[18]

Winks is correct in pointing out that any history of race and racism involves conceptual projection.[19] Although both authorized institutions and practices dominance, 'inherentism' and 'behaviourism' disagreed over whether the structures and processes of this dominance were fixed or not.[20] In the 'behaviourist' view, inequalities between and among peoples had less to do with heritable, biological traits than with the socio-cultural and institutional environment.

This form of contextualization has many merits, but political convenience is not one of them. Insisting that Churchill was a 'mere' behaviourist – cultural racialist, national chauvinist, ethnocentric[21] – serves to safeguard his name from being mixed up with the great miscreants of history. It is true that Churchill emphasized the sociocultural over the biological in thinking about human differences.[22] Yet it is also true that he believed in racial essences, division, inequality and hierarchy – a major moral failing for a man celebrated as the defender of freedom, democracy, and humanitarian universalism.[23] Indeed, it is conceptually more accurate to think of the difference between 'inherentism' and 'behaviourism' as one of degree rather than of kind.[24]

The second rhetorical strategy for talking about Churchill's racism is temporization, which is my rubric for the argument Churchill de-racialized his views of humanity over time.[25] This claim has much prima facie support. Sample his half-histories, half-autobiographies by time of publication, and it quickly appears that the early Churchill (*The River War*, for example) was more likely to deploy racial discourse than the latter one (*The World Crisis*, for example). Again, this can be explained by Churchill's rise to political leadership and the dramatic changes in the constitution of the modern world during his long career in office. The man who joined General Kitchener's troops in 1898 spoke very differently from the man who entered politics in 1900, to say nothing of the man who later sat in the Admiralty and Downing Street.[26] Furthermore, Churchill's private statements and overheard conversations suggest that he never tired of using racialized language to rank-order Europeans against one another, and Europeans

100   *S. Vucetic*

against the rest. One of his main fears in 1954, for example, was that 'new' Commonwealth immigration would turn Britain into a 'magpie society'.[27]

The third rhetorical strategy, which I call balancing, aims to offset an actor's flaws with references to his virtues. An example of this age-old morality play is Holmes' contention that the debate on Churchill's racism is misleading given that 'he did more than any other man to combat social Darwinism'.[28] The Briton can certainly be credited for leading the free world to victory against the Axis, one of the most racist forces of all time, but this line of argument inevitably involves comparisons with Stalin, who also helped defeat the Nazis.[29]

The debate over the merits and demerits of contextualization, temporization and balancing in interpreting Churchill's life is not confined to academia. Ever since the 1960s and 1970s, when the confluence of anti-colonial, anti-racist, pacifist, feminist, and gay liberation social movements led (in Western societies at least) to the mainstreaming of critique and dissent, historical figures like Churchill have been a battleground in the so-called culture wars – the intellectual as well as popular debates between the political Right and the cultural Left over beliefs and values concerning the nature of political institutions, social progress and the like.[30] Consider a 2015 *BBC News Magazine* listicle by Tom Heyden on 'The 10 Greatest Controversies of Winston Churchill's Career'.[31] The piece appears to be motived by two infamous Churchill controversies from the preceding year – the Labour candidate Benjamin Whittingham's tweet that Churchill was 'a racist and white supremacist', and the arrest of Paul Weston, chairman of the Liberty GB party, on suspicion that quoting from Churchill's 1899 book *The River War* in a public lecture constitutes racial harassment.[32] This is why, of the ten themes discussed in the article, the problem of racism can be found in no fewer than seven, namely, the indigenous peoples, the use of chemical weapons in the Middle East, the Great Bengali Famine, Ghandi and India, Jews, Islam, and Ireland.[33]

The BBC story is instructive for the way it scrutinizes both the fragments of historical materials central to debates in Churchill Studies as well as reflections upon them. The story thus not only acknowledges the problem of presentism, but it also challenges those who invoke the need for historical context only in order to delegitimize valid present-day concerns. The challenge of contextualization is even greater if one accepts that a degree of presentism can never be avoided to what philosophers of history have called the situatedness of historical knowledge.[34] This is why so many historians refuse to project *any* contemporary preoccupations backward in time without making explicit the inherent ambiguities of historical interpretation.[35] This would also be my preferred rhetorical strategy for talking about Churchill's racism: not contextualization, not temporization, not balancing, but 'explication'.

Rather than abating, academic and popular debates over 'Churchill's real feelings about race' are likely to gather pace. One reason is the aforementioned clash between conservatives and left-liberals over culture. In the US, for example, Churchill's name is known to be an object of worship at both elite and mass levels.[36] This has to do not only with the way the Americans memorialize the hot and cold wars of the twentieth century, but also with the historical development of the US's conservative 'tradition'. Following the work of Reba N. Soffer, it can in fact be argued that the heroification of Churchill in the US developed not so much via the contemporary history curriculum as through popular political philosophy books like Peter Viereck's *Conservatism: From John Adams to Churchill* (1956).[37] But therein lies both the force and the limit of America's reverence and revelry for the Briton; the more the Churchillian iconography is appropriated by and for conservatives, the more Churchill's historical record is likely to be politicized.[38]

This debate is also likely to be fuelled by the evolution of ordinary and academic understandings of race and racism. When race scholars today use Searlian language to refer to race as a human or social kind, they affirm that race has no natural (i.e. biological or genetic) foundations, while underscoring the reality of race as a social and political mechanism for ordering people.[39] The majority view is that this mechanism, first, is a product of modernity and, specifically, European (Western) colonial imperialism and, second, varies across different historical and contemporary social, economic, legal, and political contexts. However, another consensus is that race always manifests itself in interaction with class, gender and other categories of human difference to produce social and political outcomes. Viewed from this perspective, no critical inquiry into the question of what Churchill means will be complete unless it accounts for these interactions and intersections.[40] A challenge for the next BBC production on the controversies of Churchill's career, perhaps.

The citizen's speech

The textual, lexical and syntactical structures of the Fulton speech have been closely analysed by historians and communication scholars. The rhetorician Michael Hostetler summarizes the speech in terms of three 'primary metaphors': the metallurgical–theatrical 'iron curtain', referring to Soviet aggression, the corporeal 'sinews of peace', and the architectural–construction site 'temple of peace', which referred to the UN.[41] The historian David Reynolds reads the speech in terms of 'four soundbites' – the 'iron curtain', the 'lessons of appeasement', the 'special relationship', and the 'sinews of peace'.[42] Looking back in history, we know that some of these struck a chord better than others, but what is important here is their internal hierarchy, as intended by the author. Churchill's rhetorical scaffolding, as both Hostetler and Reynolds point out, was structured towards the argument that the fate of the free world hinged on the special relationship rather than on international cooperation in general or the newborn United Nations Organization (UNO) in particular. The argument goes like this: if war against tyranny is a constant of modern history, and if the UNO is unable to counter the new tyranny growing in the East, then only a common Anglo-American front can make tyrants reconsider their historical course of action. In the context of the contemporary events on the ground – the post-war Big Three condominium was collapsing under the weight of the Iran–Azerbaijan crisis, for one – and subsequent events, it is easy to see why the address is remembered as the 'Iron Curtain' speech as opposed to the 'Special Relationship' speech or, for that matter, 'The Sinews of Peace'.[43] Nevertheless, the intended 'crux' of the speech, as Churchill himself put it, was Anglo-American unity – the 'fraternal association of the English-speaking peoples' grounded in the 'special relationship between the British Commonwealth and Empire and the United States'.

The word 'race' appears in the speech once, and not in a context that deserves emphasis: 'It is from the quarrels of the strong parent races in Europe that the world wars we have witnessed, or which occurred in former times, have sprung.' So, how was it that race was *everything* that Cayton and Robeson took from it? The basic insight of semantics is that the meaning of a text is context-bound such that it depends on the different spaces and times, textual and otherwise, with which a text is engaged. The white audience of students and VIPs at the gymnasium of Westminster College probably understood the speech differently from the audiences at the historically black colleges and universities or those in Pittsburgh's Hill District, Bronzeville, Harlem, Shaw/U Street and so on. Judging by *The Atlantic Charter and Africa from an American Standpoint* (1942), a study produced by the Committee on Africa, the War, and Peace Aims, or W.E.B. Du Bois's *Color and Democracy* (1945), the African-American elites were deeply suspicious of Churchill and what he represented.[44]

Viewed another way, the fact that 'race' appears only once in the speech is precisely the issue. Thus, while Churchill's pronouncements on the importance of international cooperation in fighting tyranny and poverty are in many ways politically and morally progressive, they are fatally blunted by his inattention to racialized exclusion and oppression as a cause of said tyranny and poverty. This was no oversight. Other than the great capitalist–communist dance, the other major political context of the speech was the global anti-colonial revolt. Churchill knew this, of course, but chose to ignore it – the choice he made repeatedly throughout his career.[45] The same applies for his target audience. Hostetler acknowledges the issue of 'the cultural homogeneity in which Churchill makes his overt proposal for Anglophone global hegemony', but does so in a footnote, and by quickly drawing a curtain on further discussion: 'The underlying cultural/racial presumptions of his plan raise our hackles today, and rightly so, but they failed to raise an eyebrow in 1946.'[46] Hostetler is right except for the last part: eyebrows *were* raised in 1946.

The text of the Fulton speech can be problematized further still, starting with Churchill's use of fraternity, friendship, and kinship. On the level of daily politics, these concepts, and the tropes based on them, were code for the word 'alliance', which was still a great no–no in the US at the time.[47] On a deeper level, however, these words are code for something closer akin to what Cayton and Robeson heard in the speech. Consider the concluding sentence:

> if all British moral and material forces and convictions are joined with your own in fraternal association, the high-roads of the future will be clear, not only for us but for all, not only for our time, but for a century to come.

The Fulton address as racial discourse 103

This was no simple call for a defensive military alliance, but for a political (and economic and cultural etc.) *community* in charge of 'the future glory and safety of mankind'.

As Carole Pateman, Charles Mills, and Mona Ozouf and others have argued, brothers, friends and the family are some of the most recurring figures in modern theories of the social contract.[48] Putting aside the conceptual differences between and among these concepts, it can be said that their common purpose is to manage order in political communities. The talk of brotherhood, fraternity and family thus may help relax political tensions between Xs and Ys, but it does so only by protecting the privileges of community *leaders* – usually an all-male, all-white class of adult persons.[49]

Parallels to the Fulton speech are evident. In addition to claiming moral superiority and articulating Anglo-Americans as the special edition of humankind, Churchill's rhetoric essentially reproduced the old international hierarchy. Thus, while the UNO Charter does open some new possibilities – in the speech Churchill famously proposed that the new organization be equipped with a standing air force – in no way does it change the division of the world into what he identified as 'Powers' and 'States'. On one level, this can be interpreted as a 'classic' crude realpolitik view of the world that reduces international political life to relations of super- and subordination among sovereign nations. But on another level, as, again, Du Bois explained in *Color and Democracy*, this was a blueprint for maintaining the global colour line. The Atlantic and San Francisco Charters might help (some) 'dependent peoples' get their own states, but powerhood was reserved for, shall we say, the traditional owners of the system.

These more abstract points are important for understanding Churchill's deployment in the speech of one of his all-time favourite phrases – 'the English-speaking peoples'. Toye defines it as a 'seemingly racialized vision in which the Britons of the "White Dominions" and America were linked as part of a broader global community with a common interest in defending freedom'.[50] In the speech, the English-speaking peoples are spoken into existence on the basis of myths of a shared past – a past that is passing straight from the Magna Charta in 1215 to the joint use of military bases in 1946 – *and* the basis of a duty and destiny to promote peace, order, and good government in the world. Toye is correct to call this vision racialized; in it, non-white English-speakers are either the out-group or subordinate to white English-speakers. Moreover, Churchill patriates, in the name of an exclusive club of people, the universality of the 'title deeds of freedom' *à la* Magna Charta.[51] This is eighteenth-century colonialist rhetoric, not a 'largely Burkean defence of the modern liberal regime in its Anglo-American forms', as Daniel J. Mahoney sees it.[52]

The idea of the English-speaking peoples is one of the keys for understanding Churchill's theories of politics and of history. By my count, he used the phrase at least once in public in 1911, 1917, 1918, 1921, 1931, 1932, 1933, 1940, 1942, 1943, 1946, 1954, 1955, and 1963 – in addition to his monumental *History of the English-Speaking Peoples*. (Privately, Churchill wrote about the English-speaking peoples, then called 'communities', as early as 1898.) The rhetorical

104   *S. Vucetic*

continuity is all the more remarkable considering the drastic global transformations that occurred in this period. The phrase that graces the title of Churchill's most famous book, as Peter Clark has demonstrated, had entered the lexicon of the educated classes across the English-speaking world well before Churchill entered politics.[53] Crucially, it appears to have been coined in the context of the late nineteenth-century *liberal* Atlantic – a network of progressive intellectual and political elites who engaged each other in reflections on the changing role of government in the context of industrialization. The key moment was the 1871 Treaty of Washington in the sense that this peaceful resolution of the American Civil War-era disputes between London and Washington added grist to the mill of those who claimed that Anglo-American commonalities – language, literature, lineage, etc. – facilitated Anglo-American cooperation.

Clarke also convincingly demonstrates that it was the transatlantic Victorian liberal thought, and not simply his own Anglo-American heritage, that helped Churchill imagine the English-speaking peoples as a historical entity. Less convincing, respectfully, is Clarke's claim that, by the time Churchill first used this phrase in public the meaning of 'English-speaking peoples' had come to refer to nations and institutions rather than races. The key document here is the third edition of a pamphlet on the Irish Home Rule, published in the winter of 1911–12. Settling the Irish question, Churchill wrote in the preface, would bring Britain 'nearer in bonds of friendship and association to the United States', and thus pave the 'road to the unity of the English-speaking races'.[54] Crucially, this course was said to be sensible in the context of the coming geopolitical game: 'We see the four consolidations of the human family which are in the ascendant – the Russian power, the Yellow races, the Teutonic alliance, and the English-speaking peoples.'

Judging on what we think we know about the range of intersubjective meanings of all these phrases in this particular historical context, it is likely that Churchill was articulating the idea of racial communities as dominant power containers of world order. What is more, he probably saw them as existing in a state of mutual struggle – and quite possibly an evolutionary struggle rather than 'merely' a political one. The next section looks at this controversial point.

The last Greater Briton

The majority view in the academic literature is that the Anglo-American special relationship began during World War II.[55] This view chimes with a realpolitik understanding of international politics: absent the mortal Axis threat, there would be no close collaboration between the US and Britain, and therefore no foundation for the development of the special relationship. While several recent studies have suggested that the origins of Anglo-American specialness can be traced back to the early 1900s, 1890s and even earlier, historical consensus remains stable; by most reasonable measures – the depth and frequency of summitry diplomacy, intelligence and weapon technology sharing and joint warfare practices, above all – the special relationship owes its existence to the wartime developments in the 1940s.[56]

The Fulton address as racial discourse   105

While this periodization is sound, it tends to obscure the role played by the so-called cultural affinity – that is, by the ideas, discourses, institutions, and networks that enabled the deep and durable forms of cooperation that later came to characterize the special relationship. This is especially important in the political, social and cultural context of the Fulton address and specifically Churchill's statement about shared Anglo-American inheritance contained within it. To go back to Clarke, the phrase 'English-speaking peoples' gained currency in the wake of the 1871 Treaty of Washington. What is critical is that the same period also saw the rise of two nearby and interrelated concepts: Greater Britain and the Anglo-Saxondom.[57] A closer look at each can shed additional light on what Churchill was saying at Fulton, and why.

Greater Britain is as old as, if not older than, the idea of the English-speaking peoples. Introduced in British political discourse in 1869 by the politician and author Charles Dilke, it referred to the British and Irish Isles, the United States, Canada, Australasia, and India.[58] Dilke was on to something. According to James Belich, an informal, loosely bounded, and de-centred cultural and economic community of like-minded English-speaking peoples indeed came into existence at the time, thanks to a confluence of nineteenth-century development in political participation and ideology, transportation and communication technologies and, especially, migration and settlement.[59] The last development was revolutionary in the sense that modern history had never before witnessed such a mass, ideologically motivated and permanent transfer of population. Between the end of the Napoleonic Wars and the year of Churchill's birth, almost six million Britons moved permanently to the US, Canada, Australia, and New Zealand – a multifold increase in relation to the period before Napoleon.[60] Further, in contrast to earlier British migrants to these areas who were often convicts, soldiers and adventurers, the nineteenth-century migrants can be characterized as tightly knit communities, with considerable social and often economic capital and with high levels of mutual support. The combined effect was to reinforce and indeed 'clone' a number of key institutions and practices from Old Britain such as representative government, the common law, the diffusion of the franchise among white men, and political decentralization.[61]

This new form of settler colonialism had massive political, social, economic, and cultural consequences, the scale of which is yet to be fully analysed. As Belich puts it, Greater Britain was a veritable 'virtual nation'.[62] Importantly, Greater Britain included the US, even if only 'occasionally' the US.[63] Belich describes this fact as the 'really special relationship'.[64] No sooner than the War of 1812 ended did British capital, food, raw materials and, of course, settlers begin to cross the Atlantic in search of profit and prosperity. Only by the end of the century did some of these movements precipitously dissipate.[65]

Belich's main argument is that Greater Britain was primarily economic and cultural, yet it bears keeping in mind that this new nineteenth-century reality enabled a radical re-imagination of the political space among powerful segments of the Anglo-American ruling elite. In the 1880s, people like Andrew Carnegie in the US and J.R. Seeley in Britain publicly toyed with the idea of an Anglo-American

106   *S. Vucetic*

(re-)union, with some of their contemporaries going so far as to draw parallels between Greater Britain on the one hand and Italian and German unifications on the other.[66] Churchill's appeal for the fraternal association at Fulton heavily borrowed from this once-commonplace political discourse. According to Charmley, when Churchill spoke of Anglo-American 'unity' in the 1940s, he really meant 'union' – presumably *à la* Carnegie or Seeley.[67] Churchill was also flexible: if union was politically impossible, then 'Pax Anglo-Americana' would do.[68]

This leads us to Anglo-Saxonism. Symbiotic and complementary with Greater Britain and the English-speaking peoples, Anglo-Saxonism is a body of ideas that once posited the unity and supremacy of racially defined Anglo-Saxon Protestants. Versions of this discourse arguably go back to the English Reformation and the English Civil War and can be found in various geographic contexts throughout the modern period, certainly including the US in 1946. Compared to Greater Britain, the boundaries of Anglo-Saxondom were less elastic in the sense that its proponents rarely if ever acknowledged Irish Catholics, much less Hindu or Muslim Indians, as in-group members.[69] This is an important point: a vast and informal zone of economic and cultural exchange, Greater Britain also constituted itself via deeply racialized divisions, exclusions, and hierarchies.[70] American and British Anglo-Saxonisms developed in relation to different racialized Others, different internal tensions, and different colonial politics, but they both ended their discursive careers sometime during or after World War I.[71]

Churchill might have bucked this last trend. In biographies, his relationship to Anglo-Saxonism is sometimes reduced to a sentence or two about his professed dislike for the *Anglo-Saxon Review*, the chic quarterly founded and edited between 1899 and 1901 by his American-born mother Jennie Jerome, a.k.a. Lady Randolph Churchill. This is misleading. James Lawrence, who no one can accused of being some radical left-winger, puts it much better:

> By his mid-twenties, Churchill had absorbed the current racial dogma that identified the Anglo-Saxon race as uniquely qualified to rule and share the blessings of a civilization.... This conceit dominated his wartime and post-war dealings with America and made him enemies in both countries.[72]

Although always vigorously contested, Anglo-Saxonism was indeed one of the most pervasive and powerful discourses of identity for large segments of ruling classes on both sides of the Atlantic at the time. It was also immensely consequential politically. Consider the Great Rapprochement – the *fin-de-siècle* rise in inter-state cooperation between the US and the British Empire.[73] Once the diplomatic dust raised by the American Civil War settled after the 1871 Treaty, London and Washington found fewer and fewer reasons to fight, but war nevertheless remained a possibility. The 'war scares' over Venezuela in 1894–5 and again in 1902–3 mark another critical period for the rapprochement because they demonstrated to the domestic and international audiences that the 'two branches of the Anglo-Saxon race' had the moral and political wherewithal to resolve their colonial disputes peacefully.[74] The reciprocation of 'benevolent neutrality'

The Fulton address as racial discourse   107

in the colonial wars waged against third parties – British cheerleading for America in its war with Spain in 1898 had much to do with American support to Britain's in South Africa in 1899–1902 – was legitimated in similar phrases and had similar effects.[75] 'Pax Anglo-Saxonica' is how some continental students of geopolitics later described these developments and their potential.[76]

Absent the power and pervasiveness of Anglo-Saxonism, the Great Rapprochement would have been unlikely, which, in turn, would have hobbled the durability and depth of Anglo-American cooperation in the subsequent decades.[77] And be that as it may, Anglo-Saxonist discourses certainly helped execute a whole range of Greater Britain-traversing ideas, institutions and practices, including business and professional networks (the Rhodes scholarships); sports competitions (Sir John Astley's Anglo-Saxon Olympic Games); advocacy networks (the Anglo-American Committee, the Anglo-American League); upper-class transatlantic marriage patterns; and various political and moral reform movements. Then there was the great empire of the printing press:

> Anglo-American dialogue and Anglo-Saxonist racism were also given life by a publishing revolution in the 1890s ... [that] helped create an 'imagined community' of literate, English-speaking Americans and Britons with common affiliations and reference points, even among the less traveled.[78]

The historical importance of the transatlantic travel of books and periodicals impressed Churchill so much that he once credited, with tongue only halfway in cheek, Washington's benevolent neutrality in World War II to the American popularity of Jan Struther's fiction in 1939.[79] This literary imagined community is yet another important context for understanding the content and tone of the Fulton address.

This deeper political and historical context is what helps explain the variable reception of the Fulton address. Churchill's calls for Anglo-American unity were grounded in the long-established affiliations, reference points and, ultimately, discourses of identity shared by significant numbers of educated English-speakers, not only in America and Britain, but across Greater Britain. By the same token, this is also why the speech was denounced at the time with such vigour and, by some, also with venom, as a 'dream of the Anglo-Saxon golden age'.[80]

Conclusion

The 'iron curtain', the magnetic metaphor that almost instantaneously entered the idiom of educated people around the world, has become synonymous with Churchill's Fulton address. Together with Stalin's 'election' speech in February 1946 and George Kennan's subsequent Long Telegram, the address is almost universally regarded as a textbook document for understanding the origins of the Cold War. The same can be said about the special relationship. Although the term never took off the way 'iron curtain' did, no analysis of Anglo-American relations can ignore the Fulton address.

108 *S. Vucetic*

In this chapter, I have argued that Churchill's call for the special relationship was also a way of configuring racialized unity and superiority. This was no accident. The notion that international relations were simultaneously or even primarily inter-racial relations was a core part of the Anglo-Saxon, Greater British political identity that Churchill embodied and reproduced practically throughout his public career. Although explicitly racialized language is absent from the speech, a closer look at Churchill's constructions of old and new institutions of world order, from the nature of tyranny to the UNO, betray his commitment to racialized world order with Anglo-America at its apex.

My other argument in this chapter was that there is nothing smugly ahistorical about reading the Fulton address as racial discourse – that is, through the lenses focused upon the historical operation of race and racism. Reactions of those who spoke on behalf of African Americans reveal that these lenses were very much in use at the time. Further research would do well to recover similar contestations from the other parts of the colonized globe and consider what they imply for the ways in which Churchill's speech is commemorated today.

Notes

1 I am grateful to Sam Edwards, David Haglund, Inés Valdez and Wesley Wark for written comments and criticisms. All errors are my own.
2 Mark Solomon, 'Black Critics of Colonialism and the Cold War', in Thomas G. Paterson (ed.), *Cold War Critics: Alternatives to American Foreign Policy in the Truman Years*, Chicago: Quandrangle Books, 1971, p. 218.
3 Address at the Win-the-Peace conference, Washington, DC, April 1946. Cited in Martin Bauml Duberman, *Paul Robeson*. New York: Ballantine Books, 1989, p. 304.
4 The fact that the FBI kept a close tab on his 'subversive' activities in those years does not imply that Robeson was a communist. See, especially, Gerald Horne, *Paul Robeson*. London: Pluto Press, 2016.
5 Carol Anderson, 'From Hope to Disillusion: African Americans and the United Nations, 1944–1947', *Diplomatic History*, 20:4, Autumn 1996, pp. 531–63, at p. 543; Solomon, 'Black Critics', pp. 217–18, Duberman, *Robeson*, p. 322. The CAA, originally known as the International Committee on African Affairs, disbanded in 1955. The NAACP, which was founded in 1909 by black and white liberals, would later lead the civil rights revolution in the US.
6 On 16 March the editorial described the speech as an 'invitation to imperialism'; Solomon, 'Black Critics', p. 218.
7 Anderson, 'From Hope to Disillusion', p. 543.
8 Knowledge on this topic has greatly expanded since Fraser Harbutt's seminal research, but details about how the speech was received globally are still scant. Harbutt, *The Iron Curtain: Churchill, America and the Origins of the Cold War*, Oxford: Oxford University Press, 1986, ch. 7. US Foreign Broadcast Information Service (FBIS) Daily Reports indicate that Soviet and pro-Soviet commentators commonly described the Fulton speech as a 'racial theory'. FBIS-FRB-46–055 (19 March 1946), Eastern European Transmitters, p. 6. The only reference to non-European reactions to the speech in FBIS is to Radio Chongqing's English language broadcast of a (critical) *Ta Kung Pao* editorial on 9 March. FBIS-FRB-46–050 (12 March 1946), Far Eastern Section Articles and Speeches, G5. Irish–American reactions to the speech were negative for similar but certainly not identical reasons. John Ramsden, *Man of the Century: Winston Churchill and his Legend since 1945*, New York: Columbia University Press, 2002, pp. 368–9.

The Fulton address as racial discourse   109

9 For more, see the recent hagiographies by two Johnsons: Paul Johnson, *Churchill*, New York: Viking, 2009; and Boris Johnson, *The Churchill Factor: How One Man Made History*, London: Hodder & Stoughton, 2014.

10 While race today regularly appears in scare quotes in the academic writing, words like black, civilization and Asian usually do not, even if on the above logic they could or should. The practice of scare-quoting the word race indexes not only ontological commitments (the social construction of reality and knowledge) but also normative concerns (the moral, practical, prudential and political implications of engaging in race-talk). My own views align with those who argue that the benefits of conserving racial categories for analytical and political purposes outweigh the risks of essentialism and reification. Srdjan Vucetic, 'Against Race Taboos', in Alex Anievas, Nivi Manchanda and Robbie Shilliam (eds), *Race and Racism in International Relations, Confronting the Global Colour Line*, London: Routledge, 2014, pp. 98–114.

11 This is not just academic jargon. Political correctness debates that characterize today's anti-racist societies often arise from the uncertainty, confusion and discomfort of contemporary race-talk. Here I use race alongside racialization, a term that captures a whole gamut of ideologies, structures, and practices that are used to construct race. Vucetic, 'Against Race Taboos', p. 104.

12 On the evolution of Churchill as a historical, cultural and political object, see Ramsden, *Man of the Century*, Klaus Larres, *Churchill's Cold War: The Politics of Personal Diplomacy*, New Haven: Yale University Press, 2002, pp. xvi–xx; David Cannadine, 'Prologue: Churchill from Memory to History,' in David Cannadine and Roland Quinault (eds), *Winston Churchill in the Twenty First Century*, Cambridge: Cambridge University Press, 2004, pp. 1–7; and Richard Toye, 'The Churchill Syndrome: Reputational Entrepreneurship and the Rhetoric of Foreign Policy since 1945', *British Journal of Politics and International Relations* 10:3, 2008, pp. 364–78. Research on the truly global Churchill is still missing.

13 Churchill was known to (fondly) call himself a Victorian in the 1930s, and was called the same (insultingly) by Jawaharlal Nehru in the 1940s. See, respectively, Paul Kent Alkon, *Winston Churchill's Imagination*, Lewisburg, PA: Bucknell University Press, 2006, p. 93; and Richard Toye, *Churchill's Empire: The World that Made Him and the World that He Made*, Basingstoke: Palgrave, 2010, p. xvi. For a much-need complexification of the label Victorian in this context, see Douglas Lorimer, 'From Victorian Values to White Virtues: Assimilation and Exclusion in British Racial Discourse, *c*.1870–1914', in Phillip Buckner and R. Douglas Francis, *Rediscovering the British World*, Calgary: University of Calgary Press, 2005, pp. 109–24.

14 On the range of such contextualizations, see Toye, *Churchill's Empire*, pp. xi–xvii.

15 This episode, which Wallace recorded in his diary, is discussed in some detail by Toye, *Churchill's Empire*, pp. 240–1; and Christopher Thorne, *Allies of a Kind: The United States, Britain, and the War against Japan, 1941–1945*, New York, Oxford University Press, 1978, p. 730. Second-hand revelations are problematic by default, but they are also necessary when other forms of documentary evidence are missing (for all of his voluminous verbal production, Churchill never once penned an essay or gave a speech on race). On Churchill's racisms – the plural form is the correct one in this case – see, *inter alia*, Sarvepalli Gopal, 'Churchill and India', in R. Blake and W.R. Louis (eds), *Churchill*, Oxford: Oxford University Press, 1993, pp. 457–72; Andrew Roberts, *Eminent Churchillians*, London: Weidenfeld & Nicolson, 1994, pp. 211–42. Madhusree Mukerjee, *Churchill's Secret War: The British Empire and the Ravaging of India during World War II*, New York: Basic Books, 2010, entire; Toye, *Churchill's Empire*, especially pp. 32–3, 240–1, 116–19, 154–6, 248–9, 290–3; Lawrence James, *Churchill and Empire: Portrait of an Imperialist*, New York: Pegasus, 2014, especially pp. 47–8, 97–9, 183–5, 204–7, 321, 389, and 'Was Churchill a Racist? Oh Yes!' *Socialist Worker*, 2438, 27 January 2015.

16 Quotations are from Ronald Hyam, *Britain's Declining Empire: The Road to Decolonisation, 1918–1968*, Cambridge: Cambridge University Press, 2007, pp. 43, 41.

17 On Gandhi and race, see Sankaran Krishna, 'A Postcolonial Racial/Spatial Order: Gandhi, Ambdekar, and the Construction of the International', in Alex Anievas, Nivi Manchanda and Robbie Shilliam (eds), *Race and Racism in International Relations, Confronting the Global Colour Line*, London: Routledge, 2014, pp. 139–56.

18 Robin W. Winks, 'Winston Churchill, Intelligence and Fiction: "Mysteries Inside Enigmas"', 2 April 1995; www2.westminster-mo.edu/cm/scholar/021995.pdf (accessed 23 May 2013).

19 For more, see Michael Banton, 'The Idiom of Race: A Critique of Presentism', *Research in Race and Ethnic Relations*, 2, 1980, pp. 1–20; and Peter Mandler, '"Race" and "Nation" in Mid-Victorian Thought', in Stefan Collini, Richard Whatmore and Brian Young (eds), *History, Religion and Culture: British Intellectual History, 1750–1950*, Cambridge: Cambridge University Press, 2000, pp. 224–44.

20 Behaviourism is more commonly associated with the early twentieth-century psychology. 'Galtonianism' and '(neo-)Lamarckianism' would have been more precise terms. On these two '-isms' and their contribution to the global institutions and practices of Anglo-Saxon supremacy, see Srdjan Vucetic, *The Anglosphere: A Genealogy of a Racialized Identity in International Relations*, Stanford: Stanford University Press, 2011, ch. 2.

21 Winks' argument is functionally similar to the claim that Churchill *mostly* meant cultures or nations when talking about races. Richard Holmes, *In the Footsteps of Churchill*, London: BBC Books, 2005, p. 14; Peter Clarke, *Mr Churchill's Profession: Statesman, Orator, Writer*, London: Bloomsbury, 2012, p. 102; and Paul Addison, 'Winston Churchill's Concept of "The English-Speaking Peoples"', in Attila Pók (ed.), *The Fabric of Modern Europe: Essays in Honour of Éva Haraszti Taylor*, Nottingham: Astra, 1999, pp. 103–17, at pp. 108–9.

22 This is exemplified in the way he sometimes associated the most superior human traits with white European Protestants in general rather than those of the British stock in particular or the way he ranked Muslim Indians higher than Hindu Indians in the 1930s and 1940s.

23 His writings on the impossibility of constitutional representative government for 'coloured peoples', English-speaking and otherwise, are telling, the prime exhibit being the alt-history essay, 'If Lee Had Not Won the Battle of Gettysburg'. Originally published in *Scribner's Magazine* in 1930, this text reappeared, duly vetted by Churchill, in 1961 in *The Wisconsin Magazine of History*. Note that denial of representative government to African Americans was consistent with Victorian liberal thought in which liberal democracy was regarded as a club good reserved for people of a certain shade of white, the rest of the world being placed under a combination of paternalism and despotism. See Toye, *Churchill's Empire*, p. 121, and more generally Uday Singh Mehta, *Liberalism and Empire: A Study in Nineteenth-Century British Liberal Thought*, Chicago: University of Chicago Press, 1999. On Churchill's reservations about *mass* democracy, see Roland Quinault, 'Churchill and Democracy', in David Cannadine and Roland Quinault (eds), *Winston Churchill in the Twenty First Century*, Cambridge: Cambridge University Press, 2004, pp. 27–46.

24 For this debate, see Srdjan Vucetic, 'Black Banker, White Banker: Philosophies of the Global Colour Line', *Cambridge Review of International Affairs*, 25:1, 2013, pp. 27–48.

25 For discussions, see Toye, *Churchill's Empire*, p. xvii, and Hyam, *Britain's Declining Empire*, pp. 41–2.

26 By the mid-1930s, all liberal democratic politicians had an additional reason to distance themselves from the rhetoric of white supremacy. As Holmes puts it, 'the rise of stridently racist Nazism forced the change of vocabulary'; Holmes, *In the Footsteps of Churchill*, p. 14.

The Fulton address as racial discourse 111

27 Roberts, *Eminent Churchillians*, p. 223.

28 Holmes, *In the Footsteps of Churchill*, p. 14.

29 A priori refusal to balance good deeds against bad is a rhetorical strategy, too. See, for example, James, *Churchill and Empire*, p. 4.

30 From 2000 to 2013 the London-based Institute of Ideas reviewed such clashes in the UK context. Churchill's name figures prominently in its archive (retrievable from www.culturewars.org.uk/). Another testament to the continuity of the Churchill's racism debate is Winks' 1995 Fulton lecture, which references a culture war in *The Spectator* and elsewhere in the British media over the work by the historian Bernard Porter. Winks, 'Winston Churchill, Intelligence and Fiction'.

31 Tom Heyden, 'The 10 Greatest Controversies of Winston Churchill's Career', *BBC News Magazine*, 26 January 2015; www.bbc.com/news/magazine-29701767 (accessed 12 June 2015).

32 Context in which *The River War* receives attention today includes, but is not limited to, the current campaign against Islamist jihadism. See Thabo Mbeki, 'Address to the Parliament of the Republic of Sudan, Khartoum', 1 January 2005; www.dfa.gov.za/docs/speeches/2005/mbek1108a.htm (accessed 31 July 2010).

33 Among Churchill-watchers, these are much-debated, perennial themes that will probably never be settled. What did the Jews, Africans or his mother's alleged Iroquois heritage *really* mean to Churchill?

34 On the long-standing epistemological debates behind it, see, *inter alia*, David Reynolds, *From World War to Cold War: Churchill, Roosevelt and the International History of the 1940s*, Oxford: Oxford University Press, 2006, pp. 331–51; Daniel Little, 'Philosophy of History', in Edward N. Zalta (ed.), *The Stanford Encyclopedia of Philosophy*, 2012; http://plato.stanford.edu/archives/win2012/entries/history/ (accessed 12 June 2015); and Robert Doran (ed.), *Philosophy of History After Hayden White*, London: Bloomsbury, 2013. After all, the nationally funded broadcaster could not examine the controversies surrounding Churchill's views on race outside a certain contemporary pluralist, multicultural and, arguably, post-heroic milieu. Also see the BBC2 documentary *Churchill: When Britain Said No* (produced by Christopher Spencer, 2015). Available from www.bbc.co.uk/programmes/b05x31b6.

35 A single example will suffice. The opening paragraph zooms in on Churchill's 1937 statement to the Palestine Royal Commission in which he suggested that the genocides against Native Americans and Aboriginal Australians were justifiable in social Darwinist terms ('a stronger race, a higher-grade race, a more worldly wise race to put it that way, has come in and taken their place'). This is interpreted through voices of three individuals: John Charmley and Richard Toye, two professional historians known for their inclination to evaluate Churchill critically, plus Sir Nicholas Soames, Churchill's grandson. The argument that any judgement of the past by the standards of the present is 'ludicrous', attributed to Soames, is balanced by Toye's claim that while Churchill's views on race were historically commonplace, 'there were many others who didn't hold them'. This is then balanced with a quotation, also from Toye, that Churchill's views were essentially non-genocidal: 'Although Churchill did think that white people were superior, that didn't mean he necessarily thought it was OK to treat non-white people in an inhumane way.'

36 Christopher Hitchens, *Blood, Class and Nostalgia: Anglo-American Ironies*, New York: Farrar, Straus and Giroux, 1990. Churchill-worship in the US intensified following the events of 9/11, as Hitchens noted in the preface to the second version of his book. Hitchens, *Blood, Class and Empire: The Enduring Anglo-American Relationship*, New York: Nation Books, 2004, p. xv. Also see Toye, 'The Churchill Syndrome' and John Dumbrell, 'Winston Churchill and American Foreign Relations: John F. Kennedy to George W. Bush', *Journal of Transatlantic Studies*, 3:1, 2005, pp. 31–42.

112   *S. Vucetic*

37   Soffer describes Viereck's writings as 'Burkean Toryism' packaged for the consumption of Americans who felt alienated by the post-war expansion of liberal ideas, institutions and policies. Viereck remained popular in colleges and with general readers well into the 1970s. Reba N. Soffer, *History, Historians, and Conservatism in Britain and America: From the Great War to Thatcher and Reagan*, Oxford: Oxford University Press, 2009, p. 302.

38   The Churchill bust, as a material object in search of prominent public space, has emerged as a key battlefield in the American cultural war over the Briton's name today. Tim Stanley, 'Winston Churchill, an All-American Hero', *The Telegraph*, 31 October 2013; Amy Davidson, 'Rick Perry Meets Winston Churchill', *New Yorker*, 24 October 2011; and Srdjan Vucetic, 'What Will Obama Do with Churchill's Bust?' openDemocracy.org, 20 January 2009.

39   For one tour of this area of scholarship, see Vucetic, 'Black Banker, White Banker'.

40   Consider the 'Was Churchill a Racist? Oh Yes!' piece again. If Churchill's racism had everything to do with class-based ideological blinders, what then explains the racism of his 'progressive' rivals? See Susan Pennybacker, *From Scottsboro to Munich: Race and Political Culture in 1930s Britain*, Princeton: Princeton University Press, 2009.

41   M.J. Hostetler, 'The Enigmatic Ends of Rhetoric: Churchill's Fulton Address as Great Art and Failed Persuasion', *Quarterly Journal of Speech*, 83:4, 1997, pp. 416–28. The religious 'Tower of Babel' metaphor, referring to humanity, can also be read as a primary metaphor in the speech.

42   Reynolds, *From World War to Cold War*, pp. 257–60. Also see Spencer Warren, 'A Philosophy of International Politics', in James W. Muller (ed.), *Churchill's 'Iron Curtain' Speech Fifty Years Later*, Columbia, MO: University of Missouri Press, 1999, pp. 93–128. Also helpful is the rhetorical analysis by Henry B. Ryan, 'A New Look at Churchill's Iron Curtain Speech', *The Historical Journal*, 22, 1979, pp. 901–20.

43   Which is why some rhetoricians have chalked the speech up as 'both an artistic success and a persuasive failure' or as a 'second-level success'. Hostetler, 'The Enigmatic Ends of Rhetoric', pp. 418, 420. Assuming that the main audience was traditionally suspicious of the perfidious Albion, Churchill opted for a neutral-sounding metaphor – its Roman origins being recognizable only to a small minority of listeners – to dissect the multiple layers of sinews or tendons that unite the two nations. Harbutt, *The Iron Curtain*, p. 188. Cf. Kathleen Burk, *Britain, America, and the Sinews of War, 1914–1918*, London: Allen & Unwin, 1984.

44   For example, the Atlantic Charter rang hollow to those who heard the British prime minister declare in September 1942 that the document's principles – especially Point 3, the one about self-determination – were not really meant to apply to the 'peoples' of Africa and the Asia-Pacific. W.E.B. DuBois, *Color and Democracy: Colonies and Peace*, New York: Harcourt, Brace, 1945, p. 126.

45   If Churchill's understanding of race was inextricable from his ideas about empire, then he surely was aware of the dramatic transformations occurring around the world. In 1954 American President Eisenhower urged Churchill to give precisely a speech on colonialism, to which Churchill replied: 'I think I will stick to the old one, "The Unity of the English-speaking Peoples"'. citing his scepticism 'about universal suffrage for the Hottentots even if refined by proportional representation'; Toye, *Churchill's Empire*, p. 301.

46   Hostetler, 'The Enigmatic Ends of Rhetoric', p. 427, fn. 2.

47   It did not work. See, *inter alia*, Harbutt, *The Iron Curtain*, ch. 7; Martin Gilbert, *Churchill and America*, London: Free Press, 2005, p. 373; Robert Pilpel, *Churchill in America, 1895–1961: An Affectionate Portrait*, New York: Harcourt Brace Jovanovich, 1976, pp. 221–3; John Ramsden, 'Mr Churchill Goes to Fulton', in James W. Muller (ed.), *Churchill's 'Iron Curtain' Speech Fifty Years Later*, Columbia, MO:

The Fulton address as racial discourse   113

University of Missouri Press, 1999, pp. 15–47, at p. 37; Warren, 'A Philosophy of International Politics', pp. 97–8, 103–5; and John Lukacs, *Churchill: Visionary. Statesman. Historian*, New Haven: Yale University Press, 2002, pp. 13, 79.

48 Carole Pateman and Charles W. Mills, *Contract and Domination*, Cambridge: Polity Press, 2013 (second edition); and Mona Ozouf, 'Fraternity', in François Furet and Mona Ozouf, *A Critical Dictionary of the French Revolution*, trans. Arthur Goldhammer, Cambridge, MA: Harvard University Press, 1989, pp. 694–703.

49 These tropes, including their derivatives like fratricide and parricide, have become commonplaces in interpretations of Anglo-American history. See, for example, Kevin P. Phillips, *The Cousins' Wars: Religion, Politics, and the Triumph of Anglo-America*, New York: Basic Books, 1999.

50 Toye, *Churchill's Empire*, p. 190.

51 Like the stories of peoplehood, such patriations tend to be ethnocentric and ideological. For an overview of philosophical and methodological issues involved in such historical claims, see theses on Haitian and Iroquois 'influences' on American political development, for example. Robin Blackburn, 'Haiti, Slavery, and the Age of the Democratic Revolution', *William and Mary Quarterly*, 63:4, 2006, pp. 643–74; Donald A. Grinde, Jr, and Bruce E. Johansen, 'Sauce for the Goose: Demand and Definitions for "Proof" Regarding the Iroquois and Democracy', *William and Mary Quarterly*, 53:2, 1996, pp. 628–35.

52 Mahoney, 'Moral Principle and Realistic Judgment', in James W. Muller (ed.), *Churchill's 'Iron Curtain' Speech Fifty Years Later*, Columbia, MO: University of Missouri Press, 1999, pp. 69–81, p. 74.

53 The thesis partly relies on the mining of digital archive editions of high-circulating newspapers from 1851 onwards. Clarke, *Mr Churchill's Profession*, ch. 3.

54 'Home Rule in a Nutshell' was penned in 1911 by Jeremiah MacVeagh MP of the Nationalist Party (Ireland), and subsequently reprinted, in parts, in newspapers like *The Times*, *Manchester Guardian*, and *Daily Chronicle*. I was unable to access this document through the Churchill Archives Centre, so I rely entirely on the secondary source treatments in Clarke, *Mr Churchill's Profession*, p. 109; Paul Addison, 'Winston Churchill's Concept of "The English-Speaking Peoples"', p. 105; and Richard Toye, '"Phrases Make History Here": Churchill, Ireland and the Rhetoric of Empire', *Journal of Imperial and Commonwealth History*, 38, 2010, pp. 549–70, at p. 562.

55 John Dumbrell, *A Special Relationship: Anglo-American Relations from the Cold War to Iraq*, Basingstoke: Palgrave Macmillan, 2006, p. 11; John Charmley, *Churchill's Grand Alliance: The Anglo-American Special Relationship, 1940–57*, New York: Harcourt, 1995, p. 1.

56 Iestyn Adams, *Brothers Across the Ocean: British Foreign Policy and the Origins of the Anglo-American 'Special Relationship' 1900–1905*, London: Tauris Academic Studies, 2005; Duncan Andrew Campbell, *Unlikely Allies: Britain, America, and the Victorian Origins of the Special Relationship*, London: Hambledon Continuum, 2007; Walter Russell Mead, *God and Gold: British, America, and the Making of the Modern World*, New York: Alfred A. Knopf, 2007; and Srdjan Vucetic, 'A Racialized Peace? How Britain and America Made Their Relationship Special', *Foreign Policy Analysis*, 7:3, 2011, pp. 403–22. This minority opinion arguably goes back to Coral Bell, *The Debatable Alliance: An Essay in Anglo-American Relations*, Oxford: Oxford University Press, 1964.

57 Clarke. *Mr Churchill's Profession*, pp. 89, 97–8.

58 US, Irish, and Indian membership was always contentious in this discourse. Duncan Bell, *The Idea of Greater Britain: Empire and the Future of World Order, 1860–1900*, Princeton: Princeton University Press, 2007, p. 8.

59 James Belich, *Replenishing the Earth: The Settler Revolution and the Rise of the Angloworld*, Oxford: Oxford University Press, 2009. Cf. David Armitage, 'Greater

114 *S. Vucetic*

Britain: A Useful Category of Historical Analysis?' *American Historical Review*, 104, 1999, pp. 427–45.

60 For Belich, this revolution begins already in 1780; Belich, *Replenishing the Earth*, p. 40. The numbers cited are from ch. 2 and from John Darwin, *The Empire Project: The Rise and Fall of the British World-System, 1830–1970*, Cambridge: Cambridge University Press, 2009, pp. 41–2.

61 Belich, *Replenishing the Earth*, pp. 165–9. Violent resolution of disputes with the indigenous people also has parallels with the English conquest of Old Britain.

62 Ibid., p. 209.

63 Ibid., p. 458.

64 Ibid., ch. 16.

65 Transatlantic financial capital is a story on its own, which is said to be a key to understanding the evolution of international order. For more, consider these two 1984-vintage books: Burk, *Britain, America, and the Sinews of War* and Kees van der Pijl, *The Making of an Atlantic Ruling Class*, London: Verso, 1984.

66 Bell, *The Idea of Greater Britain*, p. 119.

67 Charmley, *Churchill's Grand Alliance*, p. 73. Churchill probably familiarized himself with Seeley's ideas at Harrow. Toye, *Churchill's Empire*, p. 18. Also: Piers Brendon, *Winston Churchill*, New York: Harper & Row, 1984, ch. 1.

68 This remained Churchill's go-to grand strategy idea until at least 1955. Lukacs, *Churchill*, p. 17. Compare with Kenneth W. Thompson, *Winston Churchill's World View: Statesmanship and Power*, Baton Rouge, LA: Louisiana State University Press, 1983.

69 Paula Hastings, 'Fellow British Subjects or Colonial "Others"? Race, Empire, and Ambivalence in Canadian Representations of India in the Early Twentieth Century', *American Review of Canadian Studies*, 38:1, 2008, pp. 3–26.

70 Belich, *Replenishing the Earth*, p. 5. Paul A. Kramer, 'Empires, Exceptions, and Anglo-Saxons: Race and Rule between the British and United States Empire, 1880–1910', *Journal of American History*, 88:4, 2002, pp. 1315–53; Srdjan Vucetic, 'The Search for Liberal Anglo-America: From Racial Supremacy to Multicultural Politics', in Peter Katzenstein (ed.), *Anglo-America: Civilizational Politics Beyond West and East*, London and New York: Routledge, 2012, pp. 120–41.

71 Whether partly or fully de-racialized, the adjective 'Anglo-Saxon' is still popular in some contexts today. Emile Chabal, 'The Rise of the Anglo-Saxon: French Perceptions of the Anglo-American World in the Long Twentieth Century', *French Politics, Culture and Society*, 30:3, 2012, pp. 1–23.

72 James, *Churchill and Empire*, p. 3. Also see ibid., pp. 259–60; Toye, *Churchill's Empire*, pp. 4, 240–1; Charmley, *Churchill's Grand Alliance*, p. 3; and Geoffrey Best, *Churchill: A Study in Greatness*, London: Penguin, 2002, p. 24.

73 The term 'Great Rapprochement' comes from the historian Bradford Perkins, who used it as a distinction from earlier Anglo-American rapprochements. Perkins. *The Great Rapprochement: England and the United States, 1895–1914*, New York: Atheneum, 1968.

74 In 1901, in his third speech in the House of Commons, Churchill argued that a war with the US would be the 'most foolish, futile and fatal of all wars'. Gilbert, *Churchill in America*, p. 45. He used the tree metaphor, too, albeit in his later writings. Addison, 'Churchill's Concept of "The English-Speaking Peoples" ', p. 105.

75 The seminal text is Stuart Anderson, *Race and Rapprochement: Anglo-Saxonism and Anglo-American Relations, 1895–1904*, Rutherford, NJ: Fairleigh Dickinson University Press, 1981. Also see Kramer, 'Empires, Exceptions, and Anglo-Saxons' and Vucetic, *The Anglosphere*, ch. 2.

76 Friedrich Meinecke, *Machiavellianism: The Doctrine of Raison d'Etat and Its Place in Modern History*, New Brunswick, NJ: Transaction Publishers, 1998 (1927), p. 432.

The Fulton address as racial discourse   115

77 Vucetic, *The Anglosphere*, pp. 51–3, 153. Expressed in the more technical language of International Relations, Anglo-Saxonism is a major reason why the 'hegemonic transition' from Pax Britannica to Pax Americana was peaceful. This makes it an outlier in the history of hegemonic transitions in the pre-nuclear era.
78 Kramer, 'Empires, Exceptions, and Anglo-Saxons', p. 1326.
79 John Sutherland, *Bestsellers: A Very Short Introduction*, Oxford: Oxford University Press, 2007, p. 13.
80 FBIS-FRB-46–054 (18 March 1946), USSR Transmitters, T4.

5 Personal diplomacy at the summit

Steve Marsh

Churchill's personal diplomacy combined indefatigable self-belief, a quest for political and strategic advantage and a commitment to peace and freedom – provided the conditions were right. Churchill was convinced that key individuals could shape positively international relations. Part of the challenge inherent in this was to understand his interlocutors. Of his WW2 experience Churchill famously divulged that 'No lover ever studied every whim of his mistress as I did those of President Roosevelt.'[1] Another part of the task was to find a stage for personal diplomacy to be effective. In the aftermath of WW2 he thus sought to resurrect the wartime meetings at the highest diplomatic level of the US, USSR and, of course, UK. These discussions could help manage East–West differences, ease Churchill's strategic concerns about what he termed Britain's 'bull's eye' status in the event of renewed war and further his determination that Britain should maintain its position at the top table of global powers.

Churchill's voluminous personal correspondence with Presidents Roosevelt and Eisenhower is testament to his investment in personal diplomacy in the interest of Anglo-American relations.[2] However, this chapter draws on archive material to examine an under-recognised contribution of his personal diplomacy, namely his development and use of regularised summitry between UK prime ministers and American presidents. In the short term he crafted an intimate style of Anglo-American summit diplomacy, encouraged detailed functional cooperation and used these fora to deliver private and public messages about Anglo-American relations within world events. In the longer term he bequeathed an expectation, style and discourse of bilateral Anglo-American summitry that pseudo-institutionalised the special relationship through its regularised performance, practice and pageantry. That he was able to do this owed much to his wartime leadership, elder statesman status and his remarkably consistent high popularity in the US.

The Churchill brand

When examining Churchill's personal diplomacy in the context of the post-WW2 Anglo-American special relationship, it needs first to be considered what imbued that diplomacy with such elite power and popular resonance on both

Personal diplomacy at the summit 117

sides of the Atlantic. The answer, at least in part, lies in 'brand Churchill', something to which Churchill consciously contributed but which also developed around him. It remains fascinatingly unpopular to criticise Churchill's beliefs and actions. Note the furore caused during the 2014 British General Election when Labour candidate Benjamin Whittingham tweeted that Churchill was 'a racist and white supremacist'. The tweet was rapidly deleted and the Labour Party both disavowed its content and issued an unreserved apology on behalf of Whittingham.[3] Yet it is quite possible to develop a historiography of Churchill far less virtuous and glowing than he himself and many others have done.[4]

In some respects one of the most amazing things about Churchill was that he survived the litany of disastrous decisions and personal controversies that ran through his life and political career long enough to deliver his 'finest hour' speech on 18 June 1940. As First Lord of the Admiralty, Churchill was a prime mover in 1915 behind the Gallipoli campaign that cost 140,000 casualties, and in 1940 he backed the disastrous invasion of Norway, which sought to prevent the country from being occupied by Nazi Germany but resulted in a German invasion and the downfall of Prime Minister Neville Chamberlain. As Chancellor of the Exchequer Churchill's Budget of 1925 infamously returned Britain to the gold standard and at a pre-war fixed rate of $4.86 to the pound. Churchill later called this the greatest mistake of his life and incurred himself a devastating critique from economist John Maynard Keynes in his *The Economic Consequences of Mr Churchill*. And then there were Churchill's beliefs in racial hierarchies and the civilisational virtues of empire, which coalesced in, for instance, controversial opposition in the 1930s to Indian independence and his denigration of Gandhi as

> a seditious Middle Temple lawyer, now posing as a fakir of a type well known in the East, striding half-naked up the steps of the Viceregal palace ... to parley on equal terms with the representative of the King–Emperor.[5]

Nor did the mantle of prime minister remove Churchill from controversy. Churchill's management of the war effort was inconsistent and even the impact of his oratory on the British people's will to fight has been questioned.[6] At the Yalta conference in 1945, critics contend that Churchill's preoccupation in saving Greece from the Soviet sphere of influence effectively sealed the fate of Eastern European countries including Poland, Hungary and Romania. And India once again embroiled Churchill in fierce criticism, this time over his perceived indifference to the 1943–4 Bengal famine that killed some three million people. In August 1944 Churchill remarked that relief would do no good because Indians 'breed like rabbits' and will outstrip any available food supply. This prompted Secretary of State for India Leo Amery to tell Churchill, 'I didn't see much difference between his outlook and Hitler's, which annoyed him no little.'[7] And once returned to office in 1951 Churchill's world view seemed to many people to be ever more inconsistent with reality. US Ambassador to Britain Walter Gifford noted in November 1951 that Churchill was considered to be

118   *S. Marsh*

'notoriously unpredictable' and 'increasingly living in the past'.[8] Not even close wartime friendships could disguise American frustration with Churchill's antiquated views. President Eisenhower and his administration felt that Churchill was 'stretching – if not outlived – his usefulness'[9] and were openly critical of his preoccupation with 'Big Three' summit meetings and his 'almost child like faith that all of the answers are to be found merely in British–American partnership'. Eisenhower even considered Churchill so governed by old prejudices and instinctive reactions that he wished he 'would turn over the leadership of the British Conservative Party to younger men'.[10]

Few would contend that Churchill was not one of the greatest orators to have ever graced the stage of international relations. Yet it is reasonable to ask what it is that made some of his speeches so memorable. Consider the Fulton speech. It is commonplace for this to be portrayed as a great success, achieving 'much of the effect Churchill desired, once the initial fuss had died down'.[11] Certainly it sparked overdue popular debate in the US about post-war Soviet intentions and American options. It also helped the British cause, especially in recasting Congressional debate about the pending Anglo-American loan from whether to bail out the British Empire to making an investment in American national security. Yet only elements of Churchill's speech struck home with positive and lasting effect. And this did not necessarily apply to what Churchill termed 'the crux of what I have travelled here to say'. It is at this point he declares:

> Neither the sure prevention of war, nor the continuous rise of world organization will be gained without what I have called the fraternal association of the English-speaking peoples. This means a special relationship between the British Commonwealth and Empire and the United States of America.[12]

However, the proposition of a 'fraternal association' sparked domestic American opposition, the Truman administration (and successive other administrations) proved leery at overt demonstrations of Anglo-American leadership and of Churchill's key metaphors it was the 'Iron Curtain' and not the 'Sinews of Peace' that underpinned the meta discourse of the Cold War. Hence it is with good reason that Hostetler asks 'Should the speech be judged for its failed main contention and the metaphors that undergirded it or for a particularly memorable metaphor mentioned only once and that two thirds of the way through the address?'[13]

Taking nothing away from the manipulation of metaphor and skilled rhetorical scaffolding, when the speech is deconstructed one might also ask, 'So what?' in the sense that it contained little that was new per se. British and American elite opinion was already hardening towards the Soviet Union as the power play in Central Europe unfolded and crisis in northern Iran deepened. Indeed, there is ample evidence to suggest that Truman knew beforehand what would be Churchill's message about the Soviet Union and his administration officials swiftly followed up with cautionary comments of their own. Equally,

Personal diplomacy at the summit 119

the metaphor of the Iron Curtain for which the speech is best known was not of Churchill's creation, originating instead in nineteenth-century theatre. Nor was he even the first to use it in the context of the post-WW2 Soviet Union; that honour fell to Nazi Minister of Propaganda Joseph Goebbels.[14] Churchill's call for Anglo-American 'fraternal association' in the face of a common enemy was also but an extension of his long-standing espousal of the virtues of Anglo-Saxonism and the English-speaking peoples. The readiness with which elements of American society interpreted his speech as a call for an Anglo-American military alliance speaks volumes to both this and his construction through his temple of peace metaphor of the UN as being virtuous but unready to uphold peace and freedom. Not even the nomenclature 'special relationship' was new. For instance, the *New York Times Herald* included the following quotation from Churchill in a news feature dating from November 1945: 'We should not abandon our special relationship with the United States and Canada about the atomic bomb and we should aid the United States to guard this weapon as a sacred trust for the maintenance of peace.'

Simply because Churchill at the time considered his Sinews of Peace speech to be the most important he had ever delivered, this was no guarantee either of impact or of perceived greatness. So why did it become so? Part of the answer lies in timing. The American people did not want to consider the prospect of renewed overseas military engagement but at the same time their confidence in continued Soviet–West cooperation was falling rapidly; a poll in February 1946 indicated only 35 per cent retained such confidence. Gallup poll data in the week following the Fulton speech throws this tension into stark contrast: 40 per cent disapproved of Churchill's speech but 71 per cent disapproved of Soviet policy towards the world. It is this unusually high flux in public opinion that offered the Fulton speech such traction. Churchill delivered it at a key moment of post-WW2 US identity formation and when tensions were being played out between internationalism and isolationism, and between the desired and perceived conditions of international politics. His Iron Curtain imagery especially helped coalesce an extant amorphous American concern about Soviet intentions.

Another part of the answer lies with the timelessness of much of the speech. Above the question was posited that, given the Fulton speech included little that was new per se, what was so special about it? Arguably the lack of 'newness' was one of its strengths, Churchill arranging the known – and cherished – in a way that led his audience along the path of his own imagination. As Isaiah Berlin once noted,

> Mr Churchill's dominant category, the single, central, organizing principle of his moral and intellectual universe, is an historical imagination so strong, so comprehensive, as to encase the whole of the present and the whole of the future in a framework of a rich and multicolored past. Such an approach is dominated by a desire – and a capacity – to find fixed moral and intellectual bearings to give shape and character, color and direction and coherence, to the stream of events.[15]

120 *S. Marsh*

At Fulton Churchill's 'othering' of the Soviet Union and association of it with war and tyranny was a model establishment of a 'we group' of virtuous Anglo-Americans and was replicable (and adjustable to new common threats) across time. References to urgency (e.g. 'Now, at this sad and breathless moment') and moral responsibility (e.g. 'with primacy in power is also joined an awe-inspiring accountability to the future') played to American manifest destiny and identity as the Beacon of Liberty. And though many Americans had qualms about Churchill's 'method of realizing our overall strategic concept',[16] the values to which he claimed joint Anglo-American inheritance were a touchstone as relevant in 1946 as they were in 1940 – or indeed as they are today. In 2011 President Obama quoted from the Fulton speech to the British Houses of Parliament: 'As Winston Churchill said, the "... Magna Carta, the Bill of Rights, Habeas Corpus, trial by jury, and English common law find their most famous expression in the American Declaration of Independence."'[17]

This leads us to the final part of the equation, the animator. What gave Churchill's speech immediate impact was not just metaphor and oratory, it was the authority imbued within and through his words. An element of this authority was structural, Churchill ensuring that Fulton would be a global platform and borrowing presidential authority from the presence of Truman – something he made fulsome reference to early in his speech. However, much more significant was 'brand Churchill'. The man who addressed Fulton was more than a man. He was an icon of Anglo-American friendship, the symbol of British bulldog spirit and an elder statesman of perceived wisdom and foresight. Churchill had been cleansed of the frailties, inconsistencies and errors inherent in his humanity by a river of historical narrative and contemporary comment that needed heroes of action and beacons of light to illuminate the grim tale of struggle, destruction and millions dead. Churchill himself contributed handsomely to this process. Blessed with an American mother and British father, his parentage conferred upon him a genetic claim to being the personification of special Anglo-American relations. His long political career also bore fruit insofar as his anti-appeasement stance in the 1930s seemingly testified to his prescience – something to which he drew much attention in his Fulton speech as a means of positioning himself as a prophet of the looming Cold War. Furthermore, Churchill was an early appreciator of the power of media within image creation. As Charmley notes, 'Churchill liked a photo opportunity before the word had been invented.'[18] Churchill cultivated an image of a man of action and of authority, frequently appearing in military uniform. He also developed instant recognisability through his headgear, large Havana cigars and flashing of his index and middle fingers in a V-sign. Perhaps not surprisingly, media developed further this larger than life image and made Churchill one of the first objects within the personalisation of politics.

When in 2002 the British public voted Churchill the most important Briton of all time, ahead of the likes of Shakespeare, Brunel, Darwin and Newton, they thus voted not for a man but for an image of a man.[19] The passage of time wove Churchill inextricably into the fabric of 'Britishness' and constructed him as an icon of Anglo-American relations. His Fulton speech became part of that myth and a touchstone of the Cold War. Churchill could not have known this when returned to office in 1951 and would probably have been amused at being 'branded'. Nevertheless, he was supremely confident of his powers of persuasion and personal standing in the US and was determined to use these to promote British interests, Anglo-American relations and an international peace that could accommodate these interests. What he most needed was a stage and for this he returned to his longstanding interest in summitry. Though unsuccessful in promoting 'Big Three' meetings with his US and Soviet counterparts, he nevertheless assiduously advocated and pursued a prestigious secondary venue of regular bilateral meetings with successive US presidents.

Developing the stage for special relations

Churchill's interest in the possibilities of summit diplomacy pre-dated WW1[20] but it was not until WW2 that there existed a logistical infrastructure capable of supporting such ambitions. Reynolds credits Churchill with introducing the term 'summit' to diplomatic lexicon and US President Barak Obama once spoke directly to the days 'when Roosevelt and Churchill could sit in a room and solve the world's problems over a glass of brandy'.[21] Churchill's conviction of the merits of personal diplomacy and of the prestige such events brought upon himself and his country could not but have been reinforced by wartime meetings of the 'Big Three'. His Fulton speech certainly called for Anglo-American 'association' and caution in the face of Soviet actions. But it also left open the prospect of dialogue. In similar vein, as leader of the political opposition in the UK, Churchill availed himself of every opportunity to push the Attlee Government towards talks 'at the highest level' with Stalin[22] and to develop similar bilateral discussions between the UK and the US. For example, on 7 December 1950 the American *Sun Journal* reported ahead of Attlee's visit to Washington to see Truman that Churchill had advised him to go, had suggested the Prime Minister make an early announcement of his visit to pre-empt any opposition lest Truman not be enthusiastic about a meeting and assured him that no attempt would be made in his absence by the Conservative Party to bring down the politically vulnerable Labour Government.[23] Even more telling of his commitment to Anglo-American summitry was his criticism of Attlee for not better using this vehicle of influence as prime minister. For example, in welcoming Attlee's report on his discussions with Truman in December 1950, Churchill opined,

> The Prime Minister spoke of the importance of renewing the series of meetings between the President and the Prime Minister which had taken place during the war and since the war. We all agree with that ... I must say it seems to me that five years is rather a long interval.[24]

Churchill, of course, got his opportunity to change this pattern of Anglo-American exchange when he led the Conservative Party to General Election victory in October 1951. The impact was almost immediate. At a personal level Churchill rated his biggest mistake during WW2 as being not going to see Truman after Roosevelt's death.[25] Shortly after his election he sought to rectify this by establishing a personal connection with the American President through a summit meeting in Washington. With US Ambassador to Britain Walter Gifford warning that Anglo-American prestige with one another had fallen ominously low,[26] and Director of the Policy Planning Staff Paul Nitze feeling that the special relationship 'has not worked at all well with Mr Morrison',[27] Churchill got his wish. In January 1952 Churchill and Truman met for Anglo-American discussions about world events. Churchill was in Washington from 5 to 10 January, and again from 16 to 19 January following a trip to Canada. For both sides this was an opportunity to improve 'the tone' of the Anglo-American relationship,[28] but for Churchill it was also a vehicle by which to 'strengthen and re-emphasize the partnership between the United States and the United Kingdom in world affairs'.[29]

This meeting in Washington was highly significant in terms of precedent-setting. Whereas Attlee's only parley at the summit with Truman had been a hurried affair and seemingly occasioned by rumours Truman might use the atomic bomb in Korea, Churchill's was a carefully planned and well-publicised set piece of international diplomacy. This was the stage for personal diplomacy that Churchill craved – and one that he was determined would be crafted to demonstrate that the UK was in a category of US ally different to all others. For instance, prior to the January 1952 summit he resolutely emphasised that 'It would not be worthwhile going unless we were "*à deux*".'[30] Churchill was also determined that bilateral Anglo-American summits would be a recurring feature in the special relationship. Not long after the Eisenhower administration came to office Churchill pushed his wartime friend for another Anglo-American summit meeting. Eisenhower, live to Churchill's motives and concerned to avoid impressions of Anglo-American condominium, insisted the French be invited.[31] Churchill resented French inclusion but within this temporary setback worked to ensure plenty of opportunity for bilateral Anglo-American talks. Thwarted in his aspiration for such a summit in summer 1953 by the stroke that he suffered on 23 June 1953, Churchill hosted a trilateral UK–US–France summit in Bermuda, 4–7 December 1953. Again his emphasis on informal and intimate talks was marked. On 12 November 1953 Churchill assured Eisenhower that 'I share your hope that we shall not spend all our time on parade.... The barbed wire to protect us from the assassin or the journalists still stands as it was.'[32] And at the summit itself Churchill secured plentiful personal time with Eisenhower. For instance, on 4 December he and Eisenhower met alone for a *tour d'horizon*, covering topics such as Korea, Egypt, the EDC, China trade and a possible summit with the Soviets. The following day he again met Eisenhower informally from 11.30 until 12.45, this time accompanied only by Lord Cherwell and Admiral Strauss to discuss atomic energy matters.

Not that this satisfied Churchill. As he later told Eisenhower, in his view of international meetings: 'Two is company; three is hard company; four is a deadlock.'[33]

Personal diplomacy at the summit   123

By the spring of 1954 he was again pushing Eisenhower for another summit. And this time he secured a strictly bilateral Anglo-American affair in Washington, the summit spanning 25–29 June 1954. What Churchill was beginning to establish was a pattern of summitry that would help pseudo-institutionalise the special relationship. Attlee had just one summit meeting with Truman. Churchill secured three summits within three years with American presidents. Once he was forced into retirement, his successors continued his precedent. Eden visited Eisenhower in Washington from 30 January to 3 February 1956. Then, following the Suez crisis, Anglo-American summits proved central to rebuilding the special relationship. Macmillan met Eisenhower for bilateral summits in Washington in October 1957, June 1958, March 1959, March 1960 and October 1960. They also met bilaterally in Bermuda in March 1957 and during Eisenhower's visit to the UK in the summer of 1959.

It might conceivably be argued that American willingness during the 1950s to engage in ever more regular summits with British prime ministers owed less to Churchill than to realpolitik calculations of Britain being the US's most important ally, to legacies of wartime friendships and to international meetings becoming easier to conduct owing to improvements in transport and communications. However, this would understate Churchill's legacy. Consider the 1960s. This decade has widely been seen as a watershed in Anglo-American relations. It marked the period in which wartime friendships no longer impacted either prime minister–president relations or high-level Anglo-American diplomats. It was also an era in which British relative decline became increasingly obvious, being evidenced in successive sterling crises, rapid decolonisation and defence retrenchment.[34] Meantime West Germany began to gather strength, de Gaulle's France topped US concern within the Atlantic Alliance and the European Economic Community became an important economic concern. Furthermore, international relations were becoming multilateralised, with the EEC, GATT and the United Nations all acquiring far greater significance.

Cast against this background one might expect bilateral Anglo-American summits to decline in regularity. Yet this was not the case. Macmillan visited Kennedy frequently. On 26 March 1961 they met in Key West for an impromptu discussion of events in Laos. Macmillan subsequently visited Kennedy for bilateral talks in Washington in April 1961 and April 1962. Conversely, Kennedy was a president who travelled. He met Macmillan in London in June 1961 and again in December that year in Bermuda. In December 1962 Kennedy and Macmillan met for the Nassau summit, which subsequently became (in)famous for the Polaris deal that kept Britain in the nuclear deterrence business following the cancellation of Skybolt. And in June 1963 Kennedy also paid Macmillan a visit at Birch Grove during his European tour, an important gesture to a prime minister then politically beleaguered by the Profumo scandal.

How is this to be explained? In part it was indeed because easier international travel and the growth of multilateralism served to supplement rather than challenge bilateral Anglo-American summits. UK prime ministers and US presidents, together with other high-level Anglo-American officials, met regularly in

124   *S. Marsh*

venues such as international peace conferences and in the wings of the United Nations. For instance, in July 1955 Eden met Eisenhower in Geneva at a summit conference with French premier Faure and Soviet premier Bulganin. Macmillan similarly met Eisenhower on 27 September 1960 in New York City while attending a UN General Assembly session. Crucially, these meetings not only maintained personal connections between Anglo-American officials but they also became important elements of bilateral summit meetings, contributing to their planning, review and follow-up. And collectively they contributed to the development of a unique Anglo-American diplomacy as diplomatic methods responded to the challenges and opportunities of globalisation.[35]

A second part of the explanation speaks even more directly to Churchill's legacy in establishing a pattern of bilateral Anglo-American summitry. Unlike Kennedy, President Johnson was not a regular international traveller, his only meetings abroad with West European leaders being on the occasions of Chancellor Adenauer's funeral in April 1967 and a brief stopover in Italy while returning from a rare tour of the Far East in December 1967. This meant a regular flow of international visitors to see Johnson in Washington, among whom were British Prime Ministers Douglas-Home and Wilson. The former had a summit with Johnson in December 1964; the latter met with him four times: December 1965, July 1966, June 1967 and February 1968. One might assume from this that Johnson was as enamoured of meeting his British counterpart as, for instance, Kennedy was. Assuredly, this was not always the case. On one occasion Johnson professed he would 'get sick and leave town' if that would prevent Wilson visiting, and another time he allegedly exploded upon hearing that Wilson wanted to visit: 'we got enough pollution over here without Harold coming over with his fly open and his pecker hanging out, peeing all over me'.[36] Yet still Wilson came. What had happened was that a pattern and expectation of Anglo-American summits had become so strong that it was politically difficult even for US presidents to decline them.

Establishing the form of special relations at the summit

Churchill's success in developing a practice of Anglo-American summits at the highest level was not, in and of itself, the sum of his ambition. After all, he was well aware that US leaders – and indeed those of the UK – would meet bilaterally and multilaterally with a host of other nations and organisations. The primary objective was for Britain to influence the US as 'a partner from the inside',[37] which meant that for Churchill's personal diplomacy to be most effective, Anglo-American summits needed an atmosphere different to those of other regular head of state meetings. To this end he had some inherent assets, a primary one being a shared language. This meant less scope for misunderstanding, capacity for discussions to cover a wider range and depth of issues in less time, and greater ease of exchange and relationship-building.

The consequent task was to craft the format of Anglo-American summits in such a way that maximised the potential for personal relationships to impact

Personal diplomacy at the summit 125

interpretation of international affairs and influence policy choices. Churchill, supremely confident of his own diplomatic prowess, had clear ideas of how to go about this. First, there needed to be as much opportunity as possible for prime minister–president talks alone. Second, provided the specialist knowledge were available for the topics at hand, the fewer officials present at working discussions the better in terms both of creating an intimate atmosphere for diplomatic exchange and of reducing the 'protective shield' erected around the president by the American professional foreign and defence bureaucracy. Third, talks should be as fluidly organised as possible to maximise the scope of personal discussions and, more strategically, to limit the ability of the US State Department especially to hold the president to predetermined positions. It is telling of these objectives that Secretary of State Acheson came to regard summitry as a 'dangerous diplomatic method'. In his view the participants were frequently ill prepared and unreliable, the process consequently 'nerve-racking' and results often 'unsatisfactory'. Even more importantly, and this was evidently Churchill's ambition given his supreme self-confidence in negotiation, 'When a chief of state or head of government makes a fumble, the goal line is open behind him.'[38]

To illustrate these points it is worth reviewing preparations for Churchill's summit with Truman in January 1952. Churchill desired opportunity to establish and develop personal relations with key American officials. As he told Truman, 'we should reach a good understanding of each other's point of view over the whole field, so that we can work together easily and intimately at the different levels as we used to do'.[39] This meant that in addition to Truman, Churchill was keen to speak to General Marshall, who 'is a link with so many',[40] and to Defence Secretary Lovett, whose acquaintance he had not yet made.[41] And the way that he desired to do this was through 'a few informal meetings or meals'.[42] This commitment to intimate 'chats' was demonstrated by his scorn of a proposed arrangement whereby he would meet Lovett accompanied by three Secretaries of the Army, Navy and Air Force, Acheson, Matthews, Gifford, General Bradley and the three Joint Chiefs of Staff:[43] 'I do not see,' he fulminated, 'how a parade of this character would give an opportunity for an "undisturbed informal talk".'[44]

A revealing battle also developed over arranging the summit meeting. US officials were live to what in December 1951 the Acting Secretary of State termed Churchill's 'idiosyncrasies concerning personal diplomacy and aversion to agenda talks'.[45] Sure enough Churchill advocated a free-ranging meeting and resisted approving a British agenda.[46] This sparked transatlantic exchanges that are interesting on several levels. Truman administration officials pressed their British counterparts for an agenda for the conference.[47] British Foreign Office officials were receptive but ran up against Churchill. The Foreign Office pushed the Prime Minister to provide the requested information. 'Truman is not,' officials cautioned, 'Mr Roosevelt, and his method of working is different.'[48] Still Churchill refused to yield. Not until Truman intervened personally in late December 1951 did the Prime Minister finally relent.[49]

These exchanges demonstrate again Churchill's commitment to informal talks and his aspiration especially that he could influence personally President

126   *S. Marsh*

Truman. Just as interestingly, the pre-summit approach of the US State Department suggests that American officials also worried that Churchill's personal diplomacy might blow the President off course. It was considered vitally important for American interests that any attempt by Churchill to overly personalise Anglo-American relations at the Washington conference be resisted firmly.[50] So anxious did American officials become about arrangements for the summit that Jock Colville of the British Private Office characterised their preparation for the conference thus: 'The White House and the State Department clutched their life-belts and prepared to repel boarders.'[51]

Churchill could not re-create with Truman the type of unscripted *tour d'horizon* talks he had enjoyed during WW2 with Roosevelt. Nevertheless, he did set a tone and style for subsequent summits that would maximise British ability to penetrate through personal diplomacy the shield erected around the President by the increasingly professional post-WW2 American foreign policy bureaucracy. For example, writing to Eisenhower shortly before the June 1954 summit meeting Churchill purred his delight at the prospect laid out thus by the President:

> I think we shall use luncheon and dinner periods for small business meetings except for Friday night, when I thought a very few members of the Cabinet and their wives should come in to meet you and Anthony. At Saturday's luncheon I shall hope to bring in a few of our top legislative people to meet you for an hour or so. None of this will be formal.[52]

Subsequent British prime ministers did all possible to follow this style, knowing it to be the best way to influence American policy from the inside.

One element of this British commitment, *à la* Churchill, was strong pressure to ensure the scheduling of social and working opportunities for the Prime Minister to be *à deux* with the President. Another was an emphasis on the form and atmosphere of summits. Britain's prime objective for the 1952 Washington talks was to improve 'the tone' of the Anglo-American relationship and to re-emphasise the intimacy of US–UK relations.[53] Likewise the Americans were anxious that 'Mr Churchill should return home in good mood'.[54] Particularly interesting, though, is that for the British especially the exchanging of views and discussions of common concern and interest were often as important as summit outcomes, if not more so. Consider perceived outcomes of the 1952 summit. US Secretary of State Acheson observed that 'Little was accomplished by way of final agreement beyond ending our differences over the Atlantic Command.' Danchev has since colourfully concluded in similar vein that 'almost no work was done other than the arduous business of socializing without adequate supplies of alcohol'.[55] Yet British officials were nigh jubilant. British Ambassador to Washington Sir Oliver Franks felt that the relationship had been 'reaffirmed and strengthened' and foresaw 'closer partnership and renewed personal trust'.[56] Lord Ismay optimistically hailed it as the most successful international conference he had ever known.[57]

Personal diplomacy at the summit   127

In December 1961 Harold Macmillan epitomised this element of the British approach to Anglo-American summits when in the aftermath of their Bermuda meeting he wrote to Kennedy:

> I hope you found the talks as helpful as I did. Their value lies not so much in the reaching of precise agreements as in the sense of understanding each other and discussing in an absolutely free and open way the problems with which we are faced.[58]

Were the Americans unaware of what this Churchillian personal diplomacy was directed towards? Of course not. McGeorge Bundy, Special Assistant to the President for National Security, specifically advised Kennedy prior to the 1961 Bermuda summit that

> The Prime Minister's main purpose is to keep you his best friend. His second purpose is to use your friendship to keep the US on his side of a number of issues on which otherwise we might be 'sticky' – as an element of this he hopes to keep the friendship with you as a defense against some of the cold, hard things McNamara tells Watkinson, or Ball tells Heath, or Seaborg tells Penny.[59]

Yet this awareness mattered little, for the reality was that these summit meetings contributed handsomely to developing the practice of intimate talks and frank exchanges between allies with similar objectives and shared heritage that over time became the norm and set their relations apart from those with any other ally. Former US Secretary of State Henry Kissinger summed matters up neatly in 1982:

> The ease and informality of the Anglo-American partnership has been a source of wonder – and no little resentment – to third countries.... The British were so matter-of-factly helpful that they became a participant in internal American deliberations, to a degree probably never before practiced between sovereign nations.[60]

Exercising 'brand Churchill': private diplomacy of 'specialness'

The final set of contributions considered here that Churchill's personal diplomacy at summits made to the special relationship lie in his message-sending, public and private. Churchill was not so lost in Britain's Elizabethan splendour that he did not appreciate either how much damage WW2 had wreaked upon Britain's wealth and capabilities or how the war had propelled the US especially to superpower status. The new asymmetry in Anglo-American relations was personally painful and professionally problematic. Journeying aboard the *Queen Mary* to meet with Truman in January 1952, Churchill lamented privately that

'They [the Americans] have become so great and we are now so small. Poor England!'[61] A root cause of these problems was Britain's economic travails, complicated further by the Korean War and strains of rearmament. Foreign Secretary Anthony Eden told the Cabinet in January 1952 that 'he had returned from North America with a renewed conviction of our need to do everything possible to re-establish our economic and financial independence'.[62] However, to Churchill's mind, that matters were so testing owed heavily to the Labour Government having allowed Britain's power, prestige and status to slip away. The jewel in the imperial crown, India, had gained independence, many other British overseas interests, such as the vitally important Anglo-Iranian Oil Company's monopoly in Iran, were under nationalist challenge, and the Anglo-American relationship had been neglected to the detriment of both its intimacy and substance.

Churchill brought to office a conviction that an effective Anglo-American relationship demanded that it be a partnership. In 1940 during negotiations on what became the Destroyers for Bases deal, he had argued: 'It doesn't do to give way like this to the Americans. One must strike a balance with them.'[63] Returned to power in autumn 1951 Churchill was determined to underscore to American and British officials that the US ought not to be able to take British support for granted or expect non-reciprocal support of national interests. Summits afforded him excellent opportunities to do so. Consider in this respect Anglo-American exchanges at the Bermuda Summit in December 1953. President Eisenhower recorded that

> Winston had much to say about the need for Washington and London to coordinate and crystallise their views whenever they had common interests in any spot in the globe ... and then present a solid front, bordering, as I understood it, almost on an ultimatum to the third party in the dispute.[64]

While Eisenhower predictably demurred, believing 'it would be too much like writing a blank check to make such an agreement in advance of knowledge of the details of the proposals', Churchill nevertheless made inroads towards his goal of Anglo-American partnership and the free and frank exchange of views therein. Secretary of State Dulles recorded that 'The Prime Minister spoke of the feeling that the UK could not differ with the US, without this creating a sense of animosity.' Eisenhower delivered the expected reassurance, stating that 'there was no sense of animosity as far as our government was concerned; that we felt strongly there could be differences which each side respected'.[65] Still more importantly, Eisenhower privately assured Churchill that 'he deprecated any such idea' and suggested that during one of the Bermuda bilateral meetings 'he and I take the occasion to tell our staffs, jointly, that we expected between them the freest and fullest kind of discussion and argument, even in those cases where they found it impossible to reach an agreement'.[66]

Complementing the affirmation of the language and diplomacy of partnership, Churchill also sent notice both of British willingness to stand firm in the face of American pressure and of dire consequences in the event that the US undercut

Personal diplomacy at the summit 129

established British positions. In regard to the former, for instance, Dulles reported at a US Cabinet meeting that during the Bermuda Summit in December 1953 Churchill especially continued the long-running Anglo-American differences over colonialism.[67] As for the latter, Churchill followed up differences at Bermuda over Egypt with a personal letter to Eisenhower on 19 December 1953 in which he warned that an American loan to Egypt during that time's Anglo-Egyptian dispute

> would, I am sure, have very grave effect in this country on Anglo-American relations ... offended Conservatives might add their voices to that section of the Socialist Party who criticise the United States. In fact I think there would be a considerable out-pouring which of course would be used in America by all who are hostile to the unity of action of the English-speaking world.[68]

Neither were these type of exchanges confined to Churchill's relationship with Eisenhower's Republican administration. At the January 1952 summit Churchill pressed Truman for a closer Anglo-American identification of interests[69] and burden-sharing arrangements.[70] He was particularly forceful in the context of the Middle East. Churchill told US officials that Britain would not have been kicked out of Abadan had he been in power, even if that had meant a 'splutter of musketry', and condemned the lack of American support at the time of British expulsion and their subsequent weakness in the face of Iranian Prime Minister Mosaddegh's impossible conduct. He further observed that British problems in Egypt, where stalled talks over the future of Britain's huge Suez base had led the Egyptian government to demand that all British troops be evacuated, were a 'bastard child of the Iranian situation'[71] and that a combined Anglo-American position would 'divide our difficulties by ten'.[72] He even pressed for a US brigade to help protect the Suez Canal.[73] The latter caused such Congressional furore that Secretary of State Acheson needed to make a public assurance that the US had made no pledges at the summit to the British concerning the Suez base. And on the oil crisis Acheson gave Foreign Secretary Eden such a 'beating' over Iran[74] that their exchanges have been described as 'probably as personal and bitter as any between Eden and Dulles'.[75] For Churchill at least, though, all of this was a price well worth paying to send the Truman administration a message of British resolution and expectation of treatment as a partner rather than supplicant.

Indeed, in his determination to impress upon all concerned the importance of Britain acting and being treated like a partner, Churchill was prepared to run significant political risks and endure criticism from his own officials as well as from those 'across the pond'. Perhaps the best example of this in his post-war summits came in 1952 over the powers and nationality of the Supreme Allied Commander Atlantic (SACLANT). The British and the Americans had agreed in principle on a single Atlantic command with an American as SACLANT at the October 1950 NATO Council meeting. Subsequent detailed discussion of SACLANT's terms of reference culminated in a further agreement by the end of

February 1951, albeit some issues such as the relationship between the British Home Station and north-eastern sub-area Atlantic command (EASTLANT) had not been determined. In addition, US Admiral William M. Fechteler became SACLANT designate and the terms of reference gradually moved to the NATO Council for ratification. However, once details of SACLANT leaked into the Danish media in February 1951, Churchill immediately led the charge against the plan, using the issue in April 1951 as part of a failed attempt to bring down the Attlee Government and entwining SACLANT with domestic British politics and the pride and the prestige of the Royal Navy.

Churchill viewed the emaciation of the once-great Royal Navy as epitomising Britain's woes and, having twice served as First Lord of the Admiralty, he was ideally placed to lead a rearguard action in its defence, which he duly did at the 1952 summit. Against the advice of British officials Churchill instructed his Chiefs of Staff to argue the case to 'Abolish the Supreme Commander'.[76] Constructive talks between Anglo-American Chiefs of Staff on Sunday 6 January 1952 delivered a series of important US operational concessions. The following day Churchill was urged at a meeting with his officials to accept the American offer. He refused and later that afternoon in the second plenary meeting of the summit laid out to Truman a series of objections to SACLANT, which prompted a 'very heated discussion' and deadlock.[77] On 8 January, in a restricted session called by Truman prior to the fourth formal meeting, the SACLANT debate was rejoined. Churchill duly sat through a further American rehearsal of why SACLANT had been agreed before again refusing to accede to the plan. The British Prime Minister then left Washington without an agreement on SACLANT for a planned mid-summit trip to Canada, where he proceeded to regale members of the Canadian government on the flaws of SACLANT and to promise to 'return to charge in Washington'.[78]

By this time it was fairly clear to the Americans that Churchill was virtually alone within the British negotiating party in holding out against SACLANT.[79] Still, though, he appeared incapable of persuasion. On 18 January Churchill locked horns with the Pentagon, a meeting unproductive other than to put the Prime Minister in a foul mood; Acheson commented that 'things did not look in very good shape by the time we assembled in the afternoon'.[80] Furthermore, for this final plenary session American and British military staffs had drawn up a communiqué that effectively ratified SACLANT. When it was given to Churchill just prior to the meeting he simply tore the document up and cast it into the air.[81]

It is thus highly surprising when cast against this backdrop that in the final plenary session Churchill did accept the principle of SACLANT, although his decision was wrapped up in facing-saving rhetoric of the US government refusing to release him from agreements made by Attlee's government and a caveat allowing him to re-raise the issue at NATO if he so chose. Why he conceded owed primarily to his ultimate objective of improving the tone and restoring the quality of Anglo-American relations. More interesting for the purposes of this chapter is why, and how, he held out as long as he did. On the latter it is clear

Personal diplomacy at the summit   131

that it was Churchill's prestige and status that facilitated actions that if undertaken by another leader might have caused serious harm to Anglo-American relations. Indeed, Lord Moran recorded explicitly, of a heated intra-British meeting on 7 January, that

> The CIGS [Slim], the First Sea Lord [McGrigor] and Pug Ismay [Secretary of State for Commonwealth Affairs] in turn urged him to accept the plan.... They were particularly anxious to avoid putting up the back of the American Navy, which had taken criticism from the PM in the most generous spirit, just because it was Mr. Churchill.[82]

As to why Churchill held out so long there was undoubtedly an emotional dimension in his attachment to the prestige of the Royal Navy. There were domestic political calculations stemming from his public opposition to SACLANT. And Churchill no doubt did favour an Anglo-American naval condominium reminiscent of the recent wartime arrangements. However, the records also reveal a determination to use the issue to send messages, especially given Churchill's private admission prior to the second plenary on 7 January that: 'There is deadlock over the Atlantic Command. I may have to submit. I might have to say to the Americans: "I am sorry you will not release me from the agreement with the Labour Government."'[83]

The first element of Churchill's message-sending strategy appears to have been the instilling of 'backbone' into British officials in their dealings with American counterparts. He was convinced that the previous administration had given way too much and too often to the Americans, and that British officials and military staff had fallen into a dangerous pattern of obeisance because of a lack of robust political leadership. This sentiment was evident in his regaling of the British Chiefs to negotiate concessions on SACLANT beyond what they thought professionally necessary. It is reflected too in Churchill's observation on 7 January 1952 that 'for five years these officers [McGrigor *et al.*] have had no lead. They have got into the way of agreeing to anything.'[84] The second message-sending element of Churchill's SACLANT strategy was to underscore that the Americans should not automatically expect British acquiescence; rather, they should treat Britain as an equal partner. Interestingly he made this case direct to the Americans and indirectly through his discussions with Canadian officials. For instance, Canadian Minister of External Affairs Lester Pearson advised Acheson that Churchill was more than willing to accept American leadership and to lend them Britain's support, but 'he is determined that this support shall be from a country which has its own strong and free voice in the collective counsels and of a kind that deserves the respect of its partners'.[85] Similarly revealing were phrases Churchill deployed at the summit meeting in an emotional defence of his position in the restricted session prior to the fourth formal meeting. After acceding to Truman's request to hear another exposition of the case for SACLANT Churchill lamented, 'the United Kingdom had lost much of its former power' whereas 'the United States had atomic power,

132   *S. Marsh*

productive power *et cetera* ... British life depended on the sea ... the British had earned equality with British blood. He said that was all the British wanted – equality, not primacy.'[86]

Exercising 'brand Churchill': public diplomacy of 'specialness'

Churchill's public diplomacy in promoting Anglo-American relations reflected both sentiment and interest. His personal belief in, and representation of, Anglo-Americana meant it was natural for him to promote publicly on both sides of the Atlantic the closest possible relations between Britain and the US. Sentimental and cultural affiliation with a special relationship needed nurturing. For example, when WW2 brought large numbers of American servicemen to Britain the government made substantial efforts to combat popular resentment at their presence – summed up in the slogan 'overpaid, oversexed and over here'. Similarly, every US serviceman was given an instruction manual about the UK to ease their integration. These efforts needed to be continued in peacetime, along with the intensified cross-cultural penetration afforded by exchange schemes, music, literature, cinema, art and so forth.

Popular support for a special relationship would help government functional objectives and, for the British people who were being pressed to make ever greater sacrifices to rearmament, it would encourage a sense of equality and world purpose even as the mantle of global leadership fell increasingly across the Atlantic. Meantime internationally, Churchill was well aware that public declarations and evidence of close Anglo-American partnership were vitally important in maintaining the impression that Britain remained at the top table of international powers. They were also key to deterring challenges to British overseas interests. Third-party expectation of American support for Britain potentially offset, or at least delayed, some of the problems caused to British interests by imperial overstretch.

Churchill was supremely confident that he could use his image and reputation to advance British interests in the US. Prior to the arranging of his speech at Fulton he had confided to Lord Moran that in travelling to America to impart his thoughts, 'I think I can be of some use over there; they will take things from me.'[87] When he returned as prime minister that confidence was undimmed. Yet while Churchill undoubtedly held himself in high esteem, how he used his stature for public diplomacy was strategic rather than arrogant. In this respect Dean Acheson insightfully dissected Churchill's cultivation of personality. Of Churchill's oration he wrote: 'His speeches were not only right and wise in content but were prepared with that infinite capacity for taking pains that is said to be genius. He used it to clothe the bedrock of sense and necessity with romanticism.' This was complemented by great attention to style: 'Everything felt the touch of his art – his appearance and gestures, the siren suit, the indomitable sign V for victory, the cigar for imperturbability.' And then there was his formidable command in debate: 'He used all the artifices to get his way, from wooing and cajolery through powerful advocacy to bluff bullying.'[88]

Personal diplomacy at the summit 133

Acheson's comments were actually made in the context of Churchill's wartime conduct but they applied with equal force to his performance as peacetime prime minister. Consider again his opposition to SACLANT, discussed above. At one moment Churchill engaged in detailed discussion of naval strategy, convoying and hunter–killer submarines. At another, he dramatically ripped up a proposed settlement. And at another he made a sorrowful plea for due American consideration: 'It was a great blow, he said, to the United Kingdom when it was told not only that it would not have the command but that it would not even have an equal voice.'[89]

It is also worth examining instances of his public performance to different audiences, of the special relationship to understand how he connected his personality with the conveying of messages about partnership, closeness and identity of purpose within contemporary Anglo-American relations. The first example comes from a luncheon for Churchill and Foreign Secretary Eden provided under the auspices of the Joint Committee of Press, Radio and Television correspondents and photographers on 28 June 1954. First he established his personal credentials. In terms of his genealogical inheritance within Anglo-American kinship Churchill drew attention to his grandfather being one of the 'principal proprietors during your civil war' of the *New York Times*. He made a tongue-in-cheek self-deprecating plea for media sympathy: 'I am sure you will consider that you must be generous, as you always are, and tender-hearted to an aged guest.' And he followed this up by underscoring his statesmanship and prescience in international relations. To this end he cited his early opposition to Russian communism: 'If I had been properly supported in 1919, I think we might have strangled Bolshevism in its cradle, but everybody turned up their hands and said "How shocking."' Poignantly he also drew attention to his Iron Curtain speech: 'I even remember making a speech at Fulton six years ago, which didn't get a very warm welcome in the United States, because it was so anti-Russian and anti-Communist.'

Churchill then moved on to the importance of regular and intimate Anglo-American consultation and cooperation. Here he invoked the wisdom of Bismarck in underscoring their unique advantage. As he inquired of his audience,

> What is the good of speaking one language if you can't put your differences to each other plainly.... One language is the biggest thing there is. As Bismarck said: 'The greatest event of the nineteenth century was the United States was found definitely to speak only' – may I say it – 'the English language.'

He also presented UK–US cooperation as a force for good in the world. Reminiscent of his advice to President Truman in January 1952 that an Anglo-American common position over the Iranian crisis would in the Middle East 'divide our difficulties by ten',[90] he told the assembled journalists that 'I am quite certain that half the evils in the world can be prevented by our going hand-in-hand together and, if necessary, shoulder to shoulder.' As for the Soviet

Union any dialogue, which he personally favoured at an appropriate moment, should be undergirded by 'exercising the strongest vigilance, and making it clear, as we are doing even now here in this building, the unbreakable unity of the English-speaking world of Britain and the United States in all these affairs.'

Finally Churchill sought to cast extant Anglo-American relations in a warm glow. Here he engaged in what would become a familiar rhetoric of special relations. He entwined the present with a shared Anglo-American past and unique wartime experience. He emphasised intimate and tested friendship at both the personal and state-to-state levels. And he exuded confidence that Britain and America would continue to move forward shoulder to shoulder. All of this is exemplified in the following passage from his press engagement:

> I have been over here in the war, since the war, and before the war in important government missions a good many times. I never have found a more friendly, tolerant atmosphere and, as for my relations with your President, they have lasted 12 years, through war and peace, and never have I felt them more high and comforting than at the present time. I feel that I have a strong personal friend with whom I can discuss matters absolutely on the dead level.[91]

On 17 January 1952 Churchill addressed a very different audience – a joint session of the US Congress. His short opening immediately positioned himself in a unique category of friend of America and again invoked the spirit of wartime cooperation. Noting that this was his third address to a joint session of Congress he observed: 'I am honoured indeed by these experiences, which I believe are unique for one who is not an American.' This was followed immediately with a rhetorical connectivity between past and present: 'It is also of great value to me ... to come over here and take counsel with many trusted friends and comrades of former anxious days.' And shortly afterwards, just as in the example above, he cited his own Fulton speech, this time in evidence of British resolve and the potential decisiveness of Anglo-American cooperation. The particular passage selected, how his introduction to it appropriated presidential authority and his subsequent reaffirmation of it are all instructive of Churchill's fusion of his personality with Anglo-American relations and of how he wove past, present and future into a beguiling logic underpinning a sense of natural 'specialness':

> As I said at Fulton in Missouri six years ago, under the auspices of President Truman:
>
> 'Let no man underrate the abiding power of the British Commonwealth and Empire. Do not suppose that we shall not come through these dark years of privation as we came through the glorious years of agony, or that half a century from now you will not see 70 or 80 millions of Britons spread about the world and united in defence of our traditions, our way of life, and of the world causes which you and we espouse. If the population of the English-speaking Commonwealth be added to that of the United States with all that

Personal diplomacy at the summit   135

such cooperation implies, in the air, on the sea, and all over the globe, and in science, industry and moral force there will be no quivering precarious balance of power to offer its temptation to ambition or adventure.'

I am very glad to be able to say the same to you here to-day.

The principal thrust of the presentation to Congress, though, was different to that made two years later to the media. It was more functionally orientated, designed both to emphasise Britain's value, and right to be treated, as a special ally, and to make a case for Anglo-American burden-sharing. The context was, of course difficult. Churchill had returned to power amid declining British prestige, growing evidence of imperial overstretch and economic problems of such magnitude that Deputy Under-Secretary of State for Foreign Affairs Roger Makins deemed Britain to be 'back in the breadline for the third time in six years'.[92] Speculation in the American press and elements of Congress was that Churchill had come to America to ask for financial aid. Interestingly, the *New York Times* picked up on British angst at this impression, and reported it in a style typical of a personalisation of politics associated with Churchill and Anglo-American relations – even using the Prime Minister's hat as a metaphor: 'Britain's feelings were emphasized when, after it was announced that Mr. Churchill would visit Washington, the British press pointedly reminded the US that Mr Churchill was coming with his hat on his head – "not in his hand".'[93]

Churchill's task was to secure American aid without appearing supplicant, and to draw greater US security contributions without it appearing that events in places like Iran and Egypt meant that 'the British Empire is in liquidation'.[94] To this end he spoke to the shifting context requiring new assessments of responsibility for Western defence, his principal focus being the Suez Canal which he argued was, as a consequence of Indian independence especially, an international rather than solely British responsibility. More generally, he painted a picture of a recovering Britain in need of assistance not so much for domestic welfare as for the common Anglo-American interest in rearmament. First he offered evidence of recovery and Britain's relative importance. British exports, he informed, had risen by two-thirds, British production was half as great again as before the war and Britain contributed to rearmament two-thirds of the rest of Europe combined. This was complemented by an invocation of the wartime spirit and conjuring of an image of a stoic British population determined to make whatever sacrifices were necessary to return Britain to greatness:

> I have not come here to ask you for money to make our life more comfortable or easier for us in Britain. Our standards of life are our business, and we can only keep our self-respect and independence by looking after them ourselves.

This Churchillian 'Declaration of Independence' was then swiftly followed by a reminder to Congress of Britain's previous sacrifice: 'During the war we bore our share of the burden and fought from first to last unconquered, and for a while alone, to the utmost limit of our resources.' Finally Churchill re-cast American aid as a shared Anglo-American commitment to defeat communism: 'I have come here to ask not for gold but for steel, not for favours but for equipment.' Not everyone was convinced. Chairman of the Joint Committee on Atomic Energy McMahon noted prior to the talks:

> Mr Churchill says publicly that he is not coming over here to seek American funds. This is, of course, nonsense – he has no choice but to solicit more money, and we have little choice except to give it to him.[95]

Nevertheless the general reception to the speech was such that British officials deemed Churchill's Congressional address 'very much of a personal triumph'.[96]

Conclusion

Churchill's use of summitry is an underrated feature of the personal diplomacy he developed in the management of Anglo-American relations. It is also an important part of his legacy for the special relationship. It was Churchill who first established the style, regularity and performance of Anglo-American summitry that runs through to the present day. Attlee had but one summit with Truman, and that was pushed by Churchill and prompted by an immediate fear of American use of the atomic bomb in Korea. Churchill was in Washington for a summit within three months of his return to office. He might not always have been successful in particular objectives, such as his pitch for an American brigade to be deployed to Suez, but the simple fact of his presence drew attention to the closeness of Anglo-American cooperation and accorded him a repeated platform from which to preach the gospel of the special relationship and the English-speaking peoples.

Similarly it was Churchill who set the mould whereby British officials would seek to guide 'the unwieldy barge'[97] that was America from within the consuls of Washington especially, but also New York and other centres of international organisation. In Britain's much reduced relative post-war position, consanguinity rather than the exercise of power was the British approach. This was never more the case than in the cultivation of close personal relations between leading officials and within the key transatlantic epistemic communities that evolved as the special relationship developed. And the pinnacle of this ambition was, of course, for the Prime Minister to establish and manipulate a close relationship with his American counterpart. The Americans understood this well – and where the practice originated. As McGeorge Bundy advised President Kennedy, 'Since the days of Churchill and Roosevelt this has been a basic British tactic.'[98]

Finally it is important to recognise the centrality of 'brand Churchill' in the establishment and use of summitry within Anglo-American relations. Churchill's wartime performance and epitimisation of the British bulldog spirit captured elite respect and popular imagination with such force that the past sins of his humanity were effectively washed away in the blood, struggle and triumph of WW2. The man who emerged was already, in the US especially, a symbol of

Personal diplomacy at the summit   137

Anglo-American cooperation and perceived to embody all that was thought to be good about Britain. Churchill recognised and added to this by cultivating his persona as a further vehicle of influence. His attire, distinctive V for victory sign and indomitable cigar gave him instant popular recognition. He enthralled the media in a way rarely, if ever, seen before, thereby giving him tremendous communication opportunities and generally sympathetic reception. And, as demonstrated by his address in January 1952 to Congress and the US Navy's tolerance of his SACLANT crusade, Churchill's prestige afforded him American indulgence and opportunities to promote the special relationship that were simply unavailable to any other statesman.

Notes

1 www.winstonchurchill.org/the-life-of-churchill/senior-statesman/1946–1949/3235-spring-1948-age-73.
2 Warren F. Kimball (ed.), _Churchill and Roosevelt: The Complete Correspondence_, Princeton: Princeton University Press, 1987; Peter G. Boyle (ed.), _The Churchill–Eisenhower Correspondence, 1953–1955_, North Carolina: University of North Carolina Press, 1990.
3 Unattributed, 'Labour Party candidate brands Sir Winston Churchill as "racist white supremacist"', _Evening Standard_, 22 September 2014; www.standard.co.uk/news/politics/labour-party-candidate-brands-sir-winston-churchill-as-racist-white-supremacist-9749623.html.
4 Roy Jenkins, _Churchill: A Biography_, London: Pan, 2002; Boris Johnson, _The Churchill Factor: How One Man Made History_, London: Hodder and Stoughton, 2015.
5 Cited in Frank Moraes, _Jawaharlal Nehru_, Chennai: Jaico Publishing House, 2007, p. 190.
6 Richard Toye, _The Roar of the Lion: The Untold Story of Churchill's World War II Speeches_, Oxford: Oxford University Press, 2013.
7 Cited by Arthur Herman, 'Without Churchill, India's Famine Would Have Been Worse', 13 September 2010; www.winstonchurchill.org/resources/in-the-media/churchill-in-the-news/966-without-churchill-indias-famine-would-have-been-worse.
8 _Foreign Relations of the United States (FRUS)_ 1952–4, Vol. 6, Part 1, Gifford to State Dept, 28 December 1951, pp. 720–3.
9 Robert H. Ferrell, _Eisenhower Diaries_, New York: W.W. Norton, 1981, diary entry 13 February 1953, p. 230.
10 Ferrell, _Eisenhower Diaries_, diary entry 6 January 1953, pp. 222–4; Dwight D Eisenhower Library (DDE), J.F. Dulles Papers, Subject series, Box 10, Churchill–Eden correspondence 1954 (3), memo for Sec. from C.W. McCardle, 9 July 1954, p. 2.
11 Richard Toye, _Churchill's Empire: The World That Made Him and the World He Made_, Basingstoke: Palgrave, 2011, pp. 267–8.
12 Winston Churchill, Sinews of Peace; www.winstonchurchill.org/resources/speeches/235–1946–1963-elder-statesman/120-the-sinews-of-peace.
13 Michael J. Hostetler, 'The Enigmatic Ends of Rhetoric: Churchill's Fulton Address as Great Art and Failed Persuasion', _Quarterly Journal of Speech_, 83:4, 1997, pp. 416–28.
14 See Ignace Feuerlicht, 'A New Look at the Iron Curtain', _American Speech_, 30:3, 1955, pp. 186–9.
15 Isaiah Berlin, 'Mr Churchill', _The Atlantic_, September 1949; www.theatlantic.com/magazine/archive/1949/09/mr-churchill/303546/.
16 Winston Churchill, Sinews of Peace; www.winstonchurchill.org/resources/speeches/235–1946–1963-elder-statesman/120-the-sinews-of-peace.

138 *S. Marsh*

17 Remarks by the President to Parliament in London, United Kingdom, 25 May 2011; www.whitehouse.gov/the-press-office/2011/05/25/remarks-president-parliament-london-united-kingdom.

18 www.bbc.com/news/magazine-29701767.

19 'Churchill Voted Greatest Briton', 24 November 2002; http://news.bbc.co.uk/2/hi/entertainment/2509465.stm.

20 Klaus Larres, *Churchill's Cold War: The Politics of Personal Diplomacy*, New Haven: Yale University Press, 2002, ch. 1.

21 Remarks by the President to Parliament in London, United Kingdom, 25 May 2011; www.whitehouse.gov/the-press-office/2011/05/25/remarks-president-parliament-london-united-kingdom.

22 Churchill on the campaign trail for the 1950 General Election, quoted in *The Western Australian*, 20 February 1950; http://trove.nla.gov.au/ndp/del/article/47830261.

23 'The Washington Merry Go Round', *The Sun Journal*, 7 December 1950; https://news.google.com/newspapers?nid=1928&dat=19501207&id=ybQ0AAAAIBAJ&sjid=UWgFAAAAIBAJ&pg=2781,6704633&hl=en.

24 HC Deb 14 December 1950 Vol. 482 cc1350–464; http://hansard.millbanksystems.com/commons/1950/dec/14/prime-ministers-visit-to-usa#S5CV0482P0_19501214_HOC_247.

25 Lord Charles Moran, *Winston Churchill: The Struggle for Survival, 1940–1965*, London: Constable, 1966, diary entry 15 October 1951, p. 47.

26 *Foreign Relations of the United States (FRUS)* 1951, Vol. 4, Gifford to Sec. State, 20 January 1951, pp. 894–9.

27 Ibid., record State-Joint Chiefs of Staff Meeting held at the Pentagon, 21 November 1951, pp. 985–9.

28 UK National Archive (UKNA), FO 371/90838, paper Makins, 'Objectives in the Washington Talks', 29 November 1951; *FRUS* 1952–4, Vol. 6, Part 1, Gifford to State Dept, 28 December 1951, pp. 720–3.

29 Harry S Truman Library (HST), PSF, Box 116, papers prepared for general information, Steering Group preparation for President and P.M. talks, 'Approach and Objectives for the Churchill Talks', u.d., p. 1.

30 UKNA, FO 371/90937, Hunt to Wilford, 15 November 1951.

31 Dwight D. Eisenhower Library (DDE), Ann Whitman File, International Series, Box 1, file: Bermuda – miscellaneous, memo by Eisenhower 'Bermuda Conference, 4–8 December 1953, 10 December 1953.

32 DDE, Ann Whitman File, International Series, Box 19, file: President–Churchill, vol. III October–December 1953 (1), Churchill to Eisenhower, 9 November 1963.

33 DDE, Ann Whitman File, International Series, Box 18, Churchill visit June 1954 (3), memo conv. 26 June 1954, p. 2.

34 See, for instance, Alan P. Dobson, 'The Years of Transition: Anglo-American Relations 1961–67', *Review of International Studies*, 16, 1990, pp. 239–58.

35 Alison R. Holmes, 'Transatlantic Diplomacy and "Global" States', in Alan P. Dobson and Steve Marsh (eds), *Anglo-American Relations: Contemporary Perspectives*, London: Routledge, 2013, pp. 105–28.

36 Citations from John W. Young, *Twentieth Century Diplomacy: Case Study in British Practice, 1963–76*, Cambridge: Cambridge University Press, 2008, p. 163; Jonathan Colman, *A 'Special Relationship'? Harold Wilson, Lyndon B. Johnson and Anglo-American Relations 'At the Summit', 1964–68*, Manchester: Manchester University Press, 2004, p. 137.

37 John Young, *The British Foreign Office and Cold War Fighting in the Early 1950s: PUSC(51)16 and the 1952 'Sore Spots' Memorandum*, Discussion Papers in Politics, Leicester: Leicester University Press, 1995.

38 Dean Acheson, *Present at the Creation. My Years in the State Department*, London: Hamilton, 1970, pp. 480–4.

Personal diplomacy at the summit 139

39 *FRUS* 1952–4, Vol. 6, Part 1, Churchill to Truman, 10 December 1951, pp. 704–5.
40 UKNA, FO 371/90938, FO to Washington Embassy, Prime Minister to Ambassador, 26 December 1951.
41 *FRUS* 1952–4, Vol. 6, Part 1, personal from Churchill, 29 December 1951.
42 Ibid., footnote 4, p. 699.
43 UKNA, FO 371/90938, Washington Embassy to FO, 28 December 1951.
44 UKNA, FO 371/90938, FO to Washington Embassy, personal from Churchill, 29 December 1951.
45 *FRUS* 1952–4, Vol. 6, Part 1, Acting Sec. State to US Embassy UK, 9 December 1951, pp. 703–4.
46 Ibid., footnote 4, p. 699.
47 UKNA, FO 371/90937, record conversation. Holmes and Makins, 12 December 1951.
48 UKNA, FO 371/90838, Makins to Strang, 29 November 1951; ibid., Eden to PM, 22 December, 1951; *FRUS* 1952–4, Vol. 6, Part 1, memcon Under Secretary of State (Webb), 10 December 1951, pp. 702–3.
49 UKNA, PRO, FO 371/90937, FO to Washington Embassy, 20 December 1951; FO 371/90938, FO to Washington Embassy, personal from Prime Minister to Truman, 23 December 1951.
50 US National Archives (USNA), RG 59, Box 2769, memo R.B. Knight to Matthews, 'Conversations between President Truman and Mr Churchill – US objectives', 10 December 1951.
51 John Colville, *Footprints in Time*, London: Collins, 1976, p. 233.
52 Letter Eisenhower to Churchill, 22 June 1954; letter Churchill to Eisenhower, 23 June 1954, reproduced in Peter G. Boyle (ed.), *The Churchill–Eisenhower Correspondence, 1953–1955*, pp. 149–50.
53 UKNA, FO 371/90838, paper Makins, 'Objectives in the Washington Talks', 29 November 1951; *FRUS* 1952–4, Vol. 6, Part 1, Gifford to State Dept, 28 December 1951, pp. 720–3.
54 Acheson, *Present at the Creation*, p. 594.
55 Acheson, *Present at the Creation*, p. 596; Alex Danchev, *Oliver Franks: Founding Father*, Oxford: Clarendon Press, 1993, p. 130.
56 UKNA, FO 371/97593, Franks to Eden, 27 January 1952.
57 UKNA, FO 371/97592, record of meeting at British Embassy Washington, 10 January 1952.
58 John F. Kennedy Library (JFK), NSF Countries, 172, UK Subjects: Macmillan correspondence 26 September 1961 to 24 December 1961, Macmillan to Kennedy, 24 December 1961.
59 JFK Library, NSF, Box 235a, President's trip, Bermuda, December 1961, folder 1 of 3, memo to the President from McGeorge Bundy, 19 December 1961.
60 Henry Kissinger, 'Reflections on a Partnership: British and American Attitudes To Postwar Foreign Policy', speech to the Royal Institute of International Affairs, in commemoration of the Bicentenary of the Office of the Foreign Secretary, 10 May 1982; www.larouchepub.com/other/2002/2901_kissinger.html.
61 Lord Moran, *Winston Churchill: The Struggle for Survival, 1940–1965*, diary entry 1 January 1952, p. 377.
62 UKNA, CAB 128/24, CC(52)4, 17 January 1952. See also FO371/90931, Makins, 'Impressions of America', 25 May 1951.
63 Churchill cited in Simon Rofe, 'Lord Lothian, 1939–40', in Michael F. Hopkins, Saul Kelly and John W. Young (eds), *The Washington Embassy: British Ambassadors to the United States, 1939–77*, Basingstoke: Palgrave, 2009, pp. 14–32, at p. 24.
64 DDE Library, Eisenhower, Dwight D, Papers as President of the US, 1953–61, Ann Whitman file, International Meetings Series, Box 3, file: Bermuda – Pres notes 12/53 (1), Bermuda, 4 December 1953.

140 *S. Marsh*

65 DDE Library, Eisenhower, Dwight D, Papers as President of the US, 1953–61, Ann Whitman file, International Meetings Series, Box 1, file: Bermuda–State Dept rpt Top Secret (1), memo of conversation by J.F. Dulles of meeting between Eisenhower and Churchill, 4 December 1953.

66 DDE Library, Eisenhower, Dwight D., Papers as President of the US, 1953–61, Ann Whitman file, International Meetings Series, Box 3, file: Bermuda – Pres. notes 12/53 (1), Bermuda, 4 December 1953.

67 DDE Library, White House Office, Office of the Staff Secretary, 1952–61, Cabinet minute series, Box 1, file: Cabinet minutes 25 September–15 December (1), Cabinet minutes 9 December 1953.

68 DDE Library, Eisenhower, Dwight D., Papers as President of the US, 1953–61, Ann Whitman file, DDE Diary Series, Box 4, file: DDE Diary December 1953, Churchill to Eisenhower, 19 December 1953.

69 UKNA, PREM 11 708, Prime Minister to Lord Cherwell, 10 November 1951; CAB 128, CC(51) 5th conclusions, 8 November 1951.

70 *FRUS* 1951, Vol. 4, Bruce to Sec. State, 19 December 1951, pp. 993–5.

71 *FRUS* 1952–4, Vol. 6, Part 1, notes Chairman of the Joint Chiefs of Staff (Bradley) of a dinner meeting aboard the SS *Williamsburg* on the evening of 5 January 1952, pp. 740–2.

72 HST, PSF, Box 116, memos and minutes of Churchill–Truman meetings, memo Knight, 9 January 1952; *FRUS* 1952–4, Vol. 6, Part 1, memo Sec. State of a dinner meeting at the British Embassy, 6 January 1952, pp. 742–6.

73 Ibid., US Delegation minutes of third formal meeting of President Truman and Prime Minister Churchill at the White House, 8 January 1952, pp. 775–90.

74 *FRUS* 1952–4, Vol. 6, Sec. Defense (Lovett) to Supreme Allied Commander Europe (Eisenhower), 24 January 1952, pp. 859–61; ibid., memo Rountree of meeting between Sec. State Acheson and Foreign Secretary Eden, 9 January 1952, pp. 821–31.

75 David Carlton, *Anthony Eden. A Biography*, London: Allen Lane, 1981, p. 307; Acheson, *Present at the Creation*, p. 600; David S. McLellan, *Dean Acheson: The State Department Years*, New York: Dodd Mead, 1976, p. 390.

76 UKNA, CAB 21/3057, Annex: II 'Atlantic Command', p. 60

77 HST Library, PSF Box 115, General File Churchill, folder: General File Churchill, Winston meeting with President Truman January 1952 folder (1), 7 January meeting, Cabinet Room.

78 *FRUS* 1952–54, Vol. 6, Part 1, The Ambassador in Canada (Woodward) to the Department of State, 14 January 1952, pp. 843–5.

79 FRUS 1952–4, Vol. 6, Part 1, Secretary of Defense (Lovett) to the Supreme Allied Commander, Europe (Eisenhower), 24 January 1952, pp. 859–61.

80 HST, Acheson Papers Box 67, Memo of Conversations 1952, folder: January, Acheson to Pearson via Woodward, 23 January 1952.

81 Acheson, *Present at the Creation*, p. 601.

82 Lord Moran, *Churchill: Taken from the Diaries of Lord Moran – The Struggle for Survival 1940–1965*, entry 7 January 1952, p. 379.

83 Lord Moran, *Churchill: Taken from the Diaries of Lord Moran – The Struggle for Survival 1940–1965*, p. 381.

84 Ibid.

85 HST, Acheson Papers Box 67, Memo of Conversations 1952, folder: January, Pearson to Acheson, 15 January 1952.

86 *FRUS* 1952–54, Vol. 6, Part 1, Memo by Special Assistant to the Secretary of State (Battle) of a Meeting between President Truman and Prime Minister Churchill, The White House, 8 January 1952, 5 pm, pp. 793–4, at p. 794.

87 Cited by C.B. Kelly, 'Excerpt: "Best Little Stories from the Life and Times of Winston Churchill"'; www.winstonchurchill.org/publications/chartwell-bulletin/104-bulletin-33-mar-2011/1094-excerpt-best-little-stories-from-the-life-and-times-of-winston-churchill.

Personal diplomacy at the summit 141

88 Acheson, *Present at the Creation*, p. 596.
89 *FRUS* 1952–54, Vol. 6, Part 1, United States Delegation Minutes of the Second Formal Meeting of President Truman and Prime Minister Churchill, The White House, 7 January 1952, 5–7 pm, pp. 766–73.
90 HST, PSF, Box 116, memos and minutes of Churchill–Truman meetings, memo Knight, 9 January 1952; *FRUS* 1952–4, Vol. 6, Part 1, memo Sec. State of a dinner meeting at the British Embassy, 6 January 1952, pp. 742–6.
91 DDE Library, JC Hagerty Papers, 1953–61, Box 70, President's press and radio conferences, file: Luncheon for Churchill and Eden under the auspices of the Jt Committee of Press, Radio and Television correspondents and photographers, 28 June 1954.
92 UKNA, FO 371/90838, paper Makins, 'Objectives in the Washington Talks', 29 November 1951.
93 'Big Two Meet to Strengthen Ties', *New York Times*, 6 January 1952, p. E1.
94 UKNA, FO 371/90838, paper Makins, 'Objectives in the Washington Talks', 29 November 1951.
95 *FRUS* 1952–4, Vol. 6, Part 1, Chairman of the Joint Committee on Atomic Energy (McMahon) to President, 5 December 1951, pp. 695–8.
96 UKNA, FO 371/97588, Washington Embassy to FO, 'Survey of American Regional Press Comment on Mr Churchill's Address to Congress', 1 February 1952.
97 UKNA, FO 371 38523, 'The Essentials of an American Policy', 21 March 1944.
98 JFK Library, NSF, Box 235a, President's trip, Bermuda, 12/61, folder 1 of 3, memo to the President from McGeorge Bundy, 19 December 1961.

6 Churchill's ambassadors – from Fulton to Suez

Tony McCulloch

Introduction

One of the many ironies in the history of the Anglo-American 'special relationship', as named by Winston Churchill in his iconic Fulton speech, was that in little more than eighteen months after his retirement as prime minister in April 1955 the Conservative Government of which he had been the head for almost four years was involved in the disastrous Suez episode – considered by many historians to have been the lowest point in Anglo-American relations from the end of the Second World War down to the present day. The responsibility for this debacle on the British side is usually allocated to Churchill's successor, Anthony Eden, and to a lesser degree his Cabinet, but what of Churchill himself and of Sir Roger Makins, the British ambassador to Washington at the time of Suez, appointed by Churchill on the recommendation of Eden? To what extent were Makins and his predecessors successful in establishing the Anglo-American 'special relationship' so desired by Churchill and why did this relationship break down during the Suez crisis?[1]

The current essay has three main aims. First, to analyse Churchill's concept of an Anglo-American 'special relationship' as set out in the Fulton speech and the reaction to it in the United States, especially the criticism, put forward by Walter Lippmann, among others, that British colonialism was a significant constraint upon an openly close relationship with the US. Second, to evaluate the political debate within the US on the Fulton speech that continued for several years after it was delivered. The public diplomacy of the British ambassadors who served in Washington in the wake of the Fulton speech forms the bulk of this section. Finally, to examine what has been called 'the descent to Suez', focusing mainly on the period from Churchill's retirement in April 1955, and the extent to which the Suez crisis can be linked to the flaws in Churchill's Fulton vision, notwithstanding the best efforts of Makins and his predecessors to maintain a close Anglo-American relationship.

'The natural term of an Ambassador's mission should be six years', Churchill wrote in 1944, 'unless he is guilty of incompetence or divergence from the Government's policy, when of course he cannot be recalled too soon.'[2] In the light of this statement it is not surprising that of the five ambassadors to the US who held office in the period from Churchill's accession to the premiership in May 1940 to his retirement fifteen years later in April 1955, the longest serving was his wartime appointment, Edward Wood, Earl of Halifax (1940–6) who stayed in Washington for over five years and was still there when Churchill delivered his Fulton speech in February 1946. Perhaps more surprising is the fact that his one peacetime appointment as ambassador to Washington, Sir Roger Makins, later 1st Baron Sherfield, served only three and a half years and was recalled by Eden on the eve of what proved to be the climax of the Suez crisis.

Halifax succeeded Philip Kerr, Lord Lothian, appointed by Neville Chamberlain from August 1939 but chiefly remembered for his contribution to Anglo-American relations after Churchill became prime minister. In between Halifax and Makins there were two ambassadors appointed during the Labour Government of Clement Attlee – Archibald Clark Kerr, Lord Inverchapel, and Sir Oliver Franks. In a very real sense these five men were all 'Churchill's ambassadors', as although Churchill was responsible for the appointment of only two of them they all served in the shadow of his wartime leadership and the establishment of what he termed the 'special relationship' between Britain and the United States. This essay has benefited from some excellent scholarship on all five ambassadors but it takes a different approach from earlier works by viewing them primarily in terms of their public diplomacy and focusing on the legacy of British colonialism after the Fulton speech, especially in relation to the Middle East, and the pitfalls for the Anglo-American relationship created by this legacy, culminating in the Suez crisis in late 1956.[3]

Lord Lothian – liberal imperialist, 1939–41

The significance of the United States and of the role of the ambassador in Washington to the successful operation of British foreign policy from 1940 can hardly be overstated. Following the fall of France in June 1940 there was no more important ally for Britain than the United States – but the nature of a British alliance with the US both then and subsequently was a matter of great sensitivity, especially on the American side of the Atlantic. Public opinion in the US was divided on the issue and suspicious of anything resembling British propaganda. Sir Ronald Lindsay, British ambassador in Washington from 1930 to 1939, was therefore reluctant to engage in public diplomacy which he feared could be construed as official propaganda and might lead to a backlash in US public opinion.[4]

But Lothian, in different circumstances and with a more gregarious personality than the taciturn Lindsay, was determined to win over American public opinion to the British cause and therefore placed much greater emphasis on public diplomacy than hitherto – a significant legacy for all of his successors. Indeed, his easy charm and gift for public relations, combined with his knowledge of the US where he was a frequent visitor in the 1930s, were Lothian's strongest assets when taking up the post of ambassador. Both of these factors helped him to overcome his earlier reputation as an 'appeaser' and critic of Churchill's warnings against the rise of Nazi Germany. Lothian was also a

144   T. McCulloch

'Liberal Imperialist' who had been a member of Lord Milner's 'Kindergarten' group of colonial civil servants in South Africa before the First World War and then Private Secretary to Lloyd George during the war. He served briefly as Under Secretary of State for India in 1931–2 and was a Liberal member of the House of Lords in the 1930s.[5]

In October 1939, soon after taking up his Washington role, Lothian gave a significant address to the Pilgrims Society in New York – a traditional rite of passage for any new British ambassador. As well as speaking to an influential audience of the 'great and the good' from American government and civil society, the Pilgrims address was invariably reported at some length in the major newspapers, especially the *New York Times*. In his speech Lothian tackled the issue of 'British propaganda' head on by saying he had been warned not to discuss the war but he felt that Britain had the right to explain its point of view to the United States and to other democracies. It was then the 'inalienable right' of Americans to make up their own mind. He suggested that Britain had no use for propaganda in the US because, as a democracy, it was content to let the facts speak for themselves. Whereas, he argued, the role of propaganda in the totalitarian states was entirely different. He accepted that Britain deserved its share of the blame for the outbreak of war but he said that Hitler's essential aim was to revise not just the Versailles Treaty but 'the whole democratic conception of international life'.[6]

Lothian also addressed the issue of British imperialism which, he conceded, might be seen as undermining Britain's democratic credentials. He referred throughout his speech to the British Commonwealth rather than the Empire and said that, in its modern form, it was 'something quite different from what most Americans believe'. It was no longer an empire 'in the old sense of the word', he said, but rather 'a vast system of international relationships, containing nearly 450,000,000 people, of many different races, religions and colours, yet living together under conditions of order and with ever increasing freedom and responsibility'. It had its fair share of problems, he acknowledged, not least in India. But Mahatma Gandhi had come out in favour of the Allied cause as had the independent Dominions like Canada and the representatives of the British colonies. This demonstrated, he argued, 'the immense gulf between British Imperialism, as it is sometimes called, and the imperialism of the totalitarian world'.[7]

It was fortunate indeed for Lothian's reputation as a highly effective ambassador and for Britain's war effort that the White House was at that time occupied by Franklin Roosevelt who judged it to be in American interests to supply Britain with 'all aid short of war'. But with FDR's death in April 1945 the case for a supportive US relationship towards Britain had to be made again – first of all with FDR's successor and fellow Democrat, Harry Truman, and later with Dwight Eisenhower, the Supreme Allied Commander at the end of the war in Europe and by 1953 a Republican president – the first for twenty years. Although American isolationism was much less in evidence after the war than before there remained a residual suspicion of British foreign policy and especially of British colonialism. The case for a close Anglo-American relationship therefore had to be made again and again – a task that Churchill took on in his Fulton address.[8]

Churchill's Fulton vision, 5 March 1946

Churchill's speech at Fulton on 5 March 1946 was delivered against the background of growing concern, both in the US and Britain, about post-war policy disagreements between the Western powers and the Soviet Union. These disagreements had been especially evident during the Potsdam Conference in the summer of 1945, after which several US spokesmen had made it clear that reaching agreement on post-war problems would not be an easy matter. John Foster Dulles, at this time Chief Adviser to James Byrnes, the US Secretary of State, gave a radio address on the Council of Foreign Ministers meeting in London in September 1945 and the differences of opinion between the US and Britain on the one side and the Soviet Union on the other. Senator Arthur Vandenberg appealed for the lifting of what he called the 'iron curtain' of secrecy between the US and the Soviet Union. Byrnes himself took to the airwaves at the end of December, detailing particular disagreements over Romania, Bulgaria, Iran and Korea. Such concerns were magnified by Stalin's speech in Moscow on 9 February 1946 that seemed to suggest that the Soviet leadership anticipated future trials of strength with the Western powers. George Kennan's 'Long Telegram', sent on 22 February 1946, resulted from these growing concerns in the West.[9]

In many ways Churchill's Fulton speech was responding to the same set of circumstances as Kennan although his remedies were public rather than private and they focused primarily on the Anglo-American relationship rather than on the US alone. Churchill certainly acknowledged the primacy of the United States in the post-war order and identified its mission as protecting the world from 'tyranny and war'. He alluded to the importance of the United Nations in ensuring world peace and to the desirability that states should have free elections and democratic principles. He then stressed the need to continue the 'special relationship' between the US and the British Empire that had come to fruition during the Second World War before highlighting the threat posed by the rapid division of Europe into two halves – the one democratic in outlook, the other Communist – divided by an Iron Curtain. Only by continuing the close wartime cooperation between the US and the British Empire, he concluded, could the United Nations Organisation be successful and the threat of another world war avoided.[10]

American reactions to Fulton – the colonial issue

Churchill's speech was in many ways a brilliant argument for the continuation of the wartime Anglo-American 'special relationship', linked as it was to the need to 'contain' Soviet power. And because of his prestige and the robust language that he employed the speech naturally attracted enormous attention both inside and outside the United States. Moreover, it raised in an acute form a number of major issues confronting the Truman administration, not least the question mark hanging over US relations with the Soviet Union. The reaction to the speech was bound to be significant and it fell to Lord Halifax, appointed by Churchill after the untimely death of Lord Lothian in December 1940, to report the details of

146   *T. McCulloch*

this reaction to the British Foreign Office and thereby to the Attlee Government that had succeeded Churchill's wartime coalition in June 1945.[11]

Referring to Churchill's criticisms of Soviet policy and use of the term 'Iron Curtain', Halifax's report – most likely drafted by Isaiah Berlin who was a member of the Embassy at this time – compared Churchill to

> a dentist who has diagnosed a severe inflammation and proposes the use of the drill, which may have to be followed by actual extraction of the diseased tooth. All but the Left-wing journalists and politicians concede that there is something wrong with the tooth in question; some are inclined to suspect that the condition may be grave indeed; but almost all shy with real or simulated horror from the idea of the drill and complain that the dentist is notorious for his love of drastic remedies, and that surely modern medicine has provided more painless methods of cure, and that so brutal a method as that recommended by Mr Churchill harks back to rough old-fashioned practices.[12]

As regards the media, the ambassador's report continued:

> Left-wing press and radio (i.e. the majority of broadcasters) denounces the speech as war-mongering, imperialistic, the call to a new anti-Comintern pact, justifying the worst Russian suspicions, etc. but even these quarters are compelled to qualify their abuses by conceding Mr Churchill's past services and complaining that it is the 'bad' Churchill rather than the 'good' Churchill who is speaking.

On the other hand

> more moderate comment is far readier to recognise the disagreeable facts forced upon their attention by Mr Churchill but tends to recoil from the drastic remedy prescribed, i.e. a close military alliance, etc. This proposal is attacked on the traditional grounds of the unpopularity of formal alliance in the United States, refusal to underwrite British imperialism, reluctance to be used to pull British chestnuts out of the fire, the 'body blow such an alliance would administer to the UNO, etc.[13]

Halifax's report thus pointed out the negative reaction to Churchill's references to the British Empire and this was very apparent in both the press and radio coverage of the Fulton speech. 'Does his fraternal military association require the United States to underwrite the present British position in Greece, Near East, India, Burma and Malaya?' asked the *Herald Tribune*. And in order to hold the line against Russian expansion would it give the US any role in 'the development of the seething peoples who now lie on the British side of it'? The more sympathetic *Christian Science Monitor* accepted that Churchill was aiming for 'the closest possible association of all English-speaking peoples'. But it

Churchill's ambassadors 147

acknowledged that his 'fears of Russian encroachment on the British Empire's Mediterranean lifeline' could be seen as the reason why he was seeking 'to inveigle the United States into jointly sharing the defence of a decadent empire'.[14]

Criticism of British colonialism was especially prevalent in the newspapers of the mid-West, most notably in Chicago – seen as a traditional stronghold of Irish-Americanism and isolationism. The *Chicago Tribune* was, of course, well known for being critical of British imperialism while the *Chicago Sun* argued that to follow Churchill's advice would lead to another world war. He had attacked Russian expansion 'while remaining silent on British imperialism' and he had used the Bible 'to justify the system of alliances dominated by a master alliance of the Anglo-Saxon Herrenvolk'. Churchill was appealing 'to an alliance to save a privileged imperial world he can't believe is dead and which would tie America to maintaining British outposts in the world against subject peoples struggling to escape the yoke'. The *Chicago Times* said that Churchill was 'a product of the past who believes in the white man's burden and consequently omitted from his speech what is less appealing to America, namely events in India, Indonesia, etc., while striking out against Soviet ambitions and tyranny'.[15]

The most incisive critique of the British colonialism that was felt to underlie the Fulton speech came from the highly influential journalist and commentator Walter Lippmann. 'The speech itself,' he wrote, 'will be received in this country as an incomplete statement as Churchill, in examining the problem of forming a united British–American front, dwelt only on Russian expansion.' According to Lippmann 'the essence of the problem' lay in the 'obscure and complex relation between the British Commonwealth and the British Empire'. He argued that Churchill had failed to face this problem and had assumed that his American audience would also fail to face it. Churchill, he continued, had suggested that the permanent defence arrangement between the US and Canada could act as a model for an arrangement between the US and all of the British Dominions but in practice this would mean establishing a permanent defence arrangement 'with the United Kingdom and the dependent empire which it governs'.[16]

The central dilemma for the US, Lippmann argued, concerned those countries under British rule or British influence that were not English-speaking and did not have any inheritance of freedom. In this case, a united front with the British Empire would be regarded in the US as 'an unattractive, unwise and ineffective policy' that could 'weaken and not strengthen the western world in the contest of influence with the Soviet Union' because 'in a united front against Russia in Asia, the United States would be incapable of differentiating its own position from that of the European empires in Asia'. It was 'precisely because the United States is neither a totalitarian state nor a colonial power,' he said, 'that it can hope to retain influence in keeping the Asiatic peoples in good relations with the western world.' Lippmann concluded that 'the United States cannot in the interests of civilisation lose its own identity in Asia by merging itself with the British Empire but must retain its separate influence'. The 'deficiencies of British

148 *T. McCulloch*

power' could not be made up entirely by the United States, he added and, ironically in view of the later Suez crisis, he suggested that Britain would have to rebuild its relationship with France if it wished to shore up its power and protect its Empire.[17]

Thus for Americans like Lippmann the Fulton speech highlighted the spectre of British colonialism and Churchill's image as a die-hard imperialist. While Churchill was not embarrassed to refer to the Empire in his speech and lauded its size and strength and its contribution to the Allied victory during the war, there was a strong element in US public opinion that was uneasy – if not downright hostile – at the notion of US support for British colonialism. This had been true of Franklin Roosevelt, especially with regard to India, and it was one of the issues that he referred to when he was seeking support from Stalin at Yalta. It was also one of the reasons why an open Anglo-American relationship – rather than the tacit understanding favoured by FDR before June 1940 – was such a sensitive issue in the US. From the American perspective the three variants of British colonialism – the Commonwealth (comprising the independent Dominions), the colonial empire, and the informal empire in the Middle East (symbolised by control of Iran's oil and the Suez Canal in Egypt) were all represented by Churchill and his Fulton speech.[18]

Fulton revisited – Churchill's Waldorf Astoria speech, 15 March 1946

Churchill's Fulton speech thus resulted in an intense debate in the US on its various contentions, not least the idea of an Anglo-American 'special relationship'. To some extent it was a renewal of the 'great debate' that had raged in 1940–1 over whether the US should intervene on behalf of Britain following the fall of France. Nor was the controversy confined to American shores. Churchill's speech was the subject of an uncomfortable discussion in the British Cabinet following suggestions in both the US and Russia that the British government had been consulted in advance and had approved of Churchill's speech. British Information Services in New York and the Ministry of Information in London had both helped to distribute advance copies of the speech to the press although ministers had not themselves seen it. Attlee told the Cabinet that he would make it quite clear to the House of Commons that the government had no knowledge of the contents of the Fulton speech before it was delivered.[19]

Churchill was still in America while the Fulton debate was in full swing and was therefore able to observe at first hand the impact of his words. In fact, his schedule during his stay in the US included no fewer than half a dozen speeches, including one at a dinner in his honour on 15 March at the Waldorf Astoria Hotel – traditional venue of ambassadorial addresses to the Pilgrims Society. The occasion was hosted by Governor Thomas Dewey and attended by the Mayor of New York, William O'Dwyer. Dean Acheson was expected to be there but was conveniently called away on urgent business at the last moment. During the ten days since Churchill's Fulton speech the international situation had taken a dramatic turn for the worse with an appeal by the Iranian government to the UN in protest at the continued presence of Soviet forces in the country. Thus when Churchill came to give his speech, entitled 'The Darkening International Scene', he was in an unrepentant mood.[20]

Churchill began by alluding to the title of his speech and the problems of the moment. 'When I spoke at Fulton ten days ago,' he said, 'I felt it was necessary for someone in an unofficial position to speak in arresting terms about the present plight of the world. I do not wish to withdraw or modify a single word.' He was sure that 'the hope which I expressed for the increasing association of our two countries' would come to pass eventually, as it was bound to do, but the main question was whether this would happen 'in a sufficiently plain and clear manner and in good time to prevent a new world struggle or whether it will come about, as it has done before, only in the course of that struggle'. He was confident that it would come in time as there was no imminent danger of military conflict and he did not feel that 'the rulers of Russia' were intent on war. But there was confusion and suspicion about their motives, for example in the case of Iran.[21]

As regards the UN, far from being a threat to the success of the new organisation, a close relationship between Britain and the US was essential for it to succeed.

> Unless they work together, in full loyalty to the Charter, the organisation of the United Nations will cease to have any reality. No one will be able to put his trust in it and the world will be left to the clash of nationalisms which have led us to two frightful wars.

He also clarified how he saw the 'special relationship' in practice. 'I have never asked for an Anglo-American military alliance or a treaty. I asked for something different and in a sense I asked for something more. I asked for a free, voluntary, fraternal association.' As he explained, 'you do not need a treaty to express the natural affinities and friendships which arise in a fraternal association'.[22]

Churchill wanted this 'fraternal association' between Britain and the US to be entirely open rather than one that was played down for whatever reason. 'It would be wrong that the fact should be concealed or ignored,' he said.

> Nothing can prevent our nations drawing ever closer to one another and nothing can obscure the fact that, in their harmonious companionship, lies the main hope of a world instrument for maintaining peace on earth and goodwill to all men.

Clearly Churchill felt that it was important that potential disturbers of the peace should realise at the outset that they would be met by joint action between the US and Britain. It was a familiar refrain – and not just by Churchill – that if only Hitler and Mussolini had realised that the US would join Britain and its Empire in confronting them they would never have launched their expansionist campaigns in Europe. Whether or not this was an accurate reading of history it was certainly a logical approach in the wake of the Second World War and it was one that eventually informed the policy of containment towards the Soviet Union adopted by the Truman administration.[23]

The North American Department of the Foreign Office felt that Churchill had done a good job of clearing the post-Fulton air in his Waldorf Astoria speech.[24] However, although he dealt explicitly with the criticisms of his Fulton speech regarding the UN issue and relations with Russia he entirely overlooked – or ignored – the other main criticism of his vision of a 'special relationship' between Britain and the United States – that this would involve the US in condoning and to some extent supporting the continuation of the British Empire in its various forms. Churchill did not mention this issue at all in his speech although, unlike at Fulton, he was careful to refer to friendship between the US and 'the British Commonwealth' rather than the Empire. The only empire he mentioned in his Waldorf Astoria speech was the Roman Empire – comparing its 'majesty and power' with that of the United States. 'We in the British Commonwealth will stand at your side in powerful and faithful friendship, and in accordance with the World Charter,' he concluded, 'and together I am sure we shall succeed in lifting from the face of man the curse of war and the darker curse of tyranny.'[25]

Of course, Churchill was the last person to apologise for the British Empire – as he still preferred to call the Commonwealth and Empire collectively. Much of his career had been spent defending it in both a military and political sense. His opposition to Indian self-government had helped to keep him out of the National Government in the 1930s and his outspokenness on this issue had blunted his early calls for action against the rising power of Germany.[26] Churchill's views on the British Empire at this time were revealed in a private speech he made at the University Club in New York a few days after his Waldorf Astoria address. 'He defended the Empire and its principles with vigour, and was warmly applauded for his presentation of its objectives,' reported one informed observer.

> He deplored Britain being 'talked out' of her rich estate in India ... but acknowledged the early need to advance India to nationhood. He expressed fear as to India's future, however, which he regarded as obscure: her people might have cause to regret any hasty assumption of the responsibilities of nationhood.[27]

Lord Halifax – Whig grandee, 1941–6

Edward Wood, Viscount Halifax, was nearing the end of his time as the British ambassador in Washington when Churchill delivered his Fulton speech. Halifax had been Viceroy of India from 1926 to 1931, a particularly turbulent period in Indian politics. His negotiations with Gandhi had received much criticism from Churchill but overall his term of office in India was regarded by Stanley Baldwin at least as a success and he had joined the Baldwin Government in June 1935. Neville Chamberlain also thought highly of him and when Anthony Eden

Churchill's ambassadors 151

resigned in April 1938 Halifax was appointed Foreign Secretary. In this capacity he was largely responsible for the appointment of Lord Lothian as British ambassador to succeed Lindsay in August 1939. A contender for the premiership when Chamberlain stood down in May 1940, Halifax deferred to Churchill who subsequently appointed him as ambassador to the US following Lothian's death in December 1940. Churchill may have been partly motivated by the desire to remove a rival from London but, whatever the motives, it proved to be, according to most accounts, a master-stroke.[28]

After an uncertain start Halifax, who had gone to Washington very reluctantly, eventually settled into his ambassadorial role. He developed an excellent relationship with Roosevelt and his key advisers – helped by the fact that he was a more of a Whig grandee than a Tory. He was also fully alive to the demands of public diplomacy and the need to represent Britain far and wide across the United States. It was his proud boast by the time he left Washington that he had visited all forty-eight states.[29] As regards the Fulton speech, Halifax's report to London detailed its very mixed reception in the United States. He also had his own private doubts about the speech – mainly concerned with the 'Iron Curtain' notion which he felt, like many US observers, would only make the Soviet Union more difficult to deal with. Interestingly, in view of Churchill's later summit diplomacy, Halifax wrote privately to suggest that Churchill should offer to meet Stalin in Moscow to discuss the worsening international situation. But Churchill declined this suggestion as likely to be compared to Chamberlain's trip to Munich in September 1938 – not an interpretation that Halifax shared.[30]

Although Halifax had his doubts about the Fulton speech he was not averse to the idea of a 'special relationship' with the US. Indeed, in his farewell speech to the Pilgrims Society in April 1946 he rivalled Churchill in his devotion to the Anglo-American ideal. Recalling his speech to the Pilgrims in March 1941 as the new British ambassador he pointed out that the Battle of Britain was only recently over at that time and most of Europe was still under German control. But December 1941 'saw the beginning of a collaboration between our two countries unique in history', he continued. 'Never before, between any two countries in war, had there been so complete a unity of military, industrial and political effort. It might almost be said that we fought as one people.' He was convinced that if this alliance had existed in 1931 then a second world war would have been avoided. The question now was whether the mistakes of the past had been learned.

> Can you and we retain during the years of peace the cooperation we learnt and practised during the years of war? To my mind the future course of history for your people and mine and perhaps for the world depends upon the answer.[31]

Still echoing Churchill, he said that the United Nations Organisation was 'the last best hope of the world' but if it was to succeed it had to receive the support of the nations that had signed up to it. The UN would take time to settle in but let our two nations who already have so much in common lead the way to this larger understanding, for if we can first win when the ground is so plainly with us we shall be that much better placed to win where the difficulties are greater and the initial advantages not so apparent.

Then, avoiding any mention of the Soviet Union, Halifax said:

Such friendship between our two countries is inspired by no selfish motive. It is directed against nobody. It is not an end, but a beginning. It has no other object than to strengthen and reinforce the will and work of the Organisation to which our loyalty is pledged.

In short, he said, the Anglo-American relationship could and should be 'the rock upon which our House of Peace is built'.[32]

Halifax then drew up a balance sheet of similarities and differences in terms of language, history, temperament, tradition and race. The most important factor, he said, was the 'priceless inheritance of common thought' based on a desire for freedom. This ensured that Britain and the US always came together on big issues even though they might differ on smaller ones. However, one area did concern him. 'I must confess,' he said,

that I have frequently deplored the extent to which the attitude of many of your people towards the British Commonwealth and Empire was affected by a tradition which leads them to be unaware of the changes of such magnitude that have taken place over the last hundred and fifty years and obscures the fact that the Commonwealth and Empire of King George VI is something very different from the Colonial Empire of King George III.

Certainly, he felt, this issue should not get in the way of friendly relations between the two countries and that they should 'go forward into the years of peace in that same comradeship which it was our salvation to find in war'. But it is significant that he raised the issue of Britain's adverse colonial image in his farewell address.[33]

Lord Inverchapel – eccentric Progressive, 1946–8

Halifax departed the USA in May 1946. Thus it was his successor, Archibald Clark Kerr – newly ennobled as Lord Inverchapel – who took over the reins in Washington during the years that followed the Fulton speech and witnessed the onset of the Cold War. Inverchapel had enjoyed a distinguished diplomatic career. He had served in Washington under Lord Bryce before the First World War and then in the Middle East, including Egypt, after the war. He had also been the British ambassador to Chile (1928–30), where he married the daughter of a Chilean aristocrat who was almost thirty years his junior. Further posts followed in Sweden (1930–4), Iraq (1935–8), China (1938–42) and the Soviet

Union (1942–6). In all of these postings his leftish sympathies served him well and he was generally regarded as a success.[34]

He was perhaps less well suited to Washington, where he was sent by the new Labour Government, as he was not keen on the social side of the ambassador's role, was not very strong on economics and was also rather eccentric in some of his ways – for example, he preferred to use a quill pen and disliked the telephone. He also divorced and remarried his Chilean partner while serving in Washington. He was obviously not a Churchill appointment and his views on the British Empire were much more progressive than those of the former prime minister. Partly for this reason, he played a significant role in trying to nullify American criticism of British colonialism in the wake of the Fulton speech and he at least realised that it was an issue that needed to be addressed.[35]

In fact, the issue was again brought to the fore in September 1946 in a speech given by FDR's former vice president, Henry Wallace, that was to some extent a rebuttal of Churchill's Fulton address six months earlier. Wallace's speech led to his dismissal by Truman and opened up a serious split in the Democratic Party at the time of the 1946 mid-term elections. To say that it created something of a political and diplomatic sensation would be putting it mildly and the fall-out from it was Inverchapel's main focus for at least a month as London sought to assess its significance for Anglo-American relations. 'Certainly we like the British people as individuals,' Wallace had said.

> But to make Britain the key to our foreign policy would be, in my opinion, the height of folly.... Make no mistake about it – the British imperialistic policy in the Near East alone, combined with Russian retaliation, would lead the United States straight to war unless we have a clearly-defined and realistic policy of our own.[36]

It was in the wake of Wallace's speech and the disastrous showing of the Democrats in the 1946 mid-term elections that Inverchapel addressed the Pilgrims Society in New York in November 1946. Unlike Churchill – and, indeed, unlike Halifax in his speech to the Pilgrims – Inverchapel took on the issue of British colonialism in a way that was most likely to win US support. No doubt this was because he was representing a Labour government and took a more liberal view of the Empire than Churchill tended to do. Indeed, he made much of 'the liberal tradition' that he said the US and Britain had in common. Liberal ideas were 'more deeply rooted and more tenaciously held than ever before by our two peoples for the reason that together we have been through the fire', he said. The 'perils of 1940' had strengthened the British national character which, he felt, had 'almost everything in common' with the American. Both were peaceloving and slow to respond to trouble but both were decisive when eventually forced to act.[37]

Inverchapel then began a measured defence of the British Empire. 'Critics chide us for being imperialists and oppressors of backward races,' he said. But the British Commonwealth of Nations was in reality 'an association of widely

154   *T. McCulloch*

scattered sovereign states united only by the common spirit of liberal institutions under one crown'. Indeed, he said, 'this Commonwealth is the first example of a United Nations organisation. Each part of it is willing to forgo some of its sovereign rights for the common good.' The Statute of Westminster had put the Dominions on an equal footing with Britain 'but no legal compulsion would ever keep such an organisation as the British Commonwealth together. That was proved in 1776.' In fact,

> our Commonwealth exists in virtue of a belief in the essentials of liberty and respect for the dignity of man. So long as we hold fast to these values, we shall remain together. We hold them more strongly now than ever before, and let no man's wisdom tell him that we are a weaker force in the world than hitherto.[38]

Great progress had also been made in the development of the colonial empire which had been inherited from the old days of imperialism that had ended in the nineteenth century, he said. 'It has been scowled at in many quarters, not least in Great Britain,' he added, by statesmen such as Gladstone. But the colonies were now seen as trusteeships rather than as territories to be exploited by Britain. Great strides had already been made towards parliamentary government in places such as Nigeria. Looking to the future, the goal was to transform the British Empire from being half Commonwealth and half Empire into 'one great, free association of peoples, Anglo-Saxons, Asiatics, Africans and Polynesians. We see these nations as equal members of a partnership called the British Commonwealth' subscribing 'to the ideas of liberty and human dignity' and joining other nations at the UN. It would be some time before that horizon was reached, he said, but much progress had already been made.[39]

It was a well-crafted speech that addressed two aspects of Britain's colonial past – the nature of the Commonwealth and the status of the colonial empire. It was an unashamedly positive gloss on the Empire that played down its considerable economic benefits. But even Inverchapel in this speech to a sympathetic audience did not tackle the issue of Britain's informal empire in the Middle East, highlighted by Henry Wallace among others. The Middle East remained a major issue during Inverchapel's time as ambassador, especially the future of Palestine and the UN mandate held by Britain, about which London and Washington had serious disagreements that were hardly lessened by Truman's decision to recognise Israel as soon as the UN mandate ended on 14 May 1948. Inverchapel returned to London two weeks later, declaring that the Washington role had been 'a very tough job' but that there had been 'a tremendous improvement' in Anglo-American relations during his two years in the United States.[40]

Sir Oliver Franks – 'Philosopher Ambassador', 1948–52

In February 1948 it was announced that Inverchapel was to be replaced by Sir Oliver Franks, an Oxford professor, economics expert and leading contributor to

Churchill's ambassadors 155

the implementation of the Marshall Plan. Franks enjoyed a very high reputation. He had excelled as a student at Oxford and was appointed a Fellow at Queen's College before taking up the post of Professor of Moral Philosophy at the University of Glasgow in 1937. With the outbreak of war he joined the Ministry of Supply in London, becoming Permanent Secretary by the end of the war. He then became Provost of Queen's College before returning to government in July 1947 as chairman of the British committee on Marshall Aid, playing a significant role in producing a united European response. He was a tall and impressive figure who quickly formed good personal relations with Truman and his Secretary of State, Dean Acheson. His first months in Washington saw the introduction of the Marshall Aid plan and the onset of the Berlin Blockade.[41]

In June 1948 Franks gave his first speech as ambassador to the National Press Club in Washington. Britain's Palestinian mandate was the main focus. Franks admitted that Britain had made mistakes but he deplored any accusations of bad faith. He felt that neither Britain nor the US had really understood the other's point of view. Both countries wanted a stable Middle East so there was common ground to build upon. More generally, he questioned whether it was helpful to see Anglo-American relations in such simple terms as 'Great Britain was an old country and the United States was a new country; that Britons were traditionalists and Americans were not'. He questioned whether the US was a young country in all respects. 'I wonder whether the American way of life is not itself a great achievement, something that has ripened,' he said. As for Britain, 'we do not feel we live in just an old country'. Britain was 'not a country burdened with tradition, but a country seething with ideas,' he argued. 'The controversy and debate would go on,' he said, because 'we are living in a country that is very much alive'.[42]

Franks spoke in a similar vein when he delivered the traditional speech to the Pilgrims Society in New York in October 1948. He began by acknowledging that Britain's economic situation made it difficult to play as full a role in European affairs as the US might like. However, Britain had been active in diplomacy, the airlift to Berlin and economic aid to Western Europe as well as the continued development of the British Commonwealth. Echoing Churchill's praise of Lend–Lease he said that the generosity and imagination of the Marshall Aid programme was 'unexampled in the history of the world'. As for the Anglo-American relationship, it had continued after the war as 'a kind of working partnership between us in the effort to deal with the many difficulties and dangers that beset us and the world'. The two countries did not always agree at first and differences often arose, but they were worked out 'because of our unity in the basic things of human living'. Between them, he declared, Britain and the United States were making 'a supreme endeavour to save the sanity of the world'.[43]

It was speeches like these two that were to earn for Franks the title of 'Philosopher Ambassador' from the *New York Times*.[44] Indeed, Franks needed to be philosophical as his time as ambassador was marked by a series of momentous events in Europe and Asia, all of which impacted upon the Anglo-American relationship – the formation of NATO; the end of the Berlin blockade and the establishment of West and East Germany as separate states; the successful testing of a Soviet atom bomb; the Chinese revolution of October 1949 that brought the Communists to power and saw the retreat of the Nationalists to Taiwan – a development that led to differences between the US and Britain over the latter's recognition of Communist China; the outbreak of the Korean War in June 1950 and the subsequent Chinese intervention; growing concern over General MacArthur's conduct of the war and the threat to use atomic weapons that saw Attlee's hurried visit to Washington in December 1950; the controversial dismissal of MacArthur in April 1951; and, last but not least, the rise of McCarthyism, with its unfortunate effect on American domestic politics and diplomacy.[45]

Throughout this period Anglo-American relations were aided by the close relationship between Franks and Dean Acheson, the American Secretary of State. Acheson was generally sympathetic to Britain as a loyal ally and privately he acknowledged that there was a special bond between the two countries because of their 'common language and history'. But he was opposed to the use of the term 'special relationship' in public, especially by the State Department, as likely to 'increase suspicion among our allies of secret plans and purposes which they did not share and would not approve'. It would also confirm to 'the Mayor Thompsons, McCarthys, McCarrans, and Jenners' that 'the State Department was a tool of a foreign power'. As he pointed out, 'Mayor Thompson of Chicago had found the key to success at the polls in his proclaimed eagerness to "hit King George on the snout"'. And before Pearl Harbor, 'Communists and "America Firsters" had joined in condemning Britain's "imperialist" war'. So it was important not to provide such groups with any ammunition that would hamper Anglo-American relations.[46]

When Franks returned to London in March 1951 for consultations with Sir Roger Makins and other Foreign Office personnel there was evident concern – as there was in Churchill's Fulton and Waldorf Astoria speeches – that the US government preferred a covert 'special relationship' to an open one. The reasons for the American attitude were not referred to in the record of the meeting but no doubt included sensitivity towards other allies such as France and various policy differences with Britain. But judging from Acheson's comments Britain's enduring colonialist image was also an important factor and it was no coincidence that he had specifically mentioned Chicago and various Irish-American politicians as sources of criticism of a public Anglo-American 'special relationship'. Furthermore, as Lippmann had pointed out after the Fulton speech, too open an association with the British Empire might hamper American efforts to win over the hearts and minds of people in the Third World.[47]

The divergence between British and US policies in the Middle East, amply demonstrated in the case of Palestine, was again in evidence during the Abadan crisis of September 1951. Like the Suez crisis several years later it followed the nationalisation of a valuable British asset by a nationalist leader – in this case the Anglo-Iranian Oil Company by Prime Minister Mohammad Mosaddegh on 2 May 1951. Not for the first time, or the last, a British ambassador in Washington was caught in the middle of a delicate issue arising in the Middle East. Franks was critical of the British-controlled company which, he said, 'had not got far enough past the stage of Victorian paternalism' and he pointed out that the 'Kipling type of technique' was unlikely to win over the Truman administration. Indeed, Acheson made it very clear to Franks that the US could not support military action. On 25 September the Iranian government announced that British technicians who refused to work for the new National Iranian Oil Company would be given a week to leave the country. On the 27th the British Cabinet seriously discussed the use of force but the American opposition to such a move persuaded Attlee and his ministers that this was not a sensible option. A week later the British employees left Abadan and the crisis was over.[48]

A general election at the end of October 1951 saw the return of Winston Churchill as Prime Minister – one month short of his seventy-seventh birthday – and of Anthony Eden as Foreign Secretary. Franks enjoyed good relations with both but he was a less influential figure for the remainder of his time as ambassador as Churchill naturally regarded himself as the leading authority on Anglo-American relations and Eden was not far behind in valuing his own opinion most highly.[49] Churchill was anxious to re-establish contact with Truman and in January 1952 he was once more in Washington. He held several talks with the President and his key officials and it was clear that confirming the 'special relationship' was uppermost in his mind, if not in Truman's. However, the main event of the visit was Churchill's address to Congress on 17 January in which he declared that:

> Under the pressure and menace of Communist aggression the fraternal association of the United States with Britain and the British Commonwealth, and the new unity growing up in Europe ... are being brought forward, perhaps by several generations, in the destiny of the world.[50]

This was obviously a veiled reference to his Fulton speech but, unlike at Fulton, Churchill also dwelt in some detail upon the Middle East – a sign of its central importance to his government. He was full of praise for Israel and pointed out that he had supported a national home for the Jews since the days of the Balfour Declaration. But his main focus was the Suez Canal. He told Congress that it was 'no longer possible' for Britain 'to bear the whole burden of maintaining the freedom of the famous waterway of the Suez Canal'. This task had become 'an international rather than a national responsibility'. There were more than 80,000 British troops in the Canal Zone and this commitment could not be borne for much longer. He appealed for support from the US, France and Turkey and said that even token reinforcements would have a stabilising effect and would help to end 'the wide disorders of the Middle East in which ... there lurk dangers not less great than those which the United States has stemmed in Korea'. It was a classic piece of Churchillian oratory – the Middle East had received the Fulton treatment.[51]

Franks' term in Washington was due to expire in June 1952 but he agreed to stay on until December. Before he departed from the US he gave another speech at the National Press Club in which he declared that US–British friendship was the foundation for the world's hopes of freedom and that, despite their differences and disagreements, should it come to 'the pinch and to the clinch' the two countries were as one.[52] He continued with this theme in a farewell speech delivered on the radio the next day. The main danger to cordial Anglo-American relations, he argued, was 'the unreasoning passion of a purely nationalistic approach'. Differences in temperament and outlook gave the Anglo-American partnership its 'strength and vitality'. But

> we should be alert to prejudices which blind us to the realities of the matter and the too-stubborn desire to follow our individual paths. These are the foes of the unity we must maintain if we are to survive in the world today.

With the benefit of hindsight Franks' words seem very prescient regarding the Suez crisis that arose during the watch of his successor.[53]

On 28 November Franks and Lady Franks sailed for Britain. Dean Acheson felt 'real and deep regret' when he first learned of Franks' departure. 'I have greatly enjoyed working with him,' he said. 'His great ability and his keen perception and knowledge of the United States and its people have enabled him to carry out his responsibilities with outstanding success.'[54] American press comment was equally positive, both on the East Coast and elsewhere. the *New York Times* referred to his 'beautiful and moving farewell to the American people' as a reminder that 'a good friend and an exceptionally keen mind are being lost – temporarily one hopes – to Anglo-American relations', while the *San Francisco Chronicle* printed the entire text of his farewell address 'because it is an expression of deep human feeling and because as such it manages to clarify and strengthen the bond between the two nations'. Clearly Franks would be a hard act to follow.[55]

Sir Roger Makins – Whitehall mandarin, 1953–6

The man selected for the task of replacing Franks was Sir Roger Makins, who was very much a Whitehall mandarin. Churchill had initially wanted a well-known public figure as ambassador along the lines of his choice of the Earl of Halifax – for example, Earl Mountbatten. But Eden preferred a top-flight official and suggested Makins, who had been an important figure in the Foreign Office since the 1930s, had already served in the US, had an American wife and was generally considered to be an expert in Anglo-American relations. By 1952 he was Deputy Undersecretary in the Foreign Office and in line for the top post. Churchill also had a high regard for him and, after meeting him over lunch at Chartwell on 20 July 1952, he agreed to the appointment. Makins eventually departed for the United States on 31 December 1952, and as Churchill was anxious to see Truman before he left office the new ambassador found himself crossing the Atlantic on the same ship as the Prime Minister, arriving in New York on 5 January 1953.[56]

Churchill's ambassadors 159

After presenting his credentials to Truman, Makins made his maiden speech to the National Press Club at the end of January 1953. Employing a theme that he would return to constantly during his time in Washington he expressed confidence that the United States and Britain continued to share common objectives despite differences on issues of secondary importance. He warned against disagreements in policy towards the Middle East which he said was a vital area for both Britain and the US. He argued that Britain was continuing to shoulder most of the defence burden in the region and that this was 'in the common interest', not just in Britain's interest. After his speech he was asked whether he thought British and American policies in the Middle East ought to be kept separate, especially in Iran, to which he replied, 'No, I don't, and especially not in Iran', stressing the strategic importance of the Middle East and its resources to both countries.[57]

A few days later Makins gave the traditional Pilgrims speech at the Waldorf Astoria. He said that the old concept of a close association between Britain and the US as the cornerstone to world peace was now broadening to include the entire North Atlantic community, which faced the twin task of forging the Atlantic alliance and then 'fashioning it into something greater and more extensive'. He argued that a military alliance kept together by the threat of Soviet attack was not enough, 'there must be something stronger than what Kipling called "ties of common funk", important though these undoubtedly are'. Anglo-American cooperation remained 'one of the central pillars' of the Atlantic alliance, he argued, while the traditional relationship was working itself into different patterns 'in the rolling mill of events' and 'would endure'.[58]

When Makins made another speech in May 1953, on 'The British Economy and the Free World', the subsequent Q and A session focused largely on the British Empire in its various forms. Asked when the British government would 'modernise its policies towards the natives in their colonial empire', Makins replied: 'It is modernising them all the time.' He then referred to new constitutions in the Gold Coast and Nigeria as well as reforms in the West Indian Federation and Malaya. 'In every colony under the British Crown there is steady progress towards self-determination and self-government. That is a continuing process which is being carried on in every part of the territories under the British Crown.' He was also quizzed about Britain's informal empire in the Middle East. 'Wouldn't Egypt be better off with Britain protecting the Suez Canal, than trying to do it themselves?' he was asked. 'I regret to say that Egypt doesn't seem to think so at the moment,' he replied, bringing laughter from his audience.[59]

By the summer of 1953 the Eisenhower administration had decided that the time had come to encourage by covert means a new, more compliant regime in Iran. There followed the Iranian coup of August 1953 engineered by the CIA and MI6 that overthrew Prime Minister Mohammad Mosaddegh and strengthened the rule of the pro-Western Shah, Mohammed Reza Pahlavi. However, the coup could not entirely restore the position of the Anglo-Iranian Oil Company which changed its name to British Petroleum and joined a consortium of companies in controlling Iranian oil output and profits. The coup suggested that

160   T. McCulloch

London and Washington could work together successfully to further their aims in the Middle East, but that covert means were preferable to the US government in dealing with obstructionist regimes rather than well-publicised military action that might disturb American public opinion and provide rhetorical ammunition for the Soviet Union. The same approach was used in Guatemala in June 1954.[60]

Further Anglo-American cooperation of a more public kind was evident when Eisenhower and Churchill met in Washington in June 1954 – a meeting that led to the so-called Potomac Charter which was to some extent a renewal of the Atlantic Charter famously agreed by Churchill and Roosevelt in the heady days of August 1941. Upon his return to Britain Churchill told the House of Commons that he

> was thrilled by the wish of the President of the United States to bring our two countries so directly together in a new declaration or charter, and to revive and renew the comradeship and brotherhood which joined the English-speaking world together in the late war, and is now, if carried into effect, the strongest hope that all mankind may survive in freedom and justice. I can well understand that such a document may incur the criticism of mischief-makers of all kinds in any country, but for myself I rejoice to have had the honour of adding my signature to it.[61]

Like the Atlantic Charter, the Potomac Declaration was couched in general terms and did not specifically refer to the Middle East. But Churchill told the Commons that he had raised the question of Egypt with the President.

> I have for some time been of the opinion that the United States have a strategic interest in Egypt as well as their interest in the international waterway of the Suez Canal and that the responsibility for both these matters should no longer be allowed to rest exclusively with Great Britain. Although, of course, the strategic importance of Egypt and the Canal has been enormously reduced by modern developments of war, it cannot be wholly excluded from American thoughts where the recent extension of NATO's southern flank to Turkey is concerned.[62]

Two weeks later, on 27 July 1954, an Anglo-Egyptian Agreement was signed in Cairo that ended the 1936 agreement negotiated when Anthony Eden first became Foreign Secretary in Baldwin's government. In effect, the new agreement brought to an end over seventy years of British occupation of the Suez Canal Zone since the Anglo-Egyptian war of 1882. British troops were to leave the Canal Zone by June 1956 although they would still be allowed to return in the event of war. The agreement was roundly criticised by some Conservative MPs – the so-called Suez Group – as an abandonment of Britain's imperial position but it was successfully defended by Churchill on the grounds not only of cost but also the new international security situation that he argued had been created by the massive American hydrogen bomb test in March 1954 at Bikini Atoll in the Marshall Islands.[63]

Churchill's ambassadors 161

For the remainder of his time as prime minister Churchill's main aim was to fulfil his ambition of a summit conference to mitigate the dangers of Cold War misunderstandings leading to a nuclear war. Having decided by March 1955 that this would not be possible at any early date he informed Eden he would be resigning on 5 April. But on 8 April a telegram from Makins suggested that Eisenhower was thinking of meeting Churchill and other Western leaders in Paris on 8 May – the tenth anniversary of VE Day – and might be open to planning a conference with the Soviet leadership. This made Churchill withdraw his plan to retire in April – much to the annoyance of Eden, who pursued the matter with Washington via the US ambassador in London rather than Makins in order to clarify Eisenhower's intentions. When the reply came back that the President was not now thinking of going to Europe, Churchill duly retired on 5 April. But this was one of a number of incidents that caused friction between Eden and his ambassador and led to Makins being recalled during the Suez crisis.[64]

Descent to Suez – and ascent to Bermuda, 1956–7

In his memoir *Descent to Suez*, Evelyn Shuckburgh provided historians with an insider's account of the development of the Suez crisis from the advent of Churchill's peacetime government in October 1951, when he was appointed Principal Private Secretary to Anthony Eden, to what he described as 'the morrow of the Suez crisis' in December 1956. In this memoir he naturally focused on the diplomacy of Anthony Eden and the shortcomings that led to the crisis, including Eden's ill health and increasing irritability and his tendency to see Nasser as another Mussolini, but he was also critical of Churchill and of Eden's ministers. As regards the British ambassadors in Washington during this period, while Franks and especially Makins were both mentioned quite frequently by Shuckburgh neither was afforded a prominent role during the crisis.[65]

In fact, Makins – like Franks – played an important and constructive part in Anglo-American relations while he was in Washington and he did his best to keep the Suez crisis from spiralling out of control. He got on well with Eisenhower and did his best to smooth over difficulties between Washington and London, even urging the Foreign Office to try to restrain press criticism of the unpopular Dulles while he was in London for a meeting in October 1953.[66] But events were against him, especially in Egypt where the revolution of July 1952 which overthrew the monarchy of King Farouk had been stimulated by a nationalist movement highly critical of British influence and power in the country. Egyptian nationalism was represented most forcefully by Gamal Abdul Nasser who by June 1956 had consolidated his hold on the republican government, following the withdrawal of British troops from the Suez Canal Zone, by becoming president. Nasser was hostile to the Baghdad Pact of Iraq, Iran, Turkey and Pakistan favoured by Eden and the British government and was prepared to buy arms from the Communist bloc if they could not be obtained from the West, hence the arms deal with Czechoslovakia in September 1955.[67]

162   T. McCulloch

The dilemma facing Britain and the United States was whether to try to win over Nasser or to confront him and secure his removal. The US government was more hopeful than the British that the former policy might work and indicated to Nasser that a loan might be made to Egypt for the construction of the Aswan High Dam if he was cooperative. Makins played a major role in the difficult and complex negotiations to arrange the massive loan required to build the dam.[68] But he had lost Eden's confidence by the time the latter became prime minister and their relations deteriorated thereafter. Essentially, he was regarded as too sympathetic to the American point of view, especially on Middle Eastern issues. He warned London that the US government was opposed to the use of force against Nasser but Eden felt he had 'gone native' and was therefore not sufficiently forceful in presenting the British point of view in Washington.[69]

On 13 July 1956 Dulles told Makins that the US was poised to withdraw the offer of funding to Egypt for the Aswan High Dam as Congress was against the idea. The ambassador said that the British view was generally supportive of this action but counselled against a blunt announcement. It was during these final deliberations on the fate of the Aswan Dam loan that on 17 July Dulles was informed that Makins would soon be leaving his Washington post. Dulles took this very badly, not only because of the timing but also because he had 'complete faith' in Makins. Indeed, the timing could hardly have been worse even though the rationale was obviously to remove an ambassador who was regarded as unsympathetic to his own government's policy.[70]

On 26 July, a week after the US withdrawal of funding from the Aswan Dam project, Nasser nationalised the Suez Canal. Eden contacted Eisenhower the next day and appealed for his support in putting 'maximum pressure' on the Egyptian government, arguing that Nasser's move threatened both British and US interests in the Middle East. On the same day, the British Cabinet agreed that Britain should act alone if Washington and Paris were not prepared to join in common action with London. At the same time, the aim of British policy was to try to arrange 'common action' with the US and France as their support – and especially that of the United States – would be necessary in the event of economic sanctions or war. In particular, Britain would have to rely on the US government to make sure that the Soviet Union did not intervene in the situation.[71]

However, despite constant pressure on the US government and what amounted to a propaganda campaign aimed at American public opinion, the British government was unable to make any progress in winning support for the use of force. There was plenty of condemnation of Nasser's action in the United States and some concern at the future control of the Canal and the potential for greater Soviet influence in Middle East but very little support for military action. Instead, Eisenhower and Dulles favoured a diplomatic solution involving the main canal users and the United Nations. A conference of twenty-two nations met in London in August 1956 but neither Nasser nor the British government was satisfied with its results. Harold Macmillan, the Chancellor of the Exchequer, met Eisenhower in Washington on 25 September but he sent back an over-sanguine report of his conversation with the President to London. Makins

Churchill's ambassadors 163

was present at the meeting and later said that he was 'amazed' that neither Macmillan nor Eisenhower had made the positions of their governments clear. However, Macmillan also met Dulles who was much clearer in his opposition to open military action, preferring to wait until a covert operation could be carried out, as in the case of Iran.[72]

Before finally departing from the US in October, Makins gave a farewell speech at a Pilgrims lunch in which he said that the Suez Canal question posed 'the most serious challenge to international confidence and good faith since the Korean conflict'. He deprecated what he regarded as the tendency to exaggerate disagreements between the US and Britain. 'We appear to have an almost pathological tendency to magnify our differences,' he said. He acknowledged that 'world issues' had strained Anglo-American relations but he argued that 'such disagreement as there is normally relates to the timing and the tactics rather than to the substance of policy'. Then, somewhat ironically in view of imminent events, he said: 'it is one of the great strengths of our relationship that when we do disagree we can sit down calmly, assess the reasons for it and understand, if we cannot share, each other's point of view'.[73]

Unbeknown to Makins, who did not discover what was happening until he returned to London, the British government was about to embark on secret negotiations with France and Israel in the Parisian suburb of Sèvres – the outcome of which was a plan to seize the Canal and to oust Nasser in the process. On 25 October Eden gave the go-ahead for British military intervention. Israeli forces duly invaded Egypt on 29 October and this was followed the next day by a British and French ultimatum to end the hostilities, which was flatly rejected by Nasser. British planes then attacked Egyptian airfields and British troops headed from Malta towards Port Said, which was captured by British and French paratroopers on 5 November. The main British and French forces arrived at Port Said on 6 November – the day of the US presidential election – and occupied the Canal.[74]

The British and French action was condemned by the US, the Soviet Union and the UN and the impact of the crisis on Britain's fragile financial situation forced Eden to order a rapid ceasefire. Eden's premiership, of course, never recovered from this humiliating turn of events and he resigned through ill health in January 1957, to be succeeded by Harold Macmillan.[75] Ironically, Makins, who was now Joint Permanent Secretary at the Treasury, had a major role to play in helping to stabilise sterling after the Suez debacle. In this capacity his contribution to Anglo-American relations was perhaps even more important than as ambassador in Washington, although it was almost unprecedented for a Foreign Service official to be given the top job at the Treasury and it was a move that was very controversial within Whitehall.[76]

As for Churchill, he issued a public statement supporting the British military action in which he said that Egypt had provoked the crisis and that British policy was intended to restore peace to the Middle East. 'I am convinced that we shall achieve our aim,' he said, and that 'our American friends will come to realise that, not for the first time, we have acted independently for the common good.'

164   T. McCulloch

The statement appeared in the press on 5 November and led Eden to write to thank him for his 'wonderful message'. Two weeks later, when Eden had agreed to withdraw British troops from the Canal Zone, Churchill was asked if he would have sent in troops, as Eden had done. 'I would never have dared,' he replied, 'and if I had dared, I would never have dared stop.' This oft-quoted remark by Churchill suggests that he would have been more cautious than Eden in risking American opposition to the use of overt military force. And while he sympathised with the Suez Group of MPs he defied them over the Anglo-Egyptian Agreement in July 1954.[77]

Conclusions

The Potomac Charter of June 1954 was in many ways the fulfilment of Churchill's mission to revive the Anglo-American 'special relationship' that had been announced by the Atlantic Charter of August 1941, forged during the Second World War and enshrined in the Fulton speech. The Potomac Declaration not only recognised the common principles underlying British and American foreign policies but it did so quite openly. It also inferred the containment of the Soviet Union and Communism while acknowledging the primacy of the United Nations. It was renewed by Eisenhower and Eden in January 1956 in the Washington Declaration and yet in less than a year the US and Britain were at loggerheads and Eden's premiership – and his reputation as a master of diplomacy – had been destroyed by Suez.[78]

Eden and his Cabinet must take much of the blame for this crisis in Anglo-American relations. Whereas the Potomac and Washington Declarations, like the original Atlantic Charter and, indeed, the Fulton address were well-considered exercises in public diplomacy the agreement between Britain, France and Israel at Sèvres was just the opposite – risky, secretive and essentially deceitful. The timing of the Israeli invasion of Egypt and the British and French intervention – just before the presidential election on 6 November – was also the height of folly given the sensitivity of that date from the US perspective. Nasser had taken advantage of the pre-election period when nationalising the Suez Canal but close allies of the US were not expected to adopt such underhand tactics. The recall of Makins during the crisis was also difficult to defend, even if he had lost Eden's confidence, as it left Britain without an ambassador in Washington at a crucial time.[79]

The Eisenhower administration also came in for its share of criticism during the Suez crisis – in the US as well as in Britain. Eisenhower's Democratic opponent in the presidential election, Adlai Stevenson, accused him and Dulles of virtually driving the British and French into a desperate act because of the lack of clarity in US policy towards Egypt and the Middle East – for example, in offering funding for the Aswan High Dam and then withdrawing it. The same line was taken by John F. Kennedy, campaigning in New York, and also by George Kennan.[80] There was much sympathy for Israel, Britain and France within the US media because of Nasser's own high-handedness and the perceived weakness and unfairness of the US response. Walter Lippmann was particularly scathing and in

Churchill's ambassadors   165

a syndicated column on 1 November, entitled 'Disaster in the Middle East', he accused the administration of treating America's closest allies with contempt. He argued that a more even-handed US response should have been adopted at the UN – recognising Egyptian provocation as well as over-reaction by Britain and France. Lippmann was sufficiently influential that his Suez column was discussed by Eisenhower and Dulles on the same day.[81]

The administration took its stand on the issue of colonialism. Vice President Richard Nixon, speaking on the campaign trail, said that the overwhelming support at the UN for the US resolution calling upon Britain and France to withdraw their troops from Suez had

> constituted a world-wide vote of confidence, the like of which has never been known before.... For the first time in history, we have showed independence of Anglo-French policies towards Asia and Africa which seemed to us to reflect the colonial tradition.[82]

More privately, Dulles told the National Security Council that the Suez invasion was 'the straight old-fashioned variety of colonialism of the most obvious sort'. The US had endeavoured to retain its good relations with Britain and France while winning over the governments of the former colonies and preventing their defection to the Communist bloc. But the US could not condone the colonialism of Britain and France otherwise it would be tied to the past rather than the future. 'It was tragic that the US felt compelled to abandon its closest long-term allies,' Dulles said, but the alternative was to condone military force to restore 'less developed nations' to colonial status.[83]

Since the Fulton speech successive British ambassadors had made some headway in explaining the nature of the British Commonwealth and Empire to the Americans. The status of the Commonwealth was no longer contentious, after the decision of India to remain a member after independence and the announcement of the London Declaration of April 1949 that defined the modern organisation.[84] The development of the colonial empire required somewhat more explanation, although an understanding had been reached in the Potomac Charter whereby 'the right of people who are capable of sustaining independence' was recognised.[85] But the third element of British colonialism – the informal empire, most notably in the Middle East – had remained a serious problem, a source of weakness as much as strength. Eden, fearful that Britain's entire position in the Middle East was under threat from Nasser, including its supply of cheap oil, felt that the Egyptian leader had to be dealt with sooner rather than later. But even those Americans who sympathised with Britain's predicament during the Suez crisis, such as Lippmann, did not condone the resort to military force. And Kennan characterised it as an 'ill-conceived and pathetic action'.[86]

After the chastening experience of Suez Churchill was anxious to repair Anglo-American relations as quickly as possible and he immediately wrote to Eisenhower to mend the British fences.[87] The President was of the same view although he also acted quickly to bolster the American position in the Middle

166   T. McCulloch

East by means of the Eisenhower Doctrine of 5 January 1957. This gave explicit support to pro-Western nations by committing the US 'to secure and protect the territorial integrity and political independence of such nations, requesting such aid against overt armed aggression from any nation controlled by international communism'.[88]

Eisenhower then invited Macmillan to a bilateral summit in March and at his suggestion the two leaders met in the British colony of Bermuda. Eisenhower later described the Bermuda meeting as the most successful international conference he attended after the Second World War, and it included a significant agreement to supply Britain with intermediate-range ballistic missiles. As Eisenhower stepped off the motor launch that took him to the dockside where Macmillan was waiting, he thanked the assembled crowd for their warm welcome and said: 'I am sure that in the next few days we can do much to strengthen the long-term bonds that have bound together the British Empire and my country.'[89]

These words were obviously music to Churchill's ears and the Bermuda summit helped to restore his Fulton dream. The British ambassadors who had served in Washington since the Fulton address, and, indeed, since Churchill had become prime minister, had all contributed in their different ways to the development of an Anglo-American 'special relationship' that was based on national self-interest and genuine cooperation as well as history and culture. Taking their lead from Lothian, they had engaged in significant public diplomacy and had sought to present a modern and forward-looking image of Britain despite the legacy of British colonialism – an image not helped by Churchill's own attachment to the Empire, both formal and informal. Churchill made his final visit to the US in May 1959 achieving his own peace with Eisenhower who bade him a friendly farewell as he departed from the White House for the last time. The 'special relationship' was alive and well, but more than ever the US was the dominant partner – now in the Middle East as elsewhere.[90]

Notes

1 For the Suez crisis in Anglo-American relations see C.J. Bartlett, *The 'Special Relationship': A Political History of Anglo-American Relations since 1945*, London: Longman, 1992; John Bayliss, *Anglo-American Defence Relations, 1939–1984*, second edition, Basingstoke: Palgrave Macmillan, 1984; John Bayliss, *Anglo-American Relations since 1939: The Enduring Alliance*, Manchester and New York: Manchester University Press, 1997; Alan Dobson, *Anglo-American Relations in the Twentieth Century*, London: Routledge, 1995; John Dumbrell, *A Special Relationship: Anglo-American Relations from the Cold War to Iraq*, second edition, Basingstoke: Palgrave Macmillan, 2006.

2 Richard Longworth (ed.), *Churchill in His Own Words*, London: Ebury Press, 2008, p. 98.

3 For example, Michael F. Hopkins, Saul Kelly, and John W. Young (eds), *The Washington Embassy: British Ambassadors to the United States, 1939–77*, Basingstoke: Palgrave Macmillan, 2009, includes the following essays: J. Simon Rofe, 'Lord Lothian, 1939–40', pp. 14–32; Nicholas J. Cull, 'Lord Halifax, 1940–46', pp. 33–51; Martin Folly, 'Lord Inverchapel, 1946–48', pp. 52–70; Michael F. Hopkins, 'Oliver Franks, 1948–52', pp. 71–90; and Saul Kelly, 'Roger Makins, 1953–56', pp. 91–109.

4 David Reynolds, *The Creation of the Anglo-American Alliance, 1937–4: A Study in Competitive Cooperation*, London: Europa, 1981, p. 11.
5 Rofe, 'Lord Lothian'; David Billington, *Lothian: Philip Kerr and the Quest for World Order*, Santa Barbara: Praeger, 2006; Rhodri Jeffreys-Jones, 'The Inestimable Advantage of Not Being English: Lord Lothian's American Ambassadorship, 1939–1940', *The Scottish Historical Review*, 63:175, 1984, pp. 105–10; David Reynolds, 'Lord Lothian and Anglo-American Relations, 1939–40', *Transactions of the American Philosophical Society*, 73:2, 1983, pp. 1–65.
6 Lord Lothian, Address to the Pilgrims Society at the Hotel Plaza, New York City, on 25 October 1939, *New York Times*, 26 October 1939.
7 Ibid.
8 For FDR's internationalism see David F. Schmitz, *The Triumph of Internationalism: Franklin D. Roosevelt and a World in Crisis, 1933–1941*, Washington, DC: Potomac, 2007; and Robert Dallek, *Franklin D. Roosevelt and American Foreign Policy, 1932–1945*, New York: Oxford University Press, 1995.
9 Wilson C. Miscamble, *From Roosevelt to Truman: Potsdam, Hiroshima and the Cold War*, Cambridge and New York: Cambridge University Press, 2008; Arnold Offner, *Another Such Victory: President Truman and the Cold War, 1945–53*, Stanford: Stanford University Press, 2002; John Lewis Gaddis, *We Now Know: Rethinking Cold War History*, Oxford: Clarendon Press, 1998.
10 UKNA (UK National Archives at Kew), FO 371, 51624, AN 649/4/45, Winston Churchill, 'Sinews of Peace' speech, Fulton, Missouri, 5 March 1946; see also Martin Gilbert (ed.), *Churchill: The Power of Words*, London: Bantam, 2012.
11 Cull, 'Lord Halifax', pp. 33–6.
12 UKNA, FO 371, 51624, AN 698/4/45, Earl of Halifax to Ernest Bevin, 8 March 1946; FO minute re Isaiah Berlin by J.C. Donnelly, 9 March 1946.
13 Ibid.
14 Ibid. British Information Services, American Press Summary Survey Special: Mr Churchill's Speech, 6/7/8 March 1946 – *Herald Tribune*, 6 March 1946, p. 20; *Christian Science Monitor*, 6 March 1946.
15 Ibid., *Chicago Sun*, 8 March 1946; *Chicago News*, 8 March 1946; *Chicago Times*, 8 March 1946.
16 Ibid., Walter Lippmann syndicated column, 6 March 1946.
17 Ibid. For Lippmann see Ronald Steel, *Walter Lippmann and the American Century*, New York: Transaction Publishers, 1999.
18 Dallek, *FDR and American Foreign Policy*; Paul Orders, 'Adjusting to a New Period in World History': Franklin Roosevelt and European Colonialism', in David Ryan and Victor Pungong (eds), *The United States and Decolonization: Power and Freedom*, London: Macmillan, 2000, pp. 63–84; William Roger Louis, *Imperialism at Bay: The United States and the Decolonization of the British Empire, 1941–45*, New York: Oxford University Press, 1987.
19 UKNA, CAB 23, Cabinet Conclusions 23 (46), 11 March 1946; see also FO 371, 51624, AN801/4/45G, 11 March 1946.
20 UKNA, FO 371, 51624, AN 755/4/45, Winston Churchill, Speech at Waldorf Astoria, 15 March 1946; see also *New York Times*, 16 March 1946, for speech and absence of Dean Acheson.
21 Ibid.
22 Ibid.
23 Ibid.
24 Ibid. FO minute by D. Brogan, 20 March 1946.
25 Ibid. Winston Churchill, Waldorf Astoria speech, 15 March 1946.
26 Sarvepalli Gopal, 'Churchill and India', in Robert Blake and William Roger Louis (eds), *Churchill*, New York: W.W. Norton, 1993, pp. 457–72.

168   *T. McCulloch*

27 UKNA, FO 371, 51624, AN 912/4/45, F.E. Evans, British Consul-General in New York to Archie Mackenzie, British Embassy in Washington, 21 March 1946 (sent to Foreign Office, 31 March 1946).
28 Cull, 'Lord Halifax', pp. 33–51; see also Andrew Roberts, *The Holy Fox: The Life of Lord Halifax*, London: Weidenfeld and Nicolson, 1991, pp. 366–402; and the Earl of Halifax, *Fullness of Days*, London: Collins, 1957, pp. 235–97.
29 Halifax, *Fullness of Days*, pp. 235–97.
30 Ibid., pp. 293–5.
31 UKNA, FO 371, 51625, AN1234/4/45, Lord Halifax, Speech to Pilgrims Society, 22 April 1946; see also *New York Times*, 23 April 1946.
32 Ibid.
33 Ibid.
34 Martin Folly, 'Lord Inverchapel', pp. 52–70; see also Donald Gillies, *Radical Diplomat: The Life of Archibald Clark Kerr, Lord Inverchapel, 1882–1951*, London, I.B. Taurus, 1999.
35 Folly, 'Lord Inverchapel', pp. 52–70.
36 UKNA, FO 371, 51626, AN 2787/2803/2809/2810/4/45, Henry Wallace speech, 12 September 1946 and FO minutes; see also *New York Times*, 13 September 1946.
37 UKNA, FO 371, 51626, AN 3558/4/45, Lord Inverchapel, Speech to the Pilgrims, Waldorf Astoria Hotel, 12 November 1946.
38 Ibid.
39 Ibid.
40 *New York Times*, 13 November 1947; Folly, 'Lord Inverchapel', pp. 64–8.
41 Hopkins, 'Oliver Franks, 1948–52', pp. 171–3. See also Michael Hopkins, *Oliver Franks and the Truman Administration: Anglo-American Relations, 1948–1952*, London: Routledge, 2002; Alex Danchev, *Oliver Franks: Founding Father*, Oxford: Clarendon Press, 1993; Peter Boyle, 'Oliver Franks and the Washington Embassy, 1948–52', in John Zametica (ed.) *British Officials and British Foreign Policy, 1945–50*, Leicester: Continuum, 1990, pp. 189–211.
42 FO 371, AN 2275/183/45, Sir Oliver Franks, speech to National Press Club, 8 June 1948; see also *New York Times*, 9 June 1948.
43 FO 371, AN 3746/183/45, Sir Oliver Franks, speech to Pilgrims at the Waldorf Astoria, New York, 13 October 1948.
44 *New York Times*, 29 November 1952.
45 Offner, *Another Such Victory: President Truman and the Cold War*; Gaddis, *We Now Know: Rethinking Cold War History*.
46 Dean Acheson, *Present at the Creation. My Years in the State Department*, London; Hamish Hamilton, 1970, pp. 387–8.
47 Bayliss, *Anglo-American Relations since 1939*, pp. 75–7 for Foreign Office meeting, March 1951.
48 Hopkins, 'Oliver Franks, 1948–52', pp. 81–4; see also W.R. Louis, *The British Empire in the Middle East, 1945–51: Arab Nationalism, the United States and Postwar Imperialism*, Oxford: Oxford University Press, 1984.
49 Martin Gilbert, *Churchill: A Life*, London and New York: BCA, 1991, pp. 897–8.
50 Ibid., pp. 899–903; *New York Times*, 18 January 1952.
51 Ibid.
52 UKNA, FO 371, 97646, AU 1892/2/45, Sir Oliver Franks, speech to National Press Club, Washington, DC, 26 November 1952; see also *New York Times*, 27 November 1952.
53 Ibid., Sir Oliver Franks, farewell speech via radio, 27 November 1952; see also *New York Times*, 28 November 1952.
54 *New York Times*, 4 October 1952.
55 FO 371 97646, AU 1892/2/45, Survey of American press comment on Sir Oliver Franks' departure from the United States, 11 December 1952.

Churchill's ambassadors 169

56 Richard Wevill, *Diplomacy, Roger Makins and the Anglo-American Relationship*, London: Ashgate, 2014, pp. 99–102; Saul Kelly, 'Roger Makins', pp. 91–3; Saul Kelly, 'A Very Considerable and Largely Unsung Success: Sir Roger Makins' Washington Embassy, 1953–56', in Jonathan Hollowell (ed.), *Twentieth Century Anglo-American Relations*, Basingstoke: Palgrave, 2001.

57 Sir Roger Makins, speech to National Press Club, 28 January 1953, *New York Times*, 29 January 1953.

58 Sir Roger Makins, speech to Pilgrims, Waldorf Astoria Hotel, 2 February 1953, *New York Times*, 3 February 1953.

59 UKNA, FO 371, 103522, AU 1056/2/45, Sir Roger Makins, speech on 'The British Economy and the Free World', to the Economic Club of Detroit, 6 May 1953.

60 Stephen Kinzer, *All the Shah's Men: An American Coup and the Roots of Middle East Terror*, Hoboken: John Wiley, 2008.

61 Winston Churchill, *House of Commons Debates*, 12 July 1954; see also James Hubbard, *The United States and the End of British Colonial Rule in Africa, 1941–1968*, Jefferson, NC: McFarland, 2011, pp. 147–8; Wevill, *Diplomacy, Roger Makins and the Anglo-American Relationship*, p. 119.

62 Ibid. For text of the 'Declaration by the President of the United States and the Prime Minister of the United Kingdom', 29 June 1954, sometimes known as the 'Potomac Charter', see Department of State *Bulletin*, 12 July 1954, p. 49.

63 Gilbert, *Churchill*, pp. 923–31; Wevill, *Diplomacy, Roger Makins and the Anglo-American Relationship*, p. 119; Gill Bennett, 'Challenging Nasser: The Suez Crisis, July 1956', in Gill Bennett, *Six Moments of Crisis: Inside British Foreign Policy*, Oxford: Oxford University Press, 2013, pp. 37–66.

64 Gilbert, *Churchill*, pp. 936–9; Wevill, *Diplomacy, Roger Makins and the Anglo-American Relationship*, pp. 123–5.

65 Evelyn Shuckburgh, *Descent to Suez: Dairies, 1951–56*, London: Weidenfeld and Nicolson, 1986; for the Suez crisis see also Keith Kyle, *Suez: Britain's End of Empire in the Middle East*, second edition, London: I.B. Taurus, 2011; W. Scott Lucas, *Divided We Stand: Britain, the US and the Suez Crisis*, London: Hodder and Stoughton, 1991; Donald Neff, *Warriors at Suez: Eisenhower Takes America into the Middle East*, New York: Simon and Schuster, 1981.

66 UKNA, FO 371, 103523, AU 1057/1/45, Sir Roger Makins to Foreign Office, 13 October 1953.

67 Wevill, *Diplomacy, Roger Makins and the Anglo-American Relationship*, pp. 125–5; Nigel Ashton, *Eisenhower, Macmillan and the Problem of Nasser: Anglo-American Relations and Arab Nationalism, 1955–59*, Basingstoke: Palgrave Macmillan, 1996.

68 Diane B. Kunz, *The Economic Diplomacy of the Suez Crisis*, Chapel Hill: University of North Carolina Press, 2009, pp. 41–56.

69 Wevill, *Diplomacy, Roger Makins and the Anglo-American Relationship*, pp. 108–31.

70 Ibid., p. 131.

71 Tony Shaw, *Eden, Suez and the Mass Media: Propaganda and Persuasion During the Suez Crisis*, London: I.B. Taurus, 2009, pp. 154–76.

72 Lucas, *Divided We Stand: Britain, the US and the Suez Crisis*, pp. 201–3.

73 Sir Roger Makins, farewell speech at lunch of Pilgrims executive committee, 11 October 1956, *New York Times*, 12 October 1956.

74 Lucas, *Divided We Stand: Britain, the US and the Suez Crisis*, pp. 243–97.

75 Ibid., pp. 298–323.

76 Wevill, *Diplomacy, Roger Makins and the Anglo-American Relationship*, pp. 137–59.

77 Gilbert, *Churchill*, pp. 948–50; Lucas, *Divided We Stand: Britain, the US and the Suez Crisis*, p. 28 for Churchill and the Suez Group.

78 Lucas, *Divided We Stand: Britain, the US and the Suez Crisis*, pp. 86–92.

79 Wevill, *Diplomacy, Roger Makins and the Anglo-American Relationship*, pp. 137–59.

80 Kyle, *Suez: Britain's End of Empire in the Middle East*, pp. 425–6.

81 Ibid., p. 426; Steel, *Walter Lippmann and the American Century*, pp. 503–4; telephone discussion, Eisenhower and Dulles, 1 November 1956, *Foreign Relations of the United States*, 1955–7, Vol. 16, Suez Crisis, 26 July–31 December 1956, Doc. 454.

82 Kyle, *Suez: Britain's End of Empire in the Middle East*, p. 426.

83 Hubbard, *United States and the End of British Colonial Rule in Africa*, pp. 149–50.

84 Amitav Banerji, 'The 1949 London Declaration: Birth of the Modern Commonwealth', *Commonwealth Law Bulletin*, 25:1, Spring 1999, pp. 1–8.

85 Hubbard, *United States and the End of British Colonial Rule in Africa*, pp. 147–8; 'Potomac Charter', 29 June 1954, Department of State *Bulletin*, 12 July 1954, p. 49.

86 Lucas, *Divided We Stand: Britain, the US and the Suez Crisis*, pp. 86–92; Kyle, *Suez: Britain's End of Empire in the Middle East*, p. 426.

87 Winston Churchill to Dwight Eisenhower, 3 November 1956, in Bayliss, *Anglo-American Relations since 1939*, pp. 82–3; Lucas, *Divided We Stand: Britain, the US and the Suez Crisis*, pp. 314–15.

88 Peter L. Hahn, 'Securing the Middle East: The Eisenhower Doctrine of 1957', *Presidential Studies Quarterly*, 36:1, March 2006, pp. 38–47.

89 Bayliss, *Anglo-American Defence Relations, 1939–1984*, pp. 88–90; Bayliss, *Anglo-American Relations since 1939*, pp. 89–91.

90 Gilbert, *Churchill*, p. 955.

7 Churchill's inter-subjective special relationship

A corpus-assisted discourse approach

Anna Marchi, Nuria Lorenzo-Dus and Steve Marsh

> In the course of my life, I have often had to eat my words, and I must confess that
> I have always found it a wholesome diet.
>
> Winston Churchill[1]

This chapter is premised on the belief that an important element of the origins and distinctiveness of the UK–US special relationship lies in the way in which Anglo-American political elites and media constructed it over time through language. After all, it is discourse that enables us to interpret and shape the world around us.[2] And as alluded to in the above epigraph, few politicians have more ably deployed discourse than Winston Churchill.

Churchill regarded his 1946 Sinews of Peace speech as the most important of his career.[3] It is best remembered for its 'iron curtain' metaphor, which initially captured a regional geopolitical division and later formed part of the Cold War meta narrative. However, our interest lies in his proposed solution – a *special relationship* between Britain and America and a fraternal association among the English-speaking peoples of the world.[4] As he told those gathered at Westminster College in Fulton, Missouri:

> If the population of the English-speaking Commonwealths be added to that of the United States with all that such co-operation implies in the air, on the sea, all over the globe and in science and in industry, and in moral force, there will be no quivering, precarious balance of power to offer its temptation to ambition or adventure.'

What is particularly instructive for us is that, conscious of American attachment to the United Nations project and their historic suspicion of entangling alliances, Churchill developed through his Sinews of Peace a discursive master-class in uncovering the connections between Britain and America, establishing common ground and positioning the 'fraternal association' as a force for good, i.e. supporting the incipient UN and safeguarding international peace. Beginning with the exceptionally close wartime experience and shared English language, Churchill subtly proceeded to develop the numerous further sinews that bound

172   *A. Marchi* et al.

the English-speaking peoples together. These included unique cooperation (e.g. shared knowledge of the atomic bomb), 'the joint inheritance' of political freedom and common law, religion, and scientific and technological leadership (evolved in the context of tackling poverty).[5]

We thus take the Sinews of Peace speech as a historical marker for the subsequent discursive construction of a modern Anglo-American special relationship. By combining diplomatic history with Corpus Assisted Discourse Analysis (CADS) we examine through government and media texts how notions of special Anglo-American relations were subsequently evolved discursively. Focusing in particular on Churchill's role in the articulation and mediation of a special relationship, we demonstrate how political and media elites in the early 1950s began to articulate and culturally embed the notion of a unique Anglo-American relationship.

The special relationship as a discursive construct

References in the literature to the importance of shared language in the special relationship are normally made in passing and within an assumed, rather than empirically proven, 'discourse of specialness'.[6] To our knowledge, there are no detailed studies of what that *discourse* may be like, that is, how a US–UK special relationship may have been discursively constructed. In treating discourse as a form of action (as performative), we adhere to foundational work in Pragmatics, specifically within Speech Act Theory,[7] which conceives of language as performative. This understanding of language has also been instrumental in other Social Sciences disciplines, which have undergone a 'discursive turn'. For instance, the Copenhagen School of Security Studies (CSSS) applied Speech Act Theory tenets directly to their main area of interest: security.[8] CSSS proposed what was at that time a radically new understanding of 'security' as a speech act and of securitisation as intersubjective, that is, as comprising a process whereby an actor uses language to elevate an issue, such as poverty, from a political to a security realm, thereby legitimising extraordinary socio-political measures to address its thus acquired security-threatening properties.[9] CSSS-influenced scholars have subsequently identified two consecutive stages within this process, namely the successful implementation of communicative and coordinative discourses. The former provides 'a common language and ideational framework through which key policy groups seek to come to agreement about a policy paradigm'; the latter serves as 'a vehicle through which policy elites seek to persuade the public that the policy paradigm is necessary and appropriate'.[10]

Our own work also sees the UK–US special relationship as emerging in part from performative discourse. We consider the process of elevating a given political issue from an 'ordinary' to an 'extraordinary' status applicable not only to perceived threats (e.g. security threats) but also to opportunities (e.g. international relations). Specifically, we argue that the UK–US relationship was raised to a 'special relationship status' through communicative and coordinative discourses. This is not to deny the role played by other, 'hard' factors.[11] Rather,

The inter-subjective special relationship 173

those factors were themselves also articulated through discourse, and jointly contributed to the emergence and development of the UK–US special relationship, shaping the intensity and emphases of its 'specialness' across time.

Our work examines the early post-WW2 period. As far as establishing a common language and ideational framework upon which to base an agreed policy paradigm (the communicative discourse stage) is concerned, we focus on the political figure of Winston Churchill. This is because of his articulation of the special relationship in the Sinews of Peace speech and the central role that he is widely accepted as having played within Anglo-American relations thereafter. Regarding the coordinative discourse stage, we focus on the principal political and media discourse contexts through which the policy paradigm was articulated for the public during that period, namely UK–US summit meetings and their print media coverage.

We use summit meetings because Diplomacy Studies' scholarship identifies them as the most important emergent diplomatic fora of the Cold War[12] and within Anglo-American relations per se, a pattern emerged between American presidents and British prime ministers whereby it was generally expected that the two leaders should personally meet on a regular basis in order to discuss important issues and policy decisions.[13] We have selected three consecutive summits spanning 1950–4. By this time British elites had abandoned both traditional policy of balancing British power against that of America and the possibility of Britain's heading a 'Third Power' grouping as an alternative to close partnership with the US.[14] Conversely, Washington had begun to reciprocate interest in close relations with the UK in the face of a series of losses to Communism, especially China, and in consequence of demands inherent in a policy of global containment. In April 1950 a US military report concluded explicitly that: 'there is and should be a special US–UK relationship.... Accordingly an examination of the relationship is necessary, not to see whether it can be retained but to see how it can be strengthened.'[15] This suggests that by the early 1950s there was an evolving transatlantic coordinative discourse around privileged (broadly defined) UK–US relations.

As for the focus on media, and specifically print media, as a further vehicle for establishing a coordinative discourse around the UK–US special relationship, this is justified by the mediatisation of political communication in general and the onset of that mediatisation process during the period under examination. Mediatisation refers to a process whereby all parts of society become progressively and increasingly more dependent on the media and their logic.[16] Media logic, and specifically news media logic, is in turn understood as the institutional, technological and sociological features of news media. The mediatisation *of politics* thus refers to the process of the media moving from mere channels of communication to active players in the political arena.[17] Professional, technological and commercial aspects conflate in this process.[18] Within these, it is worth emphasising the latter, which refers to economic forces promoting media logic in ways that increase their dependency on commercial imperatives, including the need to secure the audience's attention to sell their products through, for

174 *A. Marchi* et al.

instance, personalising politics.[19] The personalisation of politics is also in part a development of the technological aspects of mediatisation, such as the emergence of television. It would be inaccurate, however, to treat television as the catalyst of the personalisation of politics. There are important antecedents in relation to the press and radio throughout the twentieth century.[20]

The processes involved in the mediatisation and personalisation of politics are neither uniform nor linear. They are also dependent on structural and situational circumstances which, at different historical points and in different countries, may accelerate, interrupt or even reverse mediatisation and personalisation processes.[21] Umbricht's (2014) work, for instance, shows that from the 1960s to the late 2000s, mediatisation/personalisation of politics followed a straightforward upward pattern in the case of Britain, the US and Italy but not in Germany or Switzerland.

Given that British and US political systems were immersed in progressive mediatisation/personalisation processes by the 1960s, the genesis of these processes may well coincide with the 1950s: the period we have selected in our work. Both Churchill's personal investment in UK–US relations and his widely attested political charisma thus provide additional structural factors that justify our interest in that period. Was Churchill key in articulating the communicative discourse around which a policy paradigm of UK–US specialness was constructed in the early 1950s? If so, what characterised that discourse and how was it coordinated across summits and print media at the time? Before answering these questions, let us consider the specific data and analytic steps that our work draws upon.

The study

This study adopts a broad analytical framework of Corpus Linguistics. Corpus Linguistics is, in general terms, the study of language based on the use of large collections of texts (i.e. corpora) and of computational tools to interrogate them.[22] The more specific framework used in our work is Corpus-Assisted Discourse Studies (hence CADS[23]). CADS is defined as the practice of investigating particular discourse types by combining the quantitative rigour of Corpus Linguistics techniques with the social perspective of more traditional approaches to Discourse Analysis, in order to uncover '*non-obvious meaning*, that is, meaning which might not be readily available to naked-eye [perusal]'.[24] CADS, or, better, self-identified CADS researchers belong to a larger family of scholars who use corpora to study how social reality/ies are constructed, represented and transmitted linguistically.[25] CADS is characterised by the versatility of its methods, by a permeability to input from other disciplines and an adaptability to address issues and interests raised in other disciplines. Because of its explorative nature and omnivorous interests, CADS appears to have an intrinsic interdisciplinary vocation, and yet there are very few examples[26] of actual interdisciplinary research to date. The present study is an exception to this in its integration of a Diplomatic History interpretative framework and a focus on authentic language and empirical research.

The inter-subjective special relationship 175

Following the principle that frequency matters, CADS start by identifying what is numerous and salient in a corpus. The focus of analysis thus emerges bottom-up from the corpus itself, rather than being determined by a pre-defined hypothesis. Clearly there may very well be anticipations about what will be found in the corpus, and these play a key role in the way we interpret the findings, but the research path itself is dictated by the patterns one encounters. This means that the results of CADS analysis tend to hover between the corroboration of what is felt to be known and 'serendipitous'[27] discovery. Such an inductive approach does not necessarily equate to objective findings, as pattern recognition remains an inevitably interpretative activity; it does, however, mean that CADS research is replicable and accountable.

The analytic process typically moves from general to particular: from distributional information (general quantifications and word frequency lists), 'funnelling'[28] down progressively closer to the individual texts and taking into account the extra-linguistic context. While it requires extensive close reading, all corpus analysis relies on the employment of concordancing software[29] that computes statistical information, as well as being the interface between the researcher and the texts. The concordancer takes its name from the *concordance*, which is the collection of all the examples containing a target word in the corpus, as exemplified in Figure 7.1. A concordance brings together a series of fragments of text displaced from their original sequence and by juxtaposing them vertically, one after the other, it makes repetition visible and countable so that the repeated co-occurrence of items emerge to the surface.

Usually in corpus-based work, in contrast with what happens with other forms of Discourse Analysis, researchers zoom into the text using the concordancer, starting from individual words, reading vertically through the concordance, looking at other terms their target word repeatedly co-occurs with. Such repeated co-occurrences of pairs of words are called *collocates*. The principle of collocation is fundamental to the understanding of corpus work and it consists in the idea that the meaning of a word is defined by the relationships it establishes with other words 'which tend to occur in its environment'.[30] A word, for instance, may have absorbed the positive or negative evaluative meaning of the words it is repeatedly found in association with, a process known as semantic – or evaluative – prosody.

Wordlists, concordances and collocations compose the essential toolbox of CADS, such as the one we are about to present. There is one last concept (and tool) that needs introducing: that is, keywords. Keywords are the place where the search for patterns of meaning often begins and this is because all Discourse Analysis is intrinsically comparative. A primary way to do corpus comparisons is keywords analysis: the comparison of the frequent and salient words in two corpora or in two portions of a dataset. A keyword is a word 'whose frequency is unusually high in comparison with some norm'.[31] We identify keywords by comparing two wordlists, the output from which is a new list of words that are characteristic (or rather characteristically different) in the corpus/text we are examining, with reference to another text or corpus. The use of keywords as a

176   *A. Marchi* et al.

Concordance

order WASHINGTON, Jan. 16 - Winston Churchill, a stanch champion of the
President Truman and Prime Minister Churchill a fortnight ago brought the two
involved. In the world view of Winston Churchill, a strong, intimate and organic
beef dinner. The president, in turn, gave Churchill a complete set of the classes
positively of both Mr. Truman and Mr. Churchill. A certain obstinacy, a streak
see Churchill off for home Winston Churchill, a stout, stooped, Briton
Williamsburg. For this occasion, Mr. Churchill abandoned the sawed-off
not only reject the claim that Mr. Churchill abandoned anything or
talks between Gen. Eisenhower and Mr. Churchill about United States politics.
Churchill accepts US commander in
United Nations. "The invitation of Mr. Churchill, addressed to the United
the recorded voice of Prime Minister Churchill addressing the United States
, when it comes to foreign policy. Churchill advised trip Furthermore, he
should have consulted Churchill or that Churchill advised him that he should
, as previously announced. Also, Mr. Churchill advised British officials by
Churchill advises coolness to prevent a
ago last Saturday with Prime Minister Churchill. After four days in Washington,
what happened to Prime Minister Churchill after you got to Washington.
was not going to stay up talking to Mr. Churchill after nine o'clock, which is
here. Truman will avoid details The Truman-Churchill agenda however,
Eisenhower and Churchill agree on aims for peace, arms
TRUMAN, CHURCHILL AGREE ON 3 POINTS AS
, not by whether Mr. Truman and Mr. Churchill agree on this or that, but by
the point. After Mr. Truman and Mr. Churchill agreed on the principle of

Figure 7.1 Example of concordance for the word 'Churchill', retrieved using *Wordsmith*.

springboard for the analysis and the research process as a whole will be discussed in some detail below, where we finally present the most important element of CADS: the corpus.

At the core of CADS research is the corpus. Corpus design and compilation are an integral part of the research process. Given that our 'results are only as good as the corpus',[32] the corpus we collect must suit the research question. The corpus used in this study consists of approximately half a million words of archival and print media records relating to the first three post-war bilateral summit meetings (1950–4) between British prime ministers and American presidents (see Table 7.1). The corpus architecture was informed by historical knowledge and designed prior to data collection in anticipation of potentially interesting

Table 7.1 Corpus composition (tokens=number of words, texts=number of articles in the case of the press and of documents as collected and transcribed from archival material for government data)

Year	UK government		US government	
	Tokens	Texts	Tokens	Texts
1950	76,395	50	35,892	6
1952	84,639	62	76,332	60
1954	28,276	14	44,649	6
Sub-total	189,310	126	156,873	72

Year	UK press		US press	
	Tokens	Texts	Tokens	Texts
1950	28,568	27	47,355	52
1952	22,840	31	76,258	96
1954	25,490	22	53,959	56
Sub-total	76,898	80	177,572	204
Total	266,208	206	334,445	276

uses, allowing for multiple comparisons: origin (UK sub-set vs US sub-set), sources (newspapers vs governmental records), individual summits (1950 vs 1952 vs 1954), and the timeline of each summit (four weeks before the summit vs summit period vs four weeks after the summit).[33]

The analysis started with two keywords comparisons:[34] first, we compared against each other the wordlists of the newspaper (UK and US press) and government (UK and US government) sub-corpora. This produced a total of 415 keywords for the press data and 682 for the government data, which were then disambiguated and examined in detail. Keywords offer a starting point to identify the ways in which the relationship between the UK and the US is referred to. We discovered, for example, that the term *special relationship* only occurred five times in the entire corpus and was picked up just once[35] in the press.

Keywords were grouped into semantic domains: that is, individual key words were classified into lexically coherent areas of meaning, or disambiguated in context and assigned to the relevant semantic area. The same semantic domains emerged when comparing British and American data in both the media and government sub-corpora, namely: geographical/political entities; participants; military; money and resources; and interaction (i.e. verbal and mental processes). This semantic categorisation tells us what themes were central in each country's government and media (press) account of the summits. For example, they evidence an obsession with Communism throughout the US data and a preoccupation with money and resources in the US news which was absent in the UK press, but which conversely dominated the UK governmental documents. The semantic

178 *A. Marchi* et al.

categories also helped us identify the alternative lexicon of the relationship, such as: *old friendship*. In the UK press we found, for example, a strong focus on what could be called the discourse of 'harmony', with words emphasising the shared aims and agreement between the UK and the US. We also identified pervasive traces of invocation of the common language shared by the two countries. From the US government data emerged a strong focus on *cooperation* and we found a variety of references to the collaborative activities between the US and the UK. The US press especially focused on the participants and the communication between them and key above all was Winston Churchill.

The analysis that ensues follows the spotlight directed by the quantitative review of the corpus and delves into examination of the role played by Churchill as represented by the media of the time.

Churchill's role in the articulation of a communicative discourse of UK–US specialness

Corpus analysis showed that Churchill was paramount to the articulation of a discourse of UK–US specialness in the period under examination. Two kinds of evidence revealed this. First, Churchill was quantitatively key: he was by far the most mentioned individual throughout the dataset in relation to such a discourse. Second, and beyond quantification, the corpus disclosed the qualitative aspect of his keyness: his defining importance, which emerged through the review of what the data revealed of what he did at the summits and how his words and actions were reported by others.

The keywords analysis revealed that Churchill was mentioned 2.5 times more frequently in the US press than in its British counterpart and was 4.3 times more present in the US government data than in the UK's. Not only was *Churchill* one of the absolute top keywords in the US dataset (Truman's name occurred less than half as frequently and Attlee got about one-third of Churchill's mentions), he was also the most frequently named individual throughout the whole corpus. The data-driven evidence overwhelmingly points to the dominance of the figure of Churchill in the coordinative discourses both of the summits and about the summits. Thus, the historical significance of Churchill appears to be matched by the statistical significance of his ubiquity in the data. In terms of media attention, Churchill secured the media spotlight during the meetings, even when he was not physically there. The 1950 summit was attended by British Prime Minister Clement Attlee and yet American newspapers invoked Winston Churchill as the mastermind behind the event. On 7 December 1950, the *Washington Post* wrote:

> Attlee not only was careful to get Churchill's support before he left London, but Churchill even advised him on how to force Truman's hand regarding the trip. What happened is that immediately after the Prime Minister heard of Truman's atom bomb statement, he called on Churchill. Though political opponents, the two men served in the same coalition war cabinet together

The inter-subjective special relationship 179

and are personal friends. At one time Attlee was Churchill's deputy Prime Minister and handled British domestic affairs while Churchill was busy with the war. With this background of friendship, it is not hard to understand why Attlee should have consulted Churchill or why Churchill advised him that he should take the trip to Washington. Furthermore Churchill suggested that inasmuch Truman might be opposed to the trip, Attlee should make a premature announcement of his plan – thus making it impossible for Truman to decline.[36]

Beyond this individual example, comparisons between Attlee and Churchill were frequent in the corpus and when we looked at co-occurrences of *Churchill* and *Attlee*, or of either name and *predecessor* in the media texts, we invariably found that evaluation was in favour of Churchill. For instance:

Although Attlee is not showing personality like Churchill, the Administration here has regarded him as a good partner and ally.[37]

The center of the stage was held by the Western Big Two. Mr Truman and Mr Attlee are in many ways two of a kind. They stand in homespun contrast to their more spectacular predecessors, Franklin D. Roosevelt and Winston Churchill.[38]

Churchill is not only overall more frequently mentioned than the other participants by the press, but he is also more popular than other political leaders in the corpus. With respect to Attlee, this was particularly clear in the 1952 dataset, where Churchill was presented as the fixer of a relationship that had been weakened by Attlee:

The wartime prime minister, who at 77 finds himself again at the head of the British government, feels very strongly that his predecessor, Mr Attlee, lost the opportunity to maintain an intimate relationship that was built up between Britain and the United States during the war.[39]

Going back to the first extract from the *Washington Post*, the whole summit is presented as Churchill's idea and Attlee is portrayed as enveloped in Churchill's guidance (seen as actively seeking Churchill's support and advice), patronage (the reader is told that he used to work with Churchill or rather for Churchill when the latter was busy taking care of more important things, i.e. the war) and friendship. The fact that Attlee and Churchill are friends is stressed twice in the passage and the discourse of friendship works as a legitimation of Attlee, in a sort of 'a friend of my friend is my friend' manner.

Within this quantitative salience, and through collocation and concordance analysis of the mentions of Churchill in the corpus, three main roles emerged for him: Churchill as friend, Churchill as negotiator, and Churchill as the embodiment of the British bulldog spirit.

180   *A. Marchi* et al.

Churchill as 'friend'

The theme of friendship emerged already from the keywords, among which we found the word *old*, which was key in the US press and frequently found in the pattern *old friend(s)* (fifteen occurrences), or alternative lexicalisations of the concept, e.g. *old friendship, old Anglo-American collaboration, old acquaintance*. 'The Old Friend Visits Again', titled the *New York Times* (20 June 1954) over a spread of smiling and chummy photographs of Churchill with Roosevelt, Truman and Eisenhower between 1941 and 1953.

While the 'old wartime friend' motif only appeared three times in the UK data, the conceptualisation of the relationship between the two countries as a 'friendship' and its representation in terms of intimacy is very typical of the US data. This shows clearly in the way the American newspapers chose to frame Churchill's words and in their selection of Churchill's quotes. For example: 'As Mr Churchill said when he arrived and as he has emphasized repeatedly in his talks here, he is doing no more than trying to establish an "intimate relationship" between the heads of the two governments.'[40]

Walter Lippmann explicitly commented in the *Washington Post* in 1952:

> The turn will be marked, I feel sure, not by whether Mr Truman and Mr Churchill agree on this or that, but by the manners and the moods of the officials of the two countries, and of the press reports which should result from their briefings. When after a long absence two old friends meet, having some difficult business to do, what matters most is not how they do the business but whether still they are friends.[41]

The discourse of friendship and intimacy is, in particular, the way in which the American press portrayed Churchill's motives and the position of Britain in the context of the talks, thus acknowledging Churchill's aims. 'The atmosphere of respect and friendliness which Mr Churchill said he wanted to achieve with the leaders of the government has been achieved.'[42]

Related to this is the priming of Churchill's call for cooperation, stressed in the corpus by the repetition of phrases such as *common cause, common effort, common purposes, common political objectives, united action, mutual cooperation*, and so on, when reporting about Churchill. For example:

> Churchill said of his projected talks with Mr Truman that their two governments 'must understand each other's point of view and try to do all they can to help each other in the common cause'.[43]

> Churchill said that 'if we work together we may get along all right ourselves and do a lot to help our neighbours in the world.'[44]

> Mr Churchill's mission was worth while, if only because it clarified our vision of the inseparable destinies of Britain and the United States. We

The inter-subjective special relationship   181

Americans are not kindly souls handling out the necessities of life to the deserving poor. We are partners and comrades in a common effort. This is certainly what Mr Churchill wanted us to realize anew.[45]

It is interesting to note, however, that the narrative of closeness between the two countries was often accompanied by very practical implications: in US reporting of the Prime Minister's idea of unity, the newspapers tended to steer towards the shared goals and means that such unity should involve, especially acting together against Communism. This points to the interdependency of hard and soft factors in constructing the special relationship and to a goal-orientated American emphasis.

Churchill's visit was presented as a *mission*. We encountered this explicit definition ten times in the American newspapers, for instance:

Mr Churchill's mission is regarded as a public relations success.[46]

Prime Minister Churchill is going to the United States in the hope of reviving with President Truman the close relationship that existed between him and the late President Roosevelt. That is the chief purpose of Mr Churchill's mission, rather than the hope of reaching hard and fast agreements on specific problems.[47]

All the examples made clear that the mission was of a relational nature: the mission was to salvage the unuttered 'special relationship' past (the *old friendship*) and future (the *inseparable destinies*) of the two countries. From all the examples also shone through a positive attitude of the American press towards Churchill and his intents.

The emphasis on the positive relationship expressed by the press was matched in the US governmental documents corpus, where words such as *cooperative*, *cooperate*, *cooperation* and *relationship(s)* were key. The term *relationship* itself was four times more frequent in US documents than in British ones and 50 per cent of the mentions of the term referred to the Anglo-American relationship, which was qualified as *close* and three times explicitly as *special* (conversely the phrasing *special relationship* never appeared in the UK dataset). Again the semantic area of 'togetherness' was a characteristic of the US corpus (both in the media and in the government data) and so was the stress on the personal relationship with Churchill. In the US government documents Churchill was also referred to as an *old and valued friend* and mentions of him were surrounded repeatedly by expressions of appreciation and closeness. As anticipated, fascination of the American press with the British Prime Minister was palpable: 'Mr Churchill scored, as usual, a personal success.'[48]

The focus on Churchill's success as an individual is indicative of a shift towards personalisation in US politics within the period under examination. It must be noted, however, that there are important differences between the *New York Times* and the *Washington Post*. The *Washington Post*, in fact, did not share its competitor's unbounded enthusiasm for Churchill, being respectful but also sceptical:

Whether Mr Churchill can repeat the personal triumphs of his wartime visits here, however, remains to be seen. He has been out of office for five years; his hearing is now seriously impaired, and his political margin at home is far smaller than when he was Prime Minister before. Nevertheless, he has demonstrated in the last few weeks that he can still convey to his audiences a sense of the historical mission in which both the United States and Britain are involved, and as a convinced believer in the closer United States–British ties, he may very well take this opportunity to propose forms of Atlantic integration that are at least as bold as any officials here are prepared to accept.[49]

The example above is typical of the *Washington Post*'s take on Churchill: characterised by the accumulation of negative prosody, followed by a release of the tension by means of reversal of the evaluation. This scrutiny of Churchill's features, including a focus on his health problems (hearing impairment), is not only symptomatic of the advanced stage of personalisation in US politics at the time but also of the non-linearity of the process for, as discussed earlier, the US media did not subject every contemporaneous political leader to such close scrutiny.

The press also insisted on how much Churchill was liked and welcomed by the American people, who were repeatedly described as *clapping*, *cheering*, *welcoming* him and *gathering in great numbers* to do so. This emphasised the theme of friendship and the atmosphere of friendliness and cooperation built up by the press.

The popularity of the British Prime Minister in the US was registered also by the British press, including claims that Americans liked him more than their own leaders, as well as acknowledgments that Churchill's popularity was stronger in the US than in Britain.[50] *The Times* reported on 5 January 1952:

The American columnist Mr Walter Winchell devoted his entire column today to Mr Churchill, of whom he said 'his overpowering versatility places him among the immortals'. Mr Winchell said that although Mr Churchill's popularity in England had followed an erratic course, he had always been popular with Americans. 'The fact is,' he said, 'Americans today have more admiration for him than most United States leaders ... Americans welcome him as a friend.'[51]

On the other side of the Atlantic the UK press referred regularly to friendship and intimacy, the discourse of harmony and to understanding. Though references to Churchill as 'friend' were far from absent (see the example), they were nevertheless less prominent than in the US press.

[T]he man who throughout his long career has made the close friendship of Britain and the United States a first principle of his foreign policy. A few days ago even the Administration was said to regard Mr. Churchill's visit with mixed feelings. Admiration for the great statesman and affection for an

The inter-subjective special relationship   183

old friend were tinged, according to the reports, with slight apprehension as to what he might want.[52]

Among the expressions that characterised the British press corpus we found items such as *exchange views*, *harmony of views*, *identity of views*. The British press presented the summits as a way to resolve *misunderstandings*, *divergences* and *difficulties* (e.g. *elimination of all misunderstandings*, *clear up misunderstandings*, *transcend divergences*, and so on) and as a way to increase cooperation. As in the American press, at the heart of events there was a communicative intent, but on the British side the focus was on the sphere of interpretation.

> The Washington communiqué and Mr Churchill's address to Congress have been examined so minutely and interpreted so imaginatively on both sides of the Atlantic that the Prime Minister's own version of what happened was bound to seem disappointing ... there is the obvious danger, especially in the year of a Presidential election, that the agreement to differ may be interpreted as an agreement to act. Anglo-American friendship and cooperation cannot prosper unless real differences of opinion are discussed with absolute frankness; and an emergency may well leave too little time.[53]

The relevance of interpretation and disambiguation is corroborated by the insistence in the British government data on the importance of language and on the wording and tweaking of communiqués.

The UK press included the narrative of friendship initiated by Churchill himself, but not in the same way that the US press did. The friendship between the two countries was discursively constructed in the American newspapers in terms of unity, alliance and common effort, but in a rather goal-directed way: with an accumulation of references to military and diplomatic issues. The American newspapers also evidenced a strong tendency towards personalisation, of friends and of foes. As we have seen, Churchill was presented as a friend Americans are fond of and Churchill's words were reported to the effect of establishing and reinforcing the discourse of friendship. At the same time, though, the focus was steered towards the practical implications of being friends: acting together against foes, that is Communism (see 'Churchill as "negotiator"', below).

There was also evidence of personalisation in the British press. Reports emphasised the popularity of Churchill overseas, where he was presented as embodying the preferred version of Britain in the eyes of Americans (see 'Churchill as "Britain"', below). Of the discourse of friendship promoted by Churchill, the UK press boosted the communicative aspect: the talking, the harmony of feelings, the mutual understanding. In the way Churchill is reported in *The Times* we found a dense semantic area of emotion/perception (e.g. *confidence*, *hope*, *feel*), while there were far fewer references to military and contingent issues than in the US papers. Churchill's words for unity and cooperation, as selected by British reporters, were directed towards peace and negotiation (more on this in the next section) as a common cause.

184　*A. Marchi* et al.

The 'softness' of this discussion was also suggested by the vagueness of the reporting about it. While the US press gave an account of the details and the implications of the discussion as it was happening, in the UK press we predominantly found references to the overall importance of the meeting (before it happens) and its overall success (after), but very little was said in terms of specific contingent commitments and their impact on the future. If anything, the British newspaper preferred to linger on the past: the wartime closeness that gets renewed. For example:

> There may be no dramatic outcome of this visit. Its purpose, as Mr Churchill has carefully said, is to reach 'a good understanding over the whole field so that we can work together easily and intimately at the different levels as we used to do'.[54]

The *spirit of the wartime partnership* (as *The Times* calls it), albeit not a dominant theme in terms of frequency, was also evoked in the American press, particularly in terms of the personal relationship between Churchill and Roosevelt. But here it was nested in the broader utilitarian picture mentioned earlier. An extended example from the *New York Times* serves to clarify. James Reston's article, titled 'Churchill's Visit Smooths Some Rough Spots', set the scene by first remarking on the diplomatic tone and significance of the summit talks. According to Reston, 'The Truman–Churchill talks are not likely to be included among the great achievements of Mr Churchill's life, but they were useful and in some ways important.' Characterised by 'easy bantering', 'small talk' and 'probing into the roots of the relationship between the two countries', the talks apparently 'interrupted the habit of long-distance bickering which has plagued both capitals for the last two years'. They also 'improved the personal relations between the president and the prime minister and – at least equally important – between the two foreign secretaries'.

However, the bulk of Reston's article is dedicated to listing seven immediate political problems upon which a 'large measure' of Anglo-American agreement was secured:

1　They agreed that the United States and Britain should back – but not join – the revolutionary experiment of an international European army. And they agreed that this should be a part – but only a part – of the larger experiment of an integrated Atlantic community, including the United States and Britain.
2　They agreed that the United States atomic bomber bases in Britain should not be used in 'an emergency' without the consent of both governments.
3　They agreed that their differences over the recognition of China were not as important as their common interests in working together to stop the expansion of Communist aggression in Asia.
4　Accordingly, they included in their communiqué a warning to the Peiping regime that they were watching the military situation in Southeast Asia.

The inter-subjective special relationship 185

Cooperation in Mideast

5 Similarly, they agreed to work together more closely in the Middle East and the two allowed the World Bank to try to negotiate a settlement of the Iranian oil controversy with the Mosaddegh government. The British had previously given the impression that they preferred to let time destroy this government.

6 They agreed to try to relieve each other's shortage of certain raw material essential for rearmament: specifically, to give the United Kingdom more steel in exchange for more British aluminium, copper, etc.

7 Finally, they agreed to consult one another on any development which seemed to increase the danger of war.[55]

Through these points the emphasis is placed on action: Anglo-American consulting, planning and doing in the face of and in response to a common threat to peace. Moreover, the numbered checklist of agreements is very typical of American reports. We never found anything like it in the British news, which, as aforementioned, remained very vague about the contents of the talks. See, for example, *The Times* commentary on the same meeting in 1952:

> Mr Churchill's object is not to obtain new concessions from the United States or to inveigle the Administration into setting up any particular machinery, but to restore, in another form, that close relationship between the two countries which, during the war, gave to the English-speaking peoples, as he said in his speech at Fulton five years ago, a 'grand simplicity of decision'.[56]

The insistence on the existence of 'the English-speaking community' was a recurrent pattern in the UK data. It came up in the list of keywords comparing the UK press against the US press and it was one of Churchill's soundbites that is picked up in *The Times*, where we found sixteen references, (equating relatively speaking to 0.2 per 1,000 words)[57] to *English-speaking world/nations/ family/brotherhood/peoples*. In the American press the relative frequency was 0.06 per 1,000 words (that is three times less frequent than in *The Times*). The *Washington Post* ignored the line (just one mention) and the *New York Times* picked it up only peripherally. The example below from the *New York Times* (1954) shows how the actual soundbite, rather than the phrase *English-speaking world*, is the reference to the *unbroken and unbreakable* closeness of the two countries, which is built up extensively in the text:

> Flashing his 'V' for victory hand signal, Sir Winston said at the airport that his talks with the president and other United States officials had demonstrated that United States–British unity was 'unbroken and unbreakable'.
>
> The Prime Minister said he had been to the United States many times 'on serious business in difficult times' but he could not remember any meeting

186 *A. Marchi* et al.

that 'has been more worthwhile and fruitful than this one or which has been more pleasant and agreeable'.

'A great note has been struck for the unity of the Anglo-American world, the English-speaking world is unbroken and unbreakable,' he added.[58]

The context of the unbreakable unity for the US press is always and inevitably the defeat of Communism, just as Churchill's staunch anti-Communism is the very reason why he is so celebrated.

Churchill as 'negotiator'

Churchill's role as negotiator emerges from the data in several forms. Evidently one objective of the summit in January 1952 was that at a time of grave British economic weakness and burgeoning defence demands, Churchill should secure American material support. Herein Churchill was cast as a negotiator for healthy Anglo-American relations, trading stalwart British support for American containment strategy for enabling resources from the US. This is reflected in the extracts below from American newspapers:

> There is one complete concession that Mr Churchill wants to get from the United States. That is the promise of a location of about 1,000,000 pounds of steel to make up for the deficiency of Britain's steel production.[59]

> Of course Mr Churchill did not come here merely to build up goodwill. There were practical considerations of the most urgent sort. Britain and the sterling area were losing dollars at a startling rate. Britain has entered on an ambitious rearmament program which, it had become painfully clear, could not be accomplished without additional American aid.[60]

Churchill also emerges from the data as a negotiator between the US and USSR. Of course, Churchill is well known to have desired Big Three summits to try to manage the Cold War, much sometimes to the annoyance of US administrations. However, the emphasis in our data is more on how Churchill negotiates the temper of East–West relations and balances his concerns for British security in an atomic age and Anglo-American relations within a strongly anti-Communist American elite and popular context.

The US press readily reports Churchill's steadfast support for anti-Communism and his determination that specific differences should not upset Anglo-American cooperation. For instance, the main front-page headline of the *Washington Post* on 10 January 1952 read: 'Red Threat Transcends Issues, Churchill Agrees; Truman calls '52 Crucial'.[61] The US press also reports that Churchill was willing to make practical *concessions* in order to ensure the friendly relationship with America. For example:

> Anglo-US Amity Stressed Above Policies on China and Iranian Oil

The inter-subjective special relationship 187

Dedicated to the principle that no secondary 'issues shall stand in the way' of mutual Anglo-American confidence, Prime Minister Churchill has made two major concessions to obtain it. A communiqué issued yesterday after his four days talks with President Truman revealed that Churchill has agreed that neither Britain's recognition of the Communist Chinese regime, nor its rage against the government of Premier Mosaddegh will block concerted action against Russian aggression.[62]

However, having reaffirmed his established position as friend of America and opponent of Communism, Churchill is also reported as urging caution in East–West relations. For instance, US newspaper coverage of the 1954 summit picked out his urging:

Churchill urges patience in coping with Red dangers.[63]

Churchill urges East–West amity.

Churchill urged again today the 'peaceful coexistence' of the Western and the Communist world.[64]

This pattern is repeated through Churchill's own words at the press luncheon in his honour on his last summit day in the US (29 June 1954). For instance, in reply to a journalist's question: 'What are the possibilities of peaceful co-existence between Soviet Russia and Communist China, on the one hand, and non-Communist nations on the other?' Churchill says:

I am of the opinion that we ought to have a try at peaceful co-existence and a real good try for it, although anyone can see that it doesn't solve all the problems, but it may be that time, if it is accompanied by vigilance, will enable peaceful co-existence for a period of years ... I am most anxious that the real mood of the people of Russia should be known and that every opportunity should be given for its expression ... I have a sort of feeling, and I may be quite wrong – I feel it with my fingertips, that's all I've got in the matter – I have a sort of feeling that there must be a very great wish in Russia to have a better time among the masses of the people.... So I am very much in favor of patient, cool, friendly examination of what the Russian intentions are. [65]

While deeply respectful of Churchill, in an era of McCarthyism the American press was not necessarily receptive to such tones of moderation. Churchill's contributions to the press luncheon above are a specimen of diplomatic talk, marked by vagueness and indirectness. Yet these characteristics are entirely lost in the journalistic account, the *New York Times* deciding to report thus on Churchill's nearly 4,000 word-long interaction with the press:

188 *A. Marchi* et al.

Violently 'Anti-Red'

'I am not anti-Russian,' he proclaimed, rolling his famous 'r's.' 'I am violently anti-Communist, but I do beg you to give them a chance to grasp the prospects of great material well-being, and I'm rather inclined to think, if I had to make a prediction, that they would not throw away such an opportunity.'

The Prime Minister qualified this theme in two respects: the 'patient, cool, friendly examination' should be backed at all times by Allied strength, based on the 'unbreakable unity' of the United States and Britain; and second, the time of approach to the Soviet leaders should be most carefully chosen.

He conceded that such an approach must have behind it 'the consenting mind of the heads of government,' and it must not be done when other aspects of the program were not propitious, for headstrong action at the wrong time might 'darken the scene'.

The conciliatory tones of Churchill's speech are overlooked, the anti-Communism is foregrounded and stapled in the heading, the 'unbreakable unity' soundbite (from another speech) is rehearsed and once again Churchill is described as making concessions to US reservations and to the unity of Anglo-American relations.

Meantime across the Atlantic, and while US media emphasised conflict in the context of Communism (i.e. the enemy to fight together when it comes to it), British media foregrounded Churchill's preference for peace and negotiation. *The Times* dismissed as a 'waste of time' the discussion about fighting Communism and reported the same speech by Churchill in June 1954 thus:

Later he called for 'an unbreakable unity of the English-speaking world to combat the spread of Communism not only in south-east Asia but in the western sphere'. He did not think that the Kremlin leadership necessarily represented the feelings of the Soviet public; 'It does not always follow that the men in the Kremlin will always be independent of the opinion of the vast Russian masses,' he added. 'I would like to make quite sure that the Russian people would feel that they might gain far more by a quarter-century of peaceful development in their own country than they would by pressing matters to a point where we should all be led to a situation which baffles human imagination in its terror, but which I am quite sure would leave us victorious but victorious on a heap of ruins.' Sir Winston Churchill said he was in favour of patient, cool, and friendly examination of Russian intentions.[66]

This representation of Churchill as a 'negotiator' between East and West is strengthened by, and the different UK–US media reception to his calls for moderation reflect, the virulence of US anti-Communism at this time. Indeed, the US media's 'obsession with Communism' is perhaps the most immediately visible trait emerging from the keyword analysis comparing the US and the UK

The inter-subjective special relationship 189

newspapers. Words such as *Communists, Communist, Red, Reds, regime* and references to *Vietnam, Cambodia, Indochina* and *Soviet* dominate the ranks of the list of keywords. This is the case also for the government data, which display a striking preponderance of Communism-related terms in the US documents and a corresponding absence of references in the British. There are no mentions at all of *USSR* or *Soviets* in the UK government corpus and the *Kremlin* is only mentioned twice, while in the American dataset these are among the top keywords. References to *Communist/s* are 2.5 times more frequent in the US government corpus and the term *regime* appears 7.6 times more frequently in the US corpus. In the broader context of relations between the West and Communist countries, these are systematically constructed in the US data in terms of *conflict, aggression, expansion* and military language.

Finally it is noteworthy that when exploring the concordance lines for *regime*, we discover that it preponderantly appears in the following context: *Chinese Communist regime* or *Communist regime in China*. Now, references to China are equally frequent in the UK and the US data (which is why neither *China* nor *Chinese* come up in either keywords list), but in the US data the country is frequently referred to with reference to Communism. This does not happen in the UK corpus. China in the UK corpus is occasionally referred to as *Communist China* (about 5 per cent of mentions), but is normally just *China*, while in the US corpus the direct reference to *Communist* or *Red* applies to nearly 40 per cent of mentions of China. These differences clearly evidence the shock felt in the US by the 'loss' of China and well-documented subsequent divisions between London and Washington over how to deal with China and the homogeneity or otherwise of world Communism.

Churchill as 'Britain'

We have already seen how Churchill is appreciated in the US. He is presented as the embodiment of the best qualities of Britain: the 'British bulldog spirit'. He stands for Britain in a way that neither Attlee does for the UK nor American presidents do for the United States: 'it is men such as Mr Churchill and his counterparts in more obscure walks of life, in the ranks and in the factories and fields and mines and on the sea, who have made and kept Britain Britain'.[67]

In this sense there is a metonymic relationship between Churchill and Britain. This is to some extent to be expected, given the personalisation of politics around him. However, what is really interesting – for it is not commonly observed in personalisation of politics processes – is that Churchill is also presented as better than Britain itself. For example, while Churchill's personal power is acknowledged, Britain's power is contested and the country is frequently described in terms of its decline and neediness.

> He carried the immense prestige of the Empire's contribution to the victory over Germany. This illusion of power was still strong. In the eyes of the world, Mr Churchill spoke as the equal of the President of the United States.[68]

190   *A. Marchi* et al.

> British pride and sense of independence is hurt at being treated much like an occupied country.... She needs economic assistance on a large scale again.[69]

When a disagreement between Churchill's positions and Britain's at large is repeatedly raised in the news, the press stresses the fact that the British people probably will not like the substance of Churchill's agreements with Truman:

> the British people are still somewhat puzzled concerning what decisions have been made by Mr Churchill and President Truman.[70]

> With a mixture of admiration and dismay thousands of Britons heard the recorded voice of Prime Minister Churchill addressing the United States Congress.... Seldom since World War II has he spoken more cogently or more eloquently with a nicer sense of timing and the nuance of politics, national and international. Nevertheless, there was detected in his carefully phrased speech a willingness to go further with the United States in extension of the war in Korea that the average Briton wants to go.[71]

Churchill is presented as being authoritative and in charge, but, at the same time, his vision is depicted as being at odds with the popular mood of his country. The American press evaluates very positively Churchill's vision, which implies a not so enthusiastic evaluation of the average Briton's mood. Churchill represents the Britain that Americans want. Furthermore Churchill's views are presented as the preferred vision of the US media, more so than the US government's. Before the 1952 summit begins, the *Washington Post* writes:

> Even before Churchill arrived, President Truman, Secretary of State Dean G. Acheson and their advisers had rather abusively decided not to grant the British leader what he mainly wanted, which was a strengthened partnership between America and Britain. Conflict of world views was involved. In the world view of Winston Churchill, a strong, intimate and organic partnership between America and Britain is the only possible core and center of the Western alliance.... And although there were many other vital issues to discuss, his main object in coming to this country was to restore the Anglo-American partnership to the working order. The Churchill world view was formerly shared by many of the wisest American policy-makers.[72]

The punch line at the end gives a clear indication of the journalist's evaluation, implying that the current administration does not belong to the group of the 'wisest'. Another illustrative example of these sympathies may be found in the juxtaposition of Churchill and Truman as sketched in the *New York Times*:

> Churchill, 77, the descendent of the Dukes of Marlborough, educated at Harrow and Sandhurst (England's West Point), soldier, war correspondent, first Lord of the Admiralty, chastiser of appeasement, wartime prime

The inter-subjective special relationship 191

minister, dogged fighter ('We shall never surrender'), imperious defender of Empire ('I have not become the King's first minister to preside over the liquidation of the British Empire'), opponent of socialism ('the philosophy of the queue'), implacable foe of Communism. Mr Churchill is a diplomat in the Metternichian tradition. After he has been briefed by his experts, he prefers to have big men dispose large affairs in snug talks.

Truman, 57, descendent of Scots-Irish immigrants, educated in public schools of Independence, Mo., railroad timekeeper, farmer, artillery man, haberdasher, country official, investigating Senator., Vice President, president-by-death ('I never wanted the job'), president by nomination and determination ('I'm going to call that Congress back'), Fair Dealer, leader of the free world (Truman doctrine, Marshall plan, NATO). Mr Truman likes to conduct diplomacy by committee; he wants his experts by his elbow to give him constant advice.[73]

It seems that Churchill (*soldier, dogged fighter, chastiser, implacable foe of Communism, big man*) comes out as rather more impressive than Truman (merely a *president-by-death* in *constant* need of advice).

The admiration and consensus afforded to Churchill in the US press brings us back to the underlying dominant discourse of friendship and the construction of the UK–US relationship as being special. The friendliness of the relationship between the UK and the US ultimately seems to be constructed in terms of a personal friendship, even kinship, between Churchill and America. 'Churchill spoke before a battery of microphones, reading from a single sheet of typed paper. He said that "I have had a very comfortable journey from my fatherland to my mother's land" a reference to his American-born mother.'[74]

One last dominant corpus-driven pattern evidencing not only the projection of Churchill's charm, but his uniqueness and centrality in the US newspapers' reporting of the summits, is the bulk of detailed physical descriptions. Reading the American newspapers we feel as if we were looking at Churchill, as in the previous example: standing *before a battery of microphones* with his *single sheet of typed paper*. The newspapers profusely and vividly describe the British Prime Minister: the way he looked, the way he walked, the way he talked, what he wore, and the impressiveness of it all. For example:

the Prime Minister, wearing a rumpled white linen suit, made a great impression on his congressional audience, not a few of whom have been outspokenly critical of Britain's willingness to retake nice and deal with Communist China.[75]

A Victorian gentleman at the door of a DC-6, Mr. Churchill descended from the president's plane a little more slowly than he used to climb the rubble heaps in Stepney during the blitz, but he was soon tapping his cane and waving his extraordinary headgear as if he were 70 again.[76]

192   *A. Marchi* et al.

Clear markers of political personalisation – the cane, the cigar, the hat – appeared regularly in the reports. Churchill and his insignia are iconic and familiar to the US public.

> Wearing a gray Hamburg, gray storm coat with fur collar, carrying a cane and smoking a cigar, Mr Churchill continued on to his three-room suite on the main deck. Among those who accompanied the Prime Minister to the liner were Mr Baruch, Grover A. Wahlen, chairman of the Mayor's reception committee, and police Commissioner George P. Monaghan. Sarah Churchill, the Prime Minister's daughter, and her husband, Anthony Beauchamp, saw off the statesman and his party of nineteen persons.[77]

In contrast, and especially interesting, is that the newspapers take almost no interest in any other leader's appearance – which further supports the fact that personalisation of politics is not a linear process, not even under similar technological and political circumstances. In the entire corpus there was just one description of Attlee's appearance, and he was characterised as being 'dressed in the appropriate costume of Whitehall', which, it seems, could be paraphrased as being less distinctively attired than Churchill:

> Mr Attlee was first out of the plane, looking perhaps a little greyer than when he was here five years ago, but nevertheless still brisk and smiling. He was dressed in the appropriate costume of Whitehall: dark grey suit, blue polka dot tie, black Homberg hat and black overcoat, with sprig of white heather in the lapel.[78]

There were also just two mentions of Truman's outfits, which stand out similarly for their ordinariness by comparison with Churchill's *extraordinary headgear*: 'Mr Truman, who preceded him aboard, went on deck to greet Churchill. The president was wearing a brown business suit and green tie.'[79]

From the examination of collocates we find eleven close co-occurrences of *Churchill* and *hat*, which he was recurrently pictured as *doffing* and ten co-references of *cigar*.

> Mr Churchill abandoned the sawed-off stovepipe hat and appeared in the uniform of the Royal Yacht Squadron. This was a typical navy blue serge uniform with brass buttons and the usual naval officers' hat.[80]

More generally, there is constant attention paid to what is on top of Churchill's head, be it a *truncated black bowler*, a *yachting cap*, or the *grey Homburg*. The relinquishing of the hat comes to signal a sort of concession:

> As Mr Churchill stepped from his car he was cheered again by a group of persons who had waited in front of the house. He smiled and waved, and

The inter-subjective special relationship 193

then posed for pictures again. When photographers asked him to take off his hat he said 'Okay' and did so with a smile.[81]

The press even makes explicit mention of Churchill's hat as a metaphor:

> aid to London has had the psychological effect of emphasizing Britain's decline and this, in turn, has produced a resentment among Britons who do not relish a role as a 'American dependency'. Britain's feeling were emphasized when, after it was announced that Mr. Churchill would visit Washington, the British press pointedly reminded the US that Mr. Churchill was coming with his hat on his head – 'not in his hand'.[82]

A further corroboration of the meaningfulness of Churchill's iconography in the US press is its absence in the London *Times*. In *The Times* there is no reference to Churchill's (or anybody else's) looks, age or style and the word *hat* or the lemma wear appear just once in the entire corpus, in the following context:

> But photographs of Mr Churchill himself, learned disquisitions on the correct name of the hat he wears, and arguments about whether his mother was born in Brooklyn or in Rochester, New York State, take up plenty of space. And there is no sign that time has withered the affection in which he is held by the American public, or that he could ever wear out his welcome here.[83]

The hat and the discourse about the hat become the symbol and the proof of Churchill's success.

In US reports, Churchill's handling of his cigar is just as iconic as his headgear. For example:

> The 79-year-old British statesman, smiling broadly and with a big black cigar clamped in his teeth[84]

> Mr Truman played selections from Chopin while Mr Churchill sat at his side at the piano puffing a cigar.[85]

> Then he stuck the cigar in his mouth again and puffed on it. He turned to shake hands with Mr Baruch, and then faced the cameras to take his famous V for victory sign with his fingers.[86]

> Brandishing of the traditional eight inches of cigar.[87]

And the absence of the cigar also assumes a metaphorical meaning of defeat:

> On arrival, Churchill was somber, almost grim, when he walked down the ramp from Mr. Truman's airplane, the Independence, at 12:30 p.m. There was no cigar jutting like a man-of-war's bowsprit from his ruddy face. His

194   *A. Marchi* et al.

fingers were not raised in the sign which spelled 'victory' in the days of England's sorest tribulation.[88]

A common way to express Churchill's potential weakness is by reference to the Prime Minister's old age. There were thirteen mentions of his age in the US press (*77-year old/79-year-old*) and *old* is a top collocate of *Churchill* and of *Prime Minister* in the corpus. The newspapers repeatedly suggest that Churchill has aged: describing him as *visibly older* or *notably slower*, *paler*, *weaker*, etc., and making reference to his sparser hair or his leaning on his cane. At the same time we often encounter a sudden reversal, whereby Churchill emerges rather gloriously 'despite' his old age, and the public is reassured that, after all, he has not changed. the *New York Times* goes as far as celebrating his maturity to the point of epic:

> He is the most recognizable of men. The heave of his shoulders and the poise of his head, seen from behind in a flash of the television screen as he lumbered majestically up the aisle yesterday, would have been sufficient to identify him. He was not in his best voice, but the voice was nevertheless unique. It was the one which defied Hitler in the moment of Hitler's glory. It was the one which won the support of the British people by promising them nothing but blood, sweat and tears. The Mr Churchill of half a century ago, the cherubic and imprudent young MP from Oldham, has matured into a prophet that history will not forget.[89]

Similarly the adjective *old* in association with *Churchill* is characterised by a very positive semantic prosody, and Churchill is described as: *the brave old Prime Minister, the old champion, the old master, the great old man, the grand old man, the grand old warrior, good old Winnie, the old strong Churchillian voice* and, obviously, *the old friend*.

On the arrival of Churchill in 1952, the *New York Times* writes:

> Our old friend returns

> There never was a time when Winston Churchill could come to the United States and not find the red carpet rolled out for him. British correspondents in Washington and a few editorial writers in London seem to doubt the grand old warrior is as welcome this year as in other years. They really need not worry. If there is any statesman in this whole wide world for whom Americans have more affection and esteem than Winston Spencer Churchill, let them name him. They won't succeed.[90]

Conclusions

Churchill's Sinews of Peace speech is often regarded as 'an artistic success and persuasive failure' insofar as its central argument, that the US and Britain should

The inter-subjective special relationship 195

unite to face the growing Communist menace in a fraternal association of English-speaking peoples, 'never got off the ground'.[91] It is true that his call for an alliance encountered immediate, predictable and stern popular American opposition. However, our work suggests that from Fulton through to his retirement from office, and indeed beyond, Churchill's efforts to promote special Anglo-American relations were far from a 'persuasive failure'.

Churchill was, of course, selective in blending a post-war relationship of necessity with a longer progeny of shared values and culture to construct the notion of a special relationship. Skated over or simply ignored were connotations of racism within his Anglo-Saxonism, deep divides over British imperialism and a history following the American Revolution that evinced longer periods of antagonism than of friendship. That he was able to do so owed much to his being impeccably qualified to speak to the affinity of Anglo-American peoples and to the threats that challenged anew their shared way of life. After all, he was a product of Anglo-American parentage[92] and the British Embassy in Washington concluded in 1946 that his leadership during WW2 and friendship with President Roosevelt had captured the American imagination and given him 'a very large following'.[93]

British officials, such as Foreign Secretary Lord Halifax, recognised that even out of office Churchill's popularity in America meant his speeches might have 'good effect' and 'Britain would draw measure of reflected popularity'.[94] However, they could have had no idea just how central Churchill would be – as actor, referent and advocate – to the discursive construction of the special relationship. Combining diplomatic history with CADS demonstrates this as never before. First it is clear that in the early 1950s the nomenclature 'special relationship' had yet to gain currency. Churchill's great contribution in this respect was in developing – and having developed around him – an alternative lexicon that established Anglo-American closeness and familiarity from which the term 'special relationship' could later emerge. It is noteworthy that words, phrases and inferences developed by Churchill in his Sinews of Peace to highlight Anglo-American commonality feature significantly in our government and, especially, press corpus. Moreover, the speech itself evidently became a referent point establishing both the continuity of Anglo-American familiarity and, as the Cold War unfolded, the prescience of Churchill's analysis of international relations and call for close UK–US cooperation.

Our analysis also reveals Churchill to already be established as the iconic figure of special Anglo-American relations and that his personal popularity in the US enabled him to transcend American disquiet about British relative decline and his own ideas for an Anglo-American alliance. This is reflected in the three representations of Churchill that emerge from, especially, our press corpus: Churchill as friend, Churchill as accomplished negotiator and Churchill as the embodiment of Britain. Within this process Churchill as agent is self-evidently pivotal – his words, his actions and his presence. However, no other leader in our corpus secures such media attention and this reveals that Churchill's communicative impact in promoting close UK–US relations benefited also from contemporary processes of the mediatisation and personalisation of politics. There is an evident metonymic relationship between Churchill and Britain. So pronounced is the degree of personalisation of politics around him, there are even instances where Churchill is represented as being better than Britain itself.

With the caveat that more research needs to be done with a larger corpus and across and longer period of time, it is also possible to identify some interesting transatlantic coordinative and communicative differences in the early construction of the special relationship. Our semantic categorisation confirms differences in US–UK government priorities commonly presented in the extant literature. US government and media data reveals a strong focus on Communism while UK data demonstrates this to be a much lesser concern – especially next to considerations of finance and resources. More importantly for the special relationship, Anglo-American media representations of UK–US relations evince different tones and emphases. The American newspapers construct Anglo-American friendship in terms of unity, alliance and common effort. The emphasis is goal-orientated, with a foregrounding therein of military and diplomatic issues. Though Churchill commands huge respect and his words are reported widely, often the words selected by US media within its reports tend towards the practical benefits of friendship, especially working together to combat Communism.

In contrast, British media data suggests a strong investment in what we term a 'discourse of "harmony"'. There is repeated reference to shared aims and agreement, the shared common language and mutual understanding. There is far less reference to military and contingent issues and more emphasis on the semantic area of emotion/perception, including 'confidence', 'hope' and 'feel'. In coverage of the summits there is less reporting than in the US media of specific details, implications and progress and more on overall importance and relative success. While US media coverage is firmly located in the 'here and now', British coverage frequently invokes the recent past in terms of the wartime relationship and experiences. Furthermore, British media is notably more liberal in its usage of phrases such as 'English-speaking world,' suggesting continuing American reluctance to be overtly tied into such expansive identifications.

This leads us to our final – and most tentative – series of conclusions. If the discourse patterns identified here were to be repeated in our forthcoming much larger study, then our interdisciplinary analysis may not only be able to identify the way discourse helped construct the special relationship but also a key reason why its cultural 'embeddedness' has remained much stronger in the UK than in the US. As might be expected, US government data reveals a predominantly utilitarian emphasis within treating the UK differently from other partners, at least informally. Likewise, British government data not once mentions the term 'special relationship'; it too coordinates Anglo-American relations within a national interest paradigm, albeit with different emphases and a slighter greater backwards look to wartime experiences and consequences. The real difference comes in the public descriptions by government officials of the UK–US relationship and how these are used by media. US officials indulge the language of

The inter-subjective special relationship   197

friendship but foreground the practical benefits of close cooperation. This is mirrored in the US press, especially outside of its fascination with Churchill. British government officials tend to emphasise the naturalness, ease and importance of UK–US relations – a focus on 'soft' considerations taken up by British media in terms of emotion and shared mission. However, the coordinative discourse by the British government of UK–US relations is characterised predominantly by utilitarian calculations: the emphasis on unique common ground between Britain and America is designed in part at least to encourage third-party expectation of US support of British positions. British media coverage, though, plays out a Churchillian narrative of a special relationship – or at this stage its alternative lexicon – founded upon a unique combination of shared interest and common sentiment

This may help explain why over time notions of a special relationship in the US have faded and why British governments have struggled to reconcile policy with popular expectations of the special relationship. The progressively expanding power imbalance reduced quantitatively at least the scope for close Anglo-American cooperation based on calculations of mutual utility. Given US government and US media emphasis on the practical benefits of close cooperation, Britain's reduced utility would naturally question the basis of a special relationship. Churchill's departure from office would also remove the iconic figure of Anglo-American relations and lay barer the consequences of growing power disparities. Though sometimes accused of becoming misled by the mystique of the special relationship, British governments were immediately aware of the consequences of power imbalance and particularly in the post-Cold War era have periodically sought to temper public expectation of the special relationship. However, in testimony to the cultural embeddedness of the special relationship, the traditional public language of Anglo-American relations and continued British media foregrounding of the special relationship, it has proven extraordinarily difficult for British governments to develop an alternative discourse of Anglo-American relations. Prime Minister Edward Heath's 'natural relationship' faded following British entry to the European Economic Community. A media furore erupted when in 2010 the British Parliamentary Foreign Affairs Committee declared that the special relationship was 'over'. And Prime Minister Cameron and President Obama both outstayed in office their brief flirtation with the 'essential relationship'.[95]

Notes

1 Cited by Lucia Corbella, 'Sir Winston's Legacy Lives on in Calgary. Great-grandson Randolph Churchill Follows Sir Winston's Footsteps on Speaking Tour of Canada', the *Calgary Herald*, 15 May 2012; www.winstonchurchill.org/resources/in-the-media/churchill-in-the-news/1470-sir-winstons-legacy-lives-on-in-calgary-1.

2 The term here is understood in its linguistic sense, as language in its context of use and to encompass verbal as well as other modes of communication such as images. See Adam Jaworski and Nik Coupland (eds), *The Discourse Reader*, London: Routledge, 2005.

198   *A. Marchi* et al.

3 Diary of Charles Ross, entry date 7 March 1946, cited in Philip White, *Our Supreme Task: How Winston Churchill's Iron Curtain Speech Defined the Cold War Alliance*, New York: Perseus Books Group, 2012, p. 205.
4 Although the Sinews of Peace speech is often regarded as the first articulation of the 'special relationship' phrase by Churchill, he had in fact used it previously. For instance, the *New York Times Herald* included the following quotation from Churchill in a news feature dating from November 1945: 'We should not abandon our special relationship with the United States and Canada about the atomic bomb and we should aid the United States to guard this weapon as a sacred trust for the maintenance of peace.'
5 Winston S. Churchill, 'The Sinews of Peace', available at www.nato.int/docu/speech/1946/s460305a_e.htm.
6 Cf. Alan Dobson and Steve Marsh (eds), *Anglo-American Relations: Contemporary Perspectives*, London: Routledge, 2013.
7 John L. Austin, *How to Do Things with Words: The William James Lectures Delivered at Harvard University in 1955*, J.O. Urmson and Marina Sbisà (eds), second edition, Oxford: Clarendon Press, 1975 (first edition 1962).
8 Barry Buzan, Ole Wæver and Jaap de Wilde, *Security: A New Framework for Analysis*, Boulder, CO: Lynne Rienner, 1998.
9 For a study of this process in relation to post-1989 securitisation of poverty by US and the UK governments, see Nuria Lorenzo-Dus and Steve Marsh, 'Bridging the Gap: Interdisciplinary Insights into the Securitization of Poverty', *Discourse and Society*, 23:3, 2012, pp. 1–23.
10 Vivien Schmidt, 'Democracy and Discourse in an Integrating Europe and a Globalising World', *European Law Journal*, 6:3, 2000, pp. 277–300, at p. 285.
11 See, for instance, John Baylis, *Anglo-American Defence Relations, 1939–84: The Special Relationship*, London: Macmillan, 1984; Alex Danchev, *On Specialness: Essays in Anglo-American Relations*, Basingstoke: Macmillan, 1998; Alan P. Dobson, *Anglo-American Relations in the Twentieth Century: Of Friendship, Conflict and the Rise and Decline of Superpowers*, London: Routledge, 1995.
12 David Reynolds, *Summits: Six Meetings that Shaped the Twentieth Century*, New York: Allen Lane, 2007.
13 Elmer Plischke, *Modern Diplomacy: The Art of Artisans*, Washington. DC: AEI Press, 1979; Keith Hamilton and Richard Langhorne, *Practice of Diplomacy: Its Evolution, Theory and Administration*, London: Routledge, 1994.
14 United Kingdom National Archives (UKNA), FO 371 38523, 'The Essentials of an American Policy', 21 March 1944. Though in 1948 Churchill espoused a new world role for Britain as being the only power that stood astride the three great circles of Europe, the British Commonwealth and Empire, and the English-speaking world, the primacy of the transatlantic relationship was evident in a Foreign Office decision in 1949 that British interests would best be promoted by establishing a position 'closely related to the USA, and yet sufficiently independent of her, to be able to influence American policy in the directions desired'. Winston S. Churchill, 'Conservative Mass Meeting: A Speech at Llandudno, 9 October 1948', in Winston S. Churchill, *Europe Unite: Speeches 1947 and 1948*, London: Cassell, 1950, pp. 416–18; UKNA, FO371/76384, 'Third World Power or Western Preponderance', 23 March 1949.
15 United States National Archive (USNA), RG 218, Box 20, US Jt Chiefs of Staff Geographical File 1951–3, memo Chief of Staff US Army to Jt Chiefs of Staff, 19 April 1950, pp. 1–2.
16 Kent Asp and Peter Esaiasson, 'The Modernization of Swedish Campaign: Individualization, Professionalization, and Mediatization', in David L. Swanson and Paolo Mancini (eds), *Politics, Media, and Modern Democracy: An International Study of Innovations in Electoral Campaiging and Their Consequences*, Westport, CT: Praeger, 1996, pp. 73–90; Stig Hjarvard, 'The Mediatization of Society. A Theory of the Media as Agents of Social and Cultural Change', *Nordicom Review*, 29:2, 2008,

The inter-subjective special relationship   199

pp. 105–34; Winfried Schulz, 'Reconstructing Mediatization as an Analytical Concept', *European Journal of Communication*, 19:1, 2004, pp. 87–101; Jesper Strömbäck and Frank Esser, 'Shaping Politics: Mediatization and Media Interventionism', in Knut Lundby (ed.), *Mediatization: Concepts, Changes, Consequences*, New York: Peter Lang, 2009, pp. 205–23.

17 Andrea Umbricht, 'Patterns of News Making in Western Journalism: A Content Analysis of Newspapers across Six Western Democracies and Five Decades', *National Centre of Competence in Research Working Papers*, 79, Swiss National Research Foundation, 2014.

18 Frank Esser, 'Mediatization as a Challenge: Media Logic versus Political Logic', in Hanspeter Kriesi, Sandra Lavenex, Frank Esser, Jörg Matthes, Marc Bühlmann and Daniel Bochsler, *Democracy in the Age of Globalization and Mediatization*, Basingstoke: Palgrave Macmillan, 2013, pp. 155–76.

19 Linards Udris and Jens Lucht, 'Transformation of the News Media: Growing Independence from Politics – Growing Dependence on the Market', in Frank Esser and Jesper Strömbäck (eds), *Mediatization of Politics: Understanding the Transformation of Western Democracies*, Basingstoke: Palgrave Macmillan, 2014, pp. 114–36.

20 As early as the 1920s, for example, Walter Lippmann acknowledged the crucial intermediary role between politicians and the media of, then, a new type of professional communicator: the press agent (Brian McNair, *An Introduction to Political Communication* (second edition), London: Routledge, 1999). And in the 1930s and 1940s, President Roosevelt was famous for his 'fireside chats' on radio with the American people.

21 Kees Brants and Philip van Praag, 'Signs of Media Logic: Half a Century of Political Communication in the Netherlands', *Javnost, The Public*, 13:1, 2006, pp. 25–40; Jesper Strömbäck, 'Four Phases of the Mediatization: An Analysis of the Mediatization of Politics', *International Journal of Press/Politics*, 13:1, 2008, pp. 228–46.

22 For a recent comprehensive introduction, see Tony McEnery and Andrew Hardie, *Corpus Linguistics*, Cambridge: Cambridge University Press, 2012.

23 Alan Partington, 'Corpora and Discourse, a Most Congruous Beast', in Alan Partington, John Morley and Louann Haarman (eds), *Corpora and Discourse*, Bern: Peter Lang, 2004, pp. 11–20.

24 Alan Partington (ed.), *Corpora Special Issue. Modern Diachronic Corpus-Assisted Studies*, Edinburgh: Edinburgh University Press, 2010, at p. 88.

25 See Alan Partington, Alison Duguid and Charlotte Taylor, *Patterns and Meanings in Discourse: Theory and Practice in Corpus-Assisted Discourse Studies (CADS)*, Amsterdam: John Benjamins, 2013.

26 For instance: Paul Bayley and Geoffrey Williams (eds), *European Identity: What the Media Say*, Oxford: Oxford University Press, 2012.

27 Alan Partington, *The Linguistics of Laughter. A Corpus-Assisted Study of Laughter-Talk*, London: Routledge, 2006, p. 12.

28 See Anna Marchi, ' "The Moral in the Story": A Diachronic Investigation of Lexicalised Morality in the UK Press', *Corpora*, 5:2, 2010, pp. 161–90.

29 For this analysis we used two pieces of concordancing software: *Wordsmith 5.0* and *Sketchengine*. Further details about their application will be provided along with the analysis.

30 Geoffrey Leech, *Semantics*, London: Penguin, 1974, at p. 20.

31 Mike Scott, *WordSmith Tools Manual*, Oxford: Oxford University Press, 1996, at p. 53.

32 John Sinclair, *Corpus, Concordance, Collocations*, Oxford: Oxford University Press, 1991, at p. 13.

33 For reasons of space limitation, the analysis of Churchill offered in this chapter draws primarily on the press sub-corpus, which includes 482 newspaper articles from one British source (*The Times*) and two American ones (the *New York Times* and the *Washington Post*). The preliminary phase of the research, however, is based on an

200   *A. Marchi* et al.

exploration of the corpus in its entirety and it was the initial keywords analysis of the whole of the data that informed the subsequent research and led to identifying the path to pursue.

34 For a description of the process see C. Gabrielatos and Anna Marchi, 'Keyness: Appropriate Metrics and Practical Issues', talk given at CADS International Conference, 13–14 September 2012. Slides available online at: http://repository.edgehill.ac.uk/4196/.
35 In a letter to the editor in the *Washington Post*.
36 Drew Pearson, 'Attlee Likeness Cited', *Washington Post*, 7 December 1950.
37 'Parley Asked by Britons. Prime Minister, President Will Confer on Korea Crisis', *Washington Post*, 1 December 1950.
38 'West Confers Big Two and the UN', *New York Times*, 10 December 1950.
39 James Reston, 'Churchill Would Renew Wartime Ties with US', *New York Times*, 6 January 1952, p. E3.
40 James Reston, 'Truman and the Church to Thresh Out to Military and Production Problems', *New York Times*, 8 January 1952, p. 1.
41 Walter Lippmann, 'Today and Tomorrow', *Washington Post*, 7 January 1952.
42 James Reston, 'Churchill's Visit Smooths Some Rough Spots', *New York Times*, 13 January 1952, p. E3.
43 Marshall Andrews, 'Churchill and Truman in Conference', *Washington Post*, 6 January 1952.
44 Chalmers M. Roberts, 'Ike and Churchill Devote First Conference to EDC, Exchange of A-Knowledge', *Washington Post*, 26 June 1954, p. 1.
45 'Mission Accomplished', *New York Times*, 20 January 1952.
46 Raymond Daniell, 'Britons of Two Minds on Churchill's Visit', *New York Times*, 20 January 1952, p. E5.
47 Raymond Daniell, 'Churchill Would Renew Wartime Ties with US', *New York Times*, 30 December 1951, p. E3.
48 Reston, 'Churchill's Visit Smooths Some Rough Spots'.
49 James Reston, 'Agenda for Churchill Talks Excludes Economic Issues', *New York Times*, 2 January 1952, p. 1.
50 Reading through the concordance lines it becomes clear that *The Times* itself is very supportive of the Prime Minister and blames the weakness of Churchill's popularity at home on the Labour Party.
51 'Mr Churchill in US To-day Revision of Plans', *The Times*, 5 January 1952, p. 6.
52 'Grand Simplicity', *The Times*, 5 January 1952, p. 7.
53 'Speech to Congress', *The Times*, 18 January 1952, p. 5.
54 'Journey to Washington', *The Times*, 29 December 1951, p. 7.
55 Reston, 'Churchill's Visit Smooths Some Rough Spots'.
56 'Grand Simplicity', *The Times*, 5 January 1952, p. 7.
57 The term 'relatively' is used here in statistical terms to indicate normalised frequencies.
58 W.H. Lawrence, 'Eisenhower and Churchill Agree on Aims for Peace, Arms Cut and Atom Benefits', *New York Times*, 30 June 1954.
59 Daniell, 'Churchill Would Renew Wartime Ties with US'.
60 'Mission Accomplished', *New York Times*, 20 January 1952, p. E8.
61 'Red Threat Transcends Issues, Churchill Agrees; Truman Calls '52 Crucial', *Washington Post*, 10 January 1951, p. 1.
62 Alfred Friendly, 'Anglo-US Amity Stressed Above Policies on China and Iranian Oil', *Washington Post*, 10 January 1952.
63 W.H. Lawrence, 'Churchill Urges Patience in Coping with Red Dangers', *New York Times*, 27 June 1954, p. 1.
64 Dana Adams Schmidt, 'Churchill Urges East–West Amity', *New York Times*, 1 July 1954, p. 9.

The inter-subjective special relationship 201

65 'Text of Churchill's Remarks at the Press Luncheon in His Honor in Capital', *New York Times*, 29 June 1954, p. 2.

66 '"Friendly and Fruitful" Washington Talks Joint Statement by President and Prime Minister', *The Times*, 29 June 1954, p. 9.

67 'The Old Master', *New York Times*, 18 January 1952, p. 26.

68 'Big Two Meet to Strengthen Ties', *New York Times*, 6 January 1952, p. E1.

69 Raymond Daniell, 'US Air Bases a Touchy Subject among Britons', *New York Times*, 2 December 1951.

70 Daniell, 'Britons of Two Minds on Churchill's Visit', *New York Times*, 20 January 1952, p. E3.

71 Raymond Daniell, 'British Bureau Chief Yielded Too Much. Churchill's Willingness to Go Along with US in Expanded Korea War Causes Dismay', *New York Times*, 18 January 1952, p. 1.

72 Joseph and Stewart Alsop, 'Matter of Fact', *Washington Post*, 8 January 1952.

73 'Big Two Meet to Strengthen Ties', *New York Times*, 6 January 1952, p. E1.

74 C.M. Roberts, 'Ike and Churchill Devote First Conference to EDC', *Washington Post*, 26 June 1954.

75 Lawrence, 'Churchill Urges Patience in Coping with Red Dangers', *New York Times*, 27 June 1954, p. 1.

76 James Reston, 'Both Stress Unity', *New York Times*, 6 January 1952, p. 1.

77 'Churchill Departs; Honored by the City', *New York Times*, 23 January 1952.

78 James Reston, 'Allies Leave Flaming Pyongyang for Stand Above 38th Parallel; Attlee, Truman Discuss "Disaster"', *New York Times*, 5 December 1950, p. 1.

79 Marshall Andrews, 'Churchill and Truman in Conference', *Washington Post*, 6 January 1952.

80 Reston, 'Both Stress Unity'.

81 'Churchill is Here as Baruch's Guest', *New York Times*, 10 January 1952, p. 1.

82 'Big Two Meet To Strengthen Ties', *New York Times*, 6 January 1952, p. E1.

83 'Wide Scope of Washington Talks. Middle and Far East Situation Surveyed', *The Times*, 9 January 1952, p. 6.

84 Chalmers M. Roberts, 'Boys Stone Congressman. Churchill and Eden Due Here Today', *Washington Post*, 25 June 1954, p. 1.

85 'Truman Toasts Churchill as "Great Man of the Age"', *New York Times*, 8 January 1952, p. 8.

86 'Churchill is Here as Baruch's Guest', *New York Times*, 10 January 1952, p. 1.

87 Alfred Friendly, 'Joint Policy on Defense Talked with Churchill. Mutual Aid Man on Raw Materials Also Considered in Three Sessions', *Washington Post*, 8 January 1952.

88 Andrews, 'Churchill and Truman in Conference', *Washington Post*, 6 January 1952.

89 'The Old Master', *New York Times*, 18 January 1952, p. 26.

90 'Our Old Friend Returns', *New York Times*, 6 January 1952, p. E8.

91 Michael J Hostetler, 'The Enigmatic Ends of Rhetoric: Churchill's Fulton Address as Great Art and Failed Persuasion', *Quarterly Journal of Speech*, 83, 1997, pp. 416–28, at p. 416.

92 His mother was the American socialite Jennie Jerome and his father the charismatic politician Lord Randolph Churchill.

93 Cited by Henry B. Ryan, 'A New Look at Churchill's Iron Curtain Speech', *The Historical Journal*, 22:4, 1979, pp. 895–920, at footnote 61, p. 909.

94 Letter by Lord Halifax, 6 February 1946, cited by Henry B. Ryan, 'A New Look at Churchill's "Iron Curtain" Speech', at p. 902.

95 Edward Heath, *The Course of My Life*, London: Hodder & Stoughton, 1998, p. 472; Steve Marsh, 'Global Security: US–UK relations': Lessons for the Special Relationship, *Journal of Transatlantic Studies*, 12:2, 2012, pp. 182–99.

8 The architecture of a myth

Constructing and commemorating Churchill's special relationship, *c.*1919–69

Sam Edwards

On 30 January 1965, Winston Spencer Churchill was eulogised in St Paul's Cathedral. Coverage of the ceremony – at that point, the largest state funeral in history – was broadcast throughout the world, and Commonwealth Heads of State were in attendance. This was one of the last great Imperial pageants of the post-war period, resplendent with imagery and iconography that would have been familiar to Kipling; a fitting send-off to a man well-known as – and often criticised for being – a late Victorian Imperial apologist. But the theatre of this occasion was not simply Imperial in tone and tenor. Those in charge of planning the funeral also paid close attention to ensuring the day offered public expressions of Anglo-American comradeship. After all, if Churchill was the defender of the Empire, he was also a long-time advocate for the Anglo-American alliance and, at one point, for Anglo-American political federation; he was 'Anglo-American' by parentage, and after 1963, by fact (he was granted honorary American citizenship by Congress). Only right and proper then that present at the funeral as official American representative was Churchill's wartime comrade Dwight D. Eisenhower, while the proceedings – 'watched by the largest American television up to that point in history' – included a rendition of 'The Star-Spangled Banner' by a British Army band.[1] Seen in this light, the decision to perform the ceremony in St Paul's, rather than at Westminster Abbey, was apt. For while this was indeed the 'Parish Church of the British Commonwealth', it was also home to the American Memorial Chapel, dedicated in 1958 amid much Churchillian rhetoric. Just a few months later, work began on yet another Anglo-American shrine at Westminster College in Fulton, Missouri, and the ceremony surrounding the foundation stone witnessed similar rites and rituals. In this case, the eventual memorial, completed in 1969, was the resurrected seventeenth-century English church of St Mary, Aldermanbury. It was carefully placed on the exact site where the prophet of Anglo-American unity had sermonised on the 'special relationship' two decades earlier.

This chapter examines the crucial role played by such acts of commemoration in anticipating, constructing and enshrining Churchill's special relationship, an idea that the historian Jonathan Rose has identified as his 'most visionary political project'.[2] Beginning in the post-1918 period and re-emerging with new

The architecture of a myth 203

vigour during and after the Second World War, such acts of commemoration – including statues to the likes of Washington and Lincoln, memorials to American war dead and commemorative 'texts' such as Churchill's own *History of the English-Speaking Peoples* – provided invaluable forums in which to call for, perform and *imagine* Anglo-American unity. To be sure, not all were initiated or inspired by Churchill personally. Nonetheless, in form and function all were close to the spirit of what Churchill would define as the special relationship, while taken together all played a part in the Churchillian ritualisation of Anglo-American relations.

Tracing this history of memory sheds new light on the very nature of this relationship. In recent years, the historiography of the Anglo-American alliance has often been drawn to the question of whether or not, in the post-war period, it was in any way 'special', and more than one historian has contended that the 'special relationship' is little more than a 'myth'.[3] This chapter contends, however, that to dismiss the special relationship as 'myth' is rather to miss the point; it is indeed a 'myth', but not in the sense of being an untruth. Rather, in the historically and theatrically skilled hands of Churchill, the Anglo-American bond was carefully and deliberately mythologised so that it might become a quasi-religious article of political faith in which future Anglo-American generations – by habit and tradition – would have to invest. At its broadest, therefore, this chapter suggests that the twentieth-century construction of Anglo-American memorials, monuments, chapels and cemeteries did not just provide opportunities for the Churchillian myth of the 'special relationship' to be repeated and rehearsed. Rather, such commemorative structures were integral to the *active construction* of the myth; they provided its foundations and its shrines, and together with Churchill's words and warnings, they constitute its architecture.[4]

'One common Anglo-Saxon stock': hero worship and a myth of origins, *c.*1890–1940

At root, the origins of Churchill's post-1945 Anglo-American myth lay in eighteenth-century cultural Anglo-Saxonism. Inspired by the growth of English power, and driven by contemporary intellectual endeavour to uncover a native wellspring for such growth, numerous philologists, linguists and historians contended that the source of those ideas and institutions so important to eighteenth-century Englishmen – in Britain and North America – lay in the ancient Teutonic forests. Here, Germanic warriors, unconquered and uncorrupted by Rome, had found their unique capacity for self-government, a quality which their descendants took with them on their journeys west, first to the eastern shores of Britain in the fifth century, then to the eastern shores of North America in the seventeenth century (at least, so went the theory). In Britain, such sentiment affirmed contemporary belief in the superiority of British institutions over those of the Continent (where the politics and values of Absolutist and, later, Revolutionary and Napoleonic France were seen as anathema). In the American colonies, meanwhile, such cultural Anglo-Saxonism proved popular among those members of the colonial elite searching for an intellectual basis upon which to justify their rebellion against British rule. Thus, not unlike Cromwell's Parliamentarians, some Revolutionary leaders asserted that a tyrannical monarchy had usurped ancient Anglo-Saxon liberties. Thomas Jefferson (a committed Anglo-Saxonist) even suggested engraving the figures of legendary Saxon chiefs Hengist and Horsa on the newly conceived great seal of the United States.[5]

At this point, though, and as Thomas Jefferson's commitment to the American Revolution clearly suggests, such Anglo-Saxonist sentiment did not necessarily preclude or pacify Anglo-American tensions. It was not until the turn of the twentieth century that British and American Anglo-Saxonism began to find common ground. Indeed, Bradford Perkins identifies the 1890s as the moment of great 'rapprochement' between the United States and Great Britain, a rapprochement that was connected in part to the identification of a supposed transatlantic racial tie.[6] The emergence of this idea was prompted by a changed global political context, together with key domestic developments in both the United States and Britain. In particular, the rise of Darwinian science, the emergence of European industrial and military rivals, imperial encounters with racial 'others' (in the Americas as much as in Africa) and, in the United States especially, an age of mass immigration, combined to produce a climate conducive to celebrations of racialised Anglo-Saxon sentiment, at least among the Anglo-American political elite. As a result, and as Stuart Anderson explains, 'Anglo-Saxonism was a mature intellectual doctrine by the mid-1890s, ready to influence the way Britons and Americans looked at each other and the world in the years of the Anglo-American rapprochement'.[7] This now *racialised* Anglo-Saxonism dominated the discourse of Anglo-American relations throughout the early twentieth century, and even led some contemporaries – Joseph Chamberlain, Andrew Carnegie and of course Winston Churchill – to call for a racial alliance of the Stars and Stripes and Union Jack.[8] Hardly surprising that by 1918, an American military chaplain presiding over a memorial ceremony in England could say of the Anglo-American alliance that: '[o]urs is not simply the fellowship of a sudden need, the temporary alliance of a common peril; it is the reknitting of a moral and racial kinship for all time to come'.[9]

This was the backdrop to the first round of politically significant Anglo-American commemorations, of which the pre-eminent example is surely the statue of Abraham Lincoln, dedicated in Parliament Square in 1920. Lincoln had become an increasingly popular figure in Britain in the preceding decade, particularly since the genealogy of J. Henry Lea and J.R. Hutchinson had resolved the mystery of his paternal ancestry. Through painstaking research, *The Ancestry of Lincoln* (1909) traced the Lincoln line back to the village of Hingham, Norfolk, the home parish of his lineal ancestor, Samuel, who migrated to Massachusetts in 1637 and helped found a village of the same name.[10] What followed were various initiatives designed to celebrate this newly discovered transatlantic bond. In 1911, a commemorative stone was unveiled in 'New' Hingham, a gift from the residents of 'Old' Hingham.[11] In 1913, the community of New Hingham reciprocated, dedicating a memorial marker on the parish green of Old Hingham during a pilgrimage to their past.[12] In 1916, James Bryce – British Ambassador to the United States and author of an affectionate history of the American constitution – introduced a collection of Lincoln's speeches by noting that he 'came of an English stock [and] he spoke English tongue'.[13]

By 1920, following Anglo-American victory in the Great War, the ground was thus well prepared for a prominent and public celebration of Lincoln's English past. Here was the perfect opportunity to celebrate the English origins of the Great Emancipator *and* invoke memories of the recent wartime alliance. Little wonder that during his dedication speech none other than James Bryce (again) noted that Lincoln belonged 'to both branches of the old [Anglo-Saxon] race', before concluding with a statement directed to one of those Americans present: 'He is ours, Mr Root, almost as much as he is yours.'[14] Not to be outdone, Elihu Root, a well-known Anglophile, then reciprocated with an equally sentimental expression of Anglo-American unity. For while admitting that Lincoln 'never set foot on British soil' and that '[h]e never seemed to touch the life of Britain', Root nonetheless asserted that Lincoln's life and actions demonstrated that 'he was of English blood ... of English speech [and that] The English Bible and English Shakespeare ... were the bases of his education'.[15] Such sentiment was by no means unusual: the very same ideas were explored a year earlier when another statue of Lincoln was dedicated in Manchester, and again when a bust of Lincoln was unveiled in the parish church of Hingham, Norfolk, his ancestral home. During the dedication of the latter the American ambassador even explained to his largely British audience that the bust represented 'the image of a great man of the Anglo-Saxon race, whose stock is rooted in this very soil, and in whom you have, with us, an equal ground for pride'.[16]

The years in and around the First World War saw the English connections of several other famous Americans similarly celebrated in Britain. In 1909, the centenary of the death of Thomas Paine was marked in his birthplace of Thetford, Norfolk. One of those in attendance happily remarked that Paine, the author of the 'United States', was a 'stout-hearted Englishman'.[17] In 1922, a statue of George Washington, first president and friend of Paine, was unveiled at Trafalgar Square, while a year earlier his ancestral home at Sulgrave Manor in Northamptonshire was opened as a memorial to the Anglo-American alliance (significantly, the purchase of the property was funded by the same organisation behind the Lincoln statue at Westminster).[18] By the mid-1920s, the Northamptonshire past of this now anglicised hero, as well as various other 'Anglo-American' sites in Britain, had even been catalogued so that the devout could visit and pay their respects. J.F. Muirhead's *American Shrines on English Soil* (1925), for instance, includes, among other things, information about those places with either a Washington or Lincoln connection, details about Benjamin Franklin's house in London, and a special chapter about a newer 'shrine': the American war cemetery then being built at Brookwood in Surrey.[19] F.V. Morley's *Travels in East Anglia* (1923) and R.B. Mowat's *Americans in England* (1935) offer similarly affectionate takes on the Anglo-American ties that bind via discussions of particular people and places.[20]

206   *S. Edwards*

These activities and ideas, especially the heroes being honoured, were very familiar to Winston Churchill. Indeed, Churchill had a long-running interest in Abraham Lincoln and the American Civil War.[21] In 1890, while an officer cadet at Sandhurst, he wrote an essay about the war between North and South, and in later years he often contemplated a dedicated history of the conflict.[22] By the early 1930s, this interest remained, and in due course his *History of the English-Speaking Peoples*, which was nearing completion when the Second World War broke out, included a substantial section given over to Lincoln's war for freedom.[23] In a reminiscence to a journalist in 1931, Churchill even recalled the day at school in the 1880s when he had stumbled across a collection of Civil War era *Punch* cartoons, among which was the sombre – and famous – scene of Britannia laying a wreath on Lincoln's tomb following his assassination in 1865.[24] In his speeches, meanwhile, Churchill remained drawn to a Lincolnesque rhythm, cadence and phraseology for the duration of his political career. His links to George Washington were even more personal – they had a common ancestor.[25] Moreover, as the product of an Anglo-American marriage (through which he gained this Washington connection), Churchill had long been fascinated by America. He had first visited the United States in 1895, and by 1931 he had already given two American lecture tours (during one of these, in 1929, he had visited several Civil War battlefields).[26] As such, in terms of spirit and purpose, these 1920s commemorations were clearly close to Churchill, especially after he had become President of the English-Speaking Union in 1921. In terms of chronology, they were directly contemporaneous with the first period of his political career (the 1890s to the 'Wilderness' of the 1930s), while in terms of subject matter (Lincoln, Washington) they resonated with Churchill the historian and genealogist. Indeed, the main orator at the 1920 statue dedication was one of Churchill's closest political allies, Lloyd George. Understandably, therefore, the very Anglo-Saxonist sentiment that framed the dedication of Lincoln's statue in 1920 similarly framed Churchill's pronouncements on the contemporary Anglo-American alliance. In a memorandum on Anglo-American relations authored in 1925, for example, Churchill welcomes the extent to which American involvement in the First World War led to an improved appreciation of Britain, and especially to a common realisation of 'the natural affinities between the Anglo-Saxon mind'. Elsewhere in the same memorandum, he traces the origins of British friendship towards America – 'the eldest daughter of their own civilisation' – to the post-Civil War period.[27]

Writing in 1882, at the very height of the late Victorian age of 'invented traditions', and as he surveyed contemporary efforts to consolidate national boundaries as well as create new sovereign powers (Germany, Italy), Ernst Renan famously suggested that all 'nations' require a past, and that this past is often found through collective myths and memories.[28] Elsewhere, Benedict Anderson argued in an influential 1982 text that successful national identities demand 'imaginative' investment. National communities, after all, are so vast that they can never exist in reality; they rely instead on being continuously imagined and re-imagined.[29] For Anderson, not to mention Hobsbawm and Ranger, this was a key purpose of the rites and rituals of the Victorian and Edwardian age. Such occasions were not mere benign and insignificant 'superstructure'; rather, they were key components of political theatre.[30] They were the spaces within which Victorian culture created and communicated its values, ideals and history: the spaces in which this culture realised itself into existence. And crucially, by the early twentieth century, as nationalism developed into a form of civic religion, a key part of this programme of 'realisation' focused on public architecture. Indeed, for the late Victorians and early Edwardians, lacking some of the progressive confidence of the mid-nineteenth century, disorientated by social and technological change but still attached to the idea of themselves as latter-day Romans, building took on heightened symbolic importance. It was as though they sought to construct as an act of reassurance: stone and statuary were solid and lasting, and in this sense were the opium of the Imperial elite. Hence the many monuments to carefully chosen national heroes established in London in this period: Wellington (1888); Cromwell (1899); Boudicca (1902); Queen Victoria (1911); Robert Clive (1912), as well as those memorials established after 1918 to a new generation of British heroes. Here, the 'ordinary' Tommy was most conspicuous, a point clearly demonstrated by the Unknown Warrior, who in 1920 was 'entombed', like a good Anglo-Saxon, in Westminster Abbey.[31] On their own, and taken together, these various monuments were intended to construct (and, after 1918, re-construct) a collective past, and in doing so bolster and buttress national allegiance. These were elite-sponsored locations at which Britons could gather, remember and 'imagine' themselves into being; they were places of worship and veneration; they were political shrines.[32]

Seen in this context, placing a statue of Lincoln before the Palace of Westminster, or a statue of Washington before Trafalgar Square, was likewise a symbolically powerful statement. Such statues represented a conscious attempt to cultivate what might be reasonably termed an 'origins myth' for 'Anglo-America': a transatlantic entity bound not by borders, but by blood, history and 'imagination'. Some of those involved in these Anglo-American commemorative activities even drew attention to the connections between commemorating 'Great Britons' and memorialising Anglo-American heroes. During preparations for the Lincoln statue, for example, one supporter suggested that it should be judged by the same criteria as used for the recent memorial to Victoria.[33] Elsewhere, James Bryce (unsurprisingly) noted that just as he happily remembered 'King Alfred, or William Shakespeare, or Queen Elizabeth' so too did he 'remember ... thankfully and with a sense of pride George Washington, Alexander Hamilton, Abraham Lincoln'.[34] These statues, and the rhetoric which their dedication ceremonies bequeathed, are the earliest architecture of the politically powerful and resonant myth that Churchill would later attempt to enshrine as a faith: the 'special relationship'.

Consolidating the myth: discovering the special relationship, *c.*1940–58

While the early 1920s saw the first efforts to create an Anglo-American origins myth by commemorating (or, if necessary, inventing) suitably transatlantic heroes, a decade later, as Churchill retreated to the wilderness, this myth still

208   *S. Edwards*

lacked solidity and stability. In the United States, this was the era of growing isolationist sentiment and resurgent Anglophobia (at least in some quarters). In Britain, meanwhile, frustrations lingered regarding the repayment of American war loans, as well as with the perceived encroachments of American culture. And on top of all this, the discourse so long central to transatlantic relations – racial Anglo-Saxonism – was in decline. Anna Martellone suggests that in the years around the First World War, as Germany emerged as an Anglo-American rival, and as Britain's Empire reached its territorial zenith, Anglo-Saxonism began to be divested of its 'Germanic' racialism and instead was recast as 'Pan-Anglism', 'Anglo-Saxondom' or, elsewhere, 'English-speaking' unity. As a result, Anglo-Saxonism increasingly shifted from 'a racial to a linguistic conception that could be applied also to people of different origins who spoke English and lived under Anglo-Saxon institutions'.[35]

Churchill was at the forefront of this discursive 'metamorphosis'.[36] Indeed, the importance of 'English-speaking' ties would be one of his key contributions to post-war historiography, specifically in the form of his *History of the English-Speaking Peoples*, first begun in the early 1930s, and ultimately published between 1956 and 1958. To be sure, Churchill did not coin the phrase 'English-speaking'; it had been popular since at least 1868 when Charles Dilke published *Great Britain: A Record of Travel in English-Speaking Countries*, and the first decades of the twentieth century had seen the phrase used in other works of history.[37] But, unlike some of these earlier works which still conceived of language and race as intertwined, Churchill's great contribution was to pare back much of the overt racialised language previously used in Anglo-American discourse in order to reveal the older, cultural, foundations of Anglo-Saxonism. This is not to say that he abandoned racialised thought. Churchill's views on Empire, and especially of the place of India, remained stubbornly late Victorian and paternalistic throughout the war, much to the consternation of Franklin Roosevelt (and of course Ghandi). Even his paean to the English-speaking peoples included references to 'races', and to 'white men', 'black men' and red men'.[38] But, at least when it came to Anglo-American relations, he was nonetheless integral to shifting the *explicit* terms of discussion from blood and biology, to language, history and culture.

Thus, of the four volumes through which Churchill charts the emergence, development and expansion of the English-speaking peoples, three feature significant discussion of the New World, the American colonies and, ultimately, the United States. After covering the 'Birth of Britain' in Volume I (1956), which turns on the signing of Magna Carta 'on the great meadow at Runnymeade' (itself the subject, in 1957, of Anglo-American commemoration: a memorial was unveiled on the site by the American Bar Association) Churchill moves quickly to draw Americans into his narrative.[39] Thus Volume II (1956) is actually titled *The New World*, and Churchill notes in his preface that his narrative examines the 'lively and assertive communities ... which in the course of time become the United States'.[40] His subsequent discussion of these communities lingers on their thrifty, hardy, stoic qualities, and indeed their migration is presented just as cultural Anglo-Saxonism had

The architecture of a myth   209

long demanded: 'Never since the days of the Germanic invasions of Britain had such a national movement been seen. Saxon and Viking had colonised England. Now, 1,000 years later, their descendants were taking possession of America.'[41] Volume III – *The Age of Revolution* – then includes extended discussion of the 'Quarrel with America'. For Churchill, this quarrel was in large part due to the actions of George III, a man who thought himself to be an 'Englishman, born and bred' and who had the 'appearance of a typical yeoman', but who in actual fact was 'Hanoverian' in mind and manners.[42] It is the other George – Washington – who therefore emerges from the narrative as the dynamic and heroic force. A sturdy, independent, strong-willed soldier (just the sort that Churchill liked), who fought for noble and self-evident truths.[43] Volume IV – *The Great Democracies* – takes the story up to the dawn of the twentieth century, and in doing so Churchill gives a full 100 pages (indeed all of Book XI) to the American Civil War and to the man martyred at its end – Lincoln.[44]

The sum-total is an impressive and engaging work demonstrative of Churchill's mastery of history as literature. Throughout all four volumes, and by teasing out those 'moral' qualities that he understands to provide a binding force, Churchill skilfully assimilates American history into his broader narrative of the English-speaking peoples. Puritans depart, quarrels break out, a war for independence is fought. But such episodes are just momentary trials and tribulations in a longer story of essential unity of purpose. As Churchill himself outlined when explaining his work in April 1939:

> In the main, the key theme is emerging of the growth of freedom and law, of the rights of the individual, of the subordination of the State to the fundamental moral conceptions of an ever-comprehending community. Of these, the English-speaking peoples are the authors, then the trustees, and have now become the armed champions.[45]

In so many respects, this was Churchill's 'theology' of English-speaking unity and of Anglo-American relations. And, significantly, just like the theology of his lapsed Christian faith, it was offered in two parts: *The History of the English-Speaking Peoples* was thus the Old Testament charting the origins, rise, fall and reunion of the chosen people (or, in Churchill's terms above, their authorship and trusteeship of the great 'moral conceptions'). It was 'followed' by the New Testament;[46] the revealed word of the prophet himself, and of the years of heroic and victorious 'armed championship' – *The Second World War* (1954).

Such an analogy is more than mere fanciful suggestion. Taken together as a combined and collective expression of a very Churchillian myth, the two works are biblical in scope, scale and in their very form (which is consistent). Each volume is organised into 'Books', and these books in turn cover war, migration, sacrifice, martyrdom, damnation, salvation. In Volume I of *A History of the English-Speaking Peoples*, for instance, we are offered visions of an almost Edenic and merry medieval world, a world which in large measure is ended in Volume II by the flaws and failings of that fallen angel, Cromwell.[47] This

210   *S. Edwards*

'monument' to Anglophone history, a monument specifically designed to 'appeal to the United States', then concludes with Churchill hoping that the English-speaking peoples will once again 'unite' in order to stave off current and future threats to liberty.[48] Elsewhere, *A History of the English-Speaking Peoples* is full of just the sort of 'chosen people' that Churchill, always an admirer of Exodus,[49] found so compelling: the original Anglo-Saxons; the Elizabethans; and most obviously the New World Puritans, from whom would later descend those secularised and enlightened Canaanites – the Founding Fathers. The first volume of the New Testament (that is, *The Second World War*), meanwhile, is thick with prophecies declared and, in time, fulfilled (this was central to Churchill's own conception of his life, and especially of his wilderness years, during which he wandered and warned).[50] Later volumes, written at the very moment when Churchill was attempting to rekindle the contemporary Anglo-American alliance, linger on the details of his friendship with President Roosevelt and on the great Anglo-American summit gatherings.[51] In Volume III, for example, *The Grand Alliance* (1950), Churchill includes details of one of his favourite Anglo-American moments: the joint religious service involving himself, FDR and representatives from their combined militaries, and held on the deck of HMS *Prince of Wales* in August 1941 (this was the summit which ultimately bequeathed the Atlantic Charter). It was, remarked Churchill, 'a deeply moving expression of the unity of faith of our two peoples'.[52] As someone who found in the great men and grand narratives of history a spiritual replacement for traditional religion, Churchill's scholarship was ironically – or, perhaps, logically – less historical than mythological, if not indeed theological and theatrical.[53]

This approach to history would have particular consequence for one aspect of his work. For by giving prime place in Volume IV to a key event and hero (indeed, martyr), Churchill skilfully invoked an already well-established 'cipher' for Anglo-American relations: Abraham Lincoln. As Churchill clearly understood, Lincoln was the perfect figure through which to transition the terms of the Anglo-American alliance from race to culture. Even in the old era of racial Anglo-Saxonism some Britons had found inspiration in Lincoln's ideals as much as in his supposed Anglo-Saxon stock. A few years after the Great War, for example, Lloyd George, Lincoln's most famous Welsh disciple, proclaimed that 'the principles of Abraham Lincoln, will yet save the world for liberty, for peace, for good will and honest men'.[54] Throughout the Great War itself, Lincoln's 'principles' saw considerable service in Allied propaganda, while two decades later the United States Office of War Information (and Hollywood more broadly) likewise drew on the image of Lincoln and the memory of the Civil War in order to provide a historical frame of reference.[55] By 1940, therefore, Lincoln the pure blood 'Anglo-Saxon' of Brycean oratory had become Lincoln the Rooseveltian martyr for democracy and the Churchillian destroyer of tyranny (all useful ideas given the emerging global conflict).

As such, when, in 1939, Churchill sat down at Chartwell to finish drafting his history of the American Civil War, he was able to tap an established and powerful current of British thought regarding Father Abraham.[56] Moreover, in due course, the war actually saw a resurgent British interest in the Great Emancipator, especially following American entry into the conflict (and the fact that half a million US service-personnel were based specifically in East Anglia). In 1943, for example, a group of locally based American airmen made a pilgrimage to Hingham church in order to see the bust of Lincoln, while in 1944 the National Trust symbolically took a small parcel of ancestral Lincoln land into its protection. And crucially the language used to give such acts meaning exposed the contemporary discursive metamorphosis. Note, for instance, the statement offered by the donor of the ancestral Lincoln land after he gave the deeds to the National Trust. It echoes the words of James Bryce to Elihu Root in 1920, but the terms of the Anglo-American bond have been redefined:

> Abraham Lincoln is one of America's greatest historical leaders and we British, who are said to try and grab so much, cannot take him away from America, but we respectfully ask for the privilege of treating his name and *principles* as a joint heritage.[57]

This 'principled' Lincoln, the author of perhaps the most eloquent speech defending the concept of a 'people's democracy' (the Gettysburg Address), and the Lincoln depicted in Volume IV of *A History of the English-Speaking Peoples* (1958) was the Lincoln who now helped Churchill consolidate the post-war myth of the 'special relationship'. In fact, already before he put pen to paper in readiness for his trip to Fulton, several others – no doubt already very familiar with his Anglo-American ideal after six years of speeches like that given at Harvard in 1943 – had anticipated the general line that he would take. In May 1946, for example, the rector of a small church in Quidenham, Norfolk, dedicated a memorial window to fallen American airmen with words deliberately intended to invoke the long history of transatlantic connections. Speaking to a packed congregation of Britons and Americans, and in the knowledge that his speech was being broadcast across the Atlantic (and was later reported in the *New York Times*), Reverend Harper-Mitchell selected a careful phrase through which to sum up the history and heritage of the Anglo-American bond: 'From here,' he reminded his transatlantic audience, 'Lincoln came.'[58] The memorial, designed by an American serviceman and executed in stained glass by the British artist Reginald Bell, was first unveiled two years earlier, in 1944. Similar references to the Lincoln–England connection emerged in various other memorial projects. In 1945, Lincoln's words were used in a tablet dedicated to four American airmen killed in a plane crash just outside Norwich. In 1958, a Roll of Honour listing the names of all those Americans killed flying from wartime Norfolk was placed in the custody of the City of Norwich; it was accepted by the city authorities with a speech which drew inspiration – deliberately – from the Gettysburg Address.[59] Five years later, when an American Memorial Library was unveiled in Norwich, the dedication speech given by the Chargé d'Affaires of the US Embassy explained that Lincoln was the 'sixth direct descendent of Samuel Lincoln, citizen of Norwich'.[60] Only a few months before, a local author

212   *S. Edwards*

similarly remarked that although the 'bitter slaughter of the American Civil War and the placid Norfolk landscape are separated by 3,000 miles', they were nonetheless linked 'by the figure that fought to unite North with South – Abraham Lincoln'.[61]

Churchill's discovery, deployment and popularisation of the phrase 'special relationship' emerged among and within the chronology bracketed by the above memorial projects. Its first use was *c.*1940, and by 1943–4 it had already become a recurring theme in some of his correspondence. But it was of course most famously expressed at Fulton, Missouri, in March 1946 (just two months before Reverend Harper-Mitchell gave his eloquent dedication speech).[62] Churchill would duly spend much of the 1950s shaping, refining and re-stating his myth in order to give it grounding and currency. This would culminate, as discussed above, with a sophisticated theology of Anglo-American relations communicated via a multi-volume Old (1958) and New (1954) Testament. Such chronological connections are crucial, for they help us to understand a pivotal shift that would now occur in Anglo-American commemorations. For as various post-war memorial projects took shape, and as Churchill expounded on his Anglo-American vision, references to Lincoln would also begin to be eclipsed. Or, rather, such references would now be joined – explicitly and implicitly – with nods to another famous 'Anglo-American': Churchill himself.

This shift is perhaps most apparent in one of the earliest Second World War American memorials dedicated in East Anglia: a stained-glass window, established in the church of Great Cransley, in 1944. Initiated by a local unit of the American Air Force, but paid for by subscriptions from both Britain and the United States, this window took great care to assimilate the wartime Anglo-American alliance into a long history of common purpose. At the window's centre is a representation of St. George bearing sword and shield; beneath him stand two rather more recent warriors – a British and American soldier, hands clasped in friendship. The rest of the window represents the four centuries of Anglo-American history responsible for the creation of shared transatlantic ideals. In one corner is a detail featuring the Archbishop of Canterbury blessing the 1497 expedition to Newfoundland by John Cabot. Next comes a scene of the Pilgrim Fathers writing the Mayflower Compact, while close by stands seventeenth-century local Thomas Hooker, founder of the colony of Connecticut, establishing the Hertford Constitution in 1639. Elsewhere, William Penn can be seen treating with an Indian chief, before the window revisits what was by now a common and popular theme: Abraham Lincoln, son of East Anglia, stands before a crowd delivering that most eloquent rallying cry for the concept of a people's democracy: the Gettysburg Address. This is a positively Churchillian reading of Anglo-American history (indeed, it is essentially an ecclesiastical rendering of the story Churchill himself offers in Volumes II and III of the *History of the English-Speaking Peoples*). But more than just providing a pictorial and spiritually uplifting anticipation of Churchill's history, this memorial is also 'Churchillian' in the sense that Winston himself features in the iconography: in one corner is an image of President Roosevelt and Prime Minister Churchill,

The architecture of a myth 213

deep in conversation at a wartime conference. Similar Churchillian – and indeed ecclesiastical – renderings of the wartime alliance, and of Anglo-American history, featured in several subsequent memorials, most notably the American Memorial Chapel at St. Paul's and the American Military Cemetery at Madingley, near Cambridge.[63]

The British–American Commonwealth Association first launched plans for the American Memorial Chapel in 1945. This appeal declared that the Chapel would be an 'enduring British memorial to these American dead, which would serve as a shrine and a perpetual remembrance of all soldiers, sailors and airmen of the United States of America in their wartime comradeship with the British people'.[64] With an explicit nod to Churchill, *The Times* even reported the appeal under the headline 'Symbol of a Great Partnership', before explaining that the proposed memorial would 'enshrine forever the underlying moral unities which link our two peoples together'.[65] By 1952, the first part of the memorial had been completed: a book listing the names of all those Americans killed while stationed in Britain. Once again, *The Times* drew on appropriately Churchillian rhetoric in order to explain the message this book was designed to convey. As the paper explained, the memorial was intended to show 'that peace and progress in justice and security for all depended on the continuing friendship and co-operation of the English-speaking peoples'.[66] By the time of the dedication ceremony itself, held in 1958, all those who spoke were keen to invoke the language and sentiment of Churchill. Indeed, the Dean of St Paul's managed to achieve the very same rhetorical 'fusion' as was apparent in the memorial window at Great Cransley. His speech explained, for example, that the Chapel 'in a deeper sense, might remind many generations yet to come of the common effort and common sacrifice of the two English-speaking peoples and fill them with the determination to keep that comradeship alive and vigorous'.[67] Here was a Lincolnesque 'deeper sense' seamlessly bleeding into a Churchillian 'English-speaking peoples'. The dedication ceremony itself concluded with a British Army band playing 'The Battle Hymn of the Republic' (which also featured, as noted above, at Churchill's funeral in 1965), and this was then followed by the two national anthems. Those present at the unveiling included relatives of the American dead being hosted by the English-Speaking Union, the Queen, Vice President Richard Nixon (as President Eisenhower's representative) and a host of British and American generals, admirals and other political notables. Nixon, a well-known admirer of Churchill, drew the appropriate meaning from the ceremony.[68] At an official dinner engagement that evening he rose to say that 'No people in history owe more of their heritage to another than the American people to the British.'[69]

Likewise, the aesthetics of the American Memorial Chapel further explored a Churchillian reading of transatlantic history. The walls of the Chapel were made of English oak, yet engraved into the panelling were distinctly American birds, fruits and flowers. Elsewhere, the three stained-glass windows, which form the backdrop to the Chapel, were 'designed to represent the Service, Sacrifice and Resurrection of the Christian soldier in terms of biblical scenes from the Life of

Christ'. The surrounding border, meanwhile, is marked with the insignia of the forty-eight American states, the four territories and the US Army and Navy. Towards the bottom of the central window is a depiction of a ship representing those wooden vessels 'that sailed westwards 350 years ago and the great armadas which in our recent experience steamed back'. Finally, the altar rails were inscribed with various historical dates deemed significant: 607, 1300, 1666 and 1710, for these were all important years in the life of St Paul's. But the rails were also marked with the figures 1607 and 1776: the first was the date at which Jamestown was founded, the latter the date of the Declaration of Independence.[70]

A similar linking of Lincoln and Churchill was present in the very architecture of the American Military Cemetery at Madingley. Plans for this cemetery had first emerged in 1943 and initially were the subject of local protest and complaint. As one local farmer remarked: 'I feel strongly that Madingley, so beloved by Rupert Brooke and other famous Cambridge men, and with its connection with members of our Royal Family should be allowed to preserve its typical English character.'[71] Eventually, however, the Home Office pushed the plans through, and local concerns were partly placated when the American authorities agreed to 'consult' with Sir Edwin Lutyens before undertaking any construction. Work on the cemetery duly continued over the next decade, with the official unveiling taking place in the summer 1956. Significantly, while the completed cemetery did indeed alter the 'typical English character' of Madingley Hill, the commemorative architecture employed by the American Battle Monuments Commission (ABMC) did nonetheless suggest an attempt to accommodate forms, style and language sensitive to people and place.

This is most apparent at and around the Memorial Chapel (a key feature of all fourteen of the ABMC's post-war cemeteries). For instance, just outside the entrance to the Chapel is the 'Wall of the Missing'. Inscribed upon it are the names of 6,000 servicemen who have no known grave; close by is a contemplative reflecting pool. Placed at regular intervals down the length of this wall are sculptural and figurative representations of the American armed services, carved in English Portland stone: a soldier, airman, sailor and Coastguardsman. The inscription running along the top of the wall is as follows:

THE AMERICANS, WHOSE NAMES HERE APPEAR, WERE PART OF THE PRICE THAT FREE MEN FOR A SECOND TIME THIS CENTURY HAVE BEEN FORCED TO PAY TO DEFEND HUMAN LIBERTY AND RIGHTS. ALL WHO SHALL HEREAFTER LIVE IN FREEDOM WILL BE HERE REMINDED THAT TO THESE MEN AND THEIR COMRADES WE OWE A DEBT, TO BE PAID WITH GRATEFUL REMEMBRANCE OF THEIR SACRIFICE AND WITH THE HIGH RESOLVE THAT THE CAUSE FOR WHICH THEY DIED SHALL LIVE ETERNALLY.

Note the last two lines – surely inspired by Lincoln's Gettysburg Address: 'we here highly resolve that these dead shall not have died in vain'. Indeed, the

The architecture of a myth 215

placing of the wall, Chapel and reflecting pool seems a deliberate attempt to invoke the commemorative landscaping on the national Mall, dominated as it is by the Lincoln Memorial. But this Lincoln landscape is also joined, within the Chapel itself, by Churchillian history. The interior walls are dominated by vast maps of the major theatres of the war, maps which offer the very same 'grand narrative' of the conflict as does *The Second World War* (1954), completed just two years before the cemetery was dedicated in the presence of the Queen. Tellingly, this fusion of Lincolnesque architecture and Churchillian cartography perhaps owed something to the peculiar identity of the man then in charge of the ABMC. For the Secretary of the Commission, General Thomas North, was himself in fact 'Anglo-American' (born a Briton, he had joined the US Army during the First World War and duly become an American citizen).[72]

By the end of the 1950s, therefore, after four decades of dedicated cultural work, the architecture of Churchill's 'special relationship' was in place. Anglo-American heroes, most notably Lincoln, had been commemorated and, where necessary, re-invented. Anglo-American 'shrines' (often in the form of stained-glass windows, the ancient form through which to communicate biblical story and meaning) had been built, dedicated and catalogued. A 'cathedral', the American Memorial Chapel, had been unveiled and a burial ground, Madingley, consecrated. And the 'prophet' – Churchill – had offered a theology and authored a bible. The architecture was built, the myth was made and the devout had worshipped. All that now remained was to enshrine this myth and, ideally, make it a faith. For this to happen, the shift already underway in post-war commemoration would have to be continued and consolidated. In short, it was time for Churchill, rather than Lincoln, to become the key symbol of Anglo-American unity. It was time for Churchill to *become* the special relationship.

Enshrining the myth: Churchill becomes the special relationship, *c.*1961–6

Back in October 1945, Frank McCluer, Westminster College President, had contacted Churchill with the request that he deliver the forthcoming John Findley Green Foundation Lecture, a memorial endowment bequeathed in 1936 by an 'English-born woman'. Westminster College was a small institution, in rural Missouri, and McCluer's request was just one among many such invitations received by Churchill following his electoral defeat in July. But one important fact ensured that this invitation stood out: McCluer's letter of invitation had been annotated by President Harry Truman with the following brief sentences: 'This is a wonderful school in my home state. Hope you can do it. I'll introduce you.'[73] Churchill, keen for an opportunity to offer some critical commentary on contemporary world politics, accepted. As is now well known, the speech which followed in March 1946 was powerful, provocative and memorable, bequeathing two expressions which duly entered the lexicon of post-war diplomatic discourse and, later, historiography: 'Iron Curtain' and, of course 'special relationship'. In addition to welcoming the opportunity to play the role of elder statesman,

216   S. Edwards

Churchill also clearly enjoyed the setting. 'The name "Westminster" is somehow familiar to me,' he joked, 'I seem to have heard of it before.'[74]

In the years afterwards, the Faculty of Westminster were clearly pleased with the success of their coup: no other small mid-Western college had been able to secure the world's pre-eminent elder statesman for a high-profile lecture. By early 1961, just as Churchill was being canonised on American television,[75] and with backing from President Kennedy (an enthusiastic Churchill disciple[76]), the College authorities thus decided that the time was now ripe for the historic moment to be commemorated.[77] Initially, various ideas were explored, including a named scholarship programme of some description. But by the autumn of 1961 the plans had consolidated and now centred on the resurrection on the Fulton campus of a London church badly damaged during the Blitz, and since left derelict and decayed. As the College President explained in correspondence with Henry Luce, proprietor of *Life* magazine and serialiser of Churchill's *The Second World War*, a 'recent article in LIFE about Wren chapels prompted us to think about the possibility of arranging to have one of them moved from Great Britain to Fulton as this physical memorial'.[78] Luce was supportive, and so too was former President Harry Truman, who at the behest of the College authorities wrote to Churchill in September 1961 requesting that the latter 'give them permission to go ahead with their project'.[79] The church identified, and duly requested from the ecclesiastical authorities in London, was St. Mary's, Aldermanbury. Given the deliberately 'Anglo-American' dimensions of the project, this was a fitting choice: partly destroyed during the Great Fire of London, St Mary's had been rebuilt by Sir Christopher Wren in the 1670s, when the American colonies were still one with the motherland. The very architecture itself, therefore, was contemporary to the Churchillian golden age in Anglo-American relations.

At this stage, however, Churchill and his advisors still remained 'anxious' about the proposal, as they feared that it threatened to be a cause of confusion in both the United States and Britain.[80] In particular, Churchill's private secretaries – Anthony Montague Browne and Jack Colville – were both worried that the Fulton project might undermine contemporaneous efforts to fundraise for what was intended to be the major Churchill memorial, in the form of a named college within the University of Cambridge system (Churchill envisaged this as a British version of MIT).[81] In time, too, other concerns emerged: that the memorial idea was enthusiastically supported by Henry Luce (who Montague Browne disliked vehemently);[82] that the Westminster College authorities persisted in referring – revealingly – to their project as the 'Churchill Memorial' despite frequent requests that it not be personalised in this way.[83] And then there were concerns too that the College was not 'a big enough foundation to bear the weight of such large fundraising',[84] nor did some think it sufficiently substantive to be the 'whole focus of any American effort to commemorate Sir Winston'.[85]

Despite these various issues, the project did eventually receive an endorsement from Churchill, who was clearly appreciative, stating in November 1962 that he was 'honoured' by the initiative, which he hoped would 'symbolise in the

The architecture of a myth   217

eyes of the English-speaking peoples the ideals of Anglo-American associ-ation'.[86] Perhaps he saw in it the logical conclusion to all that he had been doing for the previous four decades. For if the American Memorial Chapel (1958) enshrined a very Churchillian theology in *Britain*, then that same theology none-theless still had to be enshrined in the United States, especially after Congress, with President Kennedy's warm support, had granted Churchill honorary citizen-ship in 1963. As such, while one critic declared to the Westminster College Pres-ident that the proposed memorial would 'inescapably be a stage-set' which would serve 'neither his [Churchill's] memory nor your needs', in actual fact this was the whole point and purpose: it was *supposed* to be a 'stage-set'.[87] Indeed, as a supporter had identified, the resurrected church was specifically intended to be a 'symbolic gesture' providing a space in which to 'revere' Churchill.[88] From this perspective, the plans and the place were thus entirely appropriate. For in large part due to his own pen and personality (and especially the success of Volume II of his *Second World War*), Churchill had become syn-onymous in the United States with Britain's 'Finest Hour' in 1940, and this was of course the very moment of St Mary's desecration. In chronology, therefore, church and Churchill were in this sense fused: the former had fallen to be redeemed by the latter. Second, given Churchill's long-held hopes and fears vis-à-vis the United States, where better to install a shrine to Anglo-American rela-tions than at a place named 'Westminster' in Missouri, the traditional mid-Western heartland of American isolationism? Here, his shrine might become a beacon, perhaps indeed a city on a hill, providing a place which pilgrims could visit and venerate, and at which the uncertain might be converted.

Some of the publicity material issued by the College in order to help raise funds emphasised the extent to which the project was intended as an act of resurrection. A pamphlet published in later 1963, for instance, included several images of a rather forgotten and forlorn St Mary's, overgrown with weeds, decayed and dere-lict. Elsewhere, the same pamphlet explained that St Mary's had been 'destined' for destruction, but was now to be saved and rebuilt as a 'visible testimony to the days when Britain stood alone against the forces of tyranny'.[89] In due course, there-fore, and once permission had been granted by the necessary authorities in London, the exterior stonework and columns of St Mary's were carefully dismantled and transported across the Atlantic. Former President Truman then visited the campus in 1964 to turn a symbolic shovel of soil, while the first foundation stone was laid, with much ceremony, in 1966. The exterior was complete by the spring of 1967, but it then took a further two years to finish the interior, with the Bishop of Dover (another place very much connected to Britain's 'Finest Hour') officiating at the dedication ceremony in May 1969. Churchill, of course, would not be present, having passed away in early 1965. But the St Mary's memorial, as well as his funeral ceremony in St Paul's, both offered revealing expressions of the myth which he had worked so hard to create and cultivate. Combined, these commem-orative acts represented the mythologisation of the mythmaker himself: Churchill the author of the 'special relationship' had become Churchill the *symbol* of the special relationship.

218 *S. Edwards*

Conclusions

Churchill – an occasional agnostic whose religion was, if anything, 'History' – saw in rites, rituals and rhetoric the means to *mythologise* what he had once hoped might be made actual: Anglo-American unity. His efforts in this regard were aided by many others, from the hero-worshippers of the post-1918 period, to the memorial builders of the Second World War and after. As a result, by the 1950s, Churchill's sustained cultural and commemorative endeavours, together with the creative work of many others, had produced (and occasionally appropriated) a landscape of Anglo-American memory. This landscape buttressed Churchill's myth – the 'special relationship' – with all those things which Victorians of his vintage believed were so central to nationalism as civic religion: monuments, heroes, a theology, shrines, even a chapel. As a result, by the time of his death, Churchill was ready to complete the process of mythologisation; he was ready to offer the closing chapter on a story that in so many respects he had authored. Thus, having been the prophet of Anglo-American brotherhood, and the author of the special relationship (as phrase and idea), he now became its pre-eminent *symbol*. And in this regard, his honorary American citizenship (1963), funeral (1965) and the Fulton memorial (1966–9) all fulfilled a commemorative and discursive trajectory first marked out during the Anglo-American hero worship which followed the Great War. Put differently, what had begun in 1920 with the Anglicisation of Abraham Lincoln at the Palace of Westminster had become, by 1969, the Americanisation of Winston Churchill at Westminster College. This was a fitting conclusion: already in 1949, none other than Isaiah Berlin had referred to Churchill as a 'mythical hero who belongs to legend as much as reality'.[90] Only right, then, that Churchill the legend and prophet had a shrine: St Winston's Basilica. For Churchill, who was once heard to say that 'myths have their place in epic times', it all would no doubt have made perfect sense.[91]

Notes

1 J. Rose, *The Literary Churchill: Author, Reader, Actor*, London: Yale University Press, 2015, p. 448. For details about the funeral and its planning, see Churchill Papers, Churchill College Cambridge: CHUR 1/137.
2 Ibid., p. 22.
3 For discussions and debate regarding the 'special' nature of the post-war Anglo-American alliance, see H.C. Allen, *The Anglo-American Relationship since 1783*, London: Odhams Press, 1954; C.J. Bartlett, *The Special Relationship; A Political History*, London: Longman, 1992; J. Dumbrell, *A Special Relationship: Anglo-American Relations from the Cold War to Iraq*, London: Palgrave Macmillan, 2006; W.R. Louis and H. Bull, *The Special Relationship: Anglo-American Relations since 1945*, Oxford: Oxford University Press, 1986. For the idea of the special relationship as 'myth', see especially J. Charmley, *Churchill's Grand Alliance: The Anglo-American Special Relationship, 1940–57*, London: Hodder and Stoughton, 1995.
4 My thinking about this has been particularly influenced by the scholarship of David Reynolds and Jonathan Rose. See D. Reynolds, *In Command of History: Fighting and Writing the Second World War*, London: Allen Lane, 2004; and Rose, *Literary Churchill*.

The architecture of a myth 219

5 For a discussion of cultural Anglo-Saxonism see R. Horsman, *Race and Manifest Destiny: The Origins of American Exceptionalism*, London: Harvard University Press, 1981, pp. 9–24; R. Horsman, 'Origins of Racial Anglo-Saxonism in Great Britain before 1850', *Journal of the History of Ideas*, 37:3, 1976, pp. 388–90; A. Martellone, 'In the Name of Anglo-Saxondom, For Empire and For Democracy: The Anglo-American Discourse, 1880–1920', in D.K. Adams and Cornelius A. Van Minnen (eds), *Reflections on American Exceptionalism*, Keele: Keele University Press, 1994, p. 84; S.W. Siak, ' "The Blood That Is in Our Veins Comes From German Ancestors": British Historians and the Coming of the First World War', *Albion: Quarterly Journal Concerned with British Studies*, 30:2, 1998, p. 227; S.R. Hauer, 'Thomas Jefferson and the Anglo-Saxon Language', *PMLA*, 98:5, 1983, p. 880.

6 See B. Perkins, *The Great Rapprochement: England and the United States, 1895–1914*, New York: Atheneum, 1968; P.A. Kramer, 'Empires, Exceptions, and Anglo-Saxons: Race and Rule between the British and American Empires, 1880–1910', *Journal of American History*, 88:4, 2002, pp. 1315–53.

7 S. Anderson, *Race and Rapprochement: Anglo-Saxonism and Anglo-American Relations, 1895–1904*, Rutherford: Fairleigh Dickinson University Press, 1981, p. 61.

8 Allen, *The Anglo-American Relationship*, p. 126. For Churchill's idea of an Anglo-American federation, see K. Larres, *Churchill's Cold War: The Politics of Personal Diplomacy*, New Haven: Yale University Press, 2002, p. 84.

9 *The Times*, 31 May 1918.

10 J.H. Lea and J.R. Hutchinson, *The Ancestry of Lincoln*, New York: Houghton Mifflin, 1909.

11 See L.C. Cornish, *A Pilgrimage to Old Hingham, Norfolk, England*, Hingham, MA: The Association for the Extension of Influence of Hingham Plantation, 1915. See also S. Edwards, 'From Here Lincoln Came: Anglo-Saxonism, the Special Relationship, and the Anglicization of Abraham Lincoln, *c.*1860–1970', *Journal of Transatlantic Studies*, 11:1, pp. 22–46.

12 Ibid.

13 J. Bryce, *Speeches and Letters of Abraham Lincoln, 1832–1865*, London: J.M. Dent, 1907, p. vii.

14 *The Times*, 29 July 1920.

15 Ibid.

16 *Eastern Daily Press*, 16 October 1919.

17 F.H. Millington, *The Paine Centenary: June 1909, Thetford*, Thetford: H. Green, 1909, p. 5.

18 For some details of British views on Washington, see R.C. McGrane, 'George Washington: An Anglo-American Hero', *The Virginia Magazine of History and Biography*, 63:1, 1995, pp. 3–14. For information about Sulgrave Manor, see www.sulgravemanor.org.uk/pages/31/a_symbol_of_a_special_relationship.asp (accessed 20 December 2015).

19 J.F. Muirhead, *American Shrines on English Soil*, London: The Doorland Agency, 1924.

20 F.V. Morley, *Travels in East Anglia*, London: Methuen, 1923; and R.B. Mowat, *Americans in England*, London: George C. Harrap, 1935.

21 See Rose, *Literary Churchill*, pp. 21–2, p. 46.

22 M. Gilbert, *Churchill and America*, London: Free Press, 2005, p. 11.

23 W.S. Churchill, *A History of the English-Speaking Peoples, Volume IV, The Great Democracies*, London: Cassell, 1958, pp. 105–207.

24 Churchill, quoted in Gilbert, *Churchill and America*, p. 9.

25 Ibid., p. 2.

26 Gilbert, *Churchill and America*, pp. 121–2.

27 Winston S. Churchill, 'Anglo-American Relations' (1925), CHAR 2/144. For some further details about Churchill's post-First World War views on the Anglo-American alliance, see also 'Independence Day 1918', CHAR 9/56.

220   *S. Edwards*

28 Ernst Renan, 'What is a Nation?' 11 March 1882. Full text here: http://ucparis.fr/files/9313/6549/9943/What_is_a_Nation.pdf.

29 Benedict Anderson, *Imagined Communities*, London: Verso, 2002 (first published in 1982).

30 E. Hobsbawn and T. Ranger *The Invention of Tradition*, Cambridge: Cambridge University Press, 1983.

31 See S. Goebel, *The Great War and Medieval Memory: War, Remembrance and Commemoration in Britain and Germany, 1914–1940*, Cambridge: Cambridge University Press, 2007.

32 For some details about post-1918 commemoration, see J.M. Winter, *Sites of Memory, Sites of Mourning: The Great War in European Cultural History*, Cambridge: Cambridge University Press, 1995; B. Bushaway, 'Name Upon Name: The Great War and Remembrance', in R. Porter (ed.), *Myths of the English*, Cambridge: Polity Press, 1992; T. Laqueur, 'Memory and Naming in the Great War', in J.R. Gillis (ed.) *Commemorations: The Politics of National Identity*, Princeton: Princeton University Press, 1994, pp. 150–67.

33 'The Proposed Gift to Great Britain of a Statue of Lincoln', National Archives, WO 20/106.

34 Ibid.

35 Martellone, 'In the Name of Anglo-Saxondom', pp. 83–96; see also generally Anderson, *Race and Rapprochement*.

36 Martellone, 'In the Name of Anglo-Saxondom', pp. 88–90.

37 Charles Dilke, *Greater Britain: A Record of Travel in English-Speaking Countries*, London: Macmillan, 1868. For a discussion of this text, and related ideas, see D. Bell, *The Idea of Greater Britain: Empire and the Future of the World Order, 1860–1900*, Princeton: Princeton University Press, 2007; G.W. Morris and L.S. Wood, *The English-Speaking Nations*, Oxford: Clarendon Press, 1924; R.B. Mowatt, *History of the English-Speaking Peoples*, Oxford: Oxford University Press, 1943.

38 Churchill, *A History of the English-Speaking Peoples, Volume IV*, p. 119.

39 Winston S. Churchill, *A History of the English-Speaking Peoples, Volume I: The Birth of Britain*, London: Cassell, 1956, p. 190. Significantly, Runnymeade is also the site of a British-sponsored memorial to a keen admirer of Churchill, President John F. Kennedy. This memorial was unveiled in 1965.

40 Winston S. Churchill, *A History of the English-Speaking Peoples, Volume II: The New World*, London: Cassell, 1956, p. vii.

41 Ibid., p. 142.

42 Winston S. Churchill, *A History of the English-Speaking Peoples, Volume III: The Age of Revolution*, London: Cassell, 1957, pp. 135, 142.

43 Ibid., p. 152.

44 Churchill, *A History of the English-Speaking Peoples, Volume IV*, pp. 105–207.

45 Churchill, quoted in Rose, *Literary Churchill*, p. 157.

46 *The Second World War* would of course be published prior to *The History of the English-Speaking Peoples*, but the latter was nonetheless originally conceived and started first.

47 Rose, *Literary Churchill*, pp. 421–3.

48 For the idea of *The History of the English-Speaking Peoples* as a 'monument', see Rose, *Literary Churchill*, p. 423. For the extent to which the work was intended to appeal to Americans, see Rose, *Literary Churchill*, p. 278.

49 See Rose, *Literary Churchill*, p. 178.

50 For an extended discussion of Churchill's *Second World War*, see Reynolds, *In Command of History*.

51 Ibid.

52 W.S. Churchill, *The Second World War, Volume III: The Grand Alliance*, London: Cassell, 1950, p. 384.

The architecture of a myth 221

53 For the theatrical dimensions to Churchill's scholarship, see Rose, *Literary Churchill*, p. 367, pp. 413–17.
54 David Lloyd George, *Abraham Lincoln: An Address Before the Midday Luncheon Club, Leland Hotel, Springfield Illinois, Thursday, October 18, 1923*, Cleveland: Stephen Wallis Tener, 1924, pp. 12–13.
55 See Barry Schwartz, 'Memory as a Cultural System: Abraham Lincoln in World War II', *American Sociological Review*, 61:5, 1996, pp. 908–27; E. Foner, *The Story of American Freedom*, London: Papermac, 2000, pp. 219–25.
56 For the connections between the outbreak of the Second World War and *The History of the English-Speaking Peoples*, see Rose, *Literary Churchill*, p. 266.
57 *Eastern Daily Press*, 14 February 1944.
58 Reverend Harp-Mitchell, Rector of Quidenham Church, speech at service of remembrance, 30 May 1946. Norfolk Records Office PD 97/29.
59 George Holt, Press Release, 12 December 1961, NRO, MC 2059/1, 911x7.
60 Ibid. Remarks of the Honourable Lewis G. James, American minister and Charge d'Affairs, US Embassy, 13 June 1963.
61 *Country Life*, 8 February 1962, p. 282.
62 D. Reynolds, 'Rethinking Anglo-American Relations', *International Affairs*, 65:1, 1988–9, pp. 89–111.
63 Further details about these memorials can be found in S. Edwards, *Allies in Memory: World War II and the Politics of Transatlantic Commemoration*, Cambridge: Cambridge University Press, 2015.
64 'Service of Commemoration of 28,000 Dead in Wartime Comradeship with the People of Britain', 1951, British Library.
65 *The Times*, 15 November 1945.
66 *The Times*, 9 March 1952.
67 *New York Times*, 26 November 1958. See also: National Archives, WO 32/17344.
68 Rose, *Literary Churchill*, p. 436.
69 *New York Times*, 26 November 1958.
70 For further details, see *The American Memorial Chapel in St Paul's Cathedral*, London: Pitkin Pictorials, 1958, British Library.
71 Miss Rosamund E.M. Harding to W.F. Stapleton-Harris Esq., The War Office, 23 September 1943, NA WO 32/21847.
72 See William P. Jones Papers, ABMC Memoirs (1967–74), 'Service with the American Battle Monuments Commission, 1 April 1967 to 30 June 1974', United States Army Military History Institute.
73 See P. White, *Churchill's Cold War: How the Iron Curtain Speech Shaped the Post War World*, London: Duckworth Overlook, 2012, pp. 57–62.
74 For the full and original text, see CHUR 5/4A/51–100.
75 See *Churchill: The Valiant Years* (ABC, 1960–1). For the idea that this series 'canonised' Churchill, see Rose, *Literary Churchill*, p. 435.
76 Rose, *Literary Churchill*, pp. 425–48.
77 Full details about the plans behind the memorial can be found in CHUR 2/556.
78 Letter to Mr Henry Luce, 3 October 2961, CHUR 2/566 C.
79 Harry S. Truman to Winston Churchill, 12 September 1961, CHUR 2/566 C.
80 Winston Churchill to Harry Truman, 24 September 1961, CHUR 2/566 C.
81 See, for example, Anthony Montague Browne to Duncan Sandys, 27 September 1961; Jack Colville to Anthony Montague Browne, 20 September 1961. CHUR 2/566 C.
82 See Anthony Montague Browne to Jack Colville, 13 September 1961, CHUR 2/566 C. In another letter, Montague Browne referred to Luce as 'odious'. See Anthony Montague Browne to Miss Freda Smith, 12 October 1961, CHUR 2/566 C.
83 See, for example, Anthony Montague Browne to Governor John Dalton (Missouri) 20 April 1964, CHUR 2/566 A; Anthony Montague Browne to President Davidson 11 December 1964, CHUR 2/566 A.

222   *S. Edwards*

84 Anthony Montague Browne to Jack Colville, 9 March 1964, CHUR 2/566 B.
85 Draft letter by Anthony Montague Browne to Mr Joyce Hall, March 1964, CHUR 2/566 B.
86 The Winston Churchill Memorial and Chapel, CHUR 2/566 A.
87 G.E. Kidder Smith to President Davidson, 4 August 1964, CHUR 2/566 A.
88 Professor Patrick Horsbrugh to Duncan Sandys, 31 August 1961, CHUR 2/566 C.
89 The Winston Churchill Memorial and Chapel, CHUR, 2/566 A.
90 Isaiah Berlin, quoted in Rose, *Literary Churchill*, p. 198.
91 Churchill, quoted in Rose, *Literary Churchill*, p. 154.

9 Curtains, culture and 'collective' memory[*]

David Ryan

There is a stick figure on the proverbial whiteboard in a wood-panelled lecture hall; how much better this sentence would have resonated if it had involved chalk and a blackboard, but chalk dust and contemporary health and safety regulations conspired to destroy an atmosphere. The stick figure representing President Harry S. Truman arrived on the board one day while teaching the historiography on US foreign policy and the origins of the cold war. I had presented the pitched battles between the orthodox and revisionists schools of thought, the stuff that really animated undergraduate students attracted by the Manichean battles, of seeming 'insidious arguments' on interpretation fought out over the years of the Vietnam Wars by ageing professors in tweed jackets and Oxford shirts, with cartographic references that lay somewhere between the White House and Wisconsin. For these protagonists and writers had created a world and interpretations based on the division of the continents that cut across Europe in the first instance and later Asia. Later still, there were all sorts of arrows on maps emanating from China to depict the spread of Communism in line with the dominoes that were said might fall across Southeast Asia in graphic affiliation with the US *mentalité*, 'the ideological system of the epoch in question'.[1] I had drawn a line across my globe, next to which the stick figure, Truman, now stood. Of course I had chosen the early writings of John Lewis Gaddis to represent the post-revisionists. And by transferring my line that had descended across my globe to a division within the head of Truman, I tried to explain Gaddis on the need to understand domestic politics and a whole system of representation, misperception and incomplete understanding. There was the world and more pertinently Europe as it was, and there was the world as perceived by the central protagonists; there was the world depicted in speeches and documents, in maps and cartoons – few more seminal than that of Churchill's Iron Curtain. Here was the iteration of what became a 'metapicture' that would reverberate around the world, 'a verbal representation of a visual representation'. The relationship of word and image, as W.J.T. Mitchell argues in *Picture Theory*, is not just about 'effects' and 'identity' but 'also engages the *status* of the metapicture in a wider cultural field, its positioning with respect to disciplines, discourses, and institutions'.[2]

The point is that these divisions were firmly embedded in institutional politics, culture and historiography until the advent of post-revisionism and further

224   *D. Ryan*

academic deconstructions, after the 1980s, and again after the fall of the Berlin Wall. The second point is that those deconstructions have not wholly filtered through to contemporary culture and society. The view of the cold war pitted on either side of the Iron Curtain remains a steady depiction. Various presidents, their principals, political commentators, authors, graphic artists and so forth perpetuated the image throughout the cold war and after. The Iron Curtain, both as image and as metaphor, was built up into an enduring impression of a powerful concept – the cast of mind created in 1946 endured longer than the geopolitical actuality. Collective memory retains only from the past what is useful and is capable of living in the consciousness of the culture within which it exists.[3] Moreover, collective memory is constantly refreshed by people who have an interest in perpetuating a particular memory or promoting a particular outlook. The invocation of 'Iron Curtain' in contemporary discourse serves to both send a dire warning and to reinforce a cultural process of opposition or *othering*. It is important, therefore, when examining artifacts and memory, to determine the agency behind the invocation, in this case that of the Iron Curtain.[4] Steven Rose has demonstrated that with the construction of memory in contemporary society, images are replayed endlessly, through print and digital media that produces the effect of training our memory, limiting the bounds of interpretation and strengthening perceived images.[5]

Of course, the perceptions were based on firm ground at that point in the months after the end of the Second World War. The *New York Times* had indicated that the Soviet Union had annexed 273,947 square miles, encompassing over twenty-four million people.[6] Yet there was still considerable diffidence and differences in US political culture on the appropriate US stance on Soviet expansionism and towards Moscow. There were still powerful isolationist tendencies, still some scepticism of association with the British, still some that sought accommodation with Moscow, along lines Franklin Roosevelt advanced. The clarity of the 'Good War' that emerged in the 1980s[7] built on a Manichean reading of the Second World War had yet to be transposed onto the origins of the cold war in the mid- to late 1940s. Yet some of the historiography on US foreign policy would attempt to instil that clarity, that certainty, in the triumphalist and vindicationalist literature of the 1990s and after.[8]

That transplantation of the bipolar configuration of power captured in the image was contested at first but soon grew as a sturdy metaphor yielding the fruit of its potent image throughout the Cold War. Ultimately, the Berlin Wall came to symbolise the proverbial Iron Curtain; it was the manifestation of the metaphor. Yet even after its collapse in 1989, the metaphor remained adherent and was used during the Ukrainian crises of 2014–15. Earlier, well beyond the end of the cold war, Secretary of Defense Donald Rumsfeld referenced it in 2003, observing as Saddam Hussein's statue in Firdos Square was pulled down: 'one cannot help but think of the Berlin Wall and the collapse of the Iron Curtain'.[9] It is frequently invoked in discussions on the US–Mexican Border Wall or the Gaza Wall. Incidentally, the death rates at the US wall, of people trying to enter the US, far exceed those killed trying to flee East Berlin. When

Barack Obama participated in the ritual, he noted he was not the first US president to visit, but he was proud to stand on the Eastern side. He noted that he and Angela Merkel did not look like previous German and American leaders, she a 'child of the East', he an African American. They stood as symbols, in Obama's words, that: 'No wall can stand against the yearnings of justice, the yearnings for freedom, the yearnings for peace that burns in the human heart.'[10] Still more, the Russian Deputy Foreign Minister, Sergei Ryabkov, invoked the term over US sanctions in 2014 comparing it to the 1940s.[11] The Iron Curtain had shifted momentously; he invoked the horrors of renewed cold war or worse after the events in Maidan Square, just as the original speech had invoked fears of renewed war in 1946, and served as a warning of dire alternatives. As Russia moved closer to the European Union in the post-Soviet geopolitical space there was a clear recognition of how different they were.[12] Digital searches of various media outlets reveal that the term is used for a variety of reasons: from eating and food behind the Iron Curtain, for travel in the post-communist world, on health care and cheaper options, on the Olympics, on a Soviet circus free to travel, on art, music and a variety of other activities. More pertinently, a search on the influential journal *Foreign Affairs* database for 'Iron Curtain' retrieves 282 results spanning from 1933 to 2016. It is first mentioned in 1936, but then spikes from 1946 to 1947. The period between 1947 and 1961 reveals 135 mentions; articles by Robert Gale Woolbert, 'Behind the Iron Curtain' (April 1947); Henry L. Roberts. 'The Curtain Isn't Iron' (October 1950); another by Roberts, 'East of the Iron Curtain' (October 1950). There are articles on religion and church and state behind the Iron Curtain. On the struggles behind the Iron Curtain; in July 1953 on 'The Explosion: the Uprising Behind the Iron Curtain', McGeorge Bundy's 'The Test of Yalta' January 1958. Another spike occurs around 1987 and after; from Reagan's Berlin speech to the end of the cold war. Kennan is reproduced from 1951 in the spring of 1990, 'America and the Russian Future'; Jim Hoagland on 'Europe's Destiny' in 1989; McGeorge Bundy is back with 'From Cold War Toward Trusting Peace', 1989; Walter Lippmann, Richard Nixon, John Lukacs, Zbigniew Brzezinski, Michael Howard (1989), 'The Springtime of Nations'. And of course there is a third and smaller spike in 2014–15.[13]

The Iron Curtain pivots in our culture, not only as metaphor: it also has deeply affected our cultural structures of thought and in Foucault's words, it has created a 'regime of truth' – we understand the world and various problems because they are explained in certain attractive frames and adherent ways.[14]

Gorbachev, Fulton and the '46 Model'

On 6 May 1992 the recently deposed General Secretary of the Soviet Union, Mikhail Gorbachev, toured the Churchill Museum at Fulton, Missouri, stood before the sculpture *Breakthrough*, designed by Churchill's granddaughter, Edwina Sandys, and delivered the annual John Findley Green lecture, running since the 1930s, at Westminster College.[15]

226 *D. Ryan*

Sandys' sculpture depicted human forms carved out of sections of the Berlin Wall, transported to Fulton, Missouri. The form represents not only an opening, but also liberation, and the persistence of individual liberty. Sandys and her husband, Richard Kaplan, had travelled to East Berlin in February 1990. Sections of the Wall were selling for between $60,000 and $200,000. Local officials eventually made a donation of eight sections because they thought it appropriate to locate the idea of the Berlin Wall monument 'near the site of Churchill's 1946 "Iron Curtain" speech'. She chose sections from close to the Brandenburg Gate, the graffiti, frequented by the word '*unwahr*': lies or untruths. The sculpture was dedicated on 9 November 1990; forty-four years after her grandfather had warned of the descent of the curtain, there was now a *Breakthrough*.[16] The side from which it is constantly shown is the Western side, covered in graffiti – implicitly juxtaposed with the grey, inaccessible, unpainted, dull and dour, Eastern side. The transport of sections of the 1961 wall to the site of the 1946 speech reinforced the metaphor and the message of the bipolar conflict, just as the historiography of the cold war was increasingly subject to deconstruction.[17] Another section of the wall would be erected at the Reagan Presidential Library overlooking the Simi Valley, California. The George H.W. Bush Library also displays sections of the wall, at College Station, Texas – wild horses leaping over the reduced hurdle.

Gorbachev was now deposed but through his period in office he struggled to liberate the East–West relationship from the *mentality* of the Iron Curtain framework. Not only did he move on the domestic front through *glasnost* and *perestroika* but in foreign policy his *new thinking* injected a form of realism into Soviet foreign policy; he defused tensions at the superpower level; he advanced Soviet interests in pursuit of better relations with Western Europe. His talk of the Common European Home, aggravated US policy-makers, as he identified a potential cooperative sphere running from Moscow, Bonn, Paris and London – pointedly Washington, DC, lay beyond the sphere. This in part echoed the Europe of de Gaulle and Adenauer after the Suez crisis and into the early 1960s.[18] Most explicitly, when Gorbachev delivered his speech to the United Nations in 1988 he not only advanced an agenda on disarmament, but also, in a statement that at once tried to make virtue out of necessity and was implicitly critical of the Reagan Doctrine, he declared that it was inadmissible to promote revolution from abroad.[19] In his *Memoirs*, he reflected on the speech and noted: 'the speech to the UN must [be] a "Fulton in Reverse", "anti-Fulton"'.[20]

At Fulton in 1992 Gorbachev opened with a reference to the sculpture. He observed the 'remarkable expressiveness and laconism' which conveyed the drama of the Cold War and the 'irrepressible human striving to penetrate the barriers of alienation and confrontation'. It was fitting, he noted, that it was here and that it was designed by Churchill's granddaughter.[21] Gorbachev explained that Churchill had urged audiences in 1946 to think 'super-strategically' – to look above the 'petty problems and particularities of current realities' to identify the major trends and to be guided by them. Yet his forty-five minute speech advanced a tone of admonition: 'It would be a supreme tragedy if the world, having overcome the "1946 model", were to find itself once again in a "1914 model" world.' A global effort would be needed this time to secure a more democratic and irreversible world for all of humanity and not just 'for half of it', he argued.[22]

They had missed a chance in 1946, some forty-six years earlier. Gorbachev contended that the chance they missed was to establish a world order that differed from the previous era of confrontation. He berated the Stalinist leadership for misinterpreting the period and for equating victory over fascism with the assumed victory of socialism and the aim of spreading it throughout the world. 'But,' Gorbachev swiftly turned the tables, 'the West, and the United States in particular, also committed an error. Its conclusion about the probability of open Soviet military aggression was unrealistic and dangerous.' War could not have happened, according to this account, because Stalin did not want war, he would not have pursued it, 'but primarily because the country was exhausted and destroyed; it had lost tens of millions of people, and the public hated war'.[23] The US, he argued, unleashed the arms race that went beyond normal defensive requirements; the West had not thought strategically in terms of its own interests. 'And on both sides this was justified ideologically. The conflict was presented as the inevitable opposition between good and evil – all the evil, of course, being attributed to the opponent.' The cold war continued for decades to the precipice of the abyss. 'I am stating this because the world community has paid dearly for the errors committed at this turning-point in world history.'[24]

The cold war had ended with 'a shattering of the vicious circle into which we had driven ourselves'.[25] He had tried to advance the anti-Fulton intention through his 'new thinking' and an injection of realism into Soviet foreign policy. But the Common European Home was not to be; subsequent NATO enlargement fed further suspicion and reaction. Talk of a 'new Iron Curtain' emerged as NATO expanded eastward.[26]

While Gorbachev contended that they had missed a chance back at the origins of the Cold War, Kennan concurred in 1989 that the United States purposefully had not exhausted the possibilities of negotiated accommodation. Kennan later regretted his part in solidifying the metaphor and image of the Soviet Union which had begun to gain momentum with the 1946 'long telegram' that advanced structures of thought echoed in the Truman Doctrine, the X article in *Foreign Affairs* and the Manichean disposition of NSC 68, attended by extensive and related public diplomacy exercises emanating out of NSC 59/1 which facilitated the informal propagation of the NSC 68 message through numerous activities coordinated by Edward Barratt, Assistant Secretary of State for Public Affairs. These efforts were described as a 'Marshall Plan in the field of ideas' and advanced a narrative, according to Michael Kammen, 'cohesive and patterned like a carefully designed fabric' that echoed official messages.[27] Kennan shared Churchill's perceptions, but Kennan recounted after the cold war that he thought 'Churchill took perhaps an even more military view ... than I did.'[28]

The Iron Curtain descends in US culture

Churchill's speech was pivotal in trying to cast and solidify the image of the unrelenting expansionism of the Soviet Union that could only be resisted by the union of the US and the UK. Famously, if they did not want war, they wanted the 'fruits of war and the indefinite expansion of their power and doctrines'. They did not know of Soviet immediate intentions, 'or what are the limits, if any, to their expansive or proselytizing tendencies'. Though the speech contained many intentions and agendas, in collective memory it is reduced to the famous phrases that contributed to the creation of a new West. It was a West devoid of division and difference, a West that not only segmented or *orientalised* the Other, but also encompassed the British into a new, loose and informal fraternal partnership.[29] Churchill's words that endure most significantly in collective memory capture the geopolitical image:

> From Stettin in the Baltic to Trieste in the Adriatic, an iron curtain has descended across the Continent. Behind that line lie all the capitals of the ancient states of Central and Eastern Europe. Warsaw, Berlin, Prague, Vienna, Budapest, Belgrade, Bucharest and Sofia, all these famous cities and the populations around them lie in what I must call the Soviet sphere, and all are subject in one form or another, not only to Soviet influence but to a very high and, in many cases, increasing measure of control from Moscow. Athens alone – Greece with its immortal glories – is free to decide its future at an election under British, American and French observation.[30]

It is the opening phrases, the line of geography: *from … to* that have been so frequently rendered in different form.

This 'epoch-making' passage was not contained in advance copies of the speech and it seems that it was only added on the train from Washington to Fulton, Missouri.[31] Of course, within the United States, Churchill's image and credentials were impeccable. His voice not only intoned on the necessities for the future, replayed in crackly black and white newsreel; it was not only a speech that resonated within the frame of *fighting on the beaches*, but also of Munich, of steadfastness, fortitude and resolution. Here was the rotund personification of that fortitude. Churchill infused his words with the dramatis personae that he represented, here, in Fulton in flesh and blood. 'He would dramatize [his words] and hurl them forth as if they were great boulders in the stream of history: elements of a withstanding inheritance that belonged to the English-speaking peoples at large,' Patrick Wright writes.[32] Churchill was about to publicly transform the 'big three', Yalta narrative, to a binary proposition. With the speech, Dobson writes, 'things were beginning to swing into the Cold War'. Churchill was associated with resolve, with the voice that recognised the inadequate response to 'totalitarian aggression in the 1930s. Appeasement would not be repeated.'[33] The association of Churchill with the victories of war commanded attention, boosted 'interpretive authority' and facilitated the departure from the still ambivalent discourse, though Stalin still held to the prospects of cooperation. As 'owner' of the narrative, Churchill seized the opportunity 'to narrate the world differently' where he had previously felt constrained.[34]

Though there were sectors of the American political elite and society in general that did not share his views, that reacted negatively to the message, it fell within an increasing tempo of rhetoric that wound up the so-called 'get tough' policy. Of course it followed Stalin's 9 February speech. Churchill's words fit neatly into a sequence of private and public communications: Kennan's long telegram of February 1946, its enthusiastic reception in Washington. Patrick Wright outlines a sequence of public reiterations. On 26 February 1946, presidential adviser Bernard Baruch attacked communism in a speech after visiting Churchill in Florida. The following day Senator Arthur Vandenberg echoed the theme on the Senate floor. And a day later, Secretary of State James Byrnes sang along at the Overseas Press Club, echoed by John Foster Dulles in Philadelphia on 1 March.[35] The Churchill speech had been a carefully planned first step that led to the Truman Doctrine, the Marshall Plan, containment, NATO and NSC-68. Wright argues, 'there can be no doubt either that Churchill launched the phrase into wide circulation, or that it would quickly become established as a political metaphor all over the world.' It was widely recognised as a reality before Eastern Germany wired the borders in 1952.[36]

Cumulatively, through these speeches, Churchill and others reinforced a traditional way of thinking in US political rhetoric and culture. It reinforced a tradition that had run through the history of US foreign policy that rejected John Quincy Adams' injunction not to search for 'monsters to destroy'[37] and secured the inclination to see the world in dichotomies. The metaphorical 'Iron Curtain' was 'present at the creation' of a new Manichaean world. Moreover, here was a new Other, that was grafted through familiar images with totalitarianism; and even if the British were the object of the American Other of the early nineteenth century, now the metaphor of the line of division shifted from the mid-Atlantic Monroe Doctrine to the mid-European Iron Curtain. With the terms 'Iron Curtain' and 'special relationship' 'he bequeathed to posterity a rummage bag of striking political terms whose familiarity reflects his continuing relevance', Fraser Harbutt argues.[38]

Churchill's objectives, seamlessly integrated into the Truman strategy: to 'destroy the accommodationist policies and attitudes associated with Yalta'. Despite the October 1944 Percentages Agreement between Churchill and Stalin, a matter that in Churchill's words was 'all settled in no more time than it takes to set down', various countries were divided into spheres of influence on a half-page in Moscow and affirmed by Stalin with the tick of his blue pencil.[39] Churchill now argued in 1946 that conditions would lead to inevitable war as had the attempts to appease Hitler in the 1930s.[40] Depictions of the 'Big Three', the famous photographs of Yalta and Potsdam: FDR, Churchill, Stalin and months later, Truman, Atlee with Churchill, and Stalin were discontinued.

The response to this apparently self-evident menace was the appeal to the 'fraternal association' of the Anglo-American friendship. Here at once was

230   D. Ryan

the layered employment of a weaker form of alterity, which involved both the segmentation of the world, now metaphorically divided by the Iron Curtain, and the encompassment of the Anglo-American worlds.[41]

Churchill skilfully engaged the 'grammars of identity and alterity'. Indeed one of Kennan's fortunes was that he became pivotal just as the Yalta formulation of 'one world', a world of accommodation and the anticipated four police power configuration of the world was discredited. Instead, a world view pivoting around two ways of life was emerging. Of course, the binary of orientalism has long been a feature of the Western epistemology, popularised by Edward Said in his famous 1978 book *Orientalism*. Yet what was at work in Churchill's speech was more than a two-sided proposition, because the tensions that surrounded the British signature to the Atlantic Charter of 1941, the tensions that arose because of the US public stance on colonialism and decolonisation, implied at least for this situation three worlds including the two emergent superpowers, the colonial and the coloniszed.[42] Context is all important. In this segmentary grammar, Churchill was proposing a process of 'selfing' or cooperative arrangements with the United States based on a structural level that was seen as resting above the transatlantic differences. Gerd Baumann writes,

> the intellectual beauty of this segmentary grammar of identity/alterity lies in its contextual awareness. The Other may be my foe in a context placed at a lower level of segmentation, but may simultaneously be my ally in a context placed at a higher level of segmentation.[43]

Churchill embodied the essence of authority, he spoke words that resonated, at first with a mad rush, but then rippled like concentric circles through the discourse in decades to come. His metaphor not only provided a new reading of the global situation in 1946: it rested on an old framework that had vitiated US foreign policy since its inception and before, during colonial America. The process of *othering* or *orientalising* the US opponent of the era was a regular feature of US diplomatic language and US rhetoric. The frames had worked at the time of US independence, against Native Americans, at the time of the Monroe Doctrine, against Mexicans and Latin Americans, against Nazi Germany, the Soviets and later against Islamism in the 'clash of civilisations' regime.[44]

David Gress argues in his *From Plato to NATO: The Idea of the West and Its Opponents*, such encompassment was undeniably necessary though replete with contradictions. Only at the highest level of grand narrative could the West remain coherent, based on chronicles of liberalism and pluralist democracy. Self-determination as a contributor to US identity could not be advanced successfully in the face of British colonialism and Empire, though of course the Soviet Other facilitated the adherence of the narrative publicly articulated through the new world and new sphere stretching to the Iron Curtain. Gress proposes that 'to enrol such contradictory ideas in a common front required that the distinctions be ignored or elided'.[45] Here was an attempt to contribute to a new West, a new story, a new geopolitical map and mental frame.

'A portent of change'

The Fulton speech inspired immediate dramatic headlines throughout the world. It was almost universally recognised as 'a portent of change', Harbutt contends. Though the purpose here is not to analyse the immediate reactions, suffice to say that they fell along predictable lines of endorsement and approval from the right and centre, criticism from the left and a bitter resentment from communists.[46] The *New York Times* described Churchill as 'the towering leader' of 'our whole civilization'. *Time* magazine, the *Wall Street Journal*, the *New York World Telegram* all hailed the speech in similar vein. The left considered his views reactionary and out of date. Max Lerner in *PM*, the New York paper, labelled it 'a savage ideological attack'. And *New Republic* concluded: 'altogether a bad day's work'. Many resisted the call for the Anglo-American 'alliance' though Churchill's notion of the weaker 'fraternity' was lost in the discourse; it was one thing to share the opposition to the Soviet Union, a step too far, for some, to align indefinitely with the British Empire. Henry Wallace, the former Vice President and Secretary of Commerce, representing the liberal left, declared that 'Churchill undoubtedly is not speaking either for the American people or their government or for the British people or their government'.[47] Stalin reacted furiously in an interview in *Pravda* on 13 March 1946; he denounced Churchill as a 'warmonger and accused him of advocating a racial theory of superiority of English-speaking nations', drawing in comparisons to Hitler, Roberts relates.[48]

Yet in collective memory it is only the essences and dominant images that survive, endure and resonate in public discourse. The problematic and the particularities are jettisoned by a culture seeking clarity, retaining from the past only what is capable of living in the present.[49] All of the issues and the debate on an Anglo-American fraternity settled ultimately in public discourse around the phrase 'the special relationship', and for the cold war on the 'Iron Curtain'. Yet in 1946 the fragmentation of US foreign policy evident in the division and debate ultimately gives way to consensus and a fusion of images. The image of the Iron Curtain was reinforced with narratives and statistics of Soviet expansion. Harbutt concludes,

> These points were driven home by the widespread publication of large-scale maps inevitably emphasizing the awesome geographical and strategic Soviet dominance over the Eurasian landmass and frequently illustrated, in the style of prewar geopolitics, with aggressive arrows or mailed fists radiating from Moscow, iron gates guarding Eastern Europe, and other symbols of aggressive totalitarianism and imperialism.[50]

Despite running the risk of reigniting the jaded and yet unresolved historiographical dispute on this period and US and Soviet initiatives, Melvyn Leffler argues the immediate 'Soviet threat' was negligible. His survey of Soviet and East European archives suggests Soviet policies 'were confused and contradictory, that different bureaucracies in Moscow had different goals, that links between

232 *D. Ryan*

the Kremlin and Communists abroad were intermittent and inconsistent', the communists abroad had some autonomy. Moreover, Washington did not consider the Soviet Union an imminent military threat. They did not have the capacity to be one. The Soviet Union could only compete with the United States if it could harness Western industrial infrastructures, its skilled labour and its resources. According to Leffler, Washington feared that West European communist parties would serve Moscow's interests even if they were not directly under its control. This assumption, coupled with Soviet control of Eastern Europe, constituted a long-term threat to the United States. For Leffler, this perception, 'that a whole political economy of freedom was at stake shaped the US diplomatic offensive in 1947'.[51] For Leffler, Stalin's preconceptions and paranoia facilitated his perception of enemies all around, as he related in his *Pravda* interview and earlier speech in February. He saw the initiative as an attempt to break the four-power Yalta arrangements. He wanted cooperation. Leffler writes: 'Russian, Polish, and Ukrainian documents make it clear that Stalin and his internal security services "were profoundly concerned" with how Churchill's Fulton speech might buoy the morale of rebels and insurgents' in Eastern Europe.[52]

Yet on 12 March 1946, Max Lerner wrote:

> I predict for it a great currency in America ... It more than hints at terrorism. It rolls up into a single image all the fears that the Soviet state has invoked since the Russian Revolution almost thirty years ago.[53]

The Iron Curtain provided an essential geopolitical metaphor – a mental map for the cold war, which grafted an emerging ideological frame to a cultural geography of cold war Europe.

The speech 'had a profound impact at home and abroad', Leffler writes. It 'simplified the threat', provided an ideological frame, and conflated 'Soviet expansionism' with 'Communist subversion'. While reaction to the 'fraternal' arrangement was negative, 'his warning of a totalitarian menace intent on geopolitical domination resonated deeply in their psyches'.[54]

In a short period of time the logic of bipolarity, of Soviet 'indefinite expansion' and the need for Western cohesion accumulated momentum. Stalin reacted by characterising the speech as an effort to 'sow discord'; it was, he asserted, 'a call to war with the Soviet Union'.[55]

For his part, in later years, Kennan would regret his contribution to the mindset. Writing in *The New Yorker* in 1985, he recounted that he had drafted a 'preposterously long telegram ... going right back to the beginning and describing, as though in a primer for school children, the nature, the ambitions, the calculations of these men. It is a grim and uncompromising picture.' He noted that he was on the same 'wavelength' as official Washington, 'But more important and more significant than that, I seem to have aroused a strain of *emotional and self-righteous anti-Sovietism which in later years I will wish I had not aroused.*'[56] A powerful mental map had been created that provided 'an ordered but continually adapting structure of the mind' by which people order and process information,

Curtains, culture and 'collective' memory 233

through various cultural codes, that store ideas which resonate with associated ideologies which can be recalled, or applied to a conceptual 'large scale geographical environment'.[57]

Reagan's admonition: tear down this wall

President Ronald Reagan's speech in front of the Brandenburg Gate on 12 June 1987 has gone down as one of the famous moments of his presidency. It is listed as an iconic moment. It is readily available on YouTube, informing new audiences of the apparent intentions of the administration. Reagan reflects on the speech briefly in his diary; he recalled that he addressed 'tens & tens of thousands of people', 'I got a tremendous reception' and he was interrupted twenty-eight times.[58]

Thus far history has been kind to Reagan and to the speech he delivered in Berlin in 1987. He was famed for his harsh rhetoric against the Soviet Union and communism; his reputation had been established in this area certainly since the 1950s and reinforced in October 1964, when he delivered his 'A Time for Choosing' speech, in support of Barry Goldwater. On coming to office his rhetoric was famed for its bluntness, so much so that as he ran for a second term in 1984, he was advised to tone his rhetoric down, to distance himself somewhat from the character he was in 1981 and 1982.[59] But even as the language of his speeches sent clear signals, the internal documentation from the period demonstrate that his administration sought further accommodation with the Soviets rather than the 'burial' of his public stance.

In front of the British Parliament on 8 June 1982 he famously talked of the 'hope for the long term – the march of freedom and democracy which will leave Marxism–Leninism on the ash-heap of history'. Of course, in front of this audience how could he not harken back to the pivotal image that animated his global outlook? Recounting his itinerary, he would travel from London to Bonn and thence on to Berlin, 'where there stands a grim symbol of power untamed. The Berlin Wall, that dreadful grey gash across the city'. It was then two decades old, and remained a 'fitting signature of the regime that built it'. The regimes, he indicated, 'planted by bayonets do not take root'. Free elections could not be risked behind the Iron Curtain. Reagan explained, 'From Stettin on the Baltic to Varna on the Black Sea, the regimes planted by totalitarianism have had more than thirty years to establish their legitimacy.' His reading of history was incredibly selective, even as he attributed the use of toxin warfare to the Soviet Union in Afghanistan and Southeast Asia, but failed to recall US use of chemicals in Vietnam. He cited Churchill to the effect that the Soviets sought the fruits of war if not war itself, but the West sought the prevention of war, the establishment of freedom and democracy, a mission Reagan rhetorically shared. Reagan deployed the simple image well. He had the ability to capture an essence that would resonate, just as Churchill did in 1946. Extolling the virtues of freedom and its relationship to prosperity, he talked of the Soviet decay. He compared various countries, East and West,

234 *D. Ryan*

and concluded with one of his images that would not only resonate but remain an image that could be recounted:

> one of the simple but overwhelming facts of our time is this: Of all the millions of refugees we've seen in the modern world, their flight is always away from, not towards the Communist world. Today on the NATO line, our military forces face east to prevent a possible invasion. On the other side of the line, the Soviet forces also face east to prevent their people from leaving.[60]

Lou Cannon, his early biographer relates, that 'Reagan's speech, liberally studded with quotations from Winston Churchill, struck a patriotic chord in Britain, then engaged in that leftover struggle of empire known as the Falklands War'.[61]

Yet, despite the later appeal of the performance, at the time it was noted that the speech upset many European allies that had not departed from the benefits of détente that had been built up over the 1970s and had not returned as hastily to the so-called 'second cold war' as did the United States.[62] Diggins observed that 'even Margaret Thatcher, Reagan's closest supporter, "blanched" upon hearing the expression'.[63]

The Berlin Wall had become the embodiment of the Iron Curtain and the city itself was the site of several cold war crises. John F. Kennedy famously expressed his solidarity with the people of the city in June 1963.[64] Yet intrinsically West Berlin was not important for the United States, Frank Costigliola argues, though the symbolic importance was immeasurable. The US had to be seen to preserve the city, especially after the Berlin Blockade of 1948–9 and the crises of the late 1950s and early 1960s; to do otherwise would be to risk condemnation for failing to preserve this vital outpost. Costigliola relates, 'the shock would loosen the Federal Republic of Germany from its mooring in the West', the Germans would feel betrayed by Washington, and 'America's power and credibility in Europe, and in much of the world, depended on keeping the Germans upright and facing West'. Crises in Berlin threatened the West; the uprisings in 1953 in East Germany and in Hungary in 1956 exposed the limits of the pledge associated with the Truman Doctrine. Kennedy's inauguration pledge to pay any price or bear any burden to ensure the survival and success of liberty also added new words that could be tested in this city. In part the eventual wall, initially wire and barricades were put in place to stop the outflow of refugees leaving the East through Berlin. It was a brutal act to contain the latest crisis. The potential propaganda windfall for the West of people choosing to leave in such numbers could not be tolerated; besides, the brain drain would further compound the Eastern economic plight. On 13 August 1961 the barricades were put in place. Ambrose writes, 'It was ... brutal and unprecedented. Never before in human history had a wall been built around a city to keep people *in*. Immeasurable human tragedy resulted.' Kennedy officials were privately relieved. The 'wall' was put up without the feared revolt or limitations on western access to the city. Moreover, Costigliola concludes, Washington had expected a 'Chinese

Curtains, culture and 'collective' memory 235

wall' and when the news reached Kennedy, after a brief conferral with advisors he announced, 'I am going sailing.'[65]

Reagan initially was not supposed to go to Berlin in June 1987, but altered his schedule at the request of the West German government. Reagan was the fourth president to visit the city since the wall had been erected. Here was the occasion not just to address the city, but given the favourable weather conditions and some liberalisation his voice would reach over the wall audibly and would carry through the waves to audiences further east; radio jamming was now more limited. Declaring his solidarity with the city he went on to conflate the wall with the metaphor of the Iron Curtain. In front of the Brandenburg Gate he identified,

> a vast system of barriers that divides the entire continent of Europe. From the Baltic, south, those barriers cut across Germany in a gash of barbed wire, concrete, dog runs, and guard towers. Further south, there may be no visible, no obvious wall. But there remain armed guards and checkpoints all the same – still a restriction on the right to travel, still an instrument to impose upon ordinary men and women the will of a totalitarian state.[66]

Berlin had been inserted into Reagan's agenda. The city was 750 years old, celebrations were underway, Queen Elizabeth and Mikhail Gorbachev were due to visit imminently. Reagan could include Berlin after visiting Rome and Venice for the economic summit. All of the air time that could be garnered from such historic locations distracted from the endless drips and revelations from the Congressional testimony of his administration's principals in front of the Iran-Contra hearings – each capturing a headline or more in the national dailies. Peter Robinson had been assigned to write the speech in April 1987. He had visited the city with the advance team, had talked to the US diplomatic representative in Berlin who was keen to relate what Reagan should not say: 'No chest-thumping. No Soviet-bashing. And no inflammatory statements about the Berlin Wall.' According to that State Department official, people had become used to the wall. Robinson was somewhat incredulous and used the occasion at a dinner with Berliners to enquire whether that was in fact the case: had they gotten used to it? One guest spoke of his sister who lived twenty miles away, whom he had not seen for over two decades: 'Do you think I can get used to that?' Another related uncomfortable stories of passing under watchtowers each day, looking at the guard that spoke the same language. 'We share the same history. But one of us is a zookeeper and the other is an animal, and I am never certain which is which.' Robinson relates how the hostess of the dinner had suddenly angered, 'If this man Gorbachev is serious with his talk of *glasnost* and *perestroika* he can prove it. He can get rid of this wall.' The Director of Presidential Speechwriting, Tony Dolan, and the Director of Communications, Tom Griscom, thought the injunction would work. The phrase was reworked several times. It was opposed by the State Department and the National Security Council; a telegram arrived from Berlin from the ranking US diplomat to object, in Robinson's words, that 'the

236   D. Ryan

draft was naive. It would raise false hopes. It was clumsy. It was needlessly provocative.' Redrafts by at least seven other protagonists omitted the sequence. There was a vague reference to 'One day, this ugly wall will disappear.' Which was in fact in line with the Reagan NSDD 75, which indicated the 'US must demonstrate credibly that its policy is not a blueprint for an open-ended, sterile confrontation with Moscow, but a serious search for a stable and constructive long-term basis for US–Soviet relations'.[67] Colin Powell, the deputy National Security Advisor and after the Iran-Contra related shuffles soon to be Reagan's sixth National Security Adviser, objected, as did the Secretary of State, George P. Shultz: 'I really think that line about tearing down the wall is going to be an affront to Mr Gorbachev.' The Director of Communications, Grimson, had indicated that Reagan was comfortable with it. Grimson reinforced the belief that the instruction would reverberate. Until the day before the speech the campaign against inclusion pressed on, but Reagan decided to include it: 'The boys at State are going to kill me,' he said.[68] In the publication of his speeches shortly after his presidency, Reagan's introduction reiterates the opposition by State and NSC, but observed that just because US–Soviet relations were improving it did not mean that 'we have to begin by denying the truth', which was 'what got us into such a weak position with the Soviet Union in the first place'.[69]

Though the sequence was tremendously popular with the crowd, the West Berlin mayor, Eberhard Diepgen, and the foreign policy community were not happy. Yet Douglas Brinkley later recalled, 'history has been kind to the president's speech'. It was seen as a turning point in the cold war.[70]

In a theme that brilliantly punctuates the speech at well-spaced intervals, Reagan conflated the existence of the wall, freedom, the continent and the Iron Curtain. After quoting President von Weizsacker on the German question remaining open so long as the Brandenburg Gate was closed, Reagan echoed the sentiment, widening out to the ideological level of freedom:

As long as the gate is closed, as long as this scar of a wall is permitted to stand, it is not the German question alone that remains open, but the question of freedom for all mankind. Yet I do not come here to lament. For I find in Berlin a message of hope, even in the shadow of this wall, a message of triumph.

He concluded his speech with an anecdote that surely must have been apocryphal given that the speech had been written earlier. He recounted that a moment ago, as he had looked out from the Reichstag, the symbol of German unity, he had observed words graffitied onto the wall: 'This wall will fall. Beliefs become reality.' Reagan concluded 'Yes, across Europe, this wall will fall. For it cannot withstand faith; it cannot withstand truth. The wall cannot withstand freedom.'[71]

Yet one catch-phrase resounds in history and cultural discourse, the semiotic visual endlessly sequenced into triumphal narratives that move through Reagan's arms build-up, the promise to confine the evil empire to the ash-heap of history, the instruction to Gorbachev at the wall, the ultimate breach of the wall, and then

Curtains, culture and 'collective' memory 237

the Fukuyama article on the 'end of History' all so seamlessly told through an incredible narrative arc. Reagan intoned, that if Gorbachev sought peace, prosperity for the east, liberalisation: 'Come here to this gate! Mr Gorbachev, open this gate! Mr Gorbachev, tear down this wall!'[72]

Cannon, in his biography, relates a story of the power and the internal anger with which Reagan delivered the speech. Further, he buttressed his passage with an anecdote from November 1987 after the Washington summit when Reagan again addressed Gorbachev through a public speech on the wall, indicating that it would be a 'wonderful sight' if the two could meet in Berlin and 'together take down the first bricks of that wall, and could continue taking down walls until the distrust between our peoples and the scars of the past are forgotten'.[73]

But most of this was exaggerated and extravagant theatre.[74] The cold war consensus, to which Churchill was midwife, was culturally and consciously destroyed by the Vietnam War; others argue it had in fact passed earlier, in the early 1960s.[75] It had guided administrations from Truman to Ford, Norman Graebner and others argue. Yet despite his best efforts to rebuild the consensus through his rhetoric, Reagan failed.[76] Despite the dire economic woes of the early 1980s, the administration spent extravagantly on defence. Yet they were unable to turn that military might into diplomatic advantage according to Michael Sherry. The disorganisation of the administration was coupled with the ongoing grip of the Vietnam syndrome and the reluctance to use US power, to any defined effect. 'What counted most,' Sherry writes, '... was the proper posture. Military strength was amassed to bear witness to, rather than to act on, American superiority and moral resolve.' Though the build-up came with tremendous costs, something that the Eisenhower administration was keenly aware of in the 1950s, the rhetorical bluster of Eisenhower and Dulles accompanied by the caution in policy was a strategy for Reagan, Sherry concludes, 'it seemed more a matter of hazy faith, one unaccompanied by Ike's fear of militarization's costs'.[77]

The popular and culturally resonant interpretation that links these developments with the symbolism of the 'evil empire' speech, the 'Berlin Wall' challenge and the end of the cold war has been overplayed. As Alan Dobson argues, Reagan's key strategic document regarding the Soviets 'spoke of establishing better long-term relations' and of inducements or punishment to modify behaviour, but NSDD 75 'does not seem to meet even the criteria for prevailing over, never mind defeating, the Soviets'. Reagan did not seek to end the cold war or destroy the Soviets, he sought 'constructive negotiations'.[78] The military build-up coupled with the 'aggressive rhetoric', according to Robert English, made the opportunities for a reformist leader in the Soviet Union even more difficult when set in the context of hard-line opinion in Moscow. Instead, in Graebner's words:

> Mikhail Gorbachev broke the Cold War's ideological straightjacket that had paralyzed Moscow and Washington's ability to resolve their differences. Though politically weakened, Gorbachev conceded nothing to US military

238   *D. Ryan*

superiority. Never did he negotiate from a position of weakness. In doing so, he faced greater political, even physical, risks. After considering all of this, it is difficult to avoid the conclusion that without Gorbachev, the end of the Cold War could have played out very differently and very dangerously.[79]

In Frances Fitzgerald's words: 'Gorbachev launched a political revolution in the Soviet Union. Few in Washington understood what he was doing or where he was going, and the Cold War was over before the American policy establishment knew it.'[80]

Paradigm lost: the rusting curtain?

President George H.W. Bush did refer to the changes in the Soviet Union during the presidential campaign of 1988, but once in power struggled with a paradigm to replace the clarity of the Iron Curtain.

Weeks before election day in 1988 Bush visited Fulton, Missouri, on 18 October. Seventy years after the Russian Revolution, he argued that Marxism was 'losing its luster'. Francis Fukuyama, formerly working in the State Department Policy Planning Staff, would make political capital with the declaration in the autumn of 1989 with the thesis that History had ended; there was no form of ideological development higher than that of liberal democratic capitalism.[81] But Bush also warned his audience in Fulton that there remained the need to remain vigilant, because 'Russia was a great power before the revolution' There was no time for 'complacency': 'The struggle, the rivalry, is not yet over.'[82]

For Bush, the geographical mistake aside, 'The Iron Curtain still stretches from Stettin to Trieste'. Trieste had been transferred to Italy and Yugoslavia had broken from Stalin's orbit in 1948. Yet to change the geographical coordinates of the southern end of the curtain would have lost its alliterative and familiar resonance for audiences that needed to hear *from* and *to* and *Stettin* and *Trieste*. Bush asserted that the curtain was 'rusting'. 'Shafts of light from the Western side, from our side, the free and prosperous side, are piercing the gloom of failure and despair on the other side.' The people of the east, of the Soviet Union, he recognised, were demanding more freedom, their place 'in the sun'. In his endorsement of the policy of 'peace through strength' Bush directly invoked Churchill 'when he called for a united West to use its strength to reach "a good understanding on all points with Moscow".' He concluded, 'That is what our agenda is all about.'[83]

Yet infamously, Bush struggled with the 'vision thing'. He had moved relatively quickly away from the ideological frames of his predecessor, much to the chagrin of Republican conservatives. Where Reagan had broad vision articulated through a soothing and calm rhetorical style,[84] Bush was a professional, a seasoned foreign policy expert. Tucker and Hendrickson write: 'Experts are not normally expected to indulge grand visions; leaps of the imagination in statecraft are seen as the telltale characteristic of amateurs.' Therefore, lacking the 'vision thing' was more a matter of pride than apology.

Curtains, culture and 'collective' memory 239

The end of the 1980s, however, was not the best of times for the experts. The reign of the expert is in periods when the affairs of states follow their accustomed course, not when events take a new and quite unexpected turn.[85]

For sure, Secretary of State James Baker had talked about signposts lost and the absence of a paradigm. Of course, observations on the end of the cold war had been made in 1963, in 1969, and by Jimmy Carter who talked of an America free of that inordinate fear of communism in 1977. Kissinger talked of the 'decline of the cold war, the loosening of cold-war alliances, and the assertion of national and subnational loyalties in the wake of colonial dissolution'.[86] Yet two decades later the changes seemed momentous, inexplicable beyond widening circles of freedom and the fall of the Berlin Wall, the disintegration of the Iron Curtain. The upheavals of the period related not just to the events in Eastern Europe but the demise of authoritarian regimes elsewhere too, in Latin America especially, of peoples that moved against US-supported authoritarian regimes – a phenomenon that would reach the Middle East, briefly in the Arab Spring of 2011. For Bruce Cumings, the fall of the wall could have been situated in a wider global context, of struggles from 1848 onward, of evolutionary struggles against authoritarian regimes in the East *and the West*; yet in 1989 they were reduced to morality tales; 'there are many ways by which we might come to understand the demise of authoritarian regimes, but in the US the dominant tendency was to turn these events into a celebration of ourselves'.[87]

A year into his presidency he had briefly adopted the concept of the New World Order, outlined in his 1990 State of the Union speech, based on the idea of America and a widening circle of freedom. It was largely received as vacuous. Prior to that, the early National Security Review 3, of March 1989, recognised the importance of *perestroika* as an opportunity for the United States, but it also recognised that Gorbachev's foreign policies could produce a more 'competitive superpower'. His Common European Home might be a double-edged sword potentially dividing the West. Brent Scowcroft's NSD 23, less bland, more pointed, completed in March 1989 though not signed till September, ultimately envisaged the 'integration of the Soviet Union into the international system'. Throughout the tumultuous events of 1989, the Baltic crises in 1990, to the cooperative US–Soviet alliance through the Gulf War, the Bush–Gorbachev relationship grew. Bush not only ignored his domestic economy, in Bill Clinton's estimation he ignored the 'more vigorous proponents of democratization and economic reform' in the USSR. Though the extraordinary relationship had wound down the cold war, the vision was integration of the communist system, not transcendence to its democratic alternative.[88]

Perhaps it should not be so surprising. The two leaders had cultivated a functional relationship that took comfort in the habits of diplomacy since 1985, if not the paradigms lost. The arguments on Soviet integration could be viewed in the framework of 'post-war peacemaking'. Though the cold war was not a conventional war as such, the lessons from 1815, 1918 and 1945 were instructive. Clearly the integration of at least the Western portion of Germany after the Second World War arose out of the failures of 1918. Even though the hostilities

240   *D. Ryan*

between the two would re-emerge as the 1990s progressed, at least for Bush in the early part of the decade, integration made far more sense. The prospects of complete disorder behind the old Iron Curtain with attendant questions of nationalisms and nuclear proliferation out of control were unpalatable.[89]

It is uncertain whether the sculpture outside the Bush Presidential Library, *The Day the Wall Came Down*, depicting a number of wild horses leaping over a section of the Berlin Wall, with the words 'Vision' and lines from Sting, 'free, free, set them free' is pastiche or not. The sculpture, *The Day the Wall Came Down*, by Veryl Goodnight, was first presented to Berlin on the fiftieth anniversary of the Berlin Airlift in July 1998. A second casting was made, first for the Georgia Olympic Games before being moved to the Bush Library in 1997. The image of the stallion and the four mares represents the quest for freedom and 'a victory of the human spirit'.[90] The image of the horses is apt. Soon after the cold war ended *Diplomatic History* published many articles on the events, later gathered into an edited collection. Bruce Cumings observes, 'nothing really changed in American policy. It was as if two horses were racing around a track, one broke its leg, and the other kept on running anyway.'[91] Mark Lawrence similarly quotes Nicholas Thompson's book on Nitze and Kennan, *The Hawk and the Dove*: 'Nitze became something like a coach on the sidelines of a never-ending race, exhorting his athlete to run faster each time he completed a lap, whether ahead or behind.'[92]

Between the Iron Curtain and Nitze's NSC 68 the cold war solidified. Though President George H.W. Bush attributed the fall of the wall to the people, he is increasingly credited with easing the end of the Soviet Union through 'prudence, restraint and empathy'. He told Gorbachev that he did not want to complicate his life, 'That's why I have not jumped up and down on the Berlin Wall.' At the Malta Summit he talked of a new era of 'US–Soviet relations', and aspired to an end to the division of Europe and the military standoff, goals he would reach in partnership with Gorbachev. The prospects of a USSR without Gorbachev were unpredictable, the absence of the USSR, then, inconceivable. In his diary Bush wrote, 'You would've had chaos, and the danger of military action, bloodshed, just to make a few critics feel good – crazy.'[93] In the early 1950s, after Stalin's death, Malenkov had a similar idea in peaceful coexistence: if tensions between the superpowers were relaxed, perhaps the cohesion of the West might loosen. Harper, citing Litvinov and others in Moscow, believed that the Yalta experience and the trust between Stalin and Roosevelt 'could have led to a new era in international affairs, and most important in relations between the Soviet Union and the United States … At least this feeling existed in Moscow'. In 1990, Arthur Schlesinger Jr penned an article in *The Wall Street Journal* proclaiming the vindication of Roosevelt's vision.[94]

Conclusion

Despite the US attempts to shore up Gorbachev in the final stages of his own attempt to salvage communism from the ash-heap of history, the images of the Iron Curtain and their resonance with the standard cold war narrative persist in

Curtains, culture and 'collective' memory 241

contemporary culture. The cast of mind created in the Fulton speech centred on the Iron Curtain, endured beyond the changed geopolitical reality. Though Churchill's was a message strewn among a series of other similar sentiments, its narrative authority, the clarity of the image, the resonance of the metaphor, wove through the cold war years; the Berlin Wall became a manifestation of the Curtain. I have selected but a few examples of the use of the Iron Curtain; the image, constructed of words, of metaphor, eventually of concrete and wire, became a *meta image*, an allegory 'of power and value' that was presented as a neutral reading of the geo-political landscape, the image of Europe and cold war confrontation.[95] Of course Churchill was not alone in the creation of the message, certainly he explored options for diplomacy in the 1950s, but his was the captivating image, and an image that made accommodation along lines of the 'one world' agenda advanced by Franklin Roosevelt, by pragmatists and realists, later by Nixon and Bush Senior, more difficult. That is what Gorbachev identified in the 'Fulton model' and sought to avoid in his vision of the post-cold war era, the 'imperative' in his 'river of time'; that was his intention when he stated in 1988, that his speech at the UN had to be 'Fulton in reverse'. There is poignant irony of situating sections of the Berlin Wall in Simi Valley, California and College Station, Texas – sculptures that will reinforce the traditional narrative that moved from Fulton, Missouri, to the fall of the Berlin Wall in 1989. Yet the wall endures in our cultural *mentalité*, in the stick figure on the whiteboard with a line through its head, and in our cultural and insti-tutional conception of the era, still used.

Notes

* David Ryan, 'Curtains, Culture and "Collective" Memory', *Journal of Transatlantic Studies* 2016, 14:4, pp. 401–15. Published online: 5 October 2016. Copyright © Board of Transatlantic Studies, reprinted by permission of Taylor & Francis Ltd, www. tandfonline.com on behalf of Board of Transatlantic Studies.

1 Roger Chartier, *Cultural History: Between Practices and Representations*, trans. Lydia G. Cochrane, Cambridge: Polity, 1988, p. 34.

2 W.J.T. Mitchell, *Picture Theory: Essays on Verbal and Visual Representation*, Chicago: University of Chicago Press, 1994, pp. 57, 157. See especially the essay, 'Ekphrasis and the Other', pp. 151–81.

3 Lewis A. Coser, introduction to Maurice Halbwachs, *On Collective Memory*, Chicago: University of Chicago Press, 1992, pp. 22–7.

4 Jay Winter, *Remembering War: The Great War Between Memory and History in the Twentieth Century*, New Haven: Yale University Press, 2006, p. 138.

5 Steven Rose, 'Extract from *The Making of Memory*', in James McConkey (ed.), *The Anatomy of Memory: An Anthology*, New York: Oxford University Press, 1996, pp. 55–9; Steven Rose, *The Making of Memory: From Molecules to Mind*, London: Bantam, 1992.

6 Fraser J. Harbutt, *The Iron Curtain: Churchill, America, and the Origins of the Cold War*, New York: Oxford University Press, 1986, p. 204. See also, Philip White, *Churchill's Cold War: How the Iron Curtain Speech Shaped the Post War World*, London: Duckworth Overlook, 2012.

7 Kenneth D. Rose, *Myth and the Greatest Generation: A Social History of Americans in World War II*, New York: Routledge, 2008.

8 John Lewis Gaddis, *We Now Know: Rethinking Cold War History*, Oxford: Clarendon

242 *D. Ryan*

Press, 1997; John Lewis Gaddis, *The Cold War*, London: Allen Lane, 2005; Ellen Schrecker, *Cold War Triumphalism: The Misuse of History after the Fall of Communism*, New York: The New Press, 2004; Allen Hunter (ed.), *Rethinking the Cold War*, Philadelphia: Temple University Press, 1998.

9 Donald Rumsfeld cited in Alessandra Stanley, 'A Nation at War: The TV Watch; Amid the Scenes of Joy, a Sight Less Welcome', the *New York Times*, 10 April 2003; Peter Maass, 'The Toppling: How the Media Inflated a Minor Moment in a Long War', *The New Yorker*, 10 January 2011.

10 Barack Obama, Remarks by President Obama at the Brandenburg Gate – Berlin, Germany, 19 June 2013, The White House, Briefing Room; Kate Connolly, 'Obama Speech in Berlin Looks to "Shared Values" of Iron Curtain Era', *Guardian*, 19 June 2013.

11 BBC Europe, 'Ukraine Crisis: Russia Condemns US "Iron Curtain" Sanctions', BBC, 29 April 2014; www.bbc.com/news/world-europe-27204009.

12 Richard Sakwa, *Frontline Ukraine: Crisis in the Borderlands*, London: I.B. Tauris, 2015, p. 31.

13 www.foreignaffairs.com.

14 Michel Foucault, *The Archaeology of Knowledge*, London: Routledge, 1972.

15 Cynthia Collins, 'Edwina Sandys Returns to Churchill Museum to Honour Fall of Berlin Wall', *Guardian*, 4 November 2014.

16 Anonymous, Berlin Wall History, National Churchill Museum, Dedicated by Congress, n.d.; www.nationalchurchillmuseum.org/berlin-wall-history.html.

17 Michael J. Hogan (ed.), *America in the World: The Historiography of American Foreign Relations since 1941*, Cambridge: Cambridge University Press, 1995; Gordon Martel (ed.), *American Foreign Relations Reconsidered 1890–1993*, London: Routledge, 1994.

18 See Raymond L. Garthoff, *The Great Transition: American–Soviet Relations and the End of the Cold War*, Washington, DC: The Brookings Institution, 1994, pp. 378, 400, 585–7.

19 Mikhail Gorbachev, Address to the United Nations General Assembly, 43rd Session, 7 December 1988.

20 Mikhail Gorbachev, *Zhizn'I Reformy [Life and Reforms]*, Vol. 2, Moscow: Novosti, 1995, pp. 131–2, trans. Geoff Roberts. Email to David Ryan, 22 June, 2015.

21 Mikhail Gorbachev, 'The River of Time and the Imperative', 6 May 1992, National Churchill Museum; www.nationalchurchillmuseum.org/the-river-of-time-and-the-imperative.html.

22 Ibid.

23 Ibid.

24 Ibid.

25 Ibid.; Francis X. Clines, 'At Site of "Iron Curtain" Speech, Gorbachev Buries the Cold War', *New York Times*, 7 May 1992.

26 Ian Clark, *The Post-Cold War Order: The Spoils of Peace*, Oxford: Oxford University Press, 2001, pp. 99–110; Anatol Lieven, 'A New Iron Curtain', *The Atlantic Monthly*, January 1996, pp. 20–5.

27 Michael Kammen, *Mystic Chords of Memory: The Transformation of Tradition in American Culture*, New York: Vintage, 1993, p. 572; David Ryan, 'Mapping Containment: The Cultural Construction of the Cold War', in Douglas Field (ed.), *American Cold War Culture*, Edinburgh: Edinburgh University Press, 2005, pp. 62–3; Emily Rosenberg, 'Rosenberg's Commentary', in Ernest R. May (ed.), *American Cold War Strategy: Interpreting NSC 68*, Boston: Bedford Books, 1993, pp. 161–2; Steven Casey, 'Selling NSC-68: The Truman Administration, Public Opinion, and the Politics of Mobilization, 1950–51', *Diplomatic History*, 29:4, September 2005, pp. 655–90.

28 Fred Halliday in conversation with George Kennan, *From Potsdam to Perestroika:*

Curtains, culture and 'collective' memory 243

Conversations with Cold Warriors, originally BBC Radio 4, *The World Tonight*, 7 April 1995, pp. 9, 13.

29 David Ryan, 'Necessary Constructions: The Other in the Cold War and After', in Michael Patrick Cullinane and David Ryan (eds), *US Foreign Policy and the Other*, New York: Berghahn, 2015, pp. 188–95.

30 Winston Churchill, 'The Sinews of Peace', 5 March 1946, National Churchill Museum; www.nationalchurchillmuseum.org/sinews-of-peace-history.html.

31 Patrick Wright, *Iron Curtain: From Stage to Cold War*, Oxford: Oxford University Press, 2007, p. 43.

32 Wright, *Iron Curtain*, p. 35.

33 Alan Dobson, *Anglo-American Relations in the Twentieth Century: Of Friendship, Conflict and the Rise and Decline of Superpowers*, London: Routledge, 1995, p. 95; John Dumbrell, *A Special Relationship: Anglo-American Relations in the Cold War and After*, London: Macmillan, 2001, p. 7; H.W. Brands, *What America Owes the World: The Struggle for the Soul of Foreign Policy*, Cambridge: Cambridge University Press, 1998, p. 149.

34 Ronald R. Krebs, *Narrative and the Making of US National Security*, Cambridge: Cambridge University Press, 2015, p. 187.

35 Wright, *Iron Curtain*, p. 50.

36 Ibid., p. 55.

37 See essays in Cullinane and Ryan, *US Foreign Policy and the Other*.

38 Fraser J. Harbutt, *The Iron Curtain: Churchill, America, and the Origins of the Cold War*, New York: Oxford University Press, 1988, p. 184.

39 Wright, *Iron Curtain*, p. 38.

40 Harbutt, *The Iron Curtain*, p. 189.

41 Gerd Baumann, 'Grammars of Identity/Alterity: A Structural Approach', in his and Andre Gingrich (eds), *Grammars of Identity/Alterity: A Structural Approach*, New York: Berghahn, 2004, pp. 18–24.

42 W. Roger Louis and Ronald Robinson, 'Empire Preserved: How the Americans Put Anti-Communism before Anti-Imperialism', *Times Literary Supplement* (TLS), 5 May 1995; Warren F. Kimball, *The Juggler: Franklin Roosevelt as Wartime Statesman*, Princeton: Princeton University Press, 1991; David Ryan and Victor Pungong (eds), *The United States and Decolonization: Power and Freedom*, London: Macmillan, 2000.

43 Baumann, 'Grammars of Identity/Alterity,' p. 23.

44 Cullinane and Ryan, *US Foreign Policy and the Other*; David Ryan, *US Foreign Policy in World History*, London: Routledge, 2000.

45 David Gress, *From Plato to NATO: The Idea of the West and Its Opponents*, New York: Free Press, 1998, p. 411; Ryan, 'Mapping Containment', p. 65. On cold war culture see: Stephen J. Whitfield, *The Culture of the Cold War*, Baltimore: Johns Hopkins University Press, 1991; David Campbell, *Writing Security: United States Foreign Policy and the Politics of Identity*, Minneapolis: University of Minnesota Press, 1992; Alan Nadal, *Containment Culture: American Narratives, Postmodernism, and the Atomic Age*, Durham, NC: Duke University Press, 1995; Tom Engelhardt, *The End of Victory Culture: Cold War America and the Disillusioning of a Generation*, Amherst: University of Massachusetts Press, 1995; Roland Végső, *The Naked Communist: Cold War Modernism and the Politics of Popular Culture*, New York: Fordham, 2013.

46 Harbutt, *The Iron Curtain*, p. 197.

47 Ibid., pp. 198–9.

48 Josef Stalin, Interview, *Pravda*, 13 March 1946; Geoffrey Roberts, 'Stalin and Soviet Foreign Policy', in Melvyn P. Leffler and David S. Painter (eds), *Origins of the Cold War: An International History*, New York: Routledge, 2005, p. 52.

49 Halbwachs, *On Collective Memory*.

244   *D. Ryan*

50 Harbutt, *The Iron Curtain*, p. 204.
51 Hogan, 'State of the Art: An Introduction', in his *America in the World*, p. 14; Melvyn P. Leffler, *The Specter of Communism: The United States and the Origins of the Cold War, 1917–1953*, New York: Hill and Wang, 1994, pp. 38, 42, 53, 62; Melvyn P. Leffler, *A Preponderance of Power: National Security, the Truman Administration, and the Cold War*, Stanford: Stanford University Press, 1992, pp. 5–7; Lynn Eden, 'The End of US Cold War History', *International Security*, 18:1, Summer 1993, pp. 174–207; Melvyn P. Leffler, 'National Security', in Michael Hogan and Thomas G. Paterson (eds.), *Explaining the History of American Foreign Relations*, Cambridge: Cambridge University Press, 1991, p. 211.
52 Melvyn P. Leffler, *For the Soul of Mankind: The United States, the Soviet Union, and the Cold War*, New York: Hill and Wang, 2007, pp. 51–4.
53 Lerner cited by Harbutt, *The Iron Curtain*, p. 208.
54 Leffler, *Preponderance*, p. 109.
55 Churchill's Iron Curtain speech, 5 March 1946, with commentary and Stalin's reply, 13 March 1946, reprinted in Walter LaFeber (ed.), *Eastern Europe and the Soviet Union*, Vol. II, Part 1 of Arthur Schlesinger (ed.), *Dynamics of World Power: A Documentary History of United States Foreign Policy 1945–1973*, New York: Chelsea, 1983, pp. 210–21.
56 George F. Kennan, *Memoirs 1925–1950*, Boston: Little, Brown, 1967, pp. 293–4; Ryan, *US Foreign Policy in World History*, pp. 121–2.
57 Gearóid Ó. Tuathail, 'Thinking Critically about Geopolitics', in Gearóid Ó. Tuathail, Simon Dalby and Paul Routledge (eds), *The Geopolitics Reader*, London: Routledge, 1998, pp. 3–4.
58 Ronald Reagan, *The Reagan Diaries*, ed. Douglas Brinkley, New York: Harper Collins, 2007, p. 506.
59 David Ryan, '1984, Regional Crises and Morning in America: The Predawn of the Reagan Era', in Andrew Johnstone and Andrew Priest (eds), *US Foreign Policy and American Presidential Elections: Candidates, Campaigns and Global Politics from FDR to Bill Clinton*, Lexington: University Press of Kentucky, 2017.
60 Ronald Reagan, Address to Members of the British Parliament, 8 June 1982; www.reagan.utexas.edu/archives/speeches/1982/60882a.htm.
61 Lou Cannon, *President Reagan: The Role of a Lifetime*, New York: Simon and Schuster, 1991, p. 315.
62 Fred Halliday, *The Making of the Second Cold War*, London: Verso, 1983.
63 John Patrick Diggins, *Ronald Reagan: Fate, Freedom, and the Making of History*, New York: W.W. Norton, 2007, p. 222.
64 John F. Kennedy, Remarks at the Rudolph Wilde Platz, Berlin, 26 June 1963, John F. Kennedy Presidential Library and Museum, www.jfklibrary.org/Asset-Viewer/oEX2uqSQGEGIdTYgd_JL_Q.aspx.
65 Frank Costigliola, 'The Pursuit of Atlantic Community: Nuclear Arms, Dollars, and Berlin', in Thomas Paterson (ed.), *Kennedy's Quest for Victory: American Foreign Policy 1961–1963*, New York: Oxford University Press, 1989, pp. 38–42; Stephen E. Ambrose, *Rise to Globalism: American Foreign Policy since 1938*, New York: Penguin, 1988, pp. 190–1.
66 Ronald Reagan, 'Remarks on East–West Relations at the Brandenburg Gate in West Berlin', 12 June 1987; www.reaganfoundation.org/.
67 National Security Decision Directive (NSDD 75), 'US Relations with the USSR', 17 January 1983, The Ronald Reagan Presidential Library and Museum; www.reagan.utexas.edu/archives/reference/NSDDs.html#.VssMck1tpaQ.
68 Peter Robinson, '"Tear Down This Wall", How Top Advisers Opposed Reagan's Challenge to Gorbachev – but Lost', *Prologue Magazine*, 39:2, Summer 2007: www.archives.gov/publications/prologue/2007/summer/berlin.html.
69 Ronald Reagan, *Speaking My Mind*, London: Hutchinson, 1989, p. 348.

Curtains, culture and 'collective' memory 245

70 Lucy Madison, 'Remembering Reagan's "Tear Down This Wall" Speech 25 Years Later', CBS News, 12 June 2012.

71 Ronald Reagan, 'Remarks on East–West Relations at the Brandenburg Gate in West Berlin'.

72 Ronald Reagan, 'Remarks on East–West Relations at the Brandenburg Gate in West Berlin'.

73 Reagan cited by Cannon, *President Reagan: The Role of a Lifetime*, p. 774.

74 Some believe that the speech was aimed at the right and the conservatives who criticised Reagan for accommodating Gorbachev and negotiating over the INF and arms reductions; the speech provided cover in the season of superpower summits. Will Bunch, *Tear Down This Myth: How the Reagan Legacy Has Distorted Our Politics and Haunts Our Future*, New York: Free Press, 2009, p. 25.

75 Krebs, *Narrative and the Making of US National Security*, pp. 191–264.

76 Norman A. Graebner, Richard Dean Burns and Joseph M. Siracusa, *Reagan, Bush, Gorbachev: Revisiting the End of the Cold War*, Westport: Praeger Security International, 2008, p. 72.

77 Michael S. Sherry, *In the Shadow of War: The United States since the 1930s*, New Haven: Yale University Press, 1995, p. 395.

78 Alan P. Dobson, 'The Reagan Administration, Economic Warfare, and Starting to Close Down the Cold War', *Diplomatic History*, 29:3, June 2005, pp. 532, 555. See also Beth A. Fischer, *The Reagan Reversal: Foreign Policy and the End of the Cold War*, Columbia: University of Missouri Press, 1997; Steven Kull, *Burying Lenin: The Revolution in Soviet Ideology and Foreign Policy.* Boulder: Westview Press, 1992; Robert V. Daniels, *The End of the Communist Revolution*, London: Routledge, 1993.

79 Graebner *et al.*, *Reagan*, pp. 142–6.

80 Ibid., p. 143.

81 Francis Fukuyama, 'The End of History', *The National Interest*, 16, Summer 1989, pp. 3–18; Francis Fukuyama, *The End of History and the Last Man*, London: Penguin, 1992.

82 David Lauter, 'Quotes Truman, Churchill at Site of "Iron Curtain" Speech: Bush Foresees "Greatest Age in History" ', *Los Angeles Times*, 19 October 1988.

83 Gerald M. Boyd, 'Bush Asserts "Iron Curtain" Remains, but It's "Rusting" ', the *New York Times*, 19 October 1988; Lauter, *LAT*, 19 October 1988; Mitchell Locin, 'Midwest Battlegrounds Draw Candidates: Bush Sees "Rust" in Iron Curtain', *Chicago Tribune*, 19 October 1988; 'Milestones: 1989–1992', Office of the Historian, US Department of State; https://history.state.gov/milestones/1989–1992.

84 William K. Muir, Jr, 'Ronald Reagan: The Primacy of Rhetoric', in Fred I. Greenstein (ed.), *Leadership in the Modern Presidency*, Cambridge, MA: Harvard University Press, 1988, pp. 260–95.

85 Robert W. Tucker and David C. Hendrickson, *The Imperial Temptation: The New World Order and America's Purpose*, New York: Council on Foreign Relations Press, 1992, p. 22; Chester Hartman and Pedro Vilanova (eds), *Paradigms Lost: The Post Cold War Era*, London: Pluto, 1992.

86 Henry Kissinger, Memorandum from the President's Assistant for National Security Affairs to President Nixon, 'Analysis of the Changes in International Politics since World War II and their Implications for our Basic Assumptions about US Foreign Policy', 20 October 1969, document 41, *Foundations of Foreign Policy, 1969–1972, FRUS* Vol. 1, Washington, DC: Government Printing Office, 2003, p. 131.

87 Bruce Cumings, 'Time of Illusion: Post-Cold War Visions of the World', in Ellen Schrecker (ed.), *Cold War Triumphalism: The Misuse of History after the Fall of Communism*, New York: The New Press, 2004, pp. 72–5.

88 Garthoff, *The Great*, pp. 376–7; Michael R. Beschloss and Strobe Talbott, *At the Highest Levels: The Inside Story of the End of the Cold War*, London: Warner, 1993, pp. 468–71.

246 *D. Ryan*

89 Clark, *The Post-Cold War Order*, pp. 94, 242–4. See also George Bush and Brent Scowcroft, *A World Transformed*, New York: Alfred A. Knopf, 1998, pp. 132–51.

90 Veryl Goodnight, '*The Day the Wall Came Down*: On Sculpting the American West', www.verylgoodnight.com/wall.htm; Ruth Heavy, '"The Day the Wall Came Down", Berlin: A Divided City', 7 March 2013; http://berlindividedcity.wordpress.com/2013/03/07/the-day-the-wall-came-down/.

91 Bruce Cumings, 'The Wicked Witch of the West is Dead. Long Live the Wicked Witch of the East', in Michael J. Hogan (ed.), *The End of the Cold War: Its Meaning and Implications*, Cambridge: Cambridge University Press, 1992, p. 89.

92 Mark Atwood Lawrence, 'Friends, Not Allies', review of Nicholas Thompson, *The Hawk and the Dove: Paul Nitze, George Kennan, and the History of the Cold War*, in the *New York Times*, 8 September 2009; Brian Urquhart, 'A Contest in the Cold', *New York Review of Books*, 56:20, 17 December 2009, pp. 50–7.

93 Ken Walsh, 'Bring Down Walls, 25 Years Later', *Ken Walsh's Washington*, 14 November 2014; Joseph Lelyveld, 'Prophet and Outcast Bush', *The New York Review of Books*, 63:3, 15 February 2016, n.p.

94 John Lamberton Harper, *American Visions of Europe: Franklin D. Roosevelt, George F. Kennan, and Dean Acheson*, Cambridge: Cambridge University Press, 1994, p. 123; Arthur M. Schlesinger, Jr, 'FDR's Vision is Vindicated by History', *The Wall Street Journal*, 22–23 June 1990. See also Lloyd C. Gardner, *Architects of Illusion: Men and Ideas in American Foreign Policy, 1941–1949*, Chicago: Quadrangle Books, 1970.

95 Mitchell, *Picture Theory*, p. 157.

Conclusion

Alan P. Dobson and Steve Marsh

Inspired by the seventieth anniversary in 2016 of his Sinews of Peace speech, this book set out to examine afresh Churchill's role in the creation and maintenance of what he called the Anglo-American special relationship. The approach has been twofold. First, to position Churchill's speech on the continuum of what was already a special relationship. Though it was at Fulton that he announced to the world the existence of this allegedly unique association between Britain and America, many of its ingredients drew on a prior history. Second, to offer new insights into Churchill and his role within the special relationship by eschewing the well-trodden historiographical paths of functional cooperation in favour of disciplines and subject matter that to date have been overlooked or been silent within this debate.

We as editors, at least, consider that our contributors have delivered a book true to its objectives and worthy of the issues at hand. It now falls to us to offer some more general conclusions. Kimball tells us that Fulton cannot be understood without a firm grounding in World War II alliance politics and Churchill's attitude towards the Soviet Union. So let us start there. Churchill once said of Russia: 'It is a riddle wrapped in a mystery inside an enigma.'[1] Much the same could be said of him. Who exactly was he? Extensive archive work has helped uncover what he did, what he said, where he went and who he met. And yet, as several of our contributors observe, Churchill and his role in history have not necessarily become clearer with proliferating representations and often conflicting interpretations based on selective narratives of his life and works. In an attempt to unravel some of the resulting confusion, Marchi, Lorenzo-Dus and Marsh identify a symbiotic process between Churchill and Anglo-American media as the US press especially made Churchill arguably their first object within the personalisation of politics.

Churchill encouraged and manipulated these processes to present selected images of himself, Britain and Anglo-American relations to the world. Edwards and Hendershot draw forth how in life and death Churchill became central within acts of memorialisation and commemoration that contributed to the cultural embedding of the special relationship. Ryan goes further, suggesting that in his rhetoric, metaphors and use of alterity Churchill carved for the special relationship – and wider international relations – a type of path dependency that closed off certain options and alternative courses. Perhaps this helps explain failed flirtations with alternative nomenclatures for the special relationship – such as Edward Heath's 'natural relationship' and the Cameron–Obama 'essential relationship'. These perspectives add to our understanding, but do not, of course, exhaust the possibilities for interpreting Churchill. He did indeed help to lay down a strong sense of alterity in post-war international relations, but then defying his own imagery he desperately tried to bridge the gap by opening dialogue through summitry with the Soviets after Stalin's death. Ironically, those attempts were thwarted by the Americans, who were perhaps more captured by the sense of alterity, which he had done so much to foster, than he was.

Several of our contributors also caution against taking the humanity out of Churchill by remembering him for what Marsh terms his 'brand' – a complex pastiche of selected images, wartime prestige, oratory and public demeanour. This was part of Churchill's diplomatic armoury. And it was carefully sculpted, with inconvenient, controversial and embarrassing events in Churchill's life and career being excised from the popular narrative of war hero and sage elder statesman. Marsh reminds us that this is not Churchill the man, for he actually had a very chequered career. Kimball, too, cautions against looking to Churchill for consistency, whether that be political or strategic. As a politician he clearly did not feel bound by party loyalty, twice crossing the floor of Parliament. Neither did he allow political ambition to curtail controversial deeds and words. He spent much of the 1930s cast consequently into the British political wilderness. And in international relations Kimball demonstrates in Churchill's contortions in dealing with the Soviet Union that his pragmatism would often trump principle. Above all for Kimball, Churchill's diplomacy was the art of the possible: he was supremely practical. Such views sit comfortably with the line taken by Dobson who demonstrates that Churchill's agenda at Fulton was only feasible because of the existence of longstanding commonalities in British and American political culture. Without them he would not have been able to invoke the idea of a special relationship credibly on both sides of the Atlantic: with them it was a practical strategy.

Vucetic goes further into Churchill's psyche, taking us into one of the most controversial aspects of Churchill's thinking on the English-speaking peoples and world affairs, namely racism and biological hierarchies. Vucetic's point is not to castigate Churchill by applying a contemporary moral compass to a complex Edwardian man. Rather, Vucetic shows how Churchill was influenced by the Anglo-Saxonism of the Great Rapprochement and evolved these ideas throughout his career. Churchill was undoubtedly proud of the British Empire and its colonial legacy, but he was also sensitive to changing expectations in global politics and to reaction against German National-Socialism. Whatever his personal views on race, and however they had evolved in the interwar period, he was careful in his Fulton speech to avoid giving his English-speaking peoples racial overtones. Indeed, Edwards argues that Churchill deliberately pared back much of the overt racialised language previously used in Anglo-American

Conclusion 249

discourse in order to reveal the older, cultural, foundations of Anglo-Saxonism. This de-racialisation can now be traced forwards in time to the more recent concept of an Anglo-sphere.

To discover more about what drove Churchill and informed his diplomatic practice and his attitudes we could do worse than return to his 1939 'Russian Enigma' broadcast. Seeking to predict what this enigma might do, Churchill identified one constant, namely Russian national interest. Churchill, too, had one constant. While he undoubtedly had personal ambitions, doing what he considered right for Britain was the most consistent aspect of his life and key to understanding him. To his mind, the Anglo-American special relationship was a vital part of Britain's wartime survival and post-war future.

The chapters in the second part of this book make clear that once Churchill had made his Fulton speech the special relationship was far from a 'done deal'. It took American perception of a Soviet threat both to ease the Anglo-American loan through Congress and to slowly reverse US disengagement from Europe. Of course, Churchill's own Iron Curtain metaphor was a powerful and – as Ryan elaborates – enduring contribution to this process and, indeed, to post-Cold War divisions and conflicts that re-cast Britain and America shoulder to shoulder. Nevertheless in 1951, after five frustrating years out of government, it was obvious to Churchill that the concept and practice of a special relationship needed nurture and encouragement if it were to flourish and bear fruit for British interests.

Our contributors have considered in detail some of the things Churchill did to help ensure that. McCulloch, for instance, reveals how important were British ambassadors to Washington, both in exercising influence from within American circles and in developing the intimate style of cooperation and access that was so essential to the operation and distinctive character of the special relationship. While Churchill sometimes feared their going native, and at others by-passed them in communicating with the US president and his top advisors, he nevertheless regarded Washington as the most important of all British ambassadorial appointments – a respect he held reciprocally for the US Embassy in London, which alone had direct access to Number Ten. Marsh, too, picks up on Churchill's distinctive development of diplomatic relations with the US, showing how Churchill developed and used a particular style of summitry that enabled him to send messages to multiple audiences and maximised possibilities for his personal diplomacy to influence US officials, policy and, most of all, the president.

Yet to appreciate truly Churchill's role in fashioning the Anglo-American special relationship, we should step back a little from the admirable detail and argument afforded by our contributors. What is needed is a way to place Churchill within the continuum of the development of the special relationship, from the Great Rapprochement through to the present. Here it might help to conceive of his role in two forms: animator and referent.

The starting point must be that, as Haglund, Dobson, Vucetic and Hendershot show convincingly, the roots of the special relationship can be traced back long before World War II, and one of our contributors, Warren Kimball, would trace

250   *A.P. Dobson and S. Marsh*

things right back to colonial times, if not for the actual experience of a special relationship, for the necessary ingredients of its later making. Haglund's exploration of how US strategic culture changed over time from othering Britain through to embracing Anglo-Saxonism in the Great Rapprochement and beyond reveals an important underlying element of identity shift in transatlantic relations. Vucetic echoes the existence and importance of this developing Anglo-American affiliation in his exploration of racism. And Dobson and Hendershot unravel the co-development of, and interplay between, Anglo-American culture, values and norms. Political, economic and cultural mores might have moved in different cycles but the path was generally towards convergence and recognition of commonality rather than difference.

Still, though, the interwar years offered little overt to suggest these convergent currents would culminate in a unique Anglo-American partnership. Rather, the Atlantic Ocean seemingly widened as America turned inwards to isolationism and protectionism and Britain retreated behind the wall of imperial preference and Empire. Neither did this situation change upon the outbreak of World War II. American isolationism remained strong, being reflected in the passage through Congress in the 1930s of the Neutrality Acts. The US remained militarily aloof, serving as the 'arsenal of democracy' through programmes such as Lend–Lease from March 1941 but not joining the fighting until after the Pearl Harbor attacks in December 1941.

It is at this point that much of the intimate functional wartime Anglo-American cooperation began, with the first of the Combined Boards being set up in January 1942. It is thus particularly interestingly that many scholars date the modern relationship – as Haglund does[2] – not to this but to the Destroyers for Bases deal in September 1940. At first sight one is tempted to ask why. It appears a poor return: fifty defunct US destroyers in return for an American right to build naval and/or air bases, with ninety-nine-year rent-free leases, on six British possessions in the Caribbean, plus Bermuda and Newfoundland.[3] In fact, Foreign Secretary Anthony Eden called the agreement 'a grievous blow to our authority and ultimately to our sovereignty'.[4]

Dobson notes that in 1946 Churchill defended the deal thus: 'No, we didn't trade the islands for fifty old destroyers. We did it for strategic use by the United States and for your safety and ours.' This is a valid functionalist retrospective on the exchange that locked the fate of the UK and US together. But it is not the critical point. Rather, the Destroyers for Bases deal was symbolic of Roosevelt's intent to assist Britain to the very utmost of his presidential authority and marked a morale-boosting moment at which American neutrality became more theoretical than practical. As such the deal marked a hinge-point between the unformed pre-World War II convergent currents of Anglo-American relations and the modern special relationship that was forged in war and tested repeatedly thereafter. Rightly or wrongly, it is a point of perceived dramatic change from which a mythology of the modern special relationship could be built. And if nothing else, Churchill was a consummate storyteller with an acute appreciation of the power of symbols and imagery.

Conclusion 251

Perhaps, therefore, Churchill's single greatest contribution to the modern special relationship was to conjure it into existence from existing raw materials and ongoing developments. It takes enormous skill, knowledge, understanding and courage to take much of what is already known, or felt, by people and to rearrange it into an intelligible discourse of events, sentiment and interests that appears so natural that at once it establishes a new but familiar narrative. This is what Churchill did at Fulton, Missouri – twice over. His most immediate success lay in his Iron Curtain metaphor, shifting the narrative of international relations from victory and peace to newfound threat and potential descent into conflict. The special relationship was more slow-burning, and in many ways more difficult to achieve; Marchi, Lorenzo-Dus and Marsh demonstrate that by the early 1950s this nomenclature at least was yet to gain traction in either popular imagination or diplomatic discourse. This relationship needed to be conjured using the raw material of pre-World War II Anglo-American convergence, a judicious pruning of history and the exemplar of intimate wartime cooperation and mutual dependence. And as a number of our contributors argue, it was only Churchill who had the stature, prestige and power of persuasion – public and private – who could perform this task.

Once Churchill had breathed the first sparks of life into the modern special relationship, he was its prime animator through to his death in 1965. Churchill consciously shaped the historical narrative of Anglo-American relations. For instance, as Edwards points out, Churchill's crafting of his *History of the English-Speaking Peoples* provided an invaluable forum in which to call for, perform and imagine Anglo-American unity. Churchill also knew the value of a pulpit from which to spread the word of 'fraternal association'. It was he who established the style, regularity and practice of high-profile intimate summits between prime ministers and presidents. And thereafter their performance and pageantry constantly refreshed the cultural wellspring of the special relationship.

Churchill took every opportunity possible to promote his idea of an Anglo-American special relationship, naturally combining interest and sentiment into a genuine partnership that reflected what Dean Acheson once emphasised as their common fate. In this task Churchill was aided by a combination of his prestige, popularity and media fascination with his actions and persona. Marchi, Lorenzo-Dus and Marsh argue that media discourse established three 'roles' for Churchill, namely Churchill as friend, Churchill as negotiator, and Churchill as the embodiment of the British bulldog spirit. More generally, the personalisation of politics in the US media especially blurred the distinction between Churchill as animator and Churchill as referent of Britain and the special relationship. This was important. First it provided an easy vehicle for popular imagination to connect with the special relationship. Second, it even helped Churchill promote the special relationship long after his death.

Churchill conjured the special relationship at Fulton by interweaving a narrative of a common Anglo-American past with a shared mission present. As he faded from the political scene, and ultimately died in 1965, so he transmogrified from author to referent of the special relationship – although it is difficult to establish precisely at what point Churchill became a central character in, as well as narrator of, the special relationship 'production'. He was certainly a part of its iconography well before his state funeral. Consider, for instance, his award of honorary American citizenship in 1963. What is more certain is that Churchill spans the continuum of the special relationship. In life he blended an idealised Anglo-American past to functional imperatives of war and Cold War to create a special relationship. In death he has served as a vital connector between the special relationship of the early Cold War years to the one that exists today.

British power is now to America more of a useful adjunct than an indispensable asset, but Churchill's personal stock – and the historical symbolism of the special relationship that this brings with it – remain in the US as high as ever. President Clinton announced in 1995 that the US would name an *Arleigh Burke*-class guided missile destroyer after him. George W. Bush invoked Churchill's name in developing his war on terror, and his bust, presented by Prime Minister Blair, resided alongside the Republican president in the Oval Office. As for Obama, well, he learnt in removing that bust just how badly it still plays out in the UK and at home to be perceived to insult Churchill. Indeed, John Boehner, leader of the House Republicans, summed up matters nicely in 2013. In a speech of dedication of another bronze bust of Winston Churchill – this one in the Capitol building's rotunda – he declared simply that Britain's 'bulldog' was 'the best friend the United States ever had'.[5]

Notes

1 Churchill, 'The Russian Enigma', 1 October 1939; www.churchill-society-london.org. uk/RusnEnig.html.
2 David Haglund, 'Is there a "Strategic Culture" of the Special Relationship? Contingency, Identity, and the Transformation of Anglo-American Relations', in Alan Dobson and Steve Marsh (eds), *Contemporary Anglo-American Relations: A 'Special Relationship'?*, London: Routledge, 2013, pp. 26–51.
3 Technically bases in Newfoundland and Bermuda were given freely to the US rather than as part of the Destroyers for Bases deal.
4 Cited in Galen R. Perras, *Franklin Roosevelt and the Origins of the Canadian–American Security Alliance, 1933–1945*, Westport, CN: Praeger 1998, p. 75.
5 Cited by Tim Stanley, 'Winston Churchill, an All-American Hero', *Telegraph*, 31 October 2013; www.telegraph.co.uk/news/worldnews/northamerica/usa/10417854/ Winston-Churchill-an-all-American-hero.html.

Primary sources

Archives

United Kingdom National Archives
United States National Archives
Dwight D. Eisenhower Presidential Library
Lyndon B. Johnson Presidential Library
John F. Kennedy Presidential Library

Newspapers

New York Times
The Times
Washington Post

Published collections of primary material

Foreign Relations of the United States 1951, Vol. 4.
Foreign Relations of the United States 1952–4, Vol. 6, Part 1.
Foreign Relations of the United States, 1955–7, Vol. 16, Suez Crisis, 26 July–31 December 1956.
Foundations of Foreign Policy, 1969–1972, FRUS Vol. 1, Washington, DC: Government Printing Office, 2003.
'Potomac Charter', Department of State *Bulletin*, 12 July 1954.

Books

Acheson, D., *Present at the Creation. My Years in the State Department*, London: Hamilton, 1970.
Adams, I., *Brothers Across the Ocean: British Foreign Policy and the Origins of the Anglo-American 'Special Relationship' 1900–1905*, London: Tauris Academic Studies, 2005.
Addison, P., *Churchill: The Unexpected Hero*, Oxford: Oxford University Press, 2005.
Alkon, P.K., *Winston Churchill's Imagination*, Lewisburg, PA: Bucknell University Press, 2006.
Allen, H.C., *Great Britain and the United States: A History of Anglo-American Relations, 1783–1952*, London: Oldhams, 1954.

254 *Primary sources*

Ambrose, S.E., *Rise to Globalism: American Foreign Policy since 1938*, New York: Penguin, 1988.

American Memorial Chapel in St Paul's Cathedral, London: Pitkin Pictorials, 1958.

Anderson, B., *Imagined Communities*, London: Verso, 2002.

Anderson, S., *Race and Rapprochement: Anglo-Saxonism and Anglo-American Relations, 1895–1904*, Rutherford, NJ: Fairleigh Dickinson University Press, 1981.

Arnn, L.P., *Churchill's Trial: Winston Churchill and the Survival of Free Government*, Nashville, TN: Thomas Nelson, 2016.

Ashton, N., *Eisenhower, Macmillan and the Problem of Nasser: Anglo-American Relations and Arab Nationalism, 1955–59*, Basingstoke: Palgrave Macmillan, 1996.

Austin, J.L., *How to Do Things with Words: The William James Lectures delivered at Harvard University in 1955*, ed. J.O. Urmson and M. Sbisà, second edition, Oxford: Clarendon Press, 1975 (first edition 1962).

Bartlett, C.J., *The 'Special Relationship': A Political History of Anglo-American Relations since 1945*, London: Longman, 1992.

Baruch, B., *The Public Years*, London: Odhams Press, 1961.

Bayley, P. and G. Williams (eds), *European Identity: What the Media Say*, Oxford: Oxford University Press, 2012.

Baylis, J., *Anglo-American Defence Relations, 1939–1984*, second edition, Basingstoke, Hants: Palgrave Macmillan, 1984.

Baylis, J., *Anglo-American Relations since 1939: The Enduring Alliance*, Manchester and New York: Manchester University Press, 1997.

Belich, J., *Replenishing the Earth: The Settler Revolution and the Rise of the Angloworld*, Oxford: Oxford University Press, 2009.

Bell, C., *The Debatable Alliance: An Essay in Anglo-American Relations*, Oxford: Oxford University Press, 1964.

Bell, D., *The Idea of Greater Britain: Empire and the Future of World Order, 1860–1900*, Princeton: Princeton University Press, 2007.

Bennett, G., *Six Moments of Crisis: Inside British Foreign Policy*, Oxford: Oxford University Press, 2013.

Bertram, M., *The Birth of Anglo-American Friendship: The Prime Facet of the Venezuelan Boundary Dispute – A Study of the Interrelation of Diplomacy and Public Opinion*, Lanham, MD: University Press of America, 1992.

Beschloss, M.R. and Strobe Talbott, *At the Highest Levels: The Inside Story of the End of the Cold War*, London: Warner, 1993.

Best, G., *Churchill: A Study in Greatness*, London: Penguin, 2002.

Billington, D., *Lothian: Philip Kerr and the Quest for World Order*, Santa Barbara, CA: Praeger, 2006.

Blake, R. and William Roger Louis (eds), *Churchill*, New York: W.W. Norton, 1993.

Bourne, K., *Britain and the Balance of Power in North America, 1815–1908*, Berkeley: University of California Press, 1967.

Boyle, P.G. (ed.), *The Churchill–Eisenhower Correspondence, 1953–1955*, North Carolina: University of North Carolina Press, 1990.

Brands, H.W., *What America Owes the World: The Struggle for the Soul of Foreign Policy*, Cambridge: Cambridge University Press, 1998.

Brendon, P., *Winston Churchill*, New York: Harper & Row, 1984.

Bryce, J., *Speeches and Letters of Abraham Lincoln, 1832–1865*, London: J.M. Dent, 1907.

Bunch, W., *Tear Down This Myth: How the Reagan Legacy Has Distorted Our Politics and Haunts Our Future*, New York: Free Press, 2009.

Primary sources 255

Burk, K., *Britain, America, and the Sinews of War, 1914–1918*, London: Allen & Unwin, 1984.

Burk, K., *Old World, New World: Great Britain and America from the Beginning*, New York: Grove Press, 2009.

Burley, J. (ed.), *Dworkin and His Critics: With Replies by Dworkin*, Oxford: Blackwell, 2004.

Bush, G.H., and Brent Scowcroft, *A World Transformed*, New York: Alfred A. Knopf, 1998.

Bushaway, B., 'Name Upon Name: The Great War and Remembrance', in R. Porter, (ed.), *Myths of the English*, Cambridge: Polity Press, 1992.

Buzan, B., O. Wæver and J. de Wilde, *Security: A New Framework for Analysis*, Boulder, CO: Lynne Rienner, 1998.

Campbell, C.S., Jr, *From Revolution to Rapprochement: The United States and Great Britain, 1783–1900*, New York: John Wiley & Sons, 1974.

Campbell, D., *Writing Security: United States Foreign Policy and the Politics of Identity*, Minneapolis: University of Minnesota Press, 1992.

Campbell, D.A., *Unlikely Allies: Britain, America, and the Victorian Origins of the Special Relationship*, London: Hambledon Continuum, 2007.

Cannon, L., *President Reagan: The Role of a Lifetime*, New York: Simon and Schuster, 1991.

Carlton, D., *Anthony Eden. A Biography*, London: Allen Lane, 1981.

Chapman, J., *Licence to Thrill: A Cultural History of the James Bond Films*. New York: I.B. Tauris, 2013.

Charmley, J., *Churchill's Grand Alliance: The Anglo-American Special Relationship, 1940–57*, New York: Harcourt, 1995.

Chartier, R., *Cultural History: Between Practices and Representations*, trans. Lydia G. Cochrane, Cambridge: Polity, 1988.

Churchill, R.S. (ed.), *The Sinews of Peace: Post-War Speeches by Winston S. Churchill*, London: Cassell, 1948.

Churchill, W.S., *Europe Unite: Speeches 1947 and 1948*, London: Cassell, 1950.

Churchill, W.S., *The Second World War, Volume III: The Grand Alliance*, London: Cassell, 1950.

Churchill, W.S., *A History of the English-Speaking Peoples, Volume I: The Birth of Britain*, London: Cassell, 1956, *Volume II: The New World*, London: Cassell, 1956.

Churchill, W.S., *A History of the English-Speaking Peoples, Volume III: The Age of Revolution*, London: Cassell, 1957.

Churchill, W.S., *A History of the English-Speaking Peoples, Volume IV: The Great Democracies*, London: Cassell, 1958.

Churchill, W.S. (ed.), *Never Give In: Winston Churchill's Speeches*, London: Bloomsbury Academic, 2013.

Clark, I., *The Post-Cold War Order: The Spoils of Peace*, Oxford: Oxford University Press, 2001.

Clark, W., *Less than Kin: A Study of Anglo-American Relations*, Boston: Houghton Mifflin, 1958.

Clarke, P., *Mr Churchill's Profession: Statesman, Orator, Writer*, London: Bloomsbury, 2012.

Colman, J., *A 'Special Relationship'? Harold Wilson, Lyndon B. Johnson and Anglo-American Relations 'At the Summit', 1964–68*, Manchester: Manchester University Press, 2004.

256 Primary sources

Colville, J., *Footprints in Time*, London: Collins, 1976.

Cooper, J.F., *Notions of the Americans: Picked Up By a Travelling Bachelor*, 2 vols, London: Henry Colburn, 1828.

Cornish, L.C., *A Pilgrimage to Old Hingham, Norfolk, England*, Hingham, MA: The Association for the Extension of Influence of Hingham Plantation, 1915.

Costigliola, F., *Roosevelt's Lost Alliances: How Personal Politics Helped Start the Cold War*, Princeton: Princeton University Press, 2013.

Cronin, J.E., *Global Rules: America, Britain and a Disordered World*, New Haven: Yale University Press, 2014.

Dallek, R., *Franklin D. Roosevelt and American Foreign Policy, 1932–1945*, New York: Oxford University Press, 1995.

Dalton, H., *High Tide and After: Memoirs 1945–1960*, London: Frederick Muller, 1962.

Danchev, A., *Oliver Franks: Founding Father*, Oxford: Clarendon Press, 1993.

Danchev, A., *On Specialness: Essays in Anglo-American Relations*, Basingstoke: Macmillan, 1998.

Daniels, R.V., *The End of the Communist Revolution*, London: Routledge, 1993.

Darwin, J., *The Empire Project: The Rise and Fall of the British World-System, 1830–1970*, Cambridge: Cambridge University Press, 2009.

Dewey, J., *Problems of Men*, New York: The Philosophical Library, 1946.

Dickens, C., *American Notes, May 1868*, Altenmünster: Jazzybee Verlag, 2014.

Diggins, J.P., *Ronald Reagan: Fate, Freedom, and the Making of History*, New York: W.W. Norton, 2007.

Dilke, C., *Greater Britain: A Record of Travel in English-Speaking Countries*, London: Macmillan, 1868.

Dobson, A.P., *Anglo-American Relations in the Twentieth Century: Of Friendship, Conflict and the Rise and Decline of Superpowers*, London: Routledge, 1995.

Dobson, A.P. and Marsh, S. (eds), *Anglo-American Relations: Contemporary Perspectives*, London: Routledge, 2013.

Doran, R. (ed.), *Philosophy of History After Hayden White*, London: Bloomsbury, 2013.

Dos Passos, J.R., *The Anglo-Saxon Century and the Unification of the English-Speaking Peoples*, second edition, New York: G.P. Putnam's Sons, 1903.

Du Bois, W.E.B., *Color and Democracy: Colonies and Peace*, New York: Harcourt, Brace, 1945.

Duberman, M., *Paul Robeson*. New York: Ballantine Books, 1989.

Dumbrell, J., *A Special Relationship: Anglo-American Relations in the Cold War and After*, London: Macmillan, 2001.

Dumbrell, J., *A Special Relationship: Anglo-American Relations from the Cold War to Iraq*, Basingstoke: Palgrave Macmillan, 2006.

Dumbrell, J. and A. Schäfer (eds), *America's 'Special Relationships': Foreign and Domestic Aspects of the Politics of Alliance*, London: Routledge, 2009.

Dunne, F., *Mr Dooley in Peace and War*, Boston: Small, Maynard, 1898.

Dworkin, R., *Taking Rights Seriously*, London: Duckworth, 1996.

Edwards, S., *Allies in Memory: World War II and the Politics of Transatlantic Commemoration*, Cambridge: Cambridge University Press, 2015.

Engelhardt, T., *The End of Victory Culture: Cold War America and the Disillusioning of a Generation*, Amherst: University of Massachusetts Press, 1995.

Farmelo, G., *Churchill's Bomb*, New York, Basic Books, 2013.

Ferrell, R.H., *Eisenhower Diaries*, New York: W.W. Norton, 1981.

Primary sources 257

Fischer, B.A., *The Reagan Reversal: Foreign Policy and the End of the Cold War*, Columbia: University of Missouri Press, 1997.

Fitzhugh, G., *Sociology for the South: Or The Failure of a Free Society*, Richmond: A. Morris, 1854.

Fitzhugh, G., *Cannibals All: Or Slaves Without Masters*, Boston: Harvard University Press, 1966.

Foucault, M., *The Archaeology of Knowledge*, London: Routledge, 1972.

Fukuyama, F., *The End of History and the Last Man*, London: Penguin, 1992.

Fyfe, H., *The Illusion of National Character*, London: Watts, 1940.

Gaddis, J.L., *Strategies of Containment: A Critical Appraisal of Post-war American National Security Policy*, Oxford: Oxford University Press, 1982.

Gaddis, J.L., *We Now Know: Rethinking Cold War History* Oxford: Clarendon Press, 1998.

Gaddis, J.L., *The Cold War*, London: Allen Lane, 2005.

Gardner, L.C., *Architects of Illusion: Men and Ideas in American Foreign Policy, 1941–1949*, Chicago: Quadrangle Books, 1970.

Garrison, William L., *Selections from the Writings and Speeches of William L. Garrison*, Boston: R.F. Walcutt, 1852.

Garthoff, R.L., *The Great Transition: American–Soviet Relations and the End of the Cold War*, Washington, DC: The Brookings Institution, 1994.

George, L., *Abraham Lincoln: An Address Before the Midday Luncheon Club, Leland Hotel, Springfield Illinois, Thursday, October 18, 1923*, Cleveland: Stephen Wallis Tener, 1924.

Gilbert, M., *Road to Victory*, Boston: Houghton Mifflin, 1986.

Gilbert, M., *Churchill: A Life*, London and New York: BCA, 1991.

Gilbert, M., *Churchill and America*, London: Free Press, 2005.

Gilbert, M. (ed.), *Churchill: The Power of Words*, London: Bantam, 2012.

Gillies, D., *Radical Diplomat: The Life of Archibald Clark Kerr, Lord Inverchapel, 1882–1951*, London: I.B. Taurus, 1999.

Gilpin, R.G., *War and Change in World Politics*, Cambridge: Cambridge University Press, 1981.

Goebel, S., *The Great War and Medieval Memory: War, Remembrance and Commemoration in Britain and Germany, 1914–1940*, Cambridge: Cambridge University Press, 2007.

Gorbachev, M., *Zhizn'I Reformy [Life and Reforms]*, vol. 2, Moscow: Novosti, 1995.

Graebner, N.A., Richard Dean Burns and Joseph M. Siracusa, *Reagan, Bush, Gorbachev: Revisiting the End of the Cold War*, Westport: Praeger Security International, 2008.

Green, T.H., *Liberal Legislation and Freedom of Contract*, Oxford: Slatery & Rose, 1861.

Greenleaf, W.H., *The British Political Tradition, Volume Two: The Ideological Heritage*, London: Methuen, 1983.

Gress, D., *From Plato to NATO: The Idea of the West and Its Opponents*, New York: Free Press, 1998.

Halbwachs, M., *On Collective Memory*, translated and introduced by Lewis A. Coser, Chicago: University of Chicago Press, 1992.

Halifax, Earl of, *Fullness of Days*, London: Collins, 1957.

Halliday, F., *The Making of the Second Cold War*, London: Verso, 1983.

Hamilton, K. and R. Langhorne, *Practice of Diplomacy: Its Evolution, Theory and Administration*, London: Routledge, 1994.

258 *Primary sources*

Harbutt, F., *The Iron Curtain: Churchill, America and the Origins of the Cold War*. Oxford: Oxford University Press, 1986.

Harper, J.L., *American Visions of Europe: Franklin D. Roosevelt, George F. Kennan, and Dean Acheson*, Cambridge: Cambridge University Press, 1994.

Hartman, C. and Pedro Vilanova (eds), *Paradigms Lost: The Post Cold War Era*, London: Pluto, 1992.

Heath, E., *The Course of My Life*, London: Hodder & Stoughton, 1998.

Henderson, E.A.., *Democracy and War: The End of an Illusion?*, Boulder: Lynne Rienner, 2002.

Hitchens, C., *Blood, Class and Nostalgia: Anglo-American Ironies*, New York: Farrar, Straus and Giroux, 1990.

Hitchens, C., *Blood, Class, and Empire: The Enduring Anglo-American Relationship*, New York: Nation Books, 2004.

Hobsbawn, E., and T. Ranger, *The Invention of Tradition*, Cambridge: Cambridge University Press, 1983.

Hofstadter, R., *The American Political Tradition: And the Men Who Made It*, London: Jonathan Cape, 1967.

Hogan, M.J. (ed.), *America in the World: The Historiography of American Foreign Relations since 1941*, Cambridge: Cambridge University Press, 1995.

Hollis, M., and S. Smith, *Explaining and Understanding International Relations*, Oxford: Clarendon Press, 1990.

Hollowell, J. (ed.), *Twentieth Century Anglo-American Relations*, Basingstoke: Palgrave, 2001.

Holmes, R., *In the Footsteps of Churchill*, London: BBC Books, 2005.

Hopkins, M.F., *Oliver Franks and the Truman Administration: Anglo-American Relations, 1948–1952*, London: Routledge, 2002.

Hopkins, M.F., Saul Kelly and John W. Young (eds), *The Washington Embassy: British Ambassadors to the United States, 1939–77*, Basingstoke: Palgrave Macmillan, 2009.

Horne, G., *Paul Robeson*. London: Pluto Press, 2016.

Horsman, R., *Race and Manifest Destiny: The Origins of American Exceptionalism*, London: Harvard University Press, 1981.

Hubbard, J., *The United States and the End of British Colonial Rule in Africa, 1941–1968*, Jefferson, NC: McFarland, 2011.

Hunter, A. (ed.), *Rethinking the Cold War*, Philadelphia: Temple University Press, 1998.

Hyam, R., *Britain's Declining Empire: The Road to Decolonisation, 1918–1968*, Cambridge: Cambridge University Press, 2007.

James, L., *Churchill and Empire: Portrait of an Imperialist*, New York: Pegasus, 2014.

James, R.R. (ed.), *Winston Churchill: His Complete Speeches, 1897–1963*, Vol. VII, New York and London: Chelsea House, 1974.

Jaworski, A. and N. Coupland (eds), *The Discourse Reader*, Routledge: London, 2005.

Jenkins, R., *Churchill*, London: Macmillan, 2001.

Johnson, B., *The Churchill Factor: How One Man Made History*, London: Hodder & Stoughton, 2014.

Johnson, P., *Churchill*, New York: Viking, 2009.

Johnston, A.I., *Cultural Realism: Strategic Culture and Grand Strategy in Chinese History*, Princeton: Princeton University Press, 1995.

Kagan, R., *Of Paradise and Power: America and the New World Order*, New York: Alfred A. Knopf, 2003.

Kammen, M., *Mystic Chords of Memory: The Transformation of Tradition in American Culture*, New York: Vintage, 1993.

Primary sources   259

Kennan, G., *Memoirs 1925–1950*, Boston: Little, Brown, 1967.

Keynes, J.M., *The End of Laissez-Faire*, London: Hogarth Press, 1926.

Kimball, W.F. (ed.), *Churchill and Roosevelt: The Complete Correspondence*, Princeton: Princeton University Press, 1987.

Kimball, W.F., *The Juggler*, Princeton: Princeton University Press, 1991.

Kinzer, S., *All the Shah's Men: An American Coup and the Roots of Middle East Terror*, Hoboken, NJ: John Wiley, 2008.

Knoles, G.H., *The Jazz Age Revisited: British Criticism of American Civilization during the 1920s*, Stanford: Stanford University Press, 1955.

Krebs, R.R., *Narrative and the Making of US National Security*, Cambridge: Cambridge University Press, 2015.

Kull, S., *Burying Lenin: The Revolution in Soviet Ideology and Foreign Policy.* Boulder: Westview Press, 1992.

Kunz, D.B., *The Economic Diplomacy of the Suez Crisis*, Chapel Hill, NC: University of North Carolina Press, 2009.

Kupchan, C.A., *How Enemies Become Friends: The Sources of Stable Peace*, Princeton: Princeton University Press, 2010.

Kyle, K., *Suez: Britain's End of Empire in the Middle East*, second edition, London: I.B. Taurus, 2011.

Lagadec, E., *Transatlantic Relations in the 21st Century: Europe, America and the Rise of the Rest*, London: Routledge, 2012.

Langworth, R.M. (ed.), *Churchill By Himself*, St Ives: Ebury Press, 2008.

Larres, K., *Churchill's Cold War: The Politics of Personal Diplomacy*, New Haven: Yale University Press, 2002.

Lea, J.H. and J.R. Hutchinson, *The Ancestry of Lincoln*, New York: Houghton Mifflin Co., 1909.

Leech, G., *Semantics*. London: Penguin, 1974.

Leffler, M.P., *A Preponderance of Power: National Security, the Truman Administration, and the Cold War*, Stanford: Stanford University Press, 1992.

Leffler, M.P., *The Specter of Communism: The United States and the Origins of the Cold War, 1917–1953*, New York: Hill and Wang, 1994.

Leffler, M.P., *For the Soul of Mankind: The United States, the Soviet Union, and the Cold War*, New York: Hill and Wang, 2007.

Longworth, R. (ed.), *Churchill in His Own Words*, London: Ebury Press, 2008.

Louis, W.R., *The British Empire in the Middle East, 1945–51: Arab Nationalism, the United States and Postwar Imperialism*, Oxford: Oxford University Press, 1984.

Louis, W.R., *Imperialism at Bay: The United States and the Decolonization of the British Empire, 1941–45*, New York: Oxford University Press, 1987.

Louis, W.R. and H. Bull, *The Special Relationship: Anglo-American Relations since 1945*, Oxford: Oxford University Press, 1986.

Lubbock, P. (ed.), *The Letters of Henry James, Volume I*, London: Macmillan, 1920.

Lucas, W.S., *Divided We Stand: Britain, the US and the Suez Crisis*, London: Hodder & Stoughton, 1991.

Lukacs, J., *Churchill: Visionary. Statesman. Historian*, New Haven: Yale University Press, 2002.

McCullough, D., *Truman*, New York: Simon and Schuster, 1992.

McLellan, D.S., *Dean Acheson: The State Department Years*, New York: Dodd Mead, 1976,

McNair, B., *An Introduction to Political Communication*, second edition, London: Routledge, 1999.

260 *Primary sources*

Mahan, A.T., *The Influence of Sea Power upon History 1660–1783*, New York: Dover Publications, 1987.

Manela, E., *The Wilsonian Moment*, Oxford: Oxford University Press, 2009.

Martel, G. (ed.), *American Foreign Relations Reconsidered 1890–1993*, London: Routledge, 1994.

Meacham, J., *Franklin and Winston: An Intimate Portrait of an Epic Friendship*, New York: Random House, 2003.

Mead, W.R., *God and Gold: Britain, America, and the Making of the Modern World*, New York: Alfred A. Knopf, 2008.

Mehta, U.S., *Liberalism and Empire: A Study in Nineteenth-Century British Liberal Thought*, Chicago: University of Chicago Press, 1999.

Meinecke, F., *Machiavellianism: The Doctrine of Raison d'Etat and Its Place in Modern History*, New Brunswick, NJ: Transaction Publishers, 1998 (first published 1927).

Miller, K., *Transatlantic Literature and Culture after 9/11: The Wrong Side of Paradise*, New York: Macmillan, 2014.

Millington, F.H., *The Paine Centenary: June 1909, Thetford*, Thetford: H. Green, 1909.

Miscamble, W.C., *From Roosevelt to Truman: Potsdam, Hiroshima and the Cold War*, Cambridge: Cambridge University Press, 2008.

Mitchell, W.J.T., *Picture Theory: Essays on Verbal and Visual Representation*, Chicago: University of Chicago Press, 1994.

Monger, D., *Patriotism and Propaganda in First World War Britain: The National War Aims Committee and Civilian Morale*, Liverpool: Liverpool University Press.

Moraes, F., *Jawaharlal Nehru*, Chennai: Jaico Publishing House, 2007.

Moran, Lord C.M.W., *Winston Churchill: The Struggle for Survival, 1940–1965*, London: Constable, 1966.

Morgan, K., *Labour in Power*, Oxford: Oxford University Press, 1985.

Morley, F.V., *Travels in East Anglia*, London: Methuen, 1923.

Morris, G.W., and L.S. Wood, *The English-Speaking Nations*, Oxford: Clarendon Press, 1924.

Mowat, R.B., *Americans in England*, London: George C. Harrap, 1935.

Mowat, R.B., *History of the English-Speaking Peoples*, Oxford: Oxford University Press, 1943.

Muirhead, J.F., *American Shrines on English Soil*, London: The Doorland Agency, 1924.

Mukerjee, M., *Churchill's Secret War: The British Empire and the Ravaging of India during World War II*, New York: Basic Books, 2010.

Nadal, A., *Containment Culture: American Narratives, Postmodernism, and the Atomic Age*, Durham, NC: Duke University Press, 1995.

Neff, D., *Warriors at Suez: Eisenhower Takes America into the Middle East*, New York: Simon and Schuster, 1981.

Nozick, R., *Anarchy State and Utopia*, New York: Basic Books, 1974.

Offner, A., *Another Such Victory: President Truman and the Cold War, 1945–53*, Stanford: Stanford University Press, 2002.

Olsen, L., *Citizens of London*, New York: Random House, 2010.

O'Sullivan, C., *Harry Hopkins: FDR's Envoy to Churchill and Roosevelt*, Lanham, MD: Rowman & Littlefield, 2015.

Partington, A., *The Linguistics of Laughter. A Corpus-Assisted Study of Laughter-Talk*. London: Routledge, 2006.

Partington, A. (ed.), *Corpora Special Issue. Modern Diachronic Corpus-Assisted Studies*, Edinburgh: Edinburgh University Press, 2010.

Primary sources 261

Partington, A., A. Duguid and C. Taylor, *Patterns and Meanings in Discourse: Theory and Practice in Corpus-Assisted Discourse Studies (CADS)*, Amsterdam: John Benjamins, 2013.

Pateman, C., and C. W. Mills, *Contract and Domination*, second edition, Cambridge: Polity Press, 2013.

Peabody, D., *National Characteristics*, Cambridge: Cambridge University Press, 1985.

Pennybacker, S., *From Scottsboro to Munich: Race and Political Culture in 1930s Britain*, Princeton: Princeton University Press, 2009.

Perkins, B., *The First Rapprochement: England and the United States, 1795–1805*, Berkeley: University of California Press, 1967.

Perkins, B., *The Great Rapprochement: England and the United States, 1895–1914*, New York: Atheneum, 1968.

Perras, G., *Franklin Roosevelt and the Origins of the Canadian–American Security Alliance, 1933–1945*, Westport, CT: Praeger 1998.

Pew Research Center, *Views of a Changing World*, Washington, DC: The Pew Research Center for the People and the Press, 2003.

Phillips, K.P., *The Cousins' Wars: Religion, Politics, and the Triumph of Anglo-America*, New York: Basic Books, 1999.

Pierson, P., *Politics in Time: History, Institutions, and Social Analysis*, Princeton: Princeton University Press, 2004.

Piirmäe, K., *Roosevelt, Churchill, and the Baltic Question: Allied Relations during the Second World War*, New York: Palgrave Macmillan, 2014.

Pilpel, R., *Churchill in America, 1895–1961: An Affectionate Portrait*, New York: Harcourt Brace Jovanovich, 1976; and in UK, London: New English Library, 1977.

Plischke, E., *Modern Diplomacy: The Art of Artisans*, Washington, DC: AEI Press, 1979.

Ramsden, J., *Man of the Century: Winston Churchill and his Legend since 1945*, New York: Columbia University Press, 2002.

Rawls J., *A Theory of Justice*, Oxford: Oxford University Press, 1980.

Reagan, R., *Speaking My Mind*, London: Hutchinson, 1989.

Reagan, R., *The Reagan Diaries*, edited by Douglas Brinkley, New York: HarperCollins, 2007.

Reynolds, D., *In Command of History: Fighting and Writing the Second World War*, London: Allen Lane, 2004.

Reynolds, D., *From World War to Cold War: Churchill, Roosevelt and the International History of the 1940s*, Oxford: Oxford University Press, 2006.

Reynolds, D., *Summits: Six Meetings that Shaped the Twentieth Century*, New York: Allen Lane, 2007.

Roberts, A., *The Holy Fox: The Life of Lord Halifax*, London: Weidenfeld and Nicolson, 1991.

Roberts, A., *Eminent Churchillians*, London: Weidenfeld & Nicolson, 1994.

Robinson, H.P., *The Twentieth Century American: Being a Comparative Study of the Peoples of the Two Great Anglo-Saxon Nations*, Chautauqua, NY: Chautauqua Press, 1911.

Rock, S.R., *Why Peace Breaks Out: Great Power Rapprochement in Historical Perspective*, Chapel Hill: University of North Carolina Press, 1989.

Roll, D., *The Hopkins Touch*, New York: Oxford University Press, 2013.

Rose, J., *The Literary Churchill: Author, Reader, Actor*, London: Yale University Press, 2015.

Rose, K.D., *Myth and the Greatest Generation: A Social History of Americans in World War II*, New York: Routledge, 2008.

262 *Primary sources*

Rosenberg, E., 'Rosenberg's Commentary', in Ernest R. May (ed.), *American Cold War Strategy: Interpreting NSC 68*, Boston: Bedford Books, 1993.

Ryan, D. *US Foreign Policy in World History*, London: Routledge, 2000.

Ryan, D. and Victor Pungong (eds), *The United States and Decolonization: Power and Freedom*, London: Macmillan, 2000.

Rzheshevsky, O. (ed.), *War and Diplomacy: The Making of the Grand Alliance: Documents from Stalin's Archives*, Amsterdam: Harwood Academic Publishers./Overseas Publishers Association, 1996.

Sakwa, R., *Frontline Ukraine: Crisis in the Borderlands*, London: I.B. Tauris, 2015.

Schmitz, D.F., *The Triumph of Internationalism: Franklin D. Roosevelt and a World in Crisis, 1933–1941*, Washington, DC: Potomac, 2007.

Schrecker, E., *Cold War Triumphalism: The Misuse of History after the Fall of Communism*, New York: The New Press, 2004.

Scott, A.M., *Political Thought in America*, New York: Rinehart, 1959.

Scott, M., *WordSmith Tools Manual*, Oxford: Oxford University Press, 1996.

Shaw, A., *Eden, Suez and the Mass Media: Propaganda and Persuasion During the Suez Crisis*, London: I.B. Taurus, 2009.

Sherry, M.S., *In the Shadow of War: The United States since the 1930s*, New Haven: Yale University Press, 1995.

Shuckburgh, E., *Descent to Suez: Dairies, 1951–56*, London: Weidenfeld and Nicolson, 1986.

Sinclair, J., *Corpus, Concordance, Collocations*. Oxford: Oxford University Press, 1991.

Skidelski, R., *John Maynard Keynes 1883–1946: Economist, Philosopher and Statesman*, London: Pan Books, 2004.

Snyder, J., *The Soviet Strategic Culture: Implications for Nuclear Options*, Santa Monica: RAND Corporation, 1977.

Soffer, R.N., *History, Historians, and Conservatism in Britain and America: From the Great War to Thatcher and Reagan*, Oxford: Oxford University Press, 2009.

Stafford, D., *Roosevelt and Churchill*, New York: Overlook, 2011.

Steel, R., *Walter Lippmann and the American Century*, New York: Transaction Publishers, 1999.

Steil, B., *The Battle of Bretton Woods: John Maynard Keynes, Harry Dexter White and the Making of the New World Order*, Princeton: Princeton University Press, 2013.

Sumner, W.G., *What Social Classes Owe to Each Other*, Caldwell Idaho: Caxton Printers, 1978

Sutherland, J., *Bestsellers: A Very Short Introduction*, Oxford: Oxford University Press, 2007.

Thompson, K.W., *Winston Churchill's World View: Statesmanship and Power*, Baton Rouge, LA: Louisiana State University Press, 1983.

Thorne, C., *Allies of a Kind: The United States, Britain, and the War against Japan, 1941–1945*, New York: Oxford University Press, 1978.

Tomes, J., *Balfour and Foreign Policy: The International Thought of a Conservative Statesman*, Cambridge: Cambridge University Press, 1997.

Toye, R., *Churchill's Empire: The World that Made Him and the World that He Made*, Basingstoke: Palgrave, 2010.

Toye, R., *The Roar of the Lion: The Untold Story of Churchill's World War II Speeches*, Oxford: Oxford University Press, 2013.

Tucker, R.W. and David C. Hendrickson, *The Imperial Temptation: The New World Order and America's Purpose*, New York: Council on Foreign Relations Press, 1992.

Primary sources 263

US War Department, *Over There: Instructions for American Servicemen in Britain, 1942*, Oxford: Bodleian Library, 1994.

van der Pijl, K., *The Making of an Atlantic Ruling Class*, London: Verso, 1984.

Végső, R., *The Naked Communist: Cold War Modernism and the Politics of Popular Culture*, New York: Fordham, 2013.

Vucetic, S., *The Anglosphere: A Genealogy of a Racialized Identity in International Relations*, Stanford: Stanford University Press, 2011.

Watt, D.C., *Succeeding John Bull: America in Britain's Place, 1900–1975*, Cambridge: Cambridge University Press, 1984.

Wetherell, J.E. (ed.), *The Great War in Verse and Prose*, Toronto, A.T. Wilgress, 1919.

Wevill, Richard, *Diplomacy, Roger Makins and the Anglo-American Relationship*, London: Ashgate, 2014.

White, P., *Our Supreme Task: How Winston Churchill's Iron Curtain Speech Defined the Cold War Alliance*, New York: Public Affairs, 2012: published in the UK as *Churchill's Cold War: How the Iron Curtain Speech Shaped the Post War World*, London: Duckworth Overlook, 2012.

Whitfield, S.J., *The Culture of the Cold War*, Baltimore: Johns Hopkins University Press, 1991.

Whittier, J.G., *The Poetical Works*, London: Ward, Lock, Warwick House, 1880.

Williams, F., *A Prime Minister Remembers*, London: Heinemann, 1961.

Winter, J.M., *Sites of Memory, Sites of Mourning: The Great War in European Cultural History*. Cambridge: Cambridge University Press, 1995.

Winter, J.M., *Remembering War: The Great War Between Memory and History in the Twentieth Century*, New Haven: Yale University Press, 2006.

Woods, R.W., *A Changing of the Guard: Anglo-American Relations 1941–1946*, Chapel Hill: University of North Carolina Press, 1990.

Wright, P., *Iron Curtain: From Stage to Cold War*, Oxford: Oxford University Press, 2007.

Yellin, E., *Our Mothers' War*, New York: Free Press, 2005.

Young, J.W., *The British Foreign Office and Cold War Fighting in the Early 1950s: PUSC(51)16 and the 1952 'Sore Spots' Memorandum*, Discussion Papers in Politics, Leicester: Leicester University Press, 1995.

Young, J.W., *Twentieth Century Diplomacy: Case Study in British Practice, 1963–76*, Cambridge: Cambridge University Press, 2008.

Zametica, J. (ed.), *British Officials and British Foreign Policy, 1945–50*, Leicester: Continuum, 1990.

Journals

Abbot, P., 'Leadership by Exemplar: Reagan's FDR and Thatcher's Churchill', *Presidential Studies Quarterly*, 27:2, Spring 1997, 186–206.

Aldrich, R.J., 'British Intelligence and the Anglo-American "Special Relationship" during the Cold War', *Review of International Studies*, 24, July 1998, 331–51.

Allen, H.C., 'A Special Relationship', *Journal of American Studies*, 19, December 1985, 403–13.

Anderson, C., 'From Hope to Disillusion: African Americans and the United Nations, 1944–1947', *Diplomatic History*, 20:4, Autumn 1996, 531–63.

Armitage, D., 'Greater Britain: A Useful Category of Historical Analysis?' *American Historical Review*, 104, 1999, 427–45.

264 Primary sources

Banerji, A., 'The 1949 London Declaration: Birth of the Modern Commonwealth', *Commonwealth Law Bulletin*, 25:1, Spring 1999, 1–8.

Banton, M., 'The Idiom of Race: A Critique of Presentism', *Research in Race and Ethnic Relations*, 2, 1980, 1–20.

Baylis, J., 'The Anglo-American Relationship and Alliance Theory', *International Relations*, 8, January 1985, 368–79.

Bell, C.M., 'Thinking the Unthinkable: British and American Naval Strategies for an Anglo-American War, 1918–1931', *International History Review*, 19, November 1997, 789–808.

Bennett, J.C., 'Networking Nation-States: The Coming Info-National Order', *National Interest*, 74, Winter 2003/4, 17–30.

Berenskoetter, F., 'Friends, There are No Friends? An Intimate Reframing of the International', *Millennium: Journal of International Studies*, 35, September 2007, 647–76.

Bew, J., 'Pax Anglo-Saxonica', *American Interest*, 10, May/June 2015, 40–9.

Blackburn, R., 'Haiti, Slavery, and the Age of the Democratic Revolution', *William and Mary Quarterly*, 63:4, 2006, 643–74.

Bleiker, R. and E. Hutchison, 'Fear No More: Emotions and World Politics', *Review of International Studies*, 34, January 2008, 115–35.

Brants, K. and P. van Praag, 'Signs of Media Logic: Half a Century of Political Communication in the Netherlands', *Javnost, The Public*, 13:1, 2006, 25–40.

Capoccia, G. and R.D. Kelemen, 'The Study of Critical Junctures: Theory, Narrative, and Counterfactuals in Historical Institutionalism', *World Politics*, 59, April 2007, 341–69.

Casey, S., 'Selling NSC-68: The Truman Administration, Public Opinion, and the Politics of Mobilization, 1950–51', *Diplomatic History*, 29:4, September 2005, 655–90.

Chabal, E., 'The Rise of the Anglo-Saxon: French Perceptions of the Anglo-American World in the Long Twentieth Century', *French Politics, Culture and Society*, 30:3, 2012, 1–23.

Coicaud, J., 'Emotions and Passions in the Discipline of International Relations', *Japanese Journal of Political Science*, 15, September 2014, 485–513.

Coker, C., 'The Special Relationship in the 1990s', *International Affairs*, 68, July 1992, 407–21.

Crawford, N.C., 'The Passion of World Politics: Propositions on Emotion and Emotional Relationships', *International Security*, 24, Spring 2000, 116–56.

Danchev, A., 'On Specialness', *International Affairs*, 72, October 1996, 737–50.

Danchev, A., 'Shared Values in the Transatlantic Relationship', *British Journal of Politics and International Relations*, 7, August 2005, 429–36.

Dawson, R. and R. Rosecrance, 'Theory and Reality in the Anglo-American Alliance', *World Politics*, 19, October 1966, 21–51.

Desch, M.C., 'Culture Clash: Assessing the Importance of Ideas in Security Studies', *International Security*, 23, Summer 1998, 141–70.

Dittmer, L., 'Political Culture and Political Symbolism', *World Politics*, 29, July 1977, 552–83.

Dobson, A.P., 'The Years of Transition: Anglo-American Relations 1961–67', *Review of International Studies*, 16, 1990, 239–58.

Dobson, A.P., 'The Reagan Administration, Economic Warfare, and Starting to Close Down the Cold War', *Diplomatic History*, 29:3, June 2005, 531–56.

Dobson, A.P. and S. Marsh, 'Anglo-American Relations: End of a Special Relationship?' *International History Review*, 36, August 2014, 673–97.

Primary sources 265

Dumbrell, J., 'Winston Churchill and American Foreign Relations: John F. Kennedy to George W. Bush', *Journal of Transatlantic Studies*, 3:1, 2005, 31–42.

Edelman, E., 'A Special Relationship in Jeopardy', *American Interest*, 5, July/August 2010, 25–34.

Eden, L., 'The End of US Cold War History', *International Security*, 18:1, Summer 1993, 174–207.

Edwards, S., 'From Here Lincoln Came: Anglo-Saxonism, the Special Relationship, and the Anglicization of Abraham Lincoln, *c.*1860–1970', *Journal of Transatlantic Studies*, 11:1, 2013, 22–46.

Elkins, D.J. and R. Simeon, 'A Cause in Search of Its Effect, or What Does Political Culture Explain?' *Comparative Politics*, 11, July 1979, 127–45.

Eznack, L., 'Crises as Signals of Strength: The Significance of Affect in Close Allies' Relationships', *Security Studies*, 20, April 2011, 238–65.

Feuerlicht, I., 'A New Look at the Iron Curtain', *American Speech*, 30:3, 1955, 186–9.

Fukuyama, F., 'The End of History', *The National Interest*, 16, Summer 1989.

Gardiner, A.G., 'England and America: Their Misunderstandings and Their Opportunity', *Harper's*, 149, July 1924, 145–52.

Ginsberg, M., 'National Character', *British Journal of Psychology*, 32, January 1942, 183–205.

Gleason, P., 'Identifying Identity: A Semantic History', *Journal of American History*, 69, March 1983, 910–31.

Goldstone, J.A., 'Initial Conditions, General Laws, Path Dependence, and Explanation in Historical Sociology', *American Journal of Sociology*, 104, November 1998, 829–45.

Grinde, D.A. and B.E. Johansen, 'Sauce for the Goose: Demand and Definitions for "Proof" regarding the Iroquois and Democracy', *William and Mary Quarterly*, 53:2, 1996, 628–35.

Haglund, D., 'What Good Is Strategic Culture? A Modest Defence of an Immodest Concept', *International Journal*, 59, Summer 2004, 479–502.

Haglund, D., 'Relating to the Anglosphere: Canada, "Culture", and the Question of Military Intervention', *Journal of Transatlantic Studies*, 3, Autumn 2005, 179–98.

Hahn, P.L., 'Securing the Middle East: The Eisenhower Doctrine of 1957', *Presidential Studies Quarterly*, 36:1 (March 2006), 38–47.

Hastings, P., 'Fellow British Subjects or Colonial "Others"? Race, Empire, and Ambivalence in Canadian Representations of India in the Early Twentieth Century', *American Review of Canadian Studies*, 38:1, 2008, 3–26.

Hauer, S.R., 'Thomas Jefferson and the Anglo-Saxon Language', *PMLA*, 98:5, 1983, 879–98.

Hjarvard, S., 'The Mediatization of Society. A Theory of the Media as Agents of Social and Cultural Change', *Nordicom Review*, 29:2, 2008, 105–34.

Horsman, R., 'Origins of Racial Anglo-Saxonism in Great Britain before 1850', *Journal of the History of Ideas*, 37:3, 1976, 388–90.

Hostetler, M.J., 'The Enigmatic Ends of Rhetoric: Churchill's Fulton Address as Great Art and Failed Persuasion', *Quarterly Journal of Speech*, 83:4, 1997, 416–28.

Hough, L.H., 'Address on British Day Delivered before the Chicago Association of Commerce', *Bulletin, Northwestern University*, 19:22, 1919, 2–14.

Hyde Price, A., 'European Security, Strategic Culture and the Use of Force', *European Security*, 13, January 2004, 323–43.

Inglehart, R., 'The Renaissance of Political Culture', *American Political Science Review*, 82, December 1988, 1203–30.

266 Primary sources

Ingram, E., 'The Wonderland of the Political Scientist', *International Security*, 22, Summer 1997, 53–63.

Jeffreys-Jones, R., 'The Inestimable Advantage of Not Being English: Lord Lothian's American Ambassadorship, 1939–1940', *The Scottish Historical Review*, 63:175, 1984, 105–10.

Johnston, A.I., 'Thinking about Strategic Culture', *International Security*, 19, Spring 1995, 32–64.

Kimball, W.F., 'Dangerously Contagious? The Anglo-American Special Relationship', a debate with Alex Danchev, *The British Journal of Politics and International Relations*, 7:3, 2005, 437–41.

Kimball, W.F., 'The "Special" Anglo-American Special Relationship: "A Fatter, Larger Underwater Cable"', *Journal of Transatlantic Studies*, 3:1, Spring 2005, 1–5.

Kimball, W.F., 'Sheriffs and Constables: Churchill's and Roosevelt's Postwar World', *Finest Hour: The Journal of Winston Churchill*, 141, 2008–9, 36–42.

Kramer, P.A., 'Empires, Exceptions, and Anglo-Saxons: Race and Rule Between the British and US Empires, 1880–1910', *Journal of American History*, 88:4, 2002, 1315–53.

Lane, R., 'Political Culture: Residual Category or General Theory?' *Comparative Political Studies*, 25, October 1992, 362–87.

Lieven, A., 'A New Iron Curtain', *The Atlantic Monthly*, January 1996, 20–5.

Lorenzo-Dus, N. and S. Marsh, 'Bridging the Gap: Interdisciplinary Insights into the Securitization of Poverty', *Discourse and Society*, 23:3, 2012, 1–23.

McDermott, R., 'The Feeling of Rationality: The Meaning of Neuroscientific Advances for Political Science', *Perspectives on Politics*, 2, December 2004, 691–706.

McGrane, R.C., 'George Washington: An Anglo-American Hero', *The Virginia Magazine of History and Biography*, 63:1, 1995, 3–14.

McKercher, B.J.C., '"Our Most Dangerous Enemy": Great Britain Pre-eminent in the 1930s', *International History Review*, 13, November 1991, 751–83.

Mahoney, J., 'Path Dependence in Historical Sociology', *Theory and Society*, 29, August 2000, 507–48.

Mandler, P., 'What Is "National Identity"? Definitions and Applications in Modern British Historiography', *Modern Intellectual History*, 3, August 2006, 271–97.

Marchi, A., '"The Moral in the Story": a Diachronic Investigation of Lexicalised Morality in the UK Press', *Corpora*, 5:2, 2010, 161–90.

Marsh, S., 'Global Security: US–UK Relations': Lessons for the Special Relationship', *Journal of Transatlantic Studies*, 12:2, 2012, 182–99.

Marsh, S., and J. Baylis, 'The Anglo-American "Special Relationship": The Lazarus of International Relations', *Diplomacy and Statecraft*, 17, April 2006, 173–211.

Matlary, J.H., 'When Soft Power Turns Hard: Is an EU Strategic Culture Possible?' *Security Dialogue*, 37, March 2006, 105–21.

Mattern, J.B., 'The Power Politics of Identity', *European Journal of International Relations*, 7, September 2001, 349–97.

Menon, A., 'Littler England: The United Kingdom's Retreat from Global Leadership', *Foreign Affairs*, 94, November/December 2015, 93–100.

Mercer, J., 'Emotional Beliefs', *International Organization*, 64, Winter 2010, 1–31.

Norheim-Martinsen, P.M., 'EU Strategic Culture: When the Means Becomes the End', *Contemporary Security Policy*, 32, December 2011, 517–34.

Poore, S., 'What Is the Context? A Reply to the Gray–Johnston Debate on Strategic Culture', *Review of International Studies*, 29 April 2003, 279–84.

Primary sources 267

Rasmussen, J., and J.M. McCormick, 'British Mass Perceptions of the Anglo-American Special Relationship', *Political Science Quarterly*, 108, Autumn 1993, 515–41.

Reynolds, D., 'Competitive Co-operation', *Historical Journal*, 23, March 1980, 233–45.

Reynolds, D., 'Lord Lothian and Anglo-American Relations, 1939–40', *Transactions of the American Philosophical Society*, 73:2, 1983, 1–65.

Reynolds, D., 'Re-Thinking Anglo-American Relations', *International Affairs*, 65, Winter 1988–9, 89–111.

Robb, T., 'The "Limit of What Is Tolerable": British Defence Cuts and the "Special Relationship"', *Diplomacy and Statecraft*, 22, June 2011, 321–37.

Ross, A.G., 'Coming In from the Cold: Constructivism and Emotions', *European Journal of International Relations*, 12, June 2006, 197–222.

Rutten, A.R., 'Review Essay: Politics in Time', *Independent Review*, 11, Fall 2006, 299–305.

Ryan, H.B., 'A New Look at Churchill's "Iron Curtain" Speech', *Historical Journal*, 22, December 1979, 895–920.

Sasley, B.E., 'Theorizing States' Emotions,' *International Studies Review*, 13, September 2011, 452–76.

Schmidt, V., 'Democracy and Discourse in an Integrating Europe and a Globalising World', *European Law Journal*, 6:3, 2000, 277–300.

Schulz, W., 'Reconstructing Mediatization as an Analytical Concept', *European Journal of Communication*, 19:1, 2004, 87–101.

Schwartz, B., 'Memory as a Cultural System: Abraham Lincoln in World War II', *American Sociological Review*, 61:5, 1996, 908–27.

Siak, S.W., '"The Blood That Is in Our Veins Comes from German Ancestors": British Historians and the Coming of the First World War', *Albion: Quarterly Journal Concerned with British Studies*, 30:2, 1998, 221–52.

Strömbäck, J., 'Four Phases of the Mediatization: An Analysis of the Mediatization of Politics', *International Journal of Press/Politics*, 13:1, 2008, 228–46.

Terhune, K.W., 'From National Character to National Behavior: A Reformulation', *Journal of Conflict Resolution*, 14, June 1970, 203–63.

Toye, R., 'The Churchill Syndrome: Reputational Entrepreneurship and the Rhetoric of Foreign Policy since 1945', *British Journal of Politics and International Relations* 10:3, 2008, 364–78.

Toye, R., '"Phrases Make History Here": Churchill, Ireland and the Rhetoric of Empire', *Journal of Imperial and Commonwealth History*, 38:4, 2010, 549–70.

Twomey, C.P., 'Lacunae in the Study of Culture in International Security', *Contemporary Security Policy*, 29, August 2008, 338–57.

Vucetic, S., 'A Racialized Peace? How Britain and America Made Their Relationship Special', *Foreign Policy Analysis*, 7:3, 2011, 403–22.

Vucetic, S., 'Black Banker, White Banker: Philosophies of the Global Colour Line', *Cambridge Review of International Affairs*, 25:1, 2013, 27–48.

Wallace, W. and C. Phillips, 'Reassessing the Special Relationship', *International Affairs*, 85, March 2009, 263–84.

Walzer, M., 'On the Role of Symbolism in Political Thought', *Political Science Quarterly*, 82, June 1967, 191–204.

Warner, G., 'The Anglo-American Special Relationship', *Diplomatic History*, 13, October 1989, 479–99.

Yongping, F., 'The Peaceful Transition of Power from the UK to the US', *Chinese Journal of International Politics*, 1, 2006, 83–108.

268 *Primary sources*

Book chapters

Addison, P., 'Winston Churchill's Concept of "The English-Speaking Peoples"', in A. Pók (ed.), *The Fabric of Modern Europe: Essays in Honour of Éva Haraszti Taylor*, Nottingham: Astra, 1999, 103–17.

Asp, K. and P. Esaiasson, 'The Modernization of Swedish Campaign: Individualization, Professionalization, and Mediatization', in D.L. Swanson and P. Mancini (eds), *Politics, Media, and Modern Democracy: An International Study of Innovations in Electoral Campaigning and Their Consequences*, Westport, CT: Praeger, 1996, 73–90.

Baumann, G., 'Grammars of Identity/Alterity: A Structural Approach', in G. Baumann and Andre Gingrich (eds), *Grammars of Identity/Alterity: A Structural Approach*, New York: Berghahn, 2004, 18–24.

Baylis, J., 'The "Special Relationship": A Diverting British Myth?' in C. Buffet and B. Heuser (eds), *Haunted by History: Myths in International Relations*, Oxford: Berghahn, 1998, 117–34.

Calhoun, J.C., *The South Carolina Exposition and Protest* and *A Disquisition on Government*, both in Richard K. Cralle (ed.), *The Works of John C. Calhoun*, New York: D. Appleton, 1851–6 in multiple volumes.

Cannadine, D., 'Prologue: Churchill From Memory to History', in D. Cannadine and R. Quinault (eds), *Winston Churchill in the Twenty First Century*, Cambridge: Cambridge University Press, 2004, pp. 1–8.

Costigliola, F., 'The Pursuit of Atlantic Community: Nuclear Arms, Dollars, and Berlin', in Thomas Paterson (ed.), *Kennedy's Quest for Victory: American Foreign Policy 1961–1963*, New York: Oxford University Press, 1989.

Cumings, B., 'The Wicked Witch of the West is Dead. Long Live the Wicked Witch of the East', in Michael J. Hogan (ed.), *The End of the Cold War: Its Meaning and Implications*, Cambridge: Cambridge University Press, 1992, 87–102.

Cumings, B., 'Time of Illusion: Post-Cold War Visions of the World', in Ellen Schrecker (ed.), *Cold War Triumphalism: The Misuse of History After the Fall of Communism*, New York: The New Press, 2004, 71–102.

Esser, F., 'Mediatization as a Challenge: Media Logic versus Political Logic', in Hanspeter Kriesi, Sandra Lavenex, Frank Esser, Jörg Matthes, Marc Bühlmann and Daniel Bochsler, *Democracy in the Age of Globalization and Mediatization*, Basingstoke: Palgrave Macmillan, 2013, 155–76.

Farrell, J.C. and A.P. Smith, 'Foreword', in J.C. Farrell and A.P. Smith (eds), *Image and Reality in World Politics*, New York: Columbia University Press, 1967.

Gopal, S., 'Churchill and India', in R. Blake and W.R. Louis (eds), *Churchill*, Oxford: Oxford University Press, 1993, 457–72.

Haglund, D., 'Is There a "Strategic Culture" of the Special Relationship? Contingency, Identity, and the Transformation of Anglo-American Relations', in A. Dobson and S. Marsh (eds), *Contemporary Anglo-American Relations: A 'Special Relationship'?* London: Routledge, 2013, 26–51.

Holloway, D., 'The Atomic Bomb and the End of the Wartime Alliance', in A. Lane and H. Temperley (eds), *The Rise and Fall of the Grand Alliance, 1941–45*, London: Macmillan, 1995, 207–25.

Holmes, A.R., 'Transatlantic Diplomacy and "Global" States', in A.P. Dobson and S. Marsh (eds), *Anglo-American Relations: Contemporary Perspectives*, Routledge, 2013, 105–28.

Ingram, E., 'Hegemony, Global Reach, and World Power: Great Britain's Long Cycle', in C. Elman and Miriam Fendius Elman (eds), *Bridges and Boundaries: Historians,*

Primary sources   269

Political Scientists, and the Study of International Relations, Cambridge, MA: MIT Press, 2001, 223–51.

Kimball, W.F., 'The Ghost in the Attic: The Soviet Union as a Factor in Anglo-American Wartime Planning for Postwar Germany, 1943–1945', in A.L. Funk (ed.), *Politics and Strategy in the Second World War, International Committee for the History of the Second World War and Military Affairs/Aerospace Historian*, 1976, 88–112.

Kimball, W.F., 'Principles and Compromises: Churchill, Roosevelt and Eastern Europe', in R. Langworth (ed.), *Churchill Proceedings, 1994–95*, Washington: The Churchill Center, 1998, 98–106.

Kimball, W.F., '"Fighting with Allies": The Hand-care and Feeding of the Anglo-American Special Relationship', in D. Schmitz and T.C. Jesperson (eds), *Architects of the American Century*, Chicago: Imprint Publications, 2000.

Kimball, W.F., 'The Anglo-American Relationship: Still Special after All These Years', in A. Capet (ed.), *The 'Special Relationship – La 'relation spéciale' entre le Royaume-Uni et les États-Unis*, Rouen: Université de Rouen, 2003, 207–24.

Kimball, W.F., 'Churchill and Eisenhower: Sentiment and Politics', in R. Langworth (ed.), *Churchill Proceedings, 1998–2000*, Washington, DC: The Churchill Centre, 2004, 64–74.

Kimball, W.F., 'The Sheriffs: FDR's Postwar World', in David Woolner, Warren F. Kimball and David Reynolds (eds), *FDR's World: War Peace, and Legacies*, New York: Palgrave Macmillan, 2008, 91–121.

Krishna, S., 'A Postcolonial Racial/Spatial Order: Gandhi, Ambdekar, and the Construction of the International', in A. Anievas, N. Manchanda and R. Shilliam (eds), *Race and Racism in International Relations, Confronting the Global Colour Line*, London: Routledge, 2014, 139–56.

LaFeber, W. (ed.), *Eastern Europe and the Soviet Union*, Vol. II, Part 1, in A. Schlesinger (ed.), *Dynamics of World Power: A Documentary History of United States Foreign Policy 1945–1973*, New York: Chelsea, 1983, 210–21.

Laqueur, T., 'Memory and Naming in the Great War', in J.R. Gillis (ed.), *Commemorations: The Politics of National Identity*, Princeton: Princeton University Press, 1994.

Leffler, M.P., 'National Security', in Michael Hogan and Thomas G. Paterson (eds), *Explaining the History of American Foreign Relations*, Cambridge: Cambridge University Press, 1991.

Lorimer, D., 'From Victorian Values to White Virtues: Assimilation and Exclusion in British Racial Discourse, *c.*1870–1914', in P. Buckner and R. Douglas Francis (eds), *Rediscovering the British World*, Calgary: University of Calgary Press, 2005, 109–24.

Mahoney, 'Moral Principle and Realistic Judgment', in James W. Muller (ed.) *Churchill's "Iron Curtain" Speech Fifty Years Later*, Columbia, MO: University of Missouri Press, 1999, 69–81.

Mandler, P., '"Race" and "Nation" in Mid-Victorian Thought', in S. Collini, R. Whatmore and B. Young (eds), *History, Religion and Culture: British Intellectual History, 1750–1950*, Cambridge: Cambridge University Press, 2000, 224–44.

Martellone, A., 'In the Name of Anglo-Saxondom, For Empire and For Democracy: The Anglo-American Discourse, 1880–1920', in D.K. Adams and Cornelius A. Van Minnen (eds), *Reflections on American Exceptionalism*, Keele: Keele University Press, 1994.

Mattern, J.B., 'The Difference that Language-Power Makes: Solving the Puzzle of the Suez Crisis', in F. Debrix (ed.), *Language, Agency, and Politics in a Constructed World*, Armonk, NY: M.E. Sharpe, 2003, 143–70.

270 *Primary sources*

Morton, L., 'Germany First: The Basic Concept of Allied Strategy in World War II', in K.R. Greenfield (ed.), *Command Decisions*, Washington: Office of the Chief of Military History, Department of the Army, 1960, 12–22.

Muir, W.K., Jr, 'Ronald Reagan: The Primacy of Rhetoric', in Fred I. Greenstein (ed.), *Leadership in the Modern Presidency*, Cambridge, MA: Harvard University Press, 1988.

Ozouf, M., 'Fraternity', in F. Furet and M. Ozouf, *A Critical Dictionary of the French Revolution*, trans. Arthur Goldhammer, Cambridge, MA: Harvard University Press, 1989, 694–703.

Partington, A., 'Corpora and Discourse, a Most Congruous Beast', in A. Partington, J. Morley and L. Haarman (eds), *Corpora and Discourse*, Bern: Peter Lang, 2004, 11–20.

Prelinger, E. with Barton Hacker, ' "The Spirit of Woman-Power": Representation of Women in World War I Posters', in Barton Hacker and Margaret Vining (eds), *A Companion to Women's Military History*, Leiden, Brill, 2012, pp. 453–84.

Quinault, R., 'Churchill and Democracy,' in D. Cannadine and R. Quinault (eds), *Winston Churchill in the Twenty First Century*, Cambridge: Cambridge University Press, 2004, 27–46.

Ramsden, J., 'Mr Churchill Goes to Fulton', in J.W. Muller (ed.), *Churchill's 'Iron Curtain' Speech Fifty Years Later*, Columbia, MO: University of Missouri Press, 1999, 15–47.

Rasmussen, K.B., 'Great Britain and American Hegemony', in Daniel S. Margolies (ed.), *A Companion to Harry Truman*, Chichester: Wiley-Blackwell, 2012.

Roberts, G., 'Stalin and Soviet Foreign Policy', in Melvyn P. Leffler and David S. Painter (eds), *Origins of the Cold War: An International History*, New York: Routledge, 2005.

Rofe, S., 'Lord Lothian, 1939–40', in M.F. Hopkins, S. Kelly and J.W. Young (eds), *The Washington Embassy: British Ambassadors to the United States, 1939–77*, Basingstoke: Palgrave, 2009, 14–32.

Rose, S., 'Extract from *The Making of Memory*', in James McConkey (ed.), *The Anatomy of Memory: An Anthology*, New York: Oxford University Press, 1996, 55–9.

Ryan, D., 'Mapping Containment: The Cultural Construction of the Cold War', in Douglas Field (ed.), *American Cold War Culture*, Edinburgh: Edinburgh University Press, 2005, 62–3.

Ryan, D., 'Necessary Constructions: The Other in the Cold War and After', in Michael Patrick Cullinane and David Ryan (eds), *US Foreign Policy and the Other*, New York: Berghahn, 2015, 188–95.

Ryan, D., '1984, Regional Crises and Morning in America: The Predawn of the Reagan Era', in Andrew Johnstone and Andrew Priest (eds), *US Foreign Policy and American Presidential Elections*, Lexington: University Press of Kentucky, 2017.

Sewell, H.R., Jr, 'The Concept(s) of Culture', in Victoria E. Bonnell and Lynn Hunt (eds), *Beyond the Cultural Turn: New Directions in the Study of Society and Culture*, Berkeley: University of California Press, 1999, 35–61.

Solomon, M., 'Black Critics of Colonialism and the Cold War', in T.G. Paterson (ed.), *Cold War Critics: Alternatives to American Foreign Policy in the Truman Years*, Chicago: Quandrangle Books, 1971.

Strömbäck, J., and F. Esser, 'Shaping Politics: Mediatization and Media Interventionism', in K. Lundby (ed.), *Mediatization: Concepts, Changes, Consequences*, New York: Peter Lang, 2009, 205–23.

Tuathail, G.Ó., 'Thinking Critically About Geopolitics', in Gearóid Ó. Tuathail, Simon Dalby and Paul Routledge (eds), *The Geopolitics Reader*, London: Routledge, 1998.

Primary sources 271

Udris, L., and J. Lucht, 'Transformation of the news media: growing independence from politics – growing dependence on the market', in F. Esser and J. Strömbäck (eds), *Mediatization of Politics: Understanding the Transformation of Western Democracies*, Basingstoke: Palgrave Macmillan, 2014, 114–36.

Vucetic, S., 'The Search for Liberal Anglo-America: From Racial Supremacy to Multicultural Politics', in P. Katzenstein (ed.), *Anglo-America: Civilizational Politics Beyond West and East*, London: Routledge, 2012, 120–41.

Vucetic, S., 'Against Race Taboos', in A. Anievas, N. Manchanda and R. Shilliam (eds), *Race and Racism in International Relations: Confronting the Global Colour Line*, London: Routledge, 2014, 98–114.

Warren, S., 'A Philosophy of International Politics', in J.W. Muller (ed.), *Churchill's 'Iron Curtain' Speech Fifty Years Later*, Columbia, MO: University of Missouri Press, 1999, 93–128.

Williamson, P., 'The Doctrinal Politics of Stanley Baldwin', in Michael Bentley (ed.), *Public and Private Doctrine: Essays in British History Presented to Maurice Cowling*, Cambridge: Cambridge University Press, 1993.

Newspapers/media commentary/web sources

(Atlantic Charter) Roosevelt and Churchill, 'The Atlantic Charter', *The Avalon Project*; http://avalon.law.yale.edu/wwii/atlantic.asp.

Bacevich, A., 'H-Diplo Article Review 552'; https://networks.h-net.org/node/28443/discussions/84104/h-diplo-article-review-552-monsters-everywhere-genealogy-national.

Berlin, I., 'Mr Churchill', *The Atlantic*, September 1949; www.theatlantic.com/magazine/archive/1949/09/mr-churchill/303546/.

'Bill to Aid Britain Strongly Backed', *New York Times*, 9 February 1941.

Boyd, G.M., 'Bush Asserts "Iron Curtain" Remains, but It's "Rusting"', *New York Times*, 19 October 1988

(Churchill) 'Award to Sir W. Churchill: Franklin Medal', *Glasgow Herald*, 12 January 1956.

(Churchill) National Churchill Museum; www.nationalchurchillmuseum.org/history-church-of-st-mary.html.

Churchill, W., 'The Russian Enigma', 1 October 1939; www.churchill-society-london.org.uk/RusnEnig.html.

Churchill, W., 'The Sinews of Peace', 5 March 1946, National Churchill Museum; www.nationalchurchillmuseum.org/sinews-of-peace-history.html.

Clines, F.X., 'At Site of "Iron Curtain" Speech, Gorbachev Buries the Cold War', *New York Times*, 7 May 1992.

Collins, C., 'Edwina Sandys Returns to Churchill Museum to Honour Fall of Berlin Wall', *Guardian*, 4 November 2014.

Connolly, K., 'Obama Speech in Berlin Looks to "Shared Values" of Iron Curtain Era', *Guardian*, 19 June 2013.

Corbella, L., 'Sir Winston's Legacy Lives On in Calgary. Great-grandson Randolph Churchill Follows Sir Winston's Footsteps on Speaking Tour of Canada', *Calgary Herald*, 15 May 2012; www.winstonchurchill.org/resources/in-the-media/churchill-in-the-news/1470-sir-winstons-legacy-lives-on-in-calgary-1.

Davidson, A., 'Rick Perry Meets Winston Churchill', *The New Yorker*, 24 October 2011.

272 *Primary sources*

Davidson, A., 'The Case of the Two Churchills', *The New Yorker*, 1 August 2012; www. newyorker.com/news/daily-comment/the-case-of-the-two-churchills.

Gabrielatos, C., and A. Marchi, 'Keyness: Appropriate Metrics and Practical Issues', talk given at CADS International Conference, 13–14 September 2012. Slides available online at: http://repository.edgehill.ac.uk/4196/.

Gallup Poll #300, 17 August 1943, Gallup Organization; http://brain.gallup.com/documents/questionnaire.aspx?STUDY=AIPO0300.

Gallup Poll #303, 28 September 1943; http://brain.gallup.com/documents/questionnaire.aspx?STUDY=AIPO0303.

Gallup Poll #317, 25 April 1944, Gallup Organization; http://brain.gallup.com/documents/questionnaire.aspx?STUDY=AIPO0317.

Gallup Poll #512, 20 February 1953, Gallup Organization; http://brain.gallup.com/documents/questionnaire.aspx?STUDY=AIPO0512.

Gallup Poll #524, 9 December 1953, Gallup Organization; http://brain.gallup.com/documents/questionnaire.aspx?STUDY=AIPO0524.

Gallup Poll #484, 4 January 1952, Gallup Organization; http://brain.gallup.com/documents/questionnaire.aspx?STUDY=AIPO0484.

Gallup Poll #512, 20 February 1953, Gallup Organization; http://brain.gallup.com/documents/questionnaire.aspx?STUDY=AIPO0512.

Gallup Poll #524, 9 December 1953, Gallup Organization; http://brain.gallup.com/documents/questionnaire.aspx?STUDY=AIPO0524.

Hathi Trust Digital Library, http://catalog.hathitrust.org/Record/009593532.

Heavy, R., ' "The Day the Wall Came Down", Berlin: A Divided City', 7 March 2013; http://berlindividedcity.wordpress.com/2013/03/07/the-day-the-wall-came-down/.

Goodnight, V., ' "The Day the Wall Came Down", on Sculpting the American West'; www.verylgoodnight.com/wall.htm.

Halle, K. (Katherine Murphy), #94: An Inventory of Her Personal Papers (1895–1989), John Kennedy Library, National Archives and Records Administration (NARA); www.jfklibrary.org/fa_halle.html.

Harding, W.G., *The White House*; www.whitehouse.gov/1600/presidents/warrenharding.

Herman, Arthur, 'Without Churchill, India's Famine Would Have Been Worse', 13 September 2010; www.winstonchurchill.org/resources/in-the-media/churchill-in-the-news/966-without-churchill-indias-famine-would-have-been-worse.

Heyden, T., 'The 10 Greatest Controversies of Winston Churchill's Career,' *BBC News Magazine*, 26 January 2015; www.bbc.com/news/magazine-29701767.

House of Commons Debate, 14 December 1950, Vol. 482 cc1350–464; http://hansard.millbanksystems.com/commons/1950/dec/14/prime-ministers-visit-to-usa#S5CV0482P0_19501214_HOC_247.

House Resolution 390; Congress.gov, www.congress.gov/bill/111th-congress/house-resolution/390.

Kelly, C.B., 'Excerpt: "Best Little Stories from the Life and Times of Winston Churchill" '; www.winstonchurchill.org/publications/chartwell-bulletin/104-bulletin-33-mar-2011/1094-excerpt-best-little-stories-from-the-life-and-times-of-winston-churchill.

Kennedy, J.F., Remarks at the Rudolph Wilde Platz, Berlin, 26 June 1963, Jon F. Kennedy Presidential Library and Museum; www.jfklibrary.org/Asset-Viewer/oEX2uqSQGEGIdTYgd_JL_Q.aspx.

Kissinger, H., 'Reflections on a Partnership: British and American Attitudes to Postwar Foreign Policy', speech to the Royal Institute of International Affairs, in commemoration of the Bicentenary of the Office of the Foreign Secretary, 10 May 1982; www.larouchepub.com/other/2002/2901_kissinger.html.

Primary sources 273

Krauthammer, C., 'Charles Krauthammer: Busted: Mr Pfeiffer and the White House blog', *Washington Post*, 29 July 2015; www.washingtonpost.com/opinions/charles-krauthammer-busted-mr-pfeiffer-and-the-white-house-blog/2012/07/29/gJQA8M46IX_story.html.

'Kup's Column', *Chicago Times*, 27 August 1945.

Lauter, D., 'Quotes Truman, Churchill at Site of "Iron Curtain" Speech: Bush Foresees "Greatest Age in History"', *Los Angeles Times*, 19 October 1988.

Lawrence, M.A., 'Friends, Not Allies', review of Nicholas Thompson, *The Hawk and the Dove: Paul Nitze, George Kennan, and the History of the Cold War*, New York Times, 8 September 2009

Lelyveld, J., 'Prophet and Outcast Bush', *The New York Review of Books*, 63:3, 15 February 2016.

Little, D., 'Philosophy of History', in E.N. Zalta (ed.), *The Stanford Encyclopedia of Philosophy*, 2012; http://plato.stanford.edu/archives/win2012/entries/history/.

Locin, M., 'Midwest Battlegrounds Draw Candidates: Bush Sees "Rust" in Iron Curtain', *Chicago Tribune*, 19 October 1988.

Lothian, Lord, Address to the Pilgrims Society at the Hotel Plaza, New York City, on 25 October 1939, *New York Times*, 26 October 1939.

Louis, W.R., and Ronald Robinson, 'Empire Preserved: How the Americans Put Anti-Communism before Anti-Imperialism', *Times Literary Supplement*, 5 May 1995.

Maass, P., 'The Toppling: How the Media Inflated a Minor Moment in a Long War', *The New Yorker*, 10 January 2011.

Madison, L., 'Remembering Reagan's "Tear Down This Wall" Speech 25 Years Later', *CBS News*, 12 June 2012.

Makins, Sir Roger, Farewell speech at lunch of Pilgrims executive committee, 11 October 1956, *New York Times*, 12 October 1956.

'Milestones: 1989–1992', Office of the Historian, US Department of State; https://history.state.gov/milestones/1989-1992.

Mrs Miniver, directed by William Wyler, Metro-Goldwyn-Mayer, 1942.

'Mrs Miniver,' Internet Movie Database; www.imdb.com/title/tt0035093/.

North Otago Times, 106:14291, 10 December 1918.

Obama, B. Remarks by the President to Parliament in London, United Kingdom, 25 May 2011; www.whitehouse.gov/the-press-office/2011/05/25/remarks-president-parliament-london-united-kingdom.

Pfeiffer, D., 'Fact Check: The Bust of Winston Churchill', The White House, 27 July 2012; www.whitehouse.gov/blog/2012/07/27/fact-check-bust-winston-churchill.

Public Broadcasting Service, 'What Does the World Think of Us?' 6 April 2007; www.pbs.org/now/shows/314/opinions-of-us.html.

Reagan, R., Address to Members of the British Parliament, 8 June 1982; www.reagan.utexas.edu/archives/speeches/1982/60882a.htm.

Reagan, R., 'Remarks on East–West Relations at the Brandenburg Gate in West Berlin', 12 June 1987; www.reaganfoundation.org/.

Renan, E., 'What is a Nation?' 11 March 1882; full text at http://ucparis.fr/files/9313/6549/9943/What_is_a_Nation.pdf.

Roberts, C.M., 'Ike and Churchill Devote First Conference to EDC', *Washington Post*, 26 June 1954.

Robinson, P., '"Tear Down This Wall", How Top Advisers Opposed Reagan's Challenge to Gorbachev – but Lost', *Prologue Magazine*, 39:2, Summer 2007; www.archives.gov/publications/prologue/2007/summer/berlin.html.

274 *Primary sources*

Roosevelt, F.D., 'Address of the President Delivered by Radio from Hyde Park, NY', 24 December 1943, Mid-Hudson Regional Information Center; www.mhric.org/fdr/chat27.html.

St Nicholas: An Illustrated Magazine for Boys and Girls, 46:1, New York: The Century Company, 1919.

Schlesinger, A.M., Jr, 'FDR's Vision is Vindicated by History', *Wall Street Journal*, 22–23 June 1990.

Snider, E., 'What's the Big Deal? The Great Escape', *Film.com*, www.film.com/movies/whats-the-big-deal-the-great-escape-1963.

Stalin, J., Interview, *Pravda*, 13 March 1946.

Stanley, A., 'A Nation at War: The TV Watch; Amid the Scenes of Joy, A Sight Less Welcome', *New York Times*, 10 April 2003.

Stanley, T., 'Winston Churchill, an All-American Hero', *Telegraph*, 31 October 2013.

Sulgrave Manor; www.sulgravemanor.org.uk/pages/31/a_symbol_of_a_special_relationship.asp.

The Great Escape, directed by John Sturges, the Mirisch Company, 1963.

'The Great Escape: 50th Anniversary', *Telegraph*; www.telegraph.co.uk/culture/film/9853745/The-Great-Escape-50th-anniversary.html.

The Press, New Zealand, 54:16268, 19 July 1918.

The Queenslander, ' "Britain's Day" in America', 14 December 1918.

Umbricht, A., 'Patterns of News Making in Western Journalism: A Content Analysis of Newspapers across Six Western Democracies and Five Decades', *National Center of Competence in Research Working Papers*, 79, Swiss National Research Foundation, 2014.

Unattributed, 'The Source of Anti-Britishism', *New Republic*, 52, 16 November 1927, 325–6.

Unattributed, 'Churchill on the Campaign Trail for the 1950 General Election', quoted in *The Western Australian*, 20 February 1950; http://trove.nla.gov.au/ndp/del/article/47830261.

Unattributed, 'The Washington Merry Go Round', *The Sun Journal*, 7 December 1950; https://news.google.com/newspapers?nid=1928&dat=19501207&id=ybQ0AAAAIBAJ&sjid=UWgFAAAAIBAJ&pg=2781,6704633&hl=en.

Unattributed, 'Churchill Voted Greatest Briton', 24 November 2002; http://news.bbc.co.uk/2/hi/entertainment/2509465.stm.

Unattributed, 'Labour Party Candidate Brands Sir Winston Churchill as "Racist White Supremacist"', *Evening Standard*, 22 September 2014; www.standard.co.uk/news/politics/labour-party-candidate-brands-sir-winston-churchill-as-racist-white-supremacist-9749623.html.

Unattributed, 'Was Churchill a Racist? Oh Yes!' *Socialist Worker*, 2438, 27 January 2015.

Unattributed, 'Netanyahu Will Be Speaking in Winston Churchill's Shadow', *Time*, 3 March 2015.

Unattributed, 'Little Britain', *The Economist*, 4 April 2015, 53–5.

Urquhart, B., 'A Contest in the Cold', *New York Review of Books*, 56:20, 17 December 2009.

Vucetic, S., 'What Will Obama Do With Churchill's Bust?' openDemocracy.org, 20 January 2009.

Walsh, K., 'Bring Down Walls, 25 Years Later', *Ken Walsh's Washington*, 14 November 2014.

Winks, R.W., 'Winston Churchill, Intelligence and Fiction: "Mysteries Inside Enigmas"', 2 April 1995; www2.westminster-mo.edu/cm/scholar/021995.pdf.

Index

Acheson, Dean 1, 75, 85, 125–6, 129–33, 148, 152, 156–8, 190, 251
Adenauer, Konrad 124, 226
African-American 6, 96, 102, 108, 225
American Civil War 14, 104, 106, 206, 208, 210, 212
American Memorial Chapel 8, 202, 213–15, 217
America's National Churchill Museum and Memorial 90, 225
American–Spanish War 71, 107
American War of Independence 47, 89
Amery, Leo 117
Anglo-American Loan Agreement (1946) 43–4, 54–61, 84–6, 118, 249
Anglo-American special relationship 1–12, 14–16, 19–26, 24–5, 29–37, 43, 46, 57, 59, 61, 64, 66, 68, 80–1, 84–5, 87–91, 96, 101–2, 104–5, 107–8, 116, 118–19, 122–4, 126–9, 132–3, 136–7, 142–5, 148–51, 156–7, 159, 164, 166, 171–3, 175, 177–9, 181, 183, 185, 189, 191, 195–7, 202–3, 207, 211–12, 215, 217–18, 229, 231
Anglophobia 48, 208
Anglo-Saxons and Anglo-Saxonism 7, 23–4, 32, 36, 48, 66, 70–1, 74, 96–7, 105–8, 119, 147, 154, 195, 203–10
Atlantic Charter 6, 16, 53–4, 57, 60, 77, 102–3, 160, 164, 210, 234
Attlee, Clement 11, 20, 52, 54, 56–7, 87, 121–3, 130, 136, 143, 146, 148, 156–7, 178–9, 189, 192

Baker, James 239
Baker, Newton 67
Baruch, Bernard 44, 57–8, 192–3, 229
Bellamy, Edward 51
Bentham, Jeremy 51

Berle, Adolf A. 52
Berlin 228; Blockade 155, 234, 240; Reagan speech 225, 233, 235–7; Wall 224, 226, 233–4, 237, 239–41
Berlin, Isaiah 119, 146, 218
Beveridge Report 55
Bevin, Ernest 33, 45, 57
Bill of Rights (British) 47–8, 68, 120
Blair, Tony 4, 89, 252
Blitz 72, 90, 191, 216; and the US 73–7, 79, 82, 84–5
Boothby, Lord 56
Bracken, Brendan 74
Bretton Woods 55
Britain's Day celebration 6, 64–71
Britannia 66–7, 206
British Commonwealth 20, 54, 56, 100, 102, 118, 131, 134, 144, 147–8, 150, 152–5, 157, 165, 171, 202, 213
British Empire 7, 14, 25, 30, 46, 48, 54, 56–7, 59, 65–6, 70, 72, 76, 88, 102, 106, 118, 134–5, 144–50, 152–4, 156, 159, 165–6, 189, 191, 202, 208, 230–1, 234, 248, 250
Bryan, William Jennings 51
Bryce, Lord James 152, 205, 207, 210–11, 252
Bundy, McGeorge 127, 136, 225
Bush, George H.W. 9, 226, 238–41
Bush, George W. 89, 252
Butler, R.A.B. 52
Byrnes, James 44–5, 57, 60, 145, 229

Cameron, David 90, 197, 248
Calhoun, John C. 46
Carnegie, Andrew 105–6, 204
Carter, Jimmy 239
Cayton, Horace 96, 102
Chamberlain, Joseph 204

276 Index

Chamberlain, Neville 117, 150–1
Chandler, Raymond 49
Cherwell, Lord 122
Churchill, Winston S. 1–9, 247–52;
  ambassadors 7–8, 143–66, 249; Anglo-
  American political values 5, 44–5, 47–9,
  53–4, 57–61, 250; Benjamin Franklin
  Award 87; civilizational identity 6, 64,
  68, 70, 72–91, 247; collective memory
  8–9, 223, 225–32, 234, 237, 241, 247–9;
  English-speaking peoples 2, 4, 6, 7, 20,
  21, 23, 45–8, 58–9, 70–1, 74, 79–80, 85,
  97, 102–7, 118–19, 129, 134, 136,
  146–7, 160, 171–2, 185–6, 188, 195–6,
  203, 206, 208–10, 212–13, 217, 228,
  231, 248, 251; honorary US citizen 8,
  87–8, 202, 217–18, 252; language and
  the special relationship 8, 171–97, 251;
  myth and special relationship 8, 202–3,
  206–18, 247, 251; personal diplomacy
  7, 116–37; race and identity 6–7,
  96–108, 248–9; SACLANT (Supreme
  Allied Commander Atlantic)
  controversy 129–33, 137; Soviet Union
  5, 12–16, 247; strategic culture 5, 20–1,
  24, 27, 29, 32–3, 37, 249–50; Waldorf
  Astoria speech 58–9, 148–50, 156
Civil War (American) 14, 47, 104, 106,
  133, 206, 209–10, 212
Civil War (English) 106
Clinton, Bill 89, 239, 252
Cold War 4, 9, 34, 36, 85–6, 90, 107, 118,
  120–1, 152, 161, 171, 173, 186, 195,
  197, 223–8, 231–2, 234, 236–41, 249,
  252
conferences: Atlantic 15, 77–8; Bermuda
  (1953) 122, 128–9; Bermuda (1957)
  123, 166; Bermuda (1961) 127;
  Casablanca 80; Chicago civil aviation
  57; Nassau (1962) 123; Potsdam 145;
  Quebec 80; Teheran 11, 15; Yalta
  11–12, 15–16, 20, 117, 148, 225,
  228–30, 232, 240
Conservatism and Conservatives 44,
  49–50, 52, 56–7, 96, 100–1, 118, 121,
  129, 142, 160, 238
Cooper, James Fenimore 49
Council on African Affairs 97
Croly, Herbert 51
Cromwell, Oliver 70, 204, 207, 209
Crosland, C.A.R. 52
Crossman, Richard 54

Dalton, Hugh 56

Darwin(ism) 50, 100, 120, 204
de Gaulle, Charles 123, 226
Debs, Eugene 51
Depew, Chauncey 68
Destroyers for Bases Deal 2, 5, 33, 43, 72,
  128, 250
Dewey, John 51–2, 60
Dewey, Thomas 148
Dickens, Charles 23, 48–9
Disraeli, Benjamin 46
Douglas-Home, Alec 124
Dulles, John Foster 128–9, 145, 161–5,
  229, 237
Dworkin, Ronald 51

Eden, Anthony 123–4, 128–9, 133, 142–3,
  150, 157–8, 160–5, 250
Eisenhower, Dwight D. 7–8, 13, 58, 60,
  81, 84, 88, 90, 116, 118, 122–4, 126,
  128–9, 144, 159–66, 202, 213, 237
Eliot, T.S. 28, 49
Elizabeth I Queen of Britain 207
Elizabeth II Queen of Britain 89, 213, 215,
  235
Elsey, George 79
Emerson, Ralph Waldo 14, 49
Epictetus 21–3
European Economic Community 123, 197

Fabians 51–2
Falklands War 234
Fechteler, Admiral William 130
Fitzhugh, George 46
Flagg, James Montgomery 66
Foot, Michael 54
Ford, Gerald 89
Forrestal, James 45
Franks, Sir Oliver 7, 126, 143, 154–8, 161
Fulton Missouri speech 1–11, 13–14,
  19–25, 29, 32–3, 37, 43–5, 47, 50, 54,
  58–61, 85, 88, 90, 96–7, 101–3, 105–8,
  118–21, 132–4, 142–53, 156–7, 164–6,
  171, 185, 195, 202, 211–12, 216, 218,
  225, 226–9, 231–2, 238, 241, 247–9,
  25

Gaitskell, Hugh 52
Gallup polls 77, 83–4, 90, 119
Gandhi, Mahatma 99, 117, 144, 150
Garrison, William Lloyd 46
General Agreement on Tariffs and Trade
  (GATT) 6, 53, 123
George III King of Britain 47, 152, 156,
  209

George V King of Britain 65
George VI King of Britain 152
George, Lloyd 144
Gifford, Brian Walter 117, 122, 125
Goebbels, Joseph 20, 119–20
Goldwater, Barry 223
Gorbachev, Mikhail 225–7, 235–41
Great Rapprochement 5, 7, 23, 25, 33, 70, 106, 204, 248–50
Green, T.H. 50–1, 53, 60

Halifax, Lord (Edward Wood) 7, 143, 145–6, 149–53, 158, 195
Hamilton, Alexander 207
Harding, Warren 69
Harriman, Averell 77, 81
Heath, Edward 89, 127, 197, 248
Hitchcock, Alfred 83
Hitler, Adolf 10–12, 14–16, 20, 83, 96, 117, 144, 149, 194, 229, 231
Hobhouse, L.T. 51
Hollywood 82, 110
Hopkins, Harry 11, 76
Hull, Cordell 55
Hussain, Saddam 224

International Monetary Fund (IMF) 6, 53, 55–7, 60
Inverchapel, Lord 7, 143, 152–4
Iraq War (1991) 239
Iraq War (2003) 26
Iron Curtain speech 1, 3–4, 8–12, 20, 43, 61, 85, 101–2, 107, 118–19, 133, 145–6, 151, 171, 215, 223–36, 238–41, 249, 251; *see also* Fulton Missouri speech

James, Henry 49, 70–1
Jefferson, Thomas 46, 204
Johnson, Lyndon B. 90, 124

Kai-shek, Chiang 80
Kennan, George and Long Telegram 45–6, 107, 145, 164–5, 225, 227, 229–30, 232, 240
Kennedy, John F. 9, 87, 90, 123–4, 127, 136, 164, 216–17, 234–5
Kennedy, Joseph 14
Kerr, Archibald Clark *see* Inverchapel, Lord
Kerr, Philip see Lothian, Lord
Keynes, John Maynard 53, 56–7, 60, 117
Kipling, Rudyard 3
Kissinger, Henry 127, 239
Korean War 128, 156, 190

League of Nations 69
Leahy, Admiral William 45
Lend–Lease 15, 55, 57, 77, 79, 155, 250
Liberalism and Liberals 49–51, 53, 96, 100, 230
Lifeboat (film) 83
Lincoln, Abraham 8, 46; and memorials 203–7, 209–12, 214–15, 218
Lindsay, Sir Ronald 143, 151
Lippmann, Walter 44, 59, 142, 147–8, 156, 164–5, 180, 225
Lloyd, Henry Demarest 51
Locke, John 47
Lothian, Lord 7, 143–5, 151, 166
Lovett, Robert 125

MacArthur, Douglas 84
Macmillan, Harold 123–4, 127, 162–3, 166
Magna Carta 47, 68, 103, 120, 208
McCarthy(ism) 156, 187
McCluer, Frank L. 2, 47–8, 215
Mahan, Alfred 46
Makins, Sir Roger 7, 135, 142–3, 156, 158–9, 161–4
Marshall, George C. 84, 125; and Marshall Plan/Aid 155, 191, 227, 229
Means, Gardner C. 52
Merkel, Angela 225
Meyer, Eugene 74–5
Mill, John Stuart 51
Milner, Lord 144
Miniver, Mrs (film) 82, 86
Moran, Lord 76, 131–2
Morton, H.V. 78
Mossadegh, Mohammad and Abadan oil crisis 129, 156, 159, 185, 187
Murrow, Ed 73, 75, 77, 81, 87
Mussolini, Benito 149, 161

Nasser, Gamal Abdul 161–5
National Association for the Advancement of Colored People 97
NATO (North Atlantic Treaty Organisation) 5, 33–4, 129–30, 155, 160, 191, 227, 229–30, 234
Nitze, Paul 122, 240
Nixon, Richard M. 89, 165, 213, 225, 241
Nozick, Robert 50–1

Obama, Barack 90, 120–1, 197, 225, 248, 252

Paine, Thomas 205

278 *Index*

path dependency 5, 31–6
Pearl Harbor 65, 78–9, 82, 156, 250
Pearson, Lester 131
Pershing, General John 66, 69
Pilgrims Society 68, 144, 148, 151, 153, 155, 159, 163
Potomac Charter 7, 160, 164–5
Pound, Ezra 49

RAF (Royal Air Force) 73, 82, 88; and Eagle Squadrons 73
Rawls, John 50–1
Reagan, Ronald 9, 13, 89, 225–6, 233–8
Reston, James 184
Rhodes, Cecil 46
Robeson, Paul 6, 96–7, 102
Romney, Mitt 90
Roosevelt, Elliot 78
Roosevelt, F.D. 5, 10–16, 22, 52–4, 72, 74–82, 87, 89, 116, 121–2, 125–6, 136, 144, 148, 151, 160, 179–81, 184, 195, 208, 210, 212, 224, 240–1, 250; Four Freedoms 53
Roosevelt, Theodore 51
Root, Elihu 205, 211
Rumsfeld, Donald 224

Saint Paul's Cathedral 1, 8, 65, 202
Shakespeare, William 49, 70, 120, 205
Short, Joseph 86
Shultz, George 236
Sinews of Peace speech 10–11, 13–14, 16, 101–2, 118–19, 171–3, 194–5, 247; *see also* Fulton speech; Iron Curtain
Soames, Nicholas 2
Social Darwinism 50, 100, 204
Socialism and Socialists 12, 49, 96, 191, 227, 248
Spanish–American War 46
Spencer, Herbert 50–1, 60
Stalin, Joseph 5–6, 10–13, 15–16, 44–5, 80, 96, 100, 107, 121, 145, 148, 151, 227, 229, 231–2, 238, 240
Steinbeck, John 83
Stevenson, Adlai 264
Suez Crisis 7–8, 33, 35, 89, 123, 129, 135–6, 142–3, 148, 156–65, 226
Sumner, W.G. 50, 60

Tawney, R.H. 51
Thatcher, Margaret 89, 234
The Great Escape (film) 88

Thoreau, Henry 51
Truman, Harry S. 1–2, 4, 7–8, 16, 44–6, 53–4, 58, 60, 69, 84–7, 90, 118, 120–3, 125–7, 129–34, 136, 144–5, 150, 153–5, 157–9, 178–81, 184, 186–7, 190–3, 215–17, 223, 227, 229, 234, 237; Doctrine 191, 227, 229, 234
Twain, Mark 71

Uncle Sam 66
United Nations (UN) 6, 53, 96–7, 101, 103, 108, 123–4, 145–6, 149, 151, 154, 162, 164, 171, 226
US Declaration of Independence 46–7, 65, 120, 135, 214
USS *Williamsburg* 1

Vandenberg, Arthur 145, 229
Vaughan, Major General Harry 1
Versailles Treaty 69, 144
Victoria, Queen (Victorian) 69, 98, 104, 157, 191, 202, 206–8, 218
Vietnam War 89, 223, 237
Vinson, Fred 85

Wallace, Henry 98, 153–4, 231
War of 1812 14, 105
Washington, George 79, 205–7, 209
Westminster Abbey 89, 202, 207
Westminster Cathedral 65, 89
Westminster College 2, 6, 43, 47–8, 85, 99, 102, 215–18
Whitman, Walt 49, 51
Whittier, John Greenleaf 70
Wilberforce, William 46
Winant, John 77, 81
Wilson, Harold 124
Wilson, Woodrow 51, 66–8, 98
Winster, Lord 57–8
Wood, Edward *see* Halifax, Lord
Woolton, Lord 56–7
World Trade Organization (WTO) 53
World War One (WWI; Great War) 6, 12, 23, 64–6, 68–9, 71, 91, 106, 144, 152, 205, 210, 215, 218
World War Two (WW2; Second World War) 2, 4–6, 10, 12–14, 16, 22, 24, 33, 36, 52, 55, 72, 74, 76–84, 86–91, 107, 142, 145, 150, 155, 164, 166, 179, 190, 203, 209–10, 212, 215–18, 224, 239, 247, 250–1
Wren, Sir Christopher 90, 216